CHURCH DOGM

For further resources, including the forewords to the original 14-volume edition of the *Church Dogmatics*, log on to our website and sign up for the resources webpage: http://www.continuumbooks.com/dogmatics/

KARL BARTH
CHURCH DOGMATICS

VOLUME I

THE DOCTRINE OF THE WORD OF GOD

§ 1–7

THE WORD OF GOD AS THE CRITERION OF DOGMATICS

EDITED BY
G. W. BROMILEY
T. F. TORRANCE

t&t clark

Published by T&T Clark
A Continuum Imprint
The Tower Building, 11 York Road, London, SE1 7NX
80 Maiden Lane, Suite 704, New York, NY 10038

www.continuumbooks.com

Translated by G. W. Bromiley, G. T. Thomson, Harold Knight

British Library Cataloguing-in-Publication Data
A catalogue record for this book is available from the British Library

ISBN13: 978-0-567-20290-1

Typeset by Interactive Sciences Ltd, Gloucester, and Newgen Imaging Systems Pvt Ltd, Chennai
Printed and bound in Great Britain by CPI Antony Rowe, Chippenham, Wiltshire

PUBLISHER'S PREFACE TO THE STUDY EDITION

Since the publication of the first English translation of *Church Dogmatics I.1* by Professor Thomson in 1936, T&T Clark has been closely linked with Karl Barth. An authorised translation of the whole of the *Kirchliche Dogmatik* was begun in the 1950s under the editorship of G. W. Bromiley and T. F. Torrance, a work which eventually replaced Professor Thomson's initial translation of *CD I.1*.

T&T Clark is now happy to present to the academic community this new *Study Edition* of the *Church Dogmatics*. Its aim is mainly to make this major work available to a generation of students and scholars with less familiarity with Latin, Greek, and French. For the first time this edition therefore presents the classic text of the translation edited by G. W. Bromiley and T. F. Torrance incorporating translations of the foreign language passages in Editorial Notes on each page.

The main body of the text remains unchanged. Only minor corrections with regard to grammar or spelling have been introduced. The text is presented in a new reader friendly format. We hope that the breakdown of the *Church Dogmatics* into 31 shorter fascicles will make this edition easier to use than its predecessors.

Completely new indexes of names, subjects and scriptural indexes have been created for the individual volumes of the *Study Edition*.

The publishers would like to thank the Center for Barth Studies at Princeton Theological Seminary for supplying a digital edition of the text of the *Church Dogmatics* and translations of the Greek and Latin quotations in the original T&T Clark edition made by Simon Gathercole and Ian McFarland.

London, April 2010

HOW TO USE THIS *STUDY EDITION*

The *Study Edition* follows Barth's original volume structure. Individual paragraphs and sections should be easy to locate. A synopsis of the old and new edition can be found on the back cover of each fascicle.

All secondary literature on the *Church Dogmatics* currently refers to the classic 14-volume set (e.g. II.2 p. 520). In order to avoid confusion, we recommend that this practice should be kept for references to this *Study Edition*. The page numbers of the old edition can be found in the margins of this edition.

CONTENTS

§ 1–7

§ 1 [003]

THE TASK OF DOGMATICS

As a theological discipline dogmatics is the scientific self-examination of the Christian Church with respect to the content of its distinctive talk about God.

1. THE CHURCH, THEOLOGY, SCIENCE

Dogmatics is a theological discipline. But theology is a function of the Church.

The Church confesses God as it talks about God. It does so first by its existence in the action of each individual believer. And it does so secondly by its specific action as a fellowship, in proclamation by preaching and the administration of the sacraments, in worship, in its internal and external mission including works of love amongst the sick, the weak and those in jeopardy. Fortunately the reality of the Church does not coincide with its action. But its action coincides with the fact that alike in its existence in believers and its communal existence as such it speaks about God. Its action is "theology" in both the broader and the narrower sense.

Theology is *de divinitate ratio sive sermo*[EN1] (Augustine, *De civ. Dei* VIII, 1). *Θεολόγος* est ὁ τὸν θεὸν ἐκ θεοῦ ἐνώπιον τοῦ θεοῦ εἰς δόξαν αὐτοῦ λέγων[EN2] (Coccejus, *Summa theol.*, 1699, 1, 1).

But as it confesses God the Church also confesses both the humanity and the responsibility of its action. It realises that it is exposed to fierce temptation as it speaks of God, and it realises that it must give an account to God for the way in which it speaks. The first and last and decisive answer to this twofold compulsion consists in the fact that it rests content with the grace of the One whose strength is mighty in weakness. But in so doing it recognises and takes up as an active Church the further human task of criticising and revising its speech about God. This brings us to the concept of theology in the third, strictest and proper sense of the word.

Cf. for this threefold concept of theology J. Gerhard, *Loci theol.*, 1610, *Prooem.*, 4: Theology is 1. *fides et religio Christiana, quae omnibus fidelibus doctis aeque ac indoctis communnis est, ut sic*

[EN1] argument or discourse on divinity

[EN2] A theologian is someone who speaks of God, from God, before God to God's glory

[004] *theologi dicantur*[EN3]; 2. *functio ministerii Ecclesiastici*[EN3]; 3. *accuratior divinorum mysteriorum cognitio, qua ratione theologi dicuntur, qui possunt veritatem divinam solide stabilire, eique oppositam falsitatem potenter destruere*[EN3].

Theology as a science, in distinction from the "theology" of the simple testimony of faith and life and the "theology" of the service of God, is a measure taken by the Church in relation to the vulnerability and responsibility of its utterance. It would be meaningless without justifying grace, which here too can alone make good what man as such invariably does badly. But it can be meaningful as an act of obedience to this grace, i.e., of the obedience in which here too man may believe that he is doing well even though he does not see it.

Theology saw this quite early ... *et hominum officio ipso sancto Spiritu largiente in docendis etiam ipsis doctoribus non debere cessare et tamen neque qui plantat esse aliquid neque qui rigat sed Deum qui incrementum dat*[EN4] (Augustine, *De doct. christ.* IV, 16).

The Church produces theology in this special and peculiar sense by subjecting itself to self-examination. It puts to itself the question of truth, i.e., it measures its action, its talk about God, against its being as the Church. Thus theology exists in this special and peculiar sense because before it and apart from it there is in the Church talk about God. Theology follows the talk of the Church to the extent that in its question as to the correctness of its utterance it does not measure it by an alien standard but by its own source and object. Theology guides the talk of the Church to the extent that it concretely reminds it that in all circumstances it is fallible human work which in the matter of relevance or irrelevance lies in the balance, and must be obedience to grace if it is to be well done. Theology accompanies the utterance of the Church to the extent that it is itself no more than human "talk about God," so that with this talk it stands under the judgment that begins at the house of God and lives by the promise given to the Church.

The work in which the Church submits to this self-examination falls into three circles which intersect in such a way that the centre of each is also within the circumference of the other two, so that in view of that which alone can be the centre it is as well neither to affirm nor to construct a systematic centre, i.e., the centre of a circle embracing the other three. The question of truth, with which theology is concerned throughout, is the question as to the agreement of the Church's distinctive talk about God with the being of the Church. The criterion of past, future and therefore present Christian utterance is thus

---

EN3 1. the Christian faith and religion, which is common to all the faithful, the unlearned no less than the learned, with the result that they may all be called theologians; 2. the function of the Church's ministry; 3. more specifically, knowledge of divine mysteries, for which reason they are called theologians who are able both to give firm support to divine truth and effectively refute the falsehood that opposes it

EN4 While in the teaching even of teachers the Holy Spirit is the giver, human participation must not cease, and yet neither the one who plants nor the one who waters is anything, but God who gives the growth

the being of the Church, namely, Jesus Christ, God in His gracious revealing and reconciling address to man. Does Christian utterance derive from Him? Does it lead to Him? Is it conformable to Him? None of these questions can be put apart, but each is to be put independently and with all possible force. Hence theology as biblical theology is the question of the basis, as practical [005] theology the question of the goal and as dogmatic theology the question of the content of the distinctive utterance of the Church.

What is called Church history does not correspond to any independently raised question concerning Christian talk about God, and it cannot therefore be regarded as an independent theological discipline. It is an auxiliary science indispensable to exegetical, dogmatic and practical theology.

When the Church puts to itself the question of truth in its threefold form in a way which is objective and not arbitrary, its self-examination acquires the character of a scientific undertaking which has its own place alongside other human undertakings of the same or a similar kind. It is this particular science, i.e., theological science. Naturally, however, it is only in practice and with reservations that we can claim for it either its character as a science or its distinctiveness among the sciences.

Even the asserted independence of theology in relation to other sciences cannot be proved to be necessary in principle. It is indeed unfortunate that the question of the truth of talk about God should be handled as a question apart by a special faculty, and, while we have to recognise that such a course is unavoidable in practice, we cannot find any final reasons to justify it. Only theological arrogance could argue the point on other than practical grounds. Within the sphere of the Church philosophy, history, sociology, psychology, or pedagogics, whether individually or in conjunction, might well take up the task of measuring the Church's talk about God by its being as the Church, thus making a special theology superfluous. Theology does not in fact possess special keys to special doors. Nor does it control a basis of knowledge which might not find actualisation in other sciences. Nor does it know an object of enquiry necessarily concealed from other sciences. Only by failing to recognise the actualisation of revelation, the possibility of grace and therefore its own nature, could it possibly make any such claim. Similarly, we cannot possibly prove that there is any necessity in principle for a theology of the service of God. Might it not be that Jer. 31[34] is in process of fulfilment? Philosophy and secular science generally do not have to be secular or pagan. There might be such a thing as *philosophia christiana*[EN5].

Porro si sapientia Deus est, per quem facta sunt omnia sicut divina auctoritas veritasque monstravit, verus philosophus est amator Dei[EN6] (Augustine, *De civ. Dei* VIII, 1).

[EN5] Christian philosophy

[EN6] Now, if wisdom is God through whom all things were made (as divine authority and truth have shown), then the true philosopher is a lover of God

To contest this principle is to combine despair of the world with overvaluation of the Christian world in a way which is incompatible either with Christian hope or Christian humility. Theology as a special science, like the
[006] theology of the service of God as special Christian utterance, can be justified only as a relative and factual necessity. As such it is justified.

Absolute et simpliciter Theologia non est necessaria, ne quidem toti Ecclesiae: potest enim Deus homines immediate, h.e. sine ministerio hominum Theologorum informare et convertere—sed ex hypothesi posita scil. Dei voluntate[EN7] (Quenstedt, *Theol. did. pol.*, 1685, I, *cap.* 1, *sect.* 2, *qu.* 1, *ekth.* 6).

The other sciences have not in fact recognised and adopted the task of theology. To be sure, attempts have always been made on all sides to criticise and correct the Church's talk about God. But what is required is its criticism and correction in the light of the being of the Church, of Jesus Christ as its basis, goal and content. In fact, however, even though we cannot show that this is in accordance with any necessity of principle, even those historians, pedagogues, etc., and especially philosophers who kindly take this aspect into account always miss the real problem by setting it within the sphere of their own sciences, judging the utterance of the Church about God in accordance with alien principles rather than its own principle, and thus increasing rather than decreasing the mischief which makes critical science necessary for the Church. The result is even worse when this is done in the name of "theology." In practice the achievements of the philosopher, historian, etc. can be of only indirect significance to the problem which here confronts us, i.e., by way of a specific interpretation. Directly, in all the three areas of theological enquiry philosophy, history, psychology, etc. have always succeeded in practice only in increasing the self-alienation of the Church and the distortion and confusion of its talk about God. And in the interpretation offered, as the relevant experts at once object, philosophy ceases to be philosophy, or history history. There never has actually been a *philosophia christiana*[EN8], for if it was *philosophia* it was not *christiana*, and if it was *christiana* it was not *philosophia*. If, then, the concern of the Church is not to go by default, the special function of a scientific theology, corresponding to the special function of the service of God, is in fact indispensable. Its task, not in fact discharged by other sciences, is that of the criticism and correction of talk about God according to the criterion of the Church's own principle. Theology is the science which finally sets itself this task, and this task alone, subordinating to this task all other possible tasks in the human search for truth.

Non ubique quidquid sciri ab homine potest in rebus humanis ... huic scientiae tribuens, sed illud tantummodo, quo fides saluberrima, quae ad veram beatitudinem ducit, gignitur, nutritur, defenditur,

---

[EN7] Strictly speaking, theology is not necessary, not even for the Church as a whole; for God is able to instruct and convert persons directly, that is, without the ministry of human theologians, but [it is] postulated by hypothesis as being willed by God

[EN8] Christian philosophy

roboratur[EN9] (Augustine, *De trin.* XIV, 1, 3). *Theologia ... ita est omnium arbitra et domina, ut de ipsis judicet et ipsa a nulla alia scientia judicetur; omnes enim aliae disciplinae exigendae sunt ad ejus amussim, ut quicquid habent cum Theologia non consonum reiiciatur*[EN10] (F. Turrettini, *Instit. Theol. elenchth.* I, 1679, 1, 6, 7). Cf. Thomas Aquinas, *S. theol.* I, *qu.* 1, *art.* 5.

The other sciences, too, might finally set themselves this task and this task alone, subordinating all other tasks to it. All sciences might ultimately be theology. The fact that they are not is one which we need neither bewail nor justify in the present context. But it is a fact which creates a vacuum intolerable for the Church. The separate existence of theology signifies the emergency measure on which the Church has had to resolve in view of the actual refusal of the other sciences in this respect. It can have no epistemological basis. From the standpoint of the Church itself and therefore of theology, the separate existence of the latter is theoretically very questionable. Of the efforts made to assign it a place in the system of sciences, theology itself must say that the honour is both too great, and too small. [007]

The case is much the same when we ask whether theology is really a science at all. This question is not a vital one for theology. There is no necessity of principle, nor are there any internal reasons, why it should claim to belong to this genus. On the contrary, there are good grounds why it should definitely refrain from doing so.

Among the older orthodox, so far as I am aware, Baier was the first (*Comp. Theol. posit., Prol.*, 1, 15), and then Buddeus (*Instit. dogmat.*, 1724, I, 1, 28), emphatically to call theology a *scientia*[EN11]. Perhaps in the wake of Thomas Aquinas (*S. theol.* I, *qu.* 1, *art.* 2 and 6) the older Leiden school (e.g., Walæus, *Loci comm.*, 1640, 4, *Leidener Synopsis pur. Theol.*, 1624, I, 9) spoke cautiously of *scientia vel sapientia*[EN12], while to the best of my knowledge the overwhelming majority of the older (e.g., Wolleb, *Christ. Theol. Comp.*, 1626, *Praecogn.*) and later (e.g., Mastricht, *Theol. theor.-pract.*, 1698, I, 1, 1) Reformed, and even the Lutheran Quenstedt (*Theol. did. -pol.*, 1685, I, *cap.* 1, *sect.* 1, *th.* 28), preferred the term *doctrina*[EN13]. J. Gerhard expressly rejected the description of theology as *scientia* on the following grounds: 1. *scientiae certitudo ab internis et inhaerentibus principiis, fidei vero ab externis videlicet ab autoritate revelantis pendet*; 2. *subjectum Theologiae est Christus, cujus cognitio scientifico modo haberi nequit, sed ex divina revelatione eam peti oportet*; 3. *cujusvis scientiae principium est intellectus, quando ex principiis apte cognitis ad scientiam conclusionem devenitur. At in theologia intellectus non est principium sed finis;*[EN14] 4. *scientiis ratiocinando inventis potest subesse*

EN 9 Not granting to this science everywhere everything that can be known by human beings in the realm of human affairs, but only that by which that most beneficial faith, which leads to true blessedness, is birthed, nourished, defended, strengthened

EN10 Theology ... is thus the judge and lord of all things, so that it judges concerning them and is itself judged by no other science; for all other disciplines must be examined according to its criteria, so that whatever they have that is not consonant with Theology, should be rejected

EN11 science

EN12 science or wisdom

EN13 teaching

EN14 1. the certainty of science depends on internal and inherent principles, but faith depends on external principles (viz., the authority of the revealer); 2. the subject of Theology is Christ, of whom we cannot have a scientific kind of knowledge, but a knowledge that must be sought from divine revelation; 3. the starting point of any science is understanding, such that from first principles which are appropriately known one reasons to a science as a conclusion. In

*falsum*EN15 (*Loci theol.*, 1610, *Prooem.*, 8). He and later Hollaz (*Ex. Theol. acroam.*, 1707, Prol., 1, 1) chose the term *sapientia*EN16. In the 19th century A. F. C. Vilmar is alone, so far as I am aware, in rejecting the term "science" as one which "for the time being" is too heavily loaded (*Dogmatik*, 1874, I, 38. Cf. *Die Theologie der Tatsachen wider die Theologie der Rhetorik*, 4th edn., 1876, VI f.). The passion with which G. Wobbermin assures us that "theology has the greatest possible, i.e., a thoroughly existential interest in ranking as a real science, as a science in the strict, and indeed the very strictest sense of the word" (*Richtlinien evang. Theologie*, 1929, 25), is exaggerated. For the preceding ancient and mediaeval history of the question, cf. G. Söhngen, "*Die kathol. Theologie als Wissenschaft und Weisheit*" (*Catholica, Vierteljahrschrift für Kontroverstheologie*, April, 1932).

If theology allows itself to be called, and calls itself, a "science," in so doing it declares 1. that like all other so-called sciences it is a human concern with a [008] definite object of knowledge, 2. that like all others it treads a definite and self-consistent path of knowledge, and 3. that like all others it must give an account of this path to itself and to all others who are capable of concern for this object and therefore of treading this path. But it would make not the slightest difference to its real business if it had to rank as something other than science. If it is ranked as a science, and lays claim to such ranking, this does not mean that it must allow itself to be disturbed or hampered in its own task by regard for what is described as science elsewhere. On the contrary, to the discharge of its own task it must absolutely subordinate and if necessary sacrifice all concern for what is called science elsewhere. The existence of other sciences, and the praiseworthy fidelity with which many of them at least pursue their own axioms and methods, can and must remind it that it must pursue its own task in due order and with the same fidelity. But it cannot allow itself to be told by them what this means concretely in its own case. As regards method, it has nothing to learn from them.

It does not have to justify itself before them, least of all by submitting to the demands of a concept of science which accidentally or not claims general validity.

To the question what is the "science" to which theology must fully adhere G. Wobbermin gives (*op. cit.*, p. 29) the ingenuous answer: "Striving after the most exact and complete possible knowledge of the reality accessible to us." But what good theology will include its object in the "reality accessible to us"? And will a bad theology which does this really be granted by other sciences the recognition which it seeks?

What it involves to accommodate oneself to the concept of science which is accepted and holds sway to-day, and probably not only to-day, is made strikingly clear in the essay of Heinrich Scholz "*Wie ist eine evangelische Theologie als Wissenschaft möglich?*" (*Z.d.Z.*, 1931, 8–53). In an ascending scale, the demands made upon an undertaking which aspires to rank as "science," and therefore upon theology, are listed by Scholz as follows (*op. cit.*, pp. 18–24, 24–48): 1. freedom from contradiction in all the propositions to be constructed in the

---

theology, however, understanding is not the starting point but the goal; 4. a science derived from reasoning can be based on false premises

EN15 conclusions derived from scientific investigations can be false

EN16 wisdom

so-called science ("the proposition postulate"); 2. unity in the sphere of its object ("the coherence postulate"); 3. the possibility that all the propositions presented might be tested by any "sufficiently attentive readers or hearers" ("the verifiability postulate"); 4. respect for that which is physically and biologically impossible ("the congruity postulate"); 5. freedom from all prejudgments ("the independence postulate"); and 6. the possibility of all propositions being broken up into axioms and theorems and demonstrated on this basis (this being the solemn "supreme demand which is made of a science").* Scholz is undoubtedly right when in answer to the possible objection of theologians that this concept of science is an arbitrary modern invention he argues that it, too, "has a tradition, a great, classical tradition, and that it is a splendid and worthwhile thing to work for the high estimation of this trad- [009] ition" (*op. cit.*, p. 51). In addition to a theoretical basis in the history of philosophy since Plato and Aristotle, it has on its side the historical development of at least the last two or three hundred years, and its fairly consistent practical application in Berlin, New York and Tokyo. Nor is it meant as a rigid but rather as a flexible principle which readily admits of variations in practical execution. There is thus no point in drawing attention to its internal difficulties or the ways in which it is perhaps always broken when applied, even in the natural sciences. It is still the proper concept of science for our own time. And theology can only say point-blank that this concept is unacceptable to it. Even the minimum postulate of freedom from contradiction is acceptable to theology only when it is given a particular interpretation which the scientific theorist can hardly tolerate, namely, that theology does not affirm in principle that the "contradictions" which it makes cannot be resolved. But the statements in which it maintains their resolution will be statements concerning the free activity of God and not therefore statements which "dismiss contradictions from the world" (*op. cit.*, p. 44). The remaining sections of the law as stated by Scholz can only remind the theologian that he ought to know what he is about when he transgresses them, but also that as a theologian he cannot help transgressing them. Not an iota can be yielded here without betraying theology, for any concession at this point involves surrendering the theme of theology. On the other hand, in answer to the question whether relevance or objectivity should not be regarded as one of the main postulates of the concept of science, Scholz replies (*op. cit.*, p. 52) that he has not so far met any criterion "with the help of which it can be decided even in a single seriously controverted issue whether a given line of thought is objective or not." The theologian will perhaps appreciate more than others the importance of this statement. But he will say that objectivity in this aggravatingly indefinite sense is the most general expression of the one distinctive rule to which theology may and must keep. Hence in its dealings with this concept of science it can only make the dry declaration that the concept cannot be that of theology.

An apparently more harmless because more general definition of the concept of science is given by Arthur Titius in his Berlin University address on July 26 1932: "*Ist systematische Theologie als Wissenschaft möglich?*" According to Titius, science is "present or in process of realisation wherever common work exists or is possible in the realm of knowledge. This is only the case where the object behind the knowledge is made accessible to all with the necessary clarity and can be expounded according to the methods which are common to all" (p. 5 f.). The possibility of a fulfilment of this condition by systematic theology Titius sees first (p. 11 f.) in the fact that in the newly exploited notion of the unity of the world it has a

* Editors' note. These six requirements correspond to what we would think of as (1) formal consistency, (2) inherent consistency, (3) openness to control through a community of verifiers, (4) antecedent credibility, (5) impartiality or, positively stated, according to the principle of sufficient reason, and (6) formalisability.

point of contact accessible to all who are capable of thinking at all. He then finds it (p. 14 f.) in the possibility of the myth of the direct working of God as an inner causality of a personal and miraculous nature, in the Christian form of which the theologian sees "profound truth," i.e., the truth which even those who reject this myth must recognise in its "significance" etc. He sees it finally (p. 27 f.) in the psychological, sociological and moral significance of the Christian religion as this may be plainly grasped by any man. "Hence theology may be integrated with scholarship" if only there is accorded to it as to all historical and scientific learning the possibility of making appropriate use of the more basic contemplation which is "a kind of intuition in virtue of which aesthetic elements enter into the process of cognition and help to determine it" (p. 30). In this way theology may indeed be integrated into knowledge. But in respect of the very three elements which are supposed to vindicate it as a science, namely, the idea of unity, the possibility of myth, and the humanistic relevance of
[010] Christianity, it can only be described as completely empty from the theological standpoint, so that theology integrated along these lines must be flatly disowned as theology. How can it be otherwise if the intention is to make the theme of theology accessible to all men with the requisite clarity and to depict it according to methods which are valid for all? Whatever may be the concept of science, this object of knowledge cannot be handled in this way.

If theology allows itself to be called, or calls itself, a science, it cannot in so doing accept the obligation of submission to standards valid for other sciences.

Similarly, it cannot justify itself before other sciences on the score of propounding for discussion by them a concept of science which does not exclude but includes a good theology. To set itself in a systematic relationship to other sciences, theology would have to regard its own separate existence as necessary in principle. But this is the very thing which it cannot do. It cannot think of itself as a link in an ordered cosmos, but only as a stop-gap in a disordered cosmos. But how can there possibly be a concept of knowledge common to this stop-gap and the disordered cosmos? Any attempt of this kind must founder at once upon the conflict of will whether or not to take up the theme of theology. And from the theological standpoint this conflict is no mere problem to be solved by a synthetic construction.

Since the days of Schleiermacher, many encyclopaedic attempts have been made to include theology in the sciences. But the common objection may be made against all of them that they overlook the abnormality of the special existence of theology and therefore essay that which is radically impossible. The actual result of all such attempts has always been the disturbing or destructive surrender of theology to a general concept of science and the mild unconcern with which non-theological science, perhaps with a better sense of realities than theologians with their desire for synthesis, can usually reply to this mode of justifying theology.

Thus even the task of drafting a better concept of science in basic self-justification can only be rejected on the part of theology.

The only way which theology has of proving its scientific character is to devote itself to the task of knowledge as determined by its actual theme and thus to show what it means by true science. No science has any manorial rights to the title, nor does any theory of science have absolute power either to grant or withhold the title. Even conventions brought into currency by a general concept of science have no claim to final respect. Whether or not a person or thing is what it claims to be is always decided by the event which either substantiates or refutes the claim and not by even the most weighty stipulations concerning the justification or non-justification of the claim. We must leave it to this event. Theology has no reason not to call itself a science. It may well prove to be more of a science than many or even all the sciences grouped under the above convention.

There are three practical reasons why we should quietly insist on describing [011]
theology as a science.

1. In so doing, theology brings itself into line. As a human concern for truth, it recognises its solidarity with other such concerns now grouped under the name of science. It protests against the idea of an ontological exaltation above them such as might easily be suggested by its emphatic and distinctive designation by older writers as *doctrina*[EN17] or even *sapientia*[EN18]. It remembers that it is only a science and therefore that it is secular even as it works in its own relatively special way and in the highest spheres.

2. In not just resigning the title to others, with all due respect to the classical tradition it makes a necessary protest against a general concept of science which is admittedly pagan. It cannot do any harm even to the most stalwart representatives of this concept, or indeed to the whole university, to be reminded by the presence of the theologian among them that the quasi-religious certainty of their interpretation of the term is not in fact undisputed, that the tradition which commences with the name of Aristotle is only one among others, and that the Christian Church certainly does not number Aristotle among its ancestors.

3. Finally, in grouping itself among the sciences for all the radical and indeed indissoluble difference in the understanding of the term, theology shows that it does not take the heathenism of their understanding seriously enough to separate itself under another name, but that it reckons them as part of the Church in spite of their refusal of the theological task and their adoption of a concept of science which is so intolerable to theology. It believes in the forgiveness of sins, and not in the final reality of a heathen pantheon. If there can be no question of establishing this belief, there can be even less of denying it. But such a denial might well underlie too clear-cut a distinction between theology and the sciences.

These are the external and less basic reasons which we have for not making this distinction.

[EN17] teaching
[EN18] wisdom

2. DOGMATICS AS AN ENQUIRY

Dogmatics is the self-examination of the Christian Church in respect of the content of its distinctive talk about God. The true content which is sought we shall call dogma. This term, and therefore the word "dogmatics," will be explained in § 7. In this initial approach we may simply say that when we describe the true content of the Church's talk about God as the object of human work or investigation, we presuppose that it has both the capacity and
[012] the need to serve as the object of human enquiry. In other words, we presuppose that the "science of dogma" is both possible and necessary. Neither proposition is self-evident. Each must be sustained.

1. Dogmatics as an enquiry presupposes that the true content of Christian talk about God can be known by man. It makes this assumption as in and with the Church it believes in Jesus Christ as the revealing and reconciling address of God to man. Talk about God has true content when it conforms to the being of the Church, i.e., when it conforms to Jesus Christ ... *εἴτε προφητίαν, κατὰ τὴν ἀναλογίαν τῆς πίστεως*[EN19] (Rom. 12^{6}). It is in terms of such conformity that dogmatics investigates Christian utterance. Hence it does not have to begin by finding or inventing the standard by which it measures. It sees and recognises that this is given with the Church. It is given in its own peculiar way, as Jesus Christ is given, as God in His revelation gives Himself to faith. But it is given. It is complete in itself. It stands by its claim without discussion. It has the certainty which a true standard or criterion must have to be the means of serious measurement. Dogmatics presupposes that, as God in Jesus Christ is the essence of the Church, having promised Himself to it, so He is the truth, not merely in Himself, but also for us as we know Him solely by faith in Jesus Christ. To the extent that dogmatics receives this standard by which it measures talk about God in Jesus Christ, in the event of the divine action corresponding to the promise given to the Church, it is possible for it to be knowledge of the truth. What is or is not the true content of such talk about God is dear at once and with complete fulness and certainty in the light in which we are here set. The fulfilment of this knowledge, the event of human action, the appropriation corresponding to this address in which, through the stages of intuitive apprehension to formulated comprehension, the revelation of the *analogia fidei*[EN20] and the resultant clarity in dogmatics (in dogmatics too, but not first or solely in dogmatics) take creaturely form, is, of course, a second event compared with the divine action itself, united with it in faith, yet also in faith to be distinguished from it. The second event, however, does not abolish the first. In, with and under the human question dogmatics speaks of the divine answer. It knows even as it seeks. It teaches even as it learns. In human uncertainty like any other science, it establishes the most certain truth

[EN19] ... whether prophecy, according to the analogy of faith
[EN20] analogy of faith

ever known. In relation to its subject, every statement in dogmatics, as a statement of faith, must be ventured with the assurance of speaking divine and not just human truth. In distinction from the academic reserve of, e.g., a philosophical proposition, it cannot evade the severity of the dogmatic. The necessary corrective is supplied by the matter itself: "in relation to its object … as a statement of faith." The intractability of faith and its object guarantees that divine certainty cannot become human security. But it is this intractable faith [013] and its intractable object which make possible the certain divine knowledge which is at issue in dogmatics.

ὁ δὲ πνευματικὸς ἀνακρίνει μὲν τὰ πάντα, αὐτὸς δὲ ὑπ' οὐδενὸς ἀνακρίνεται. τίς γὰρ ἔγνω νοῦν κυρίου, ὃς συμβιβάσει αὐτόν; ἡμεῖς δὲ νοῦν χριστοῦ ἔχομεν[EN21] (1 Cor. 2[15f.]). *Viderint, qui Stoicum et Platonicum et dialecticum Christianismum protulerunt. Nobis curiositate opus non est post Christum Jesum nec inquisitione post evangelium*[EN22] (Tertullian, *De praescr.* 7). *Aliud est, de silvestri cacumine videre patriam pacis et iter ad eam non invenire et frustra conari per invia … et aliud tenere viam illuc ducentem cura coelestis imperatoris munitam*[EN23] (Augustine, *Conf.* VII, 21, 27). *Civitas Dei … habens de rebus quas mente et ratione comprehendit etiamsi parvam … tamen certissimam scientiam*[EN24] (*De civ. Dei* XIX, 18). *Tolle assertiones, et Christianismum tulisti*[EN25] (Luther, *De servo arb.*, 1525, *W.A.* 18, 603, 32). *Spiritus sanctus non est scepticus, nec dubia out opiniones in cordibus nostris scripsit, sed assertiones ipsa vita et omni experientia certiores et firmiores*[EN26] (*ibid.*, 605, 32). *Veritas periclitari potest, perire non potest. Impugnatur quidem, sed non expugnatur, Quia verbum Domini manet in aeternum*[EN27] (*Comm. on Gal.* 1[7], 1535, *W.A.* 40[1], 115, 15). *Sic ego omnino nihil audio contrarium meae doctrinae; sum enim certus et persuasus per Spiritum Christi meam doctrinam de Christiana justitia veram ac certam esse*[EN28] (*Comm. on Gal.* 3[1], *W.A.* 40[1], 323, 28). *Haec est ratio, cur nostra Theologia certa sit: Quia rapit nos a nobis et ponit nos extra nos, ut non nitamur viribus, conscientia, sensu, persona, operibus nostris, sed eo nitamur, quod est extra nos, Hoc est, promissione et veritate Dei, quae fallere non potest*[EN29] (*Comm. on Gal.* 4[6], *W.A.* 40[1], 589,25). *Ut certa est cuilibet sano haec sententia: bis quattuor sunt octo … ita sint certi nobis et immoti articuli fidei, comminationes et promissiones divinae … Quare illam dubitationem philosophicam seu*

EN21 The spiritual person judges all things but is himself to be judged by no one. For who has known the mind of the Lord so as to instruct him? But we have the mind of Christ

EN22 Let them watch out who proffer some Stoic and Platonic and dialectical Christianity. We have no need for curiosity after Jesus Christ, nor of academic investigation after the gospel

EN23 It is one thing to see the fatherland of peace from a wooded peak and not to find the path to it and to try to come upon it in vain through byways … and another to hold to the road that leads there, built by the solicitude of the ruler of heaven

EN24 The city of God … has of those things which it comprehends by intellect and reason admittedly limited … but nonetheless most certain knowledge

EN25 Take away assertions and you have taken away Christianity

EN26 The Holy Spirit is no skeptic, nor has he inscribed only doubts or opinions in our hearts, but assertions that are more certain and steadfast than life itself and any experience

EN27 The truth can be endangered, but cannot perish. It can be assailed, but not subdued. For the word of the Lord endures forever

EN28 Therefore I listen to nothing at all contrary to my doctrine; for I am certain and fully persuaded by the Holy Spirit that my doctrine concerning Christian righteousness is true and certain

EN29 This is the reason why our Theology is certain: It snatches us away from ourselves and places us outside ourselves, so that we do not rely on our own powers, conscience, feeling, person, or works, but rely on that which is outside of us, that is, on God's promise and truth, which cannot fail

ἐποχὴν *nequaquam admittamus ad doctrinam ecclesiae a Deo traditam ... Non alenda est hic aut laudanda dubitatio, sed sit fides certa assensio ...* [EN30] (Melanchthon, *Loci comm.*, 1559, *C. R.* 21, 604 f.). The "critical question" with which Eberhard Grisebach thinks it necessary to approach the work of theology has the value of sharpening the insight, not unfamiliar to some theologians, that the statements of dogmatics can have no other certainty than that which may be had by statements of faith with reference to their object, and that neither object nor faith stands at the disposal of the dogmatician. To the extent that such criticism passes from the investigation of theological certainty to its denial, it destroys itself and may be ignored. And theologians of this school may well be asked how long they think they can live on repetition of the "critical question."

It was obviously with reference to this aspect of the possibility of dogmatics as enquiry that the Reformed orthodox adopted the dangerously abbreviated definition of theology as *doctrina revelata*[EN31] or *patefacta*[EN31]. Yet among the later writers of this school we also find the more exact statement that *evidentia*[EN32] and *certitudo*[EN32] are proper to theological propositions in respect of their *ratio objectiva*[EN33], i.e., revelation, and the *habitus*[EN34], i.e., faith, in which we affirm them (F. Burmann, *Syn. Theol.*, 1678, I, 2, 60), *Ea cognitio est vera, etiamsi non sit adaequata, quia quae de Deo cognoscuntur ... carent omni mendacio, licet plus in re ipsa sit, quam a nobis intellegi potest*[EN35] (Coccejus, *Summa theol.*, 1669, I, 4).

2. Dogmatics as an enquiry presupposes that the true content of Christian talk about God must be known by men. Christian speech must be tested by its conformity to Christ. This conformity is never clear and unambiguous. To the finally and adequately given divine answer there corresponds a human question which can maintain its faithfulness only in unwearied and honest persist-
[014] ence. There corresponds even at the highest point of attainment the open: "Not as though I had already attained." Dogmatics receives even the standard by which it measures in an act of human appropriation. Hence it has to be enquiry. It knows the light which is intrinsically perfect and reveals everything in a flash. Yet it knows it only in the prism of this act, which, however radically or existentially it may be understood, is still a human act, which in itself is no kind of surety for the correctness of the appropriation in question, which is by nature fallible and therefore stands in need of criticism, of correction, of critical amendment and repetition. For this reason the creaturely form which the revealing action of God assumes in dogmatics is never that of knowledge attained in a flash, which it would have to be to correspond to the divine gift,

---

[EN30] Just as the sentence 'Twice four equals eight' is certain to anyone of sound mind ... so the articles of faith – the divine threats and promises – should be certain and unshaken to us .... For this reason we in no way admit that doubt or 'suspension of judgment' of the philosophers in matters having to do with the doctrine given over to the church by God ... Such doubt must be neither supported nor praised, but let faith be a most certain assent

[EN31] revealed or disclosed doctrine

[EN32] obviousness and certitude

[EN33] objective character

[EN34] disposition

[EN35] Such knowledge is true, even if it may not be fully adequate, because what is known of God ... is free of every falsehood, although there is more to the subject matter itself than what can be known by us

but a laborious movement from one partial human insight to another with the intention though with no guarantee of advance.

Βλέπομεν γὰρ ἄρτι δι' ἐσόπτρου ἐν αἰνίγματι ... ἄρτι γινώσκω ἐκ μέρους[EN36] (1 Cor. 13[12]). And with a like application we may also recall 2 Cor. 4[7]: *Ἔχομεν δὲ τὸν θησαυρὸν τοῦτον ἐν ὀστρακίνοις σκεύεσιν, ἵνα ἡ ὑπερβολὴ τῆς δυνάμεως ᾖ τοῦ θεοῦ καὶ μὴ ἐξ ἡμῶν*[EN37]. *Diximusne aliquid et sonuimus aliquid dignum Dei? Imo vero nihil me aliud quam dicere voluisse sentio: Si autem dixi, non hoc est, quod dicere volui*[EN38] (Augustine, *De doctr. Christ.* I, 6). *Cur non te sentit, Domine Deus, anima mea, si invenit te? An non invenit, quem invenit esse lucem et veritatem? ... An et veritas et lux est, quod vidit, et tamen nondum te vidit, quia vidit te aliquatenus, sed von vidit te, sicuti es? Domine Deus meus, formator et reformator meus, dic desideranti animae meae, quid aliud es, quam quod vidit ut pure videat quod desiderat*[EN39] (Anselm of Canterbury, *Prosl.* 14). *Et ut omne aenigma est sermo obscurus, nodosus, involutus, intellectu difficilis: ita nostra Theologia ratione obiecti est inevidens, complectens mysteria profundissima et in hac mortalitate cognitu difficillima*[EN40] (Hollaz, *Examen Theol. acroam.*, 1707, *Prol.* I, 8).

The fact that it is in faith that the truth is presupposed to be the known measure of all things means that the truth is in no sense assumed to be to hand. The truth comes, i.e., in the faith in which we begin to know, and cease, and begin again. The results of earlier dogmatic work, and indeed our own results, are basically no more than signs of its coming. They are simply the results of human effort. As such they are a help to, but also the object of, fresh human effort. Dogmatics is possible only as *theologia crucis*[EN41], in the act of obedience which is certain in faith, but which for this very reason is humble, always being thrown back to the beginning and having to make a fresh start. It is not possible as an effortless triumph or an intermittent labour. It always takes place on the narrow way which leads from the enacted revelation to the promised revelation.

... *ἐκ πίστεως εἰς πίστιν*[EN42] (Rom. 1[17]). Augustine in an important passage evolves the doctrine that *credere*[EN43] must precede *intelligere*[EN44] to the extent that it is established by the

---

EN36 For now we see in a mirror dimly ... now I know in part

EN37 But we have this treasure in earthen vessels, to show that the transcendent power belongs to God and not to us

EN38 Have we said anything or spoken anything worthy of God? I feel I have done nothing more than to have wanted to say something [of this sort], but if I have spoken, it is not what I wanted to say

EN39 Lord God, why does my soul not feel You, if it has found You? Or has it not found the one whom it finds to be light and truth? ... Or is it both truth and light which it sees, and yet it still does not see You, because it sees You after a fashion, but does not see You as you are? O Lord my God, who shape and reshape me, tell my desiring soul what You are that is other than it sees, so that it may see clearly what it desires

EN40 So just as every riddle is a secret form of speech, convoluted, complicated, difficult to understand, so is our theology by reason of its object obscure, comprehending the deepest mysteries and most difficult to grasp in this mortal sphere

EN41 a theology of the cross

EN42 ... from faith to faith

EN43 believing

EN44 understanding

vox de coelo[EN45] (*verbum Dei*[EN46]), but that it must follow it to the extent that it is to be established by the *sermo propheticus*[EN47] (*verbum meum*[EN48]). as in Mark 9[22]. Faith as faith in God
[015] stands on its own feet and is the basis of knowledge. Faith as the faith of man requires knowledge and is established by it (*Sermo* 43, 4–9).

Here our way diverges from that of Roman Catholic dogmatics, and we must also enter a *caveat*[EN49] against a certain tendency in the older Protestant tradition. Dogmatics is the science of dogma. Only in a subordinate sense, and strictly in conjunction with the primary, is it also the science of dogmas. The task of dogmatics, therefore, is not simply to combine, repeat and transcribe a number of truths of revelation which are already to hand, which have been expressed once and for all, and the wording and meaning of which are authentically defined.

Even on the Roman Catholic view there does seem to be "a true progress of the teaching Church," namely, in knowledge and understanding in the development, application and expression of revealed truth (Diekamp, *Kath. Dogmatik*, 6th edn., Vol. I, 1930, 19 f. Cf. Vincent of Lerins and his doctrine of *profectus religionis*[EN50], *Common.* I, 22 f.). In this context, however, the truth of revelation means the "apostolic deposit" infallibly proposed by the teaching office of the Church in the two forms of Holy Scripture and oral apostolic tradition (Diekamp, *op. cit.*, p. 24 f.). This deposit is thus identical with a sum of sacred texts. The task of dogmatics is "to mediate a fuller understanding of these truths by inferences'' (*op. cit.*, p. 76 f.). Moreover it is presupposed that the meaning of these truths or texts has already been mediated and authoritatively proclaimed by the teaching office, so that even in this task of understanding there can be no question of anything but transcription in a rather higher sense: *Hinc sacrorum quoque dogmatum is sensus perpetuo est retinendus, quem semel declaravit sancta mater Ecclesia, nec unquam ab eo sensu altioris intelligentiae specie et nomine recedendum*[EN51] (*Conc. Vatic., Sess. III, Constit. de fide cath., c.* 4).

This only too practicable view, by its direct equation of divine ascription and human appropriation in the dogmas, fails to recognise the divine-human character of the being of the Church. The being of the Church is Jesus Christ, and therefore an indissolubly divine-human person, the action of God towards man in distinction from which human appropriation as attested in the dogmas believed by the Church may be very worthy and respectable but can hardly be called infallible and therefore withdrawn from further enquiry whether this is how it should be. The concept of truths of revelation in the sense of Latin propositions given and sealed once for all with divine authority in both wording and meaning is theologically impossible if it is a fact that revelation is true in the free decision of God which was taken once for all in Jesus Christ, that it is

[EN45] voice from heaven
[EN46] the word of God
[EN47] prophetic speech
[EN48] my word
[EN49] warning
[EN50] progress of religion
[EN51] Hence also that understanding of the sacred dogmas must be retained in perpetuity which Holy Mother Chuch has once declared, nor can there ever be a departure from that sense in the form or name of a higher understanding

thus strictly future for us, and that it must always become true in the Church in the intractable reality of faith. The freely acting God Himself and alone is the truth of revelation. Our dogmatic labours can and should be guided by results which are venerable because they are attained in the common knowledge of the Church at a specific time. Such results may be seen in the dogmas enshrined in the creeds. But at no point should these replace our dogmatic [016] labours in virtue of their authority. Nor can it ever be the real concern of dogmatics merely to assemble, repeat and define the teaching of the Bible.

This is how Melanchthon seems to have understood the task (*Loci comm.*, 1559, *C.R.* 21, 601). Rather more crudely Heidanus (*Corp. Theol. christ.*, 1686, *Prol.*, 1 f.) taught that Holy Scripture is *non scripta ut systema quoddam, sed historica nobis facta Ecclesiae ab initio mundi ad finem describit*[EN52]. Hence it is the task of *Loci communes*[EN53] to present *res. S. Scriptura contentas certo et concinno ordine ... ut certo methodo res divinas complecti et eas suo ordine collocare possitis et sicut Pharmacopolae solent medicamenta sua certis capsulis distinguere et disponere, ita vos omnia suis quaque locis digerere possitis*[EN54].

Exegetical theology investigates biblical teaching as the basis of our talk about God. Dogmatics, too, must constantly keep it in view. But only in God and not for us is the true basis of Christian utterance identical with its true content. Hence dogmatics as such does not ask what the apostles and prophets said but what we must say on the basis of the apostles and prophets. This task is not taken from us because it is first necessary that we should know the biblical basis.

Although exegesis and dogmatics are constantly interwoven in his work, for Calvin too *Institutio religionis christianae*[EN55] means the direction of Christian thought and speech to its own contemporary responsibility.

As the Church accepts from Scripture, and with divine authority from Scripture alone, the attestation of its own being as the measure of its utterance, it finds itself challenged to know itself, and therefore even and precisely in face of this foundation of all Christian utterance to ask, with all the seriousness of one who does not yet know, what Christian utterance can and should say to-day.

Nam et ego tecum credo et inconcusse credo ... sed nunc molimur id quod in fidem recepimus, etiam intelligendo scire ac tenere firmissimum[EN56] (Augustine, *De lib. arb.* I, 3 6; cf. 4, 10). *Quod enim hortante ipso quaerimus eodem ipso demonstrante inveniemus, quantum haec in hac vita et a nobis*

EN52 not written as a kind of system, but gives us a factual account of the Church's history from the beginning of the world to its end

EN53 (a theological textbook organized around) common topics

EN54 the matters contained in Holy Scripture in a fixed and appropriate order ... so that you can comprehend divine matters by an assured method and put them in their proper order and, just as apothecaries are accustomed to distinguish and arrange their medicines in particular capsules, you might be able to organize all matters relating to theological topics

EN55 Institutes of the Christian Religion

EN56 For I believe with you and believe firmly ... but now we strive to know also by understanding and thus to hold as utterly certain that which we have received in faith

talibus inveniri queat[EN57] (*ib.*, II, 2, 6). The purpose of Anselm of Canterbury regarding the question raised by his interlocutor is *non tam ostendere, quam tecum quaerere*[EN58] (*Cur Deus homo?* I, 2). His aim in *intellectus fidei*[EN59] is not a repetition of the believer's *legere*[EN60], but a genuine *intus legere*[EN61] of Scripture and dogma, though not on the basis of their accepted authoritative givenness: ... *quatenus auctoritate Scripturae penitus nihil in ea (scil. meditatione) persuaderetur* (*Monol. Prol.*) ... *ut quod fide teneamus ... sine Scripturae auctoritate probari possit*[EN62] (*Ep. de incarn.*, 6). For the distinction between dogmatic enquiry and authoritative quotation we might also refer to the well-known though not wholly unobjectionable formula of Anselm: *remoto Christo ... quasi nihil sciatur de Christo*[EN63] (*Cur Deus homo?*, *Prol.*). *Quaedam disputatio ordinatur ad removendam dubitationem an ita sit; et in tali disputatione theologica maxime utendum est auctoritatibus, quas recipiunt illi, cum quibus disputatur ... Quaedam vero disputatio est magistralis in scholis non ad removendum errorem, sed ac instruendum auditores, ut inducantur ad intellectum veritatis quam intendit; et tunc oportet rationibus inniti investigantibus veritatis radicem et facientibus scire, quomodo sit verum, quod dicitur*[EN64] (Thomas Aquinas, *Quodlib.*, 4, 18).

[017] This aspect of the matter, i.e., the necessity of dogmatics as an enquiry, was in the minds of the orthodox Lutherans when they used to distinguish theology quite expressly from Holy Scripture as *ex verbo Dei exstructa*[EN65] (e.g., J. Gerhard, *Loci comm.*, 1610, *Prooem.* 31) *docens ... ex divina revelatione*[EN66] (Baier, *Comp. Theol. pos.*, 1686, *Prol.* 38), etc. (So, too, among the Reformed writers, Burmann, *Syn. Theol.*, 1678, I, 2, 41.)

3. DOGMATICS AS AN ACT OF FAITH

Dogmatics is a part of the work of human knowledge. But this part of the work of human knowledge stands under a particularly decisive condition. Like all work of human knowledge, it naturally demands the intellectual faculties of attentiveness and concentration, of understanding and appraisal. Like all serious work of human knowledge, it demands the best will to utilise these faculties and ultimately the giving of the whole man to this utilisation. Over and above this, however, it demands Christian faith, which does not simply come of

---

[EN57] For what we seek, exhorted by him, we will find, being shown by him, to the extent that these things can be found by such as us in this life

[EN58] not so much to demonstrate as to inquire with you

[EN59] the understanding of the faith

[EN60] reading

[EN61] inward reading

[EN62] that nothing at all in this (meditation) should be settled on the authority of Scripture alone (Monol. Prol.) ... so that what we hold by faith ... might be proved without reference to Scripture's authority (*Ep. de incarn.* 6)

[EN63] with Christ out of the picture ... as though nothing were known of Christ

[EN64] Some disputations are directed to removing doubt as to whether something is the case: and in this kind of theological disputation, it is especially useful to cite authorities which those with whom one is disputing acknowledge ... But another kind of disputation is that conducted by teachers in the schools, not for the removing of error, but for the instructing of students, so that they might be led to an understanding of the truth at which it aims; and in these cases it is preferable to be supported by those who investigate the logical basis of the truth and are thereby able to show how it is that what is taught is true

[EN65] built up from the word of God (e.g., J. Gerhard, Loci com., 1610, Prooem. 31)

[EN66] teaching ... on the basis of divine revelation

itself even with the deepest and purest surrender to this task. Dogmatics is a function of the Christian Church. The Church tests itself by essaying it. To the Church is given the promise of the criterion of Christian faith, namely, the revelation of God. The Church can pursue dogmatics. Even in the Church dogmatics need not be the work of a special dogmatic science. But there is no possibility of dogmatics at all outside the Church. To be in the Church, however, is to be called with others by Jesus Christ. To act in the Church is to act in obedience to this call. This obedience to the call of Christ is faith. In faith the judgment of God is acknowledged and His grace extolled. In faith self-examination is necessary in view of responsibility before God. Faith grasps the promise that we shall be led into all truth (Jn. 16[13]). Faith knows God. Faith is the determination of human action by the being of the Church and therefore by Jesus Christ, by the gracious address of God to man. In faith, and only in faith, human action is related to the being of the Church, to the action of God in revelation and reconciliation. Hence dogmatics is quite impossible except as an act of faith, in the determination of human action by listening to Jesus Christ and as obedience to Him. Without faith it would be irrelevant and meaningless. Even in the case of the most exact technical imitation of what the Church does, or the most sincere intention of doing what the Church does, it would be idle speculation without any content of knowledge.

H. Scholz (*Z.d.Z.*, 1931, 34) poses the question, expressly in relation to dogmatics: "Can we or can we not construct a form of Christianity, and do so in such a way that it is worth our while to contemplate this form and immerse ourselves in it, unless for better or for worse we ourselves actually believe in this Christianity?" His own answer, which fortunately is only [018]
indirect, is to the effect "that we may confidently evolve from Platonism or Aristotelianism, from Leibniz or Kant, a picture which ought to impress any who are susceptible to such spiritual pictures, and in such a way that for better or for worse we are neither Platonists nor Aristotelians, neither Leibnizians nor Kantians, but what it is our destiny to be." Our comment is that, so long as we understand by Christianity the creaturely and cultural reality of a view of life and the world alongside Platonism, Aristotelianism, etc., and so long as we understand by a form or picture of Christianity the representation of it in its creatureliness according to the laws of the knowledge of such a reality, then the construction of an impressive form of Christianity without believing in it for better or for worse, is certainly an attractive and rewarding possibility. But there can be no question of this in dogmatics. In dogmatics Christianity means the proper content of talk about God ventured in the fear of God. Form means the statements in which we formulate our provisional answers in investigation of this content. The problem of impressiveness for the spiritually susceptible is bluntly replaced by that of responsibility to God. The third point reminds us that in dogmatics there can be no construction outside the real encounter between God and man, which is faith. Nor can the real content, i.e., Jesus Christ, be simply equated with creaturely reality. For He is revelation, divine-human reality. If there is such a reality, and if there is knowledge of it, as the Church and dogmatics presuppose, then this knowledge can only be that of faith, and we have good reason to ask if faith is really faith unless it is for better or for worse. *Omnis recta cognitio Dei ab obedientia nascitur*[EN67] (Calvin, *Instit.* I, 6, 2). Plato's claim to make us Platonists might be

[EN67] All right knowledge of God is born of obedience

transformed without loss into an impressive exposition of Platonism. Christ's claim to obedience is identical with the being of the Church and cannot therefore be evaded by any dogmatics which is not prepared to forswear itself and become a mere survey of human thought. Dogmatics does not presuppose that it is our destiny to believe as Christians, but rather that our destiny not to do so is not final, and therefore that we shall not be disobedient to the heavenly voice (Ac. 26^{19}),

Faith, however, is not a determination of human action which man can give to it at will or maintain at will once it is received. On the contrary, it is the gracious address of God to man, the free personal presence of Jesus Christ in his activity. Hence, if we say that dogmatics presupposes faith, or the determination of human action by hearing and as obedience to the being of the Church, we say that at every step and with every statement it presupposes the free grace of God which may at any time be given or refused as the object and meaning of this human action. It always rests with God and not with us whether our hearing is real hearing and our obedience real obedience, whether our dogmatics is blessed and sanctified as knowledge of the true content of Christian utterance or whether it is idle speculation.

It is in this light that we have to ponder what was once much discussed as the demand for regeneration or conversion in the theologian and what is to-day being debated afresh as the prerequisite of what is called existentiality in theological thinking. Urgent warnings that theologising is powerless unless there is a relationship between the theme and the theologian in which the true and total man is claimed may be found already in Anselm, who tells
[019] us that the *credere*[EN68] underlying *intelligere*[EN69] cannot be merely a *credere id*[EN70] but must be a *credere in id, quod credi debet*[EN71] (*Monol.* 76–78). *Rectitudo fidei et intellectus*[EN72] necessarily involves a *rectitudo volendi*[EN73] (*De concordia, qu.* III, 2 and 6). *Non solum ad intelligendum altiora prohibetur mens ascendere sine fide et mandatorum Dei obedientia, sed etiam. aliquando, datus intellectus subtrahitur ... neglecta bona conscientia*[EN74] (*Ep. de incarn.* 1). *Non est ... securus transitus a scientia ad sapientiam; oportet ergo medium ponere, scilicet sanctitatem*[EN75] (Bonaventura, *In Hex.* XIX, 3). Against certain supposed "mystical" theologians, whose actual experience was the very opposite of all negative theology, and who knew nothing of the Christian's love for death and hell, the younger Luther wrote the words: *Vivendo, immo moriendo et damnando fit theologus, non intelligendo, legendo aut speculando*[EN76] (*Op. in Psalm. W.A.* 5, 163, 28). "Doctors of arts, medicine, law and philosophy, can be made by the pope, the emperor, and the universities; but be quite sure that no one can make a doctor of Holy Scripture save only the Holy Ghost from heaven, as Christ says in John vi: 'They must all be taught of God

---

EN68 believing
EN69 understanding
EN70 believing something
EN71 believing in that which ought to be believed
EN72 rightness of faith and understanding
EN73 rightness of willing
EN74 Without faith and obedience to the commandments of God not only is the mind prevented from rising to the understanding of higher things, but sometimes even the given understanding is removed ... when good conscience is neglected
EN75 There is no ... secure transition from knowledge to wisdom; there needs to be a means in between, namely holiness
EN76 By living, no: by dying and being damned does one become a theologian, not by knowing, reading, or speculating

himself.' Now the Holy Ghost does not ask after red or brown robes, or what is showy, nor whether a man is young or old, lay or clerical, monastic or secular, virgin or married. Indeed, He once spake by an ass against the prophet that rode on it. Would God we were worthy that such doctors be given us ...." (Luther, *An d. chr. Adel deutch. Nation v. d. chr. Standes Besserung,* 1520, *W.A.* 6, 460, 28), Even Melanchthon (e.g., *Apol. Conf. Aug., De justif.* 9 and 37, *C.R.* 27, 430 and 434) was ready to insist that true knowledge of salvation is not gained by empty speculations, but only *in agone conscientiae et in acie*[EN77]. The theological significance of all this is brought out in the age of orthodoxy by the fact that *theologia concretive considerata*[EN78], i, e,. as event rather than concept, is described as *habitus θεόδοτος per verbum a Spiritu sancto homini collatus*[EN79] (J. Gerhard, *Loci theol.*, 1610, *Prooem.*, 31). It can be said: *Post lapsum non nascuntur theologi, sed fiunt scil. a Deo docti per verbum scriptum*[EN80] (Quenstedt, *Theol. did. pol.*, 1685, l, *cap.* 1, *sect.* 2, *qu.* 2, *ekth.* 2). Thus true theology is an actual determination and claiming of man by the acting God. That there is at this point an acute danger of anthropologising theological knowledge is shown by the rather equivocal assertion of Anselm that if we compare the proclamation and hearing of the Word of God with sowing (*agricultura*), then the *semen*[EN81], i.e., the Word of God, is *immo non verbum sed sensus qui percipitur per verbum*[EN82] (*de Concordia, qu.* III, 6). For here there is at least the threat of the unfortunate transition from a divine determining to a human determination, if not expressly to a human achievement, as was the opinion of Bonaventura, who understood and could describe that *sanctitas*[EN83] as a *vita timorata, inpolluta, religiosa, aedificatoria*[EN84] (*In Hex.* XIX, 20 f.). If we follow up this line, then the *sensus*[EN85], the human determination, the experience and attitude of the knowing subject are made the criterion of theological knowledge. It was obviously in an attempt to avoid this danger that the middle and later orthodoxy (e.g. Quenstedt, *op. cit.*, *ekth.* 5; Hollaz, *Ex. theol. acroam.*, 1707, *Prol.*, 1, 18–21; Buddeus, *Instit. theol. dogm.*, 1724, l, 1, 49) made a distinction between objective theological *habitus*[EN86] on the one side and faith or the regeneration of the theologian on the other: *Constat, habitum Theologiae reapse separare posse a fide salvifica*[EN87] (Heidan, *Corp. Theol. christ.*, 1686, L, 1, 3). It hardly need be said that this is not in keeping with the thought of Luther. It carries with it the far worse implication that faith, regeneration and conversion are now to be regarded quite definitely as a human experience and attitude. How little certainty there was in the whole matter is shown by the fact that it was thought necessary to hedge around with every conceivable reservation and restriction the possibility of an unconverted theologian living only by the *habitus*[EN88], i.e., of a *theologia irregenitorum*[EN89], which had to be admitted on the basis of the distinction. We need not be surprised that Pietism abandoned the distinction and demanded of the student of theology at least a serious striving for per- [020]
sonal conversion (A. H. Francke, *Method. stud. theol.*, 1723, *cap.* 2). But the very fact that it can speak only of striving is an indication how self-evident has become the idea that faith is

---

EN77 in the struggle of the conscience and in conflict
EN78 theology viewed concretely
EN79 a God-given disposition conveyed to the individual through the word by the Holy Spirit
EN80 After the fall theologians are not born, but are rather made by God, being taught by the written word
EN81 seed
EN82 not so much the word as the meaning which is perceived through the word
EN83 holiness
EN84 life that is devout, free from blemish, pious, constructive
EN85 emotional meaning
EN86 disposition
EN87 It is manifest that the disposition for Theology really can be separated from saving faith
EN88 disposition
EN89 theology of the unregenerate

to be decisively regarded as a determination of human reality. So far as concerns this subjective presupposition, Rationalism (e.g., G. J. Planck, *Einl. i. d. theol. Wissensch.*, 1794, Vol. I, 62 f.) was not prepared to insist on the need for Christian religiosity, but only for religiosity in general. But this did not help the situation. And when Schleiermacher as a theologian was prepared to speak, "out of the irresistible inner necessity of his nature" (*Reden ü. d. Rel.*, 1799, 5), only of that which was "the innermost impulse of his being" (*loc. cit.*), thus expounding "his own view as an object for the rest" (*op. cit.*, p. 182), he had obviously lost altogether any sense of what Anselm, Luther and Melanchthon were after with their demand for *sensus*[EN90] and *experientia*[EN91] as the presupposition of true theology. "It may be presupposed that no one becomes a theologian, or makes the science of the Christian religion his calling, without having an inner relation to religion or Christianity, just as no one will pursue any branch of science without a love for its theme"—such is their concern as translated into the language of 19th century Liberalism (H. Mulert, *Evangelische Kirchen und theologische Fakultäten*, 1930, p. 16 f.). The anthropologising of theology was complete. And it is a serious question whether the same is not to be said of the existential element which is demanded to-day from theological thinking and utterance under the influence of Kierkegaard, but supremely if sometimes unconsciously in continuation of the Pietist tradition. It is perhaps laughable though highly suspicious that in line with the contemporary vogue even G. Wobbermin has set out to reinterpret his theology, which is in no sense either interested in Kierkegaard or orientated to him, as a theology of existential religious psychology (*Wort Gottes und evangelischer Glaube*, 1931, 14 f.). If this existential element is sought in the fact that the statements of theology must be accounts of the human situation of the theologian as radically revealed in faith; if it is demanded that its utterances must be "the cry of a man who like Christophorus breaks under the far too heavy burden of what must now in any circumstances take place in modern Germany"; if, e.g., the proposition that we are all sinners is not to be a mere phrase, but "I am to speak it for concrete reasons, being brought by a definite occasion to an awareness that this hopeless failure of mine springs from a self-centredness ... which I share with all my fellows" (K. Heim, *Glaube und Denken*, 1931, 409), then these are psychologisms and legalisms under the yoke of which we do not have to bend and should not do so. The time has come to go back with a new understanding to the pre-Pietist doctrine of the theological *habitus*[EN92] in virtue of which the theologian is what he is by the grace of God quite irrespective of his greater or lesser likeness to Christophorus, and without any need for existential outcry, etc. A reaction in this sense, a new relating of Christophorus to Christ, has indeed appeared already. We have been told afresh that "theological statements are possible only on the basis of the presence of the Gospel, the message and proclamation." A proposition with theological intention is one which is true "quite apart from the existential position of the speaker, receiving its meaning for the hearers only on the basis of this independence" (K. F. Schumann, *Der Gottesgedanke und der Zerfall der Moderne*, 1929, 348 f.). Or again with a sharp polemical application: "The ἀκοὴ πίστεως[EN93] is not to be understood as the existential decision of faith in apprehension of the promise" (H. M. Müller, *Glaube und Erfahrung bei Luther*, 1929, 90). "Where the existential element is in any way made the theme of theology, service is offered to the *humanum*[EN94] .... There is only one alternative: Either we understand our own existence as being in faith, or we await God's contin-

[EN90] emotional meaning
[EN91] experience
[EN92] disposition
[EN93] hearing of faith
[EN94] the realm of what is human

gent visitation in the real end of this existence" (*op. cit.*, p. 187). This reaction is timely and useful. Yet the original demand of Anselm, Luther and Melanchthon, in which the older and newer doctrine of the *theologia regenitorum*[EN95], of existential theology, has its *particula veri*[EN96], must not be lost to view. Even if only from the standpoint of the end, or from without, God's contingent visitation does affect the existence of man, and therefore the gift of its promise by faith is a divine determination and claiming of the concrete being of man, of myself. Without this, theology would become the irrelevant wisdom of spectators outside the Church. There would be knowledge only in the dependent form of an imitative formal participation in the knowledge of the Church and faith. If the latter were to fail, then, as Anselm rightly stated, such a theology would lose its power of knowledge. But theology neither does nor can at any time find human safeguards against the danger of becoming the irrelevant wisdom of spectators outside the Church, and therefore a-theology. Faith, regeneration, conversion, existential thinking on the basis of a preceding existential encounter, are no doubt indispensable prerequisites of dogmatic work, yet not to the extent that they imply an experience and attitude, a desire and activity, a knowledge and achievement of the theologian, so that his theology is a personal cry, an account of his biographical situation, but to the extent that they imply the grace of divine predestination, the free gift of the Word and Holy Spirit, the act of calling the Church, which must always come upon the theologian from the acting God in order that he may really be what he does and what his name suggests. [021]

Naturally, the Church can and should undertake and execute its own self-examination of itself with the human application of human means. But whether in so doing it acts as the Church and therefore knows God in faith; whether the result of its action is true and important criticism and correction and not a worse perversion of Christian utterance, does not depend upon itself. Clearly, the presence of any distinctive and decisive determination of dogmatics, the decision as to what is or is not true in dogmatics, is always a matter of the divine election of grace. In this respect the fear of the Lord must always be the beginning of wisdom. This is the often discovered difficulty of all theology, especially dogmatic theology.

Cognovi, explicationem dogmatum Ecclesiae propter multas causas opus esse difficillimum et quamquam necessarium est, tamen plenum esse ingentium periculorum [EN97](Melanchthon, *Loci communes*, 1559, *C.R.* 21, 602). It was more than a monkish trick of style when Anselm referred to the *imbecillitas scientiae meae*[EN98] (*Cur Deus homo?* I, 25) and Bonaventura to the *pauper portiuncula scientiolae nostrae*[EN99] (*Breviloq., Prooem.*), and when on the first page of his *Sentences* Peter Lombard compared his achievement to the widow's mite or the two pence which the Good Samaritan gave to the inn-keeper with the promise to pay him more when he returned. The story is also told of Thomas Aquinas, whose *Summa theologica* obviously remained a torso, that when asked to write more he replied: "Reginald, I cannot, for all that I have written is like chaff to me. I hope that God will soon put an end to my life and thinking" (M. Grabmann, *Das Seelenleben des hl. Thomas v. Aq.*, 1924, 51). As against this, the other story

EN95 theology of the regenerate

EN96 element of truth

EN97 I know that the explanation of the Church's dogmas is for many reasons an extremely difficult though necessary task, but it is full of enormous dangers

EN 98 feebleness of my knowledge

EN 99 poor little portion of our little knowledge

that when he was engaged in the christological part of the work Christ appeared to him with the words: *Bene scripsisti de me, Thoma*[EN100]! seems to be less in accord with the facts! Thomas himself was rightly prepared to leave it to eschatology to invest the *doctor ecclesiae*[EN101] with a halo (*S. theol.* III, *qu.* 96, *art.* 6).

[022] Dogmatics must always be undertaken as an act of penitence and obedience. But this is possible only as it trusts in the uncontrollable presence of its ontic and noetic basis, in the revelation of God promised to the Church, and in the power of faith apprehending the promise. This is no less true in the case of the teacher than the scholar, of the author of dogmatic works than the reader. The act of faith, which means, however, its basis in the divine predestination, the free act of God on man and his work, is always the condition by which dogmatic work is made possible but by which it is also called in question with final seriousness.

Paul Althaus finds the problem of theology as a science in the conflict between critical attitude and Church connexion, which are both necessary to the theologian but which seem to be irreconcilably opposed (*Grundriss der Dogmatik*, 1929, § 1). There is a lack of true and final seriousness in this problem. As Althaus himself shows, it can be solved on both sides in a comparatively easy and amicable way. The older theologians rightly found the difficulty of theology, and sought to overcome it, on a different level: *Non ego te duco, sed ille, de quo loquimur, sine quo nihil possumus, nos ducit, ubicumque viam veritatis teneamus*[EN102] (Anselm, *Cur Deus homo?*, II, 9). *In Theologia ... datur subiectum plane divinum, quod est ... omni re prius, ut nullam principiati rationem habere possit, unde ... fit, ut duas hasce rationes simul contineat, sitque subjectum, de quo agit Theologia et simul etiam ejus principium*[EN103] (F. Turrettini, *Inst. Theol. el.* I, 1679, L, 1, *qu.* 5, 9). *Ille enim solus idoneus est de se testis, qui quod sibi gratum est, docere nos possit et cui nihil gratum esse potest, nisi a se profectum et naturae suae conveniens. Quod quale sit nemo novit nisi ipse. At id quomodo nobis innotescat, nisi nobis ab ipso patefiat el reveletur?*[EN104] (Heidanus, *Corp. Theol. chr.*, 1686, L, 1, 7). *Quemadmodum in spiritualibus nemo mortalium sibi ipse quidquam absque gratiae viribus aut dare aut tribuere, ita multo minus ea largire potest, quae ad theologiae habitum requiruntur*[EN105] (Buddeus, *Instit. Th. dogm.*, 1724, I, 1, 51). In his work *Die Entstehung der chr. Theologie und des kirchl. Dogmas*, 1927, 54 f., 87 f., A. v. Harnack explains in relation to both past and present that there are and always have been two kinds of theology. The first is a charismatic theology from within. In this, speaking from the standpoint of a believer, the theologian is convinced of its truth by its inner power of persuasion, and is

EN100 You have written rightly of me, Thomas

EN101 teacher of the church

EN102 To whatever extent we keep to the way of truth, it is not I who lead you, but He of whom we speak leads us, without whom we can do nothing

EN103 In Theology ... we begin with a wholly divine subject, which is ... prior to everything else, so that it can have no more fundamental principle than itself, whence ... it happens, that it combines two characteristics, so that it is at the same time the subject which Theology investigates and also the principle of its investigation

EN104 For He alone is able to be a witness to Himself, who is able to instruct us what is pleasing to Himself and to whom nothing can be pleasing unless it proceeds from Him and accords with His nature. What this might be no one knows except Himself. And how is it to be made known to us, unless it should be disclosed and revealed to us by Him?

EN105 Just as in spiritual matters no mortal can either give or confer anything upon himself without the powers of grace, so much the less is he able to bestow those things which are necessary to the practice of theology never without an awareness "that he can speak as a theologian only with the assistance of the Spirit of God, and that his work is thus charismatically determined." Paul is the founder of this kind of theology, but it can never become either ecclesiastical or scientific. It shapes confession and preaching, but not fellowship. The second is a theology from without. It "places the relevant religion in the circle of other objects of knowledge, and describes its reality and truth accordingly to generally valid historical, psychological and theoretical principles of knowledge." Its fathers are the 2nd-century apologists, and it alone creates fellowship and can be ecclesiastical and scientific. "We may bewail this, since the inadequacy of such a theology is manifest; but no one can alter the fact, and he who tries to do so destroys and confuses theology. His proper task is to preach." It is only fitting that this final declaration of one whom I also honour as a teacher should be allowed to speak for itself without either commentary or criticism.

Humanly speaking, there is no way to overcome this fundamental difficulty which afflicts theology alone among the sciences, and dogmatics alone within theology. There is no feasible way of creating this specifically decisive condi- [023] tion of dogmatics. We may summon up good intentions, but even the best of intentions are of no avail at this point. Nor can we evoke of ourselves the Christian faith which decisively constitutes the theological *habitus*[EN106]. The popular suspicion of theology, and especially of dogmatics, is only too well founded. There always seems to be an element of presumption in it, and all the exertions seem to lead to such meagre results. We always seem to be handling an intractable object with inadequate means. And this appearance is too solidly grounded in the nature of the study itself to be permanently overcome by a mere change of methods.

The mystery of the *ubi et quando visum est Deo*[EN107] (*Conf. Aug.*, Art. 5; cf. for an understanding of this statement the passages adduced by Hans Engelland, *Melanchthon*, 1931, 568 f.) has accompanied not only Christian talk about God in general, but dogmatics in particular, through all the stages of its history. Nor can it be any different in the future.

We maintain that humanly speaking there is nothing to alleviate the difficulty. We simply confess the mystery which underlies it, and we merely repeat the statement that dogmatics is possible only as an act of faith, when we point to prayer as the attitude without which there can be no dogmatic work.

Hoc intelligere quis hominum dabit homini? quis angelus angelo? quis angelus homini? A te petatur, in te quaeratur, ad te pulsetur: sic accipietur, sic invenietur, sic aperietur[EN108] (Augustine, *Conf.* XIII, 38, 53). *Non solum admonendi sunt studiosi venerabilium Litterarum, ut in scripturis sanctis genera locutionem sciant ... verum etiam, quod est praecipium et maxime necessarium, orent ut intelligant. In eis quippe Litteris, quarum studiosi sunt, legunt quoniam Dominus dat sapientiam et a facie ejus*

EN106 disposition

EN107 where and when God pleases

EN108 Who of human beings is able to give this understanding to another human being? What angel can give it to an angel? What angel to a human being? From You it must be asked, from You it must be sought, it is at Your door that one must knock: thus it will be received, thus it will be found, thus the door will be opened

scientia et intellectus a quo et ipsum studium, si pietate praeditum est, acceperunt[EN109] (*De doct. chr.* III, 37). We are already reminded of Anselm's *Proslogion*, 1—a passage to which we shall return in § 6, 4. Thomas Aquinas set the following prayer at the head of his *Summa theologica*: *Concede mihi quaeso, misericors Deus, quae tibi sunt placita ardenter concupiscere, prudenter investigare, veraciter agnoscere et perfecte implere ad laudem nominis tui*[EN110]. Relevant, too, is the intention of A. H. Francke in his treatment *De oratione* in a whole section of his directions for the study of theology. Nor is it to be regarded as baroque adornment that Hollaz transforms his treatment of each specific *Locus*[EN111] into a *Suspirium*[EN112], his talk about God becoming quite expressly address to God.

Prayer can be the recognition that we accomplish nothing by our intentions, even though they be intentions to pray. Prayer can be the expression of our human willing of the will of God. Prayer can signify that for good or evil man justifies God and not himself. Prayer can be the human answer to the divine hearing already granted, the epitome of the true faith which we cannot assume of ourselves. We do not speak of true prayer if we say "must" instead of "can." According to Rom. 8[26f] the way from "can" to "must" is wrapped in the
[024] mystery at the gates of which we here stand. With this reference we do not give anyone a means by which he can count on succeeding in his work. It must be said, however, that it is hard to see how else there can be successes in this work but on the basis of divine correspondence to this human attitude: "Lord, I believe; help thou mine unbelief."

[EN109] Students of these venerable Books are to be advised not only to get to know the forms of expression in the holy Scriptures ... but also – what is of special importance and most necessary – that they should pray for understanding. For in these Books of which they are students they read that 'the Lord gives wisdom; from his mouth come knowledge and understanding' [Prov. 2:6], and from Him they have received their zeal for knowledge, if it is joined with piety

[EN110] Grant my request, merciful God, that I may earnestly desire, soberly examine, truly recognize, and perfectly complete those things that are pleasing to You, to the praise of Your name

[EN111] topic

[EN112] sigh

§ 2 [025]

THE TASK OF PROLEGOMENA TO DOGMATICS

Prolegomena to dogmatics is our name for the introductory part of dogmatics in which our concern is to understand its particular way of knowledge.

1. THE NECESSITY OF DOGMATIC PROLEGOMENA

Prolegomena to a science, in so far as they are necessary and possible, will always consist decisively in discussions and expositions of how knowledge is attained in it. By prolegomena to dogmatics (*praecognita Theologiae*[EN1], as many older writers called it with even greater fulness of meaning), we understand the attempt to give an explicit account of the particular way of knowledge taken in dogmatics, or, as we might also say, of the particular point from which we are to look, think and judge in dogmatics. It cannot be taken for granted that this question can be explicitly raised and answered, and therefore that there can be such a thing as dogmatic prolegomena. Or again, the question might be answered quite simply by the manner in which dogmatics goes its way. The assumptions made might perhaps emerge and prove themselves in application. What is said might obviate any need for a foreword. The lack of prolegomena, or at least of extensive prolegomena, might well indicate, not a naive attitude, but one which is scientifically mature and well-considered. Nor need such an attitude rest on an illusion. It might well have a solid basis in the simplicity of truth, in supreme scientific soundness. *Ab esse ad posse valet consequentia*[EN2] might well be its justification. It must be remembered that the great representatives of early and mediaeval dogmatics were sometimes content with the briefest reflections on the way of knowledge taken by them.

For instance, in the *Ἔκδοσις ἀκριβὴς τῆς ὀρθοδόξου πίστεως*[EN3] of John Damascene we find two introductory chapters on the knowability of God which might be claimed as prolegomena. Peter Lombard begins his *Sentences* with a short preface in which there is no discussion of method. In the *Summa theologica* Thomas Aquinas has a first *Quaestio* with ten articles on the concept of *doctrina sacra*[EN4], and in his *Summa c. gent.* there are 8 introductory sections on faith and knowledge. Among the Reformers Zwingli in his *Comm. de vera et falsa religione*, 1525, kept to the same tradition with a brief discussion of the term *religio*. His *Fidei ratio*, 1530, plunges at once into the doctrine of the Trinity after an address to the Emperor, [026]
and his *Fidei christianae expositio*, 1531, follows up the address to the French king with a

---

EN1 theological preliminaries
EN2 A deduction from reality to possibility is valid
EN3 Exact Exposition of the Orthodox Faith
EN4 sacred doctrine

development of the concept of God. Among more recent writers A. Schlatter, *Das christliche Dogma*, 2nd edn., 1923, is able to dispense almost completely with prolegomena.

But the phenomenon is not unequivocal. It might be explained by a profound realism, but it might also be explained by a less profound arrogance and self-assurance. From the theological standpoint, both possibilities have to be taken into account, and we must not be overhasty in deciding between them.

I still think it rash to conclude that in the rapid application of older writers to their main task we have the expression of a *theologia gloriae*[EN5] which does not see its own difficulties (cf. E. Brunner, *Z.d.Z.*, 1930, 397). On the other hand, I fear that in the first edition of the present book (p. 10 f.) I myself was guilty of a romanticising philosophy of history, which I must now reject, when I described the earlier procedure as that of a classical age and our modern approach as that of a decadent age.

The situation of the Church which is the sphere of dogmatic work is not always the same but lays various special conditions on this work. What is now forbidden did not always have to be. On the other hand, what was once permitted may now be forbidden. We are now forbidden to take up the main content of dogmatics without express and explicit discussion of the problem of the way of knowledge. The only question is—and it is decisively important—on what ground this is forbidden, and therefore on what ground dogmatic prolegomena are necessary.

At this point the customary procedure, followed with new zeal in modern work, is to indicate the change in general cultural awareness and the general world-picture which has taken place in the last 300 years and called theology as such in question. Attention is drawn to the wave of paganism which obviously seems to be engulfing everything and to carry with it a particular threat to the Church and theology. Note is taken of the radicalism of rational thought which supposedly distinguishes our age from all others and which negates all revelation as such.

"Already in the second half of the seventeenth century, and even more so in the first half of the eighteenth, so many questions, objections and doubts were brought by naturalists, rationalists and free-thinkers against the doctrines of the Christian faith and their scholarly presentation that a short introduction was not enough and preliminary discussion became indispensable before dogmatics could begin" (Carl Daub, *Prolegomena zur Dogmatik*, 1839, 3). "The problem to-day is not the nature of God but His existence, not what is revealed but whether there is such a thing as revelation, not rationalistic corruption at individual points but the questioning of the miracle of revelation as such. It is the problem of the sign and norm of all Christian theology, of the concept of revelation and not its contents. In short, it is the problem of reason and revelation" (E. Brunner, *Z.d.Z.*, 1930, 414).

[027] This altered situation, we are told, is what makes dogmatic prolegomena necessary to-day. If dogmatics is to be existential theology and not to fall victim to a "dangerous Chinese Wall mentality," then in addition to its primary task as

---

[EN5] theology of glory

the reflection of the Church on the Word of God there must be recognised and tackled a second task which arises out of this situation.

In his essay "*Die andere Aufgabe der Theologie*" (*Z.d.Z.*, 1929, 255 f.), to which I particularly refer, E. Brunner proposes to give to this preparatory dogmatic discipline the name of eristics rather than apologetics. But does he not make out the older apologetics to be worse than it was, in order to be able to mark himself off from it, when he characterises it *in toto*[EN6] as a "feeble and anxious defensive before a tribunal of reason, as the self-justification of Christians before a world which has lost confidence in them" (*op. cit.*, p. 258)? Is the difference between C. E. Luthardt's *Apologetische Vorträge* (1870 f.), for example, and Karl Heim's *Glauben und Denken* (1931), any other than that between the better and the worse, or the outmoded and the modern? Would it not be clearer to accept the name apologetics without apology? Eristics is hardly likely to escape the scourge of Overbeck with which the earlier apologetics is chastised according to Brunner.

On this view the task of dogmatics consists in the "conflict against the self-assurance of the modern spirit," "against the rational axiom of the final efficacy of reason." It consists in the "contesting of this reason which is self-sufficient and therefore opposes the Word," and in the "liberation of the reason which in this illusion and isolation of reason secretly yearns for the divine Thou."

Karl Heim says much the same thing with rather greater restraint (*op. cit.*, 433): "In accordance with the lowly position of service ... occupied by knowledge in relation to life, only a negative task can be ascribed to Christian philosophy. It must deprive man of assurance. It must mercilessly reveal in its impossibility all that man has always undertaken, and thus point him to a position of reserve in which he is assured in face of the question of eternity constantly posed to him afresh."

Nevertheless, there is "in man a point of contact for the divine message which is not disturbed by sin." There is a "questing after God" which is natural to man.

By this concept of a point of contact, which is so important to him, E. Brunner understands the "self-evident knowledge which man can have even as an unbeliever and which as such is taken up into his believing" (*Theologie und Ontologie, Z.Th.Z.*, 1931, 112).

In connexion with this point of contact it has "to be shown how by the Word of God human reason is partly disclosed to be the source of error which is hostile to life, and partly fulfilled in its own incomplete searching."

E. Brunner, *Z.d.Z.*, 1929, 257, 260, 262, 264, 267, 273 f. Cf. also *Z.d.Z.*, 1930, 398, 410; *Gott und Mensch*, 1930, 55 f.

This basis of the necessity of dogmatic prolegomena is to be rejected for three reasons. [028]

1. It is to be rejected because there is no theological foundation for the assumed difference between our own and earlier times. Has there ever been an age in which theology has not basically confronted a radical negation of the

---

[EN6] as a whole

revelation believed in the Church? Have not antiquity and the Middle Ages, as theologians realised only too well, had their rationalists, atheists and secularists as forerunners of our specifically modern heathenism? If we are concerned to-day for the tactical situation of belief in revelation, was it not much more seriously threatened in the second half of the 18th century? Above all, did the plenitude of gods, demons and miracles which distinguished the ancient view of the world from our own really signify from the Christian standpoint a true gain as compared with the dedivinisation which marks the present time? Did the pre-Kantian and pre-Copernican cultural consciousness, in which there was more place than in our own for this or that revelation, or for revelation in general, genuinely make easier the situation of the Christian Church and its dogmatics, and thus constitute a serious reason for the paucity of prolegomena in earlier writers? On the other hand, has the modern cultural consciousness and view of the world, with its particular threat to all revelation, to revelation as a whole and in general, really created for Christian dogmatics a situation of greater peril in which there is a very different kind of need for assurance and debate? Both questions could be given an affirmative answer if the revelation believed in the Church were to be understood as a specific instance within the genus of revelation as a whole and in general. But this is not so, if we may provisionally make this simple affirmation. Knowledge of the revelation believed in the Church does not stand or fall with the general religious possibility that is made easier by the ancient view of things and more difficult by the modern. On the contrary, the struggle between the unbelieving reason of man and the revelation believed in the Church has always been with fundamentally the same seriousness the problem of Christian utterance in general and of dogmatics in particular. Hence we need not regard the tragedy of modern godlessness as anything out of the ordinary, nor treat it as tragically as is presupposed in this conception of the necessity of dogmatic prolegomena.

2. This conception is also mistaken, however, because it carries with it a complex of problems for dogmatic prolegomena which results in the abandonment rather than the serious acceptance of the task of dogmatics. In dogmatics the Church has to measure its talk about God by the standard of its own being, i.e., of divine revelation. Its talk about God, however, is that of the intrinsically godless reason of man which is inimical to belief. At every point,
[029] therefore, dogmatics is a struggle between this reason of man and the revelation believed in the Church. This struggle, however, takes place in the Church itself, so that it is not orientated to the contradiction of reason but to the declaration of revelation. Its interest is not in the exhibition of a point of contact for the divine message to man but wholly and utterly in the divine message itself as it has gone out and been received. Even its question of knowledge cannot, then, be put as follows: How is human knowledge of revelation possible?—as though there were doubt whether revelation is known, or as though insight into the possibility of knowledge of divine revelation were to be

expected from investigation of human knowledge. It can only take this form: What is true human knowledge of divine revelation?—on the assumption that revelation itself creates of itself the necessary point of contact in man. But if this relationship is set aside, if the contradiction of human reason is made the subject of enquiry and its overcoming the goal, the sphere of the Church is abandoned and "another task" is indeed substituted for the task of dogmatics.

"Eristic theology is distinguished from dogmatic by the fact that it has more regard to the one with whom it speaks about faith, that it addresses itself more ... to his resistance, and that to this extent it speaks more *ad hominem*[EN7]" (E. Brunner, *Z.d.Z.*, 1929, 269). As though dogmatics were speaking rather to angels! But if there is an emphatic intention of speaking "to men," not merely the dogmatic attitude but the theological attitude in general is jeopardised.

However legitimate or possible this other task may be, the task of dogmatics is set aside when it is pursued. No progress is thus made towards the answering of its own specific question of knowledge nor towards the establishment of its own body of knowledge. Undertaken in relation to this complex of problems, prolegomena to dogmatics do not so much lead up to the real work of dogmatics as lead away from it.

Nor is it merely the zeal of the discoverer which leads Emil Brunner, particularly in his 1929 essay, to set the work of real dogmatics in a very unfavourable light as compared with that of eristics.

3. It must also be asked, however, whether in this conception of the necessity of dogmatic prolegomena too little justice is not done even to the concern in which it clearly has its basis, namely, the "responsibility and relevance" (E. Brunner, *Z.d.Z.*, 1930, 397) of theological thinking. Is it really going to protect dogmatics from isolation, and secure for it the undoubtedly desirable connexion with the unbelieving contemporary world, if it loses sight of its theme at the very first step and with mysterious omnipotence applies itself to the strange task of "shattering the axiom of reason" (E. Brunner, *Z.d.Z.*, 1929, 265)? We do not think so. Theological thinking which by the grace of God is truly responsible and relevant, and stands in true connexion with contemporary society, will even to-day show itself to be such by not allowing itself to be [030]
drawn into discussion of its basis, of the question of the existence of God or of revelation. On the contrary, it will refrain from attempted self-vindication as its theme demands, and thus show its responsibility and relevance by simply fulfilling itself as thinking on this basis, and therefore by simply existing as the witness of faith against unbelief. There can be no question, of course, that with the Christian Church generally dogmatics, too, has everywhere to speak in the antithesis of faith to unbelief and therefore apologetically and polemically. But there has never been any effective apologetics or polemics of faith against

[EN7] to the individual person

unbelief except that which is not deliberately planned, which cannot possibly be planned, which simply happens as God Himself acknowledges the witness of faith. There are three reasons why all planned apologetics and polemics have obviously been irresponsible, irrelevant and therefore ineffective.

(*a*) In such apologetics faith must clearly take unbelief seriously. Hence it cannot take itself with full seriousness. Secretly or openly, therefore, it ceases to be faith. What unbelief expects of faith is quite simply that it should be an event. It is not in our hands to produce this event. But faith is certainly not an event in conscious wrestling with unbelief. Does not the credal statement concerning the remission of sins itself forbid any discussion in which the unbelief of the partner in discussion is taken seriously, and he is therefore addressed as a worldling and riveted to his unbelief? Is there really any hope even apagogically that in this way he will be taught the injustice of his prejudices against faith?

(*b*) In all independently ventured apologetics and polemics there may be discerned the opinion that dogmatics has done its work.

Karl Heim begins the preface to his *Glaube und Denken*, 1931, with the astonishing statement: "We have enough dogmatic handbooks, which provide excellent introductions to the teaching of the Evangelical Church." Enough? Excellent?

The theologian who gives himself to these crafts is obviously of the opinion that he has both the time and the authority to abandon the concern for dogmatics, and instead of working at the thing itself to begin to discuss it with others. This confident distraction is quite out of place, and cannot in the long run or at bottom succeed in making itself convincing.

(*c*) An independent eristics at least runs the risk that once its task is completed dogmatics will think that its conflict with unbelief has been brought to an end in the form of such prolegomena, and that it will thus lose the necessary awareness of the constant exposure to assault of all its statements. In other words, dogmatics may well come to act as an eristics which is *praenumerando*[EN8]
[031] assured, and thus be guilty of a genuine Chinese Wall mentality, the building of the Great Wall of China being obviously a thoroughly eristic enterprise.

Theology is genuinely and effectively apologetic and polemical to the extent that its proper work, which cannot be done except at the heart of the conflict between faith and unbelief, is recognised, empowered and blessed by God as the witness of faith, but not to the extent that it adopts particular forms in which it finally becomes only too clear to the opposing partner that it is either deceiving him when it proposes to deal with him on the ground of common presuppositions, or that it is not quite sure of its own cause in so doing. Either way, there can be no shattering of the axiom of reason along these lines, but only as theology goes its own way sincerely and with no pretence. Apologetics and polemics can only be an event and not a programme.

[EN8] in advance

It is thus true of theology too: "For this reason we must note that if we do not uphold the Gospel with its own strength, but rather with our own resources, all will be lost, so that no matter how well we defend it, it will crumble to pieces. Let us have no anxiety that the Gospel needs our help. It is sufficiently strong of itself, and may be committed to God alone, whose it is ... Hence it is a poor and miserable thing that this feeble rabble of sophists opposes it. For what do these poor bats hope to accomplish with their petty flappings? Let them come! By the grace of God they have no true learning ... In all these things there is no better counsel than to preach the Gospel simply and purely, praying God that He will direct and lead us" (Luther, *Sermon vom Glauben und guten Warken*, 1522, *W.A.* 10^3, 354, 1.15). "It is thus settled that the Word of God can have no other master, judge or protector than God Himself. It is His Word, and therefore, as He utters it quite apart from human merit or counsel, so He Himself will uphold and defend it without human help or strength. If any man seek human protection or comfort in this respect, he will undoubtedly fall and miss both, being abandoned by both God and man" (*Fastenpostille*, 1525, *W.A.* 17^2, 108, 1.26).

To be truly imperious, the necessity of dogmatic prolegomena, i.e., of an explicit account of the particular way to be taken in dogmatics, must be an inner necessity grounded in the matter itself. If it rests on a conflict in which faith finds itself, then, if this conflict is to be serious, it must be a conflict of faith with itself. The conflict of faith with unbelief can be truly significant only as and when it is a conflict of faith with itself, since in faith unbelief has in some sense expressed itself and claims a hearing. This paradoxical fact is a real fact. Faith does not stand only, or even in the first and most important sense, in conflict with unbelief. It stands in conflict with itself, i.e., with a form or forms of faith in which it recognises itself in respect of form but not of content, in which it so seriously fails to do so in the latter respect that, although in them it must genuinely recognise faith, and even Christian faith, so far as form is concerned, it can only understand this faith as another faith so far as concerns content. This other faith is the faith in which we hear unbelief express itself. As we take up the task of dogmatics, we come up against this fact of another faith. [032]
That is to say, as we try to ask about the being of the Church, about Jesus Christ, as the norm of Church action, we find that even in the understanding of this norm, in the knowledge of Jesus Christ as the Lord of the Church, we are so much at one with some that we can at once address ourselves to the task with them, but so little at one with others even in this presupposition, i.e., in the way in which we understand it, that we cannot pursue the dogmatic task together with them. We have to state quite definitely that our own understanding of the being of the Church is in no sense the only one, that alongside it other and quite different understandings are also present, that the only possible fellowship with the representatives of these other understandings is that of conflict with them, and that the different and even alien element in them cannot be regarded by us as another possibility of faith perhaps as yet unknown to us, but only as a possibility which is hostile to faith, and therefore as unbelief, even though it must still be understood as a possibility of faith in virtue of its formal presuppositions. The paradoxical fact to which we refer is that of heresy. By heresy we understand a form of Christian faith which we

cannot deny to be a form of Christian faith from the formal standpoint, i.e., in so far as it, too, relates to Jesus Christ, to His Church, to baptism, Holy Scripture and the common Christian creeds, but in respect of which we cannot really understand what we are about when we recognise it as such, since we can understand its content, its interpretation of these common presuppositions, only as a contradiction of faith.

This paradoxical element in the factor of heresy has been finely brought out in the words of Irenaeus: *Similia enim loquentes fidelibus ... non solum dissimilia sapiunt, sed et contraria et per omnia plena blasphemiis, per quae interficiunt eos, qui per similitudinem verborum dissimile affectionis eorum in se attrahunt venenum; sicut quis aquae mixtum gypsum dans pro late, seducat per similitudinem coloris, sicut quidam dixit superior nobis de omnibus qui quolibet modo depravant quae sunt Dei, et adulterant veritatem: In Dei lacte gypsum male miscetur*[EN9] (*C. o. haer.* III, 17, 4).

Because of its paradoxical nature, heresy is for faith an important factor. Or, as we might say, unbelief in the form of heresy is for faith an important factor—which is not the case when it is present as pure unbelief. Because in heresy it is present as a form of faith, it must be taken seriously at this point, and there can and must be serious conflict between faith and heresy.

The early, mediaeval and post-Reformation Church right up to Pietism and the Enlightenment engaged in conflict with Jews, pagans and atheists only for the most part incidentally, and never with anything like the same emphasis or zeal as it did with heretics. Even when this included the by no means laudable nor even necessary mutual abuse or even burnings of
[033] those past days, there was meaning in it. since the Church and heretics were talking very differently about the same theme, and therefore not talking past one another but in opposition to one another. There was thus a headlong collision such as can only take place between contending brothers. The much vaunted progress made between the 17th and 18th centuries consisted in the decision to tolerate one another, i.e., to abandon one another to the appropriate fate. This was the first breach in the fellowship hitherto continually maintained in conflict.

In the conflict between the Church and heresy, however, it is a matter of engagement from different angles with the thing itself, and not of mere talk about it condemned at the very outset to be sterile of results. The theme is the same. This is why there can be strife. We have to do with differing interpretations of the same theme. This is why there has to be strife. So different is the interpretation of the Church from that of heretics that the menacing question arises whether they are not really dealing with different themes, and therefore whether the opposing and different faith is not really to be understood as unbelief. The conversation between the Church and heretics would not be so

---

[EN9] For though they say things that sound similar [to what] the faithful [say], ... not only do they hold opinions which are different, but event contrary [to the truth] and thoroughly full of blasphemies, through which they destroy those who through the likeness of the words draw toward themselves the poison which does not suit their constitution; just as when someone who gives plaster mixed with water instead of milk may deceive on account of the likeness of the colour; as a man greater than I has said of all those who in whatever way pervert the things of God and corrupt the truth: 'Lime is wickedly mixed with God's milk.'

serious if it were conducted elsewhere than under the shadow of this menacing question. But so long and so far as the conversation goes on, this question is not decided in such sort that the Church and heretics can have no further dealings. The conversation itself, and its very sharpness, prove the contrary. In this conversation the Church must wrestle with heresy in such a way that it may itself be the Church. And heresy must attack the Church because it is not sufficiently or truly the Church. Neither can perform its task without recourse to the continually problematical formal presuppositions which they have in common. Though divided in the content of faith, both sides appeal to certain common forms of faith and thus maintain, even if only by raising that menacing question, a common ground of faith which does at least always come into consideration. Only when the Church and heresy no longer confront one another, or have no more to say to one another, is the distant but indisputable bow of peace which overarches them broken or robbed of its significance. In true encounter with heresy faith is plunged into conflict with itself, because, so long and so far as it is not free of heresy, so long and so far as heresy affects it, so long and so far as it must accept responsibility in relation to it, it cannot allow even the voice of unbelief which it thinks it hears in heresy to cause it to treat it as not at least also faith but simply as unbelief. It must understand it as a possibility of faith. To be sure, it will see it as a profoundly incomprehensible one, which can be regarded only as a possibility of the disruption and destruction of faith, as a possibility against which it must be on guard. Yet it must still understand it as a possibility of faith, and therefore and to this extent—hence the need for powerful defence—as its own possibility, as a possibility within and not without the Church, hard though it may be to think of it as such. This [034] is the reason why this conflict is a serious conflict. This is the reason why the task of giving an explicit account of the way of knowledge taken in dogmatics can and must be an inner necessity grounded in the matter itself.

We stand before the fact of heresy. Concretely, we stand before the fact of Roman Catholicism in the form which it gave itself in the 16th century in the battle against the Reformation. Again, within the organised unities of the Evangelical Churches themselves, we stand before the fact of pietistic and rationalistic Modernism as rooted in mediaeval mysticism and the humanistic Renaissance. The fact of the modern denial of revelation, etc., is quite irrelevant compared with this twofold fact. For here, in its antithesis to Roman Catholicism and Protestant Modernism, the Evangelical faith stands in conflict with itself. For these two things are not irrelevant paganisms, nor do they seek to be such. If we take them for what they purport to be, they encounter us as possibilities of faith, and therefore of our own faith, within and not without the Church. And as we listen to them, not evading the formal justice of their claim, we are forced to say that in them we do not recognise faith and the Church. We so fully fail to recognise faith and the Church in them that the question is unavoidable whether these are not possibilities of simple unbelief, whether the Roman Catholic or Protestant Modernist theologian is not to be regarded as "an heathen man and a publican" (Mt. 18[17]). But our encounter with heresies would not be a true encounter; we should be quickly rid of them; we should not hear them any more, if we were to regard this question as settled. If they really confront us as a fact, and if this question is not therefore settled, it turns against ourselves and there is demanded of us purification, reckoning and responsibility in respect of our own understanding of the being of the Church and our own knowledge of Christ. That we pursue Evangelical and not some other theology is, of course, something that we can as little discuss or establish as that we are baptised and believe. In relation to ourselves, too, we can only start with the fact in so far as it is posited as such. But heresies force us to see clearly to what extent, in what sense and with what inner foundation we stand on the one side and not the other, and thus understand revelation, not in Roman Catholic or Modernist terms, but in Evangelical terms.

That we must hear this demand decisively in the existence of heresies is an ancient insight: *Improbatio quippe haereticorum facit eminere quid Ecclesia tua sentiat et quid habeat sana doctrina*[EN10]. (Augustine, *Conf.* VII, 19, 25, cf. *De cat. rud.* 24, 44, *De civ. Dei* XVI, 2, 1). *Ob hoc haereseon non statim divinitus eradicantur auctores, ut probati manifesti fiant, id est, ut unusquisque, quam tenax et fidelis et fixus catholicae fidei sit amator, appareat*[EN11] (Vincent of Lerins, *Common.* I,
[035] 20, 25, cf. 19, 24). *Quia perversi homines apostolicam doctrinam et caeteras doctrinas et scripturas pervertunt ad sui ipsorum perditionem ... ideo necessaria fuit temporibus procedentibus explicatio fidei*[EN12] (Thomas Aquinas, *S. theol.* II[2], *qu.* 1, *art.* 10).

The purification required of us, however, will at once and necessarily be a purification in respect of the way of knowledge which we take. The ways diverge from the very source of knowledge. Already in relation to this source we must thus be at unity with ourselves in respect of the divergent possibilities. But what else is this source or basis of knowledge but the being of the Church, which itself can obviously be so diversely interpreted that whatever follows is quite different, as may be seen at every point in the debate between the Church and heresies? To clarify the Evangelical understanding of those apparently or genuinely identical formal presuppositions is thus the inner necessity of dogmatic prolegomena now resting upon us.

Heretical trends and even whole heretical churches such as e.g., the Marcionite, Donatist and Arian, were known, of course, both in the early and mediaeval Church. It must still be said, however, that only since the Reformation has heresy become a generally and fundamentally experienced problem. If there was nothing new formally, it was something quite new materially that the Evangelical Church of a Luther or Calvin should see heresy in the Papacy and Roman Catholicism of the 16th and 17th centuries, and *vice versa*. It was then for

---

[EN10] Indeed, the rejection of heretics sets in relief what your Church believes and what sound doctrine teaches

[EN11] The authors of heresies are not immediately destroyed by God in order that the proven ones might be made manifest, i.e., that it becomes apparent to what extent each person is a firm and faithful and steadfast lover of the catholic faith

[EN12] Because perverse men pervert apostolic doctrine and other teachings and the Scriptures to their own destruction ... with the passing of time it was necessary to provide expositions of the faith

the first time that the Church learned what is meant by divergent faith. That is why there have had to be all types of dogmatic prolegomena from that day forward. We find the first traces of them in the preambles on the Scripture principle which begin to appear especially in the Reformed confessions, first in the *Conf. Tetrapol.*, 1530, and then in most of those which follow. With the new material knowledge of Jesus Christ, which brought about the Reformation, especially in relation to the interconnexion of the forgiveness of sins and the Christian life, there was linked from the very first, comprehended in the doctrine of the sole normativeness of Holy Scripture, a new formal theology which inevitably demanded explicit and independent expression in face of the contradiction which confronted the matter itself and in face of the fact that this contradiction was that of divergent faith rather than of unbelief. The growing need in this respect may be gauged by the development of introductory discussions of the Scripture principle even in the different editions of the *Loci* of Melanchthon. As the first example of radically exhaustive prolegomena in our sense we shall have to claim the first ten chapters of the 1559 edition of Calvin's *Institutio.* Basic formal definitions in repudiation of the Evangelical Scripture principle were no less necessary for the opposing dogmatics of Roman Catholicism. We find the first visible step in this direction in the definitions of the dignity of Church tradition alongside or even in preference to Holy Scripture at the head of the rulings of the Council of Trent. And it is consistent and understandable that since the Vatican decree the prolegomena of Roman Catholic dogmatics should circle around the concept of the teaching office of the Church, unified in the Papacy, as the true source of revelation and of the corresponding "Catholic faith." The task of giving such an account of the formal presuppositions became even more urgent, and dogmatic prolegomena acquired even more evident importance and comprehensiveness, when pietistic and rationalistic Modernism became a third partner in the debate, particularly active and triumphant on the Evangelical side, yet not without interrelationships on the Roman Catholic. Even though this has neither been expelled from the Evangelical Churches nor under- [036] taken to form its own Church, we must differentiate ourselves from it no less than from Roman Catholicism. The faith which is in conflict with doubt of the truth, with the question of the existence of God, is very different from the faith which asks whether the God whose existence is no problem is gracious or whether man must despair of himself. The first is Modernistic faith, the second Evangelical, and the two can recognise one another only in respect of identical formal presuppositions. They are one in Christ, and yet they are not one. Modernistic faith has felt this no less than Evangelical or Roman Catholic faith. For this reason, when it began to develop its own dogmatics, it found its own approach to the matter as it thought it should understand it in the distinctive 18th and 19th century doctrine of "religion." The significance of Schleiermacher consists above all in the fact that in his doctrine of Christian piety as the being of the Church he gave this heresy a formal foundation which not merely brought to culmination the preceding era but also proved prophetic for that which was to follow. He is not the inaugurator but the great and mature classical exponent of Modernism whom the latter must never allow itself to be prevented from following if it has a true understanding of itself.

2. THE POSSIBILITY OF DOGMATIC PROLEGOMENA

How are dogmatic prolegomena possible as a preliminary understanding of the way of knowledge to be pursued? Such an understanding obviously presupposes a place from which this way is visible and intelligible. What is this place?

The answer proposed to theology since the days of the Enlightment and with a new urgency in our own time, the answer of Modernistic dogmatics, is that the Church and faith are to be understood as links in a greater nexus of being. Hence dogmatics is to be understood as a link in a greater nexus of scientific problems, from the general structural laws of which its own specific conditions of knowledge are to be deduced and its own specific scientific character known. This nexus of problems, however, is that of an ontology, and since Descartes this necessarily means that of a comprehensively explicated self-understanding of human existence which may also at a specific point become the pre-understanding of an existence in the Church or in faith, and therefore the pre-understanding and criterion of theological knowledge.

It was Idealistic philosophy which once led Schleiermacher and De Wette to understand human existence as a sum of capacities or tendencies or activities of human self-consciousness, and within this to discover at the central point, in the form of feeling or direct self-consciousness, an original disposition or basis for the piety which is to find historical actualisation, and therewith the noetic principle of Christian dogmatics as the self-explanation of this specific historically actual piety. The understanding of existence here presupposed was, of course, far too naive both formally and materially in relation to the real problems of human existence. This modern ontology, better instructed theoretically by Kier-
[037] kegaard and practically by world war and revolution, interprets human existence not merely secondarily but from the very outset as history, and materially not so much as capacity but rather as "being projected into nothingness" (M. Heidegger, *Was ist Metaphysik?*, 1929, 20). And it was understandable that a theology which was itself seeking a more essential understanding of the New Testament should attempt to interpret existence according to this understanding as prior to faith, i.e., that it should try to find in it the ontologically existential possibility of the existential event of faith, and by means of its analysis attain to a prior understanding of Christian utterance, Christian theology and above all exegesis (R. Bultmann, *Der Begriff der Offenbarung im N.T.*, 1929; *Die Geschichtlichkeit des Daseins und der Glaube, Z.Th.K.*, 1930, 339 f.). The methodological relationship of Bultmann's conception to that of Schleiermacher and De Wette should not be overlooked. "That theology should begin with a definition of existence, or man ... is at root a piece of Liberalism. One might have thought that the attempt to speak of believing man apart from God had shown itself to be impracticable" (Heinrich Barth, *Philosophie, Theologie und Existenzproblem, Z.d.Z.*, 1932, 113 f.). Cf. on this point the extolling of Bultmann by G. Wobbermin (*Richtlinien evangel. Theologie*, 1929, 102, 110 n., 116, 143).

Dogmatic prolegomena on the basis of this conception obviously consist first in the demonstration that in a general ontology or anthropology there is actually a place for this ontic factor, for the being of the Church or faith, and that human existence is practicable also as believing existence. They then consist in the concrete historical reminder that this particular ontic factor is in fact present as an event and is thus the object of ontic science. They finally consist in the establishment of the rules suggested by this ontological-ontic foundation for this science, and therefore for the criticism and correction of Christian utterance.

1. Anthropological possibility, 2. historico-psychological reality and 3. method do in fact constitute the schema which is actually followed in the introductions to Schleiermacher's

Der christliche Glaube (§ 3–10, § 11–19, § 20–31) and De Wette's *Lehrbuch der christlichen Dogmatik*, 1831 (§ 1–27, § 28–45, § 46–61), and which would have to be followed by the introduction to a dogmatics in the sense of Bultmann.

The statements of such prolegomena do not in this case aim to be themselves statements of dogmatic knowledge. Hence the prefix *pro* in the word prolegomena has here the force of "prior."

In the words of Schleiermacher, "the statements made at this point cannot themselves be dogmatic too" (*Der. ch. Gl.*, § 1, 1).

The statements of such prolegomena have instead the character, in part of statements borrowed from metaphysics, anthropology (Schleiermacher's ethics), religious philosophy and religious history, and in part of purely methodological discussions. What dogmatic knowledge is, is thus in fact affirmed *praenumerando*[EN13] quite apart from dogmatics, and might be affirmed even by those who have no mind to concern themselves any further with the subject.

The possibility of this solution stands or falls with the answer to the question [038] whether there really is a nexus of being superior to the being of the Church and consequently a nexus of scientific problems superior to dogmatics. Is there in fact an existential potentiality which is different from the actuality of revelation and in the light of which the latter is to be understood? Is there, as possibility, something generally human of which this specific human phenomenon may be regarded as an actualisation? Is there an existentially ontological *prius*[EN14] to this ontically existential factor? If this presupposition is granted, then prolegomena of this kind are possible. This presupposition, however, does not have a neutral but a highly theological character. If there is involved a statement of what dogmatics is from outside dogmatics, this is correct only to the extent that the statement is made outside a specific dogmatics, namely, Reformation and Evangelical, or indeed Roman Catholic, dogmatics, but for this reason all the more definitely within Modernistic dogmatics. The assertion of an existentially ontological *prius* to ontically existential faith, or the definition of faith as a mode of the historical being of human existence, is a cardinal proposition of the faith which understands the being of the Church and itself decisively as a definition of the reality of man, of piety.

Schleiermacher's assertion that his introduction is not itself dogmatics is quite untenable. Even his disciple A. Schweizer has seen and stated that in it we do not have "merely an introductory account but the very basis of the doctrine of faith," and in relation to the task of dogmatic prolegomena he has thus declared that "a particular part of the doctrine of the faith itself must be advanced as the foundation in which the Christian consciousness of faith takes account of itself quite apart from the differentiation of the different elements residing in it" (*Die christliche Glaubenslehre*, 2nd edn., 1877, Vol. I, 92 f.). The assertion of Schleiermacher is to be judged in the light of the definitions of the Church which he gives a little later, namely, that it is "a fellowship which arises and can continue only by free human

---

[EN13] in advance
[EN14] prior condition

actions," and "a fellowship in relation to piety" (*D. ch. Gl.*, § 2, 2; § 3, 1). These definitions, which are decisive for all that follows and which obviously characterise Modernism, have their origin in English Congregationalism (cf. e.g., *Arts.* 20, 23 and 24 of the *Platform of the Savoy Declaration*, 1658). They and they alone could authorise Schleiermacher to commence his basic work of introduction with statements borrowed from ethics. And of themselves they are sufficient to characterise these borrowed statements as dogmatics, i.e., dogmatically heretical statements.

We regard this Modernist faith as also Christian to the extent that the being of the Church implies in fact a determination of human reality. But we cannot regard it as Christian to the extent that it interprets the possibility of this reality as a human possibility, to the extent that it fails to recognise that this determination of human reality derives and is to be considered only from outside all human possibilities, i.e., from the acting God Himself, to the extent that it
[039] seeks to interpret its history, not in terms of itself, but in terms of a general capacity or of the general historicity of human existence. If this faith falls, so does this interpretation of faith, so too the presupposition of an anthropological *prius* of faith, and so finally the possibility of prolegomena of this kind.

Heinrich Barth (*op. cit.*, p. 105) understands by "existence" the "concrete decision for a possibility which finds actualisation in this decision." But as distinct from M. Heidegger and R. Bultmann he says that it is "referred to something beyond itself" (p. 117), namely, to "the criterion which transcends it" (p. 108), which "for its part has the significance of existence" (p. 109), and which is identical with the "idea" of existence (p. 110). This "existence in limitation," H. Barth thinks, "might be called an 'analogy' of the knowledge of God, to borrow the old Scholastic term." The theatre of the dialectic of existence interpreted in this way is history, and in such sort that "each historical phase represents something unique which cannot be repeated," Something unique of this kind thus meets us in that element of history which the theologian understands as "the history of revelation, in which the truth of existence, and therefore the meaning and possibility of response to it, shine out in an absolutely unique way never previously known" (p. 118 f.). The interrelation of philosophy and theology is thus to be defined as follows: "The philosophy of existence starts with existence in general; since it uses only the existence already before it as its point of contact, it can have no confidence that further thought will give it a clear picture of the 'new existence' of biblical man. It is thus reasonable, and grounded in the nature of the problem of existence, that it should leave the further work of reflection to a special science, i.e., theology," What "constitutes this as a special science is the positive factor of a certain historical element. To this extent theology is a 'positive' science" (p. 121). "Theology has as its theme the believing existence of biblical man and the self-understanding of his certainty of existence as stated in the message of Scripture. Theology must devote its reflection to this historical factor in a distinctive sense" (p. 122). "The possibility of a sifting and clarifying conception of the existential insights which there confront us" is what takes form specifically in the attempt at dogmatics (p. 122 f.). Now undoubtedly we have here a spirited and impressive effort to overcome the anthropological narrowness of Heidegger's philosophy of existence on the ground and with the weapons of this philosophy itself. We are given a philosophical scheme in which there is no place for an anthropological *prius* of faith and therefore for the patronising and conditioning of theology which are not overcome in Heidegger or Bultmann. Three points are to be noted in H. Barth's understanding. 1. The juxtaposition of the general and the particular does not imply a rationalistic attempt to master the particular, i.e., the problem of special historical reality, by subsuming it under a general concept. 2. The truth of existence which shines forth in the history of revelation is not to be regarded as identical with the general truth of existence, with which existential philosophy as such is concerned, but rather as the light which shines forth here and not elsewhere. The philosophical or general concept of existence does not offer knowledge of God, but only an analogy to such knowledge. Thus philosophy neither can nor does seek to integrate or subordinate theology to its own nexus of problems, but simply attempts to display its own attitude to dogmatics, which it may well do on the basis of that transcendent understanding. 3. Only in retrospect from revealed truth, i.e., by way of recapitulation and not anticipation, does the philosophical concept of existence seek to be an analogy to the knowledge of God. In no sense, therefore, can it be accepted as an instrument of the knowledge of God. It is only to be wished that this self-interpretation of the "critical philosophy of existence" could [040] have been brought into the public debate in a far more unmistakeable form than is the case in the essay quoted (cf., e.g., the definition of theology given on p. 122 or the description of theology as one such unique factor on p. 119). It is also to be wished that towards this end the use of such loaded categories as the general and the particular, positive and historical, might have been abandoned. Again, it must be left to philosophy to assume responsibility for the assertion that in that transcendent knowledge of human existence we have an "analogy" to the knowledge of God, since this assertion cannot possibly be a theological statement. For it is hard to see what theological foundation could be found for it. A sharp warning should thus be given to the theologian that this new use of the "old Scholastic term" cannot give any philosophical certainty to his work, so that he must not be enticed by any fresh possibility of natural theology. Even the "critical philosophy of existence" cannot give rise to any dogmatic prolegomena. If the assertion of analogy is really to be regarded as recapitulatory rather than anticipatory, then this warning is also to be found in the meaning of this philosophy itself.

In distinction from the conception already contested, Roman Catholic dogmatics describes the place from which it ascertains its way of knowledge as the self-originating and self-grounded reality of divine revelation and the corresponding supernatural faith. Here, then, dogmatic prolegomena consist in the assertion that in the form of Holy Scripture, Church tradition, and the living teaching apostolate of the Church infallibly representing and interpreting both, there is to be found the objective principle of knowledge, and in the form of the *fides catholica*[EN15], which accepts revelation as proposed by the Church, there is to be found the subjective principle.

On this point, cf., e.g., M. J. Scheeben, *Handbuch der kathol. Dogmatik*, Vol. I, 1874; B. Bartmann, *Lehrbuch der Dogmatik*, 7th imp., Vol, I, 1928. How fluid even this conception can be in detail may be seen from the fact that on the one side J. Kuhn's *Einleitung in die katholische Dogmatik*, written in 1846 in debate with Idealism like the work of J. A. Möhler, can consist almost exclusively in a doctrine of faith, whereas on the other side the introduction to F. Diekamp's *Katholische Dogmatik*, Vol. l, 6th imp., 1930, can consist no less exclusively in a doctrine of the sources of dogmatics, i.e., of the objective principle of knowledge.

It is self-evident that these assertions are already statements of faith and therefore in their scientific form dogmatic statements. But we can regard

---

[EN15] catholic faith

these statements, too, only as those of another faith and an alien dogmatics. Their presupposition is that the being of the Church, Jesus Christ, is no longer the free Lord of its existence, but that He is incorporated into the existence of the Church, and is thus ultimately restricted and conditioned by certain concrete forms of the human understanding of His revelation and of the faith which grasps it. Again, there can be no mistaking the common Christian character of this faith to the extent that the concept of the acting God, of that which is radically beyond all human possibilities, is taken seriously as the
[041] source of dogmatic knowledge, at least in intention. But again our fellowship with this faith is broken by the way in which grace here becomes nature, the action of God immediately disappears and is taken up into the action of the recipient of grace, that which is beyond all human possibilities changes at once into that which is enclosed within the reality of the Church, and the personal act of divine address becomes a constantly available relationship. Roman Catholic faith believes this transformation. It can recognise itself and God's revelation in this constantly available relationship between God and man, in this revealedness. It affirms an *analogia entis*[EN16], the presence of a divine likeness of the creature even in the fallen world, and consequently the possibility of applying the secular "There is" to God and the things of God as the presupposition, again ontological, of that change or transformation, of that depriving of revelation and faith of their character as decision by evasion and neutralisation.

Inhorresco in quantum dissimilis ei sum; inardesco in quantum similis ei sum[EN17] (Augustine, *Conf.* XI, 9, 11). *Id quod in Deo perfecte est, in rebus aliis per quandam deficientem participationem invenitur ... Et sic creatura habet quod Dei est; unde et Deo recte similis dicitur*[EN18] (Thomas Aquinas, *S. c. gent.*, cc I, *c.* 29). Cf. also *Conc. Later.* IV, 1215, *De trin., etc., c.* 2 in Denzinger's *Enchiridion,* No. 432 towards the end, and the relevant comments of E. Przywara, *Religionsphilosophie kath. Theol.*, 1926, 22 f. and *passim.*

If this faith is not ours; if we know nothing of such a change and its presupposition; if we can as little say: "There is revelation," as we can: "There is faith," then we cannot possibly adopt the standpoint which yields this particular dogmatic knowledge.

The only possibility of a conception of dogmatic knowledge remaining to us on the basis of Evangelical faith is to be marked off on the one hand by the rejection of an existential ontological possibility of the being of the Church and on the other hand by the rejection of the presupposition of a constantly available absorption of the being of the Church into a creaturely form, into a "There is." On the one side we have to say that the being of the Church is *actus*

EN16 analogy of being

EN17 I shudder when I think how unlike Him I am; I glow when I think how like Him I am

EN18 That which is in God perfectly is found in other things according to a kind of imperfect participation ... And in this way the creature has what is God's and for this reason is rightly said to be like God *purus*[EN19], i.e., a divine action which is self-originating and which is to be understood only in terms of itself and not therefore in terms of a prior anthropology. And on the other side we have also to say that the being of the Church is *actus purus,* but with the accent now on *actus,* i.e., a free action and not a constantly available connexion, grace being the event of personal address and not a transmitted material condition. On both sides we can only ask how it may be otherwise if the being of the Church is identical with Jesus Christ. If this is true, then the place from which the way of dogmatic knowledge is to be seen and understood can be neither a prior anthropological possibility nor a subsequent ecclesiastical reality, but only the present moment of the speaking and hearing of Jesus Christ Himself, the divine creation of light in our hearts.

λάμπειν ἐν ταῖς καρδίαις ἡμῶν[EN20] (2 Cor. 4^6, compared by Paul with the "Let there be light" of Gen. 1^3). [042]

In the light of the fact that Jesus Christ is the being of the Church, the free personal decision may be expected concerning what is the proper content of Christian utterance and therefore concerning what should be the way to its knowledge, i.e., to the knowledge of dogma. Like the attempt to know dogma, any understanding of the orientation of this attempt can only be a particular form of the expectation of the decision of the Lord of the Church based upon and prepared by His promise.

Now this means that we find confirmation of the insight which is self-evident in the sphere of Roman Catholic dogmatics and which cannot finally be avoided in Modernist dogmatics, namely, that prolegomena to dogmatics are possible only as part of dogmatics itself. The prefix *pro* in prolegomena is to be understood loosely to signify the first part of dogmatics rather than that which is prior to it.

In order to give an account of the way of knowledge pursued in dogmatics, we cannot take up a position which is somewhere apart from this way or above the work of dogmatics. Such a place apart or above could only be an ontology or anthropology as the basic science of the human possibilities among which consideration is somewhere given to that of faith and the Church. But any supposed reality of the Church in which the decision of the Lord of the Church is already anticipated can only be viewed as such a place apart or above. In both cases, i.e., in both Modernist and Roman Catholic prolegomena, it can be known and said in advance, before actually embarking on dogmatics, what will be the proper way of knowledge. Evangelical dogmatics cannot proceed along these lines. It can only venture to embark on its way, and then on this way, admittedly perhaps as its first task, yet genuinely on this way, concern itself with the knowledge of the correctness of this way. It knows that there can be no entering the self-enclosed circle of this concern from without,

---

[EN19] pure act

[EN20] shining in our hearts

whether from a general human possibility or an ecclesiastical reality. It realises that all its knowledge, even its knowledge of the correctness of its knowledge, can only be an event, and cannot therefore be guaranteed as correct knowledge from any place apart from or above this event. In no circumstances, therefore, can it understand the account which is to be rendered in prolegomena as an attempt to secure such a guarantee. This account can be given only within, even if at the beginning of, the dogmatic work which is not guaranteed from that point apart or above.

We perceive the possible point of departure for such an account in the fact that the Christian Church ventures to talk of God, or to regard what it says as talk about God. This fact itself, quite apart from the possible or actual contents
[043] of what is said, is obviously a part of talk about God. It says of God that the Church speaks of Him. This statement, however it is meant and however it may be explained, is as little self-evident and as much in need of explanation as all the other material statements which the Church may venture to make about God. Like them, it needs to be criticised and corrected. It must be the subject of enquiry with what right the Church comes to say this, and in what sense it does so. This right and sense are obviously identical with the norm by which what it says is to be measured, i.e., with the norm of the remaining content of its utterance concerning God. The knowledge of this right and sense is identical with the knowledge of the correctness of its insights, of the right way which it must take in the criticism and correction of its insights. If there should be specific reflection concerning this way as such—and we have seen that there should—then it must consist in the question, itself dogmatic, as to the true content of the presupposed statement concerning the talk about God which takes place in the Church. This statement has a true content when it is related to a prior Word of God Himself spoken to the Church which speaks about God. Only when and to the extent that such a Word of God is spoken by God Himself to the Church is there any right or sense in speaking about God in the Church. Only when there is such a Word of God is there a criterion, namely, this Word itself, of the correctness of such speech and therefore of the correct criticism and correction of such speech, i.e., of dogmatics. In the prolegomena to dogmatics, therefore, we ask concerning the Word of God as the criterion of dogmatics. In so doing, and therefore already on the way, we give an account of the way which we tread.

Basically, the theme of dogmatic prolegomena as understood in this sense is obviously none other than that which the older Protestant theology, in its resistance to Roman Catholicism and then to incipient Modernism, treated under the title *De scriptura sacra*[EN21]. We shall see that the cardinal statement of the doctrine of the Word of God which we shall try to develop in what follows is indeed materially the same as the assertion of the authority and normativeness of Holy Scripture as the witness to divine revelation and the presupposition of

---

[EN21] On Holy Scripture

Church proclamation. But in the modern situation, both as regards Roman Catholicism and also Modernism, what falls to be said about Holy Scripture as the criterion of dogmatics needs a comprehensive elucidation of context. Hence we shall attempt a doctrine of the Word of God and not merely of Holy Scripture, i.e., a doctrine of Holy Scripture in the context of an embracing doctrine of the Word of God. Even the older dogmaticians in their development of the topic 'On Holy Scripture' could not in fact avoid decisive references to the contents of Christian utterance concerning God. That is, they could not avoid anticipating material dogmas, e.g., the doctrine of reconciliation, the Holy Spirit, faith, or the Church. We, too, must anticipate in this way, [044]
and we must do so to an even greater extent if we are to achieve true clarity. The most striking anticipation of this kind will consist in the fact that we shall treat of the whole doctrine of the Trinity and the essentials of Christology in this connexion, namely, as constituent parts of our answer to the question of the Word of God. We cannot pose the question of formal dogma without immediately entering at these central points upon material dogma. Indeed, what is thought to be formal dogma is itself highly material in fact. The only point is that here at the beginning of the whole work it is not to be estimated solely according to its material significance, but specifically according to its formal significance as the foundation of dogmatic knowledge as such.

[047]

§ 3

CHURCH PROCLAMATION AS THE MATERIAL OF DOGMATICS

Talk about God in the Church seeks to be proclamation to the extent that in the form of preaching and sacrament it is directed to man with the claim and expectation that in accordance with its commission it has to speak to him the Word of God to be heard in faith. Inasmuch as it is a human word in spite of this claim and expectation, it is the material of dogmatics, i.e., of the investigation of its responsibility as measured by the Word of God which it seeks to proclaim.

1. TALK ABOUT GOD AND CHURCH PROCLAMATION

Not all human talk is talk about God. It could be and should be. There is no reason in principle why it should not be. God is the Lord from whom and to whom we exist. Even the realities and truths distinct from Him and us which usually form the concrete occasion and subject of human speech exist from Him and to Him. Hence there is no genuinely profane speech. In the last resort, there is only talk about God. Yet serious reflection on human talk about God must take as its starting-point the fact that this is not at all the case, that it is quite impossible to interpret human talk as such as talk about God. We do not know man, i.e., ourselves, as man in his original estate and therefore as the man of the kingdom of glory. Of this man it might well be said that all his talk is talk about God. But we do not know ourselves as this man. We know ourselves only as the man to whom mercy is shown as one who is fallen, lost and condemned. We know ourselves only as man in the kingdom of grace, of the present age between the time of creation and that of redemption. We stand under the sign of a decision constantly taken between the secularity and the sanctification of our existence, between sin and grace, between a being as man
[048] which forgets God, which is absolutely neutral in relation to Him and therefore absolutely hostile, and one which in His revelation is awakened by faith to being in the Church, to the appropriation of His promise. This cleavage continually applies, however, to human speech as well. It is not identical with the distinction between secular and religious utterance. Religious utterance is, of course, externally marked off from secular by the fact that God is its more or less explicit theme. It is also marked off internally by the intention expressly or tacitly orientated to this subject, by the more or less sincere purpose, directly or indirectly to speak about God. But the cleavage still takes place intrinsically

within secular existence. Neither the subject nor the intention makes human speech sanctified talk about God, just as conversely it does not have to be secular because it does not have this subject or intention. This distinction, like the distinction between a believing and religious and an unbelieving and worldly attitude, is only a symptom, and not even an unequivocal symptom, of the true and final distinction between secular and sanctified existence. Nevertheless, it is a necessary symptom. The ongoing event of the final distinction, the event in which God Himself acts, casts its shadow before in the event of this provisional distinction in which man is at work.

It cannot, therefore, be generally correct to characterise this provisional distinction as the "human cleavage between sacramental daemonism and secular exorcism" (Paul Tillich, *Relig. Verwirklichung*, 1930, 64), To be sure, it is not co-extensive with the divine distinction, and to this extent it can be characterised in such terms. But as a symptom of the divine distinction it can be a pointer to its reality, and it is not, therefore, exhaustively defined in this way. Again, it does not rest on careful discussion if it is stated generally that from God's standpoint the historical Church has no advantage over historical society, that revelation is addressed equally to society and the Church, and that the "invisible community" can be equally proclaimed and actualised "from the religious and the cultural angles" (P. Tillich, *Kirche und Kultur*, 1924, 10 f., 16 f., 19). Certainly, God is not bound to the historical Church. He is free and able to raise up children to Abraham from the stones. But this does not alter the fact that the antithesis between the Church and society can be a symptom of the divine distinction, and a pointer to its truth, not in the abstract equality but in the concrete inequality of the two sides. Finally, it is wrong to interpret this antithesis in general as basically non-essential (*op. cit.*, p. 9) and thus to make it the subject of a general protest from the standpoint of "the far side of being" (*Rel. Verwirklichung*, 46). For our standpoint is neither the time of creation nor that of redemption, and therefore it is not that of a far side of being. It is the present between the times, the time of the *regnum gratiae*[EN1], in which the symptom of this human cleavage, for all its ambiguous relativity and its provisional character, can always be highly essential as a pointer to the divine distinction.

The event in which God acts consists wholly in the fact that men are visibly awakened, separated and gathered by God to being in the visible Church. A visible distinction which arises within the secular sphere between religious and profane is now, not intrinsically but in this event of divine election, confirmed and maintained and therefore characterised as a genuine indication of the [049] antithesis of judgment and grace in which, even though men do not act towards others, God Himself acts towards men. Only in faith, of course, is this event visible as such; only in faith is being in the Church visible as divine election and sanctification. What is visible in itself is simply an event within the secular sphere. Its significance can be missed, but it cannot actually be taken away from it again.

"He thus shows with certainty that the preaching of the Gospel is not an eternal, lasting, static doctrine, but like a moving shower of rain which strikes what it strikes and misses what it misses. Nor does it return nor halt, but is followed by the sunshine and warmth which lick

---

[EN1] kingdom of grace

it up, etc. Hence our experience that in no place in the world has the Gospel remained pure and simple beyond a man's memory, but has stood and increased so long as those have remained who brought it, and its light has then gone out when they themselves passed on, being succeeded at once by schismatics and false teachers" (Luther, *Fastenpostille*, 1525, *W.A.* 17^{II}, 178, 28).

The one who is awakened and gathered to being in the Church has every cause for the full assurance of faith, but none at all for certainty or overconfidence.

Why not? *Τὸ φῶς ἐν τῇ σκοτίᾳ φαίνει καὶ ἡ σκοτία αὐτὸ οὐ κατέλαβεν*[EN2] (Jn. 1^5). So it is with us.

Yet even though it is infinitely threatened in this way as seen from without, the being of man in the Church *ubi et quando visum est Deo*[EN3] is a true and concrete event, a visible being in the visible Church. In the same sense there is human talk which, as talk about God, is truly and concretely distinguished from other human talk, not in itself and as such, but in virtue of the divine confirmation and preservation, yet in virtue of the divine confirmation and preservation of that which truly and and concretely distinguishes it from other human talk. If the being of the Church, Jesus Christ as the acting person of God, sanctifies the being of man in the visible sphere of human occurrence as being in the Church, then He also sanctifies its talk as talk about God taking place in the Church.

Not all talk in the Church's worship seeks to be proclamation. It does not seek to be such when it is talk addressed by man to God. The Church's prayers and hymns and confessions of faith obviously are what they purport to be only to the extent that so far as possible they cease to attempt the impossible task of proclaiming something to God or the unworthy one of incidentally proclaiming something to man. They are the response to God of the praise, confession and thanksgiving of those to whom proclamation concerning Him has come. They are the sacrifice the bringing of which can have before God only the meaning of a confirmation of what He has done to man, and in respect of
[050] which man can obviously have no intentions in relation to others who may also be present.

We think of Luther's demand in his sermon at the dedication of the Castle Church at Torgau in 1544, "that nothing else should take place therein than that our dear Lord Himself should speak with us through His holy Word, and we again speak with Him through prayer and praise ..." (*W.A.* 49, 588, 15; cf. 592, 17; 594, 26). "Thirdly, that when we have heard God's Word we should bring before God our common holy smoke or incense, i.e., that we should together call upon Him and pray to Him" (599, 25).

But there are also other elements in the life of the Church in which what we

---

[EN2] The light shines in the darkness, and the darkness has not overcome it
[EN3] where and when God pleases

say about God is addressed to our fellow-men but which cannot seek to be proclamation. To this group belongs a function which from the very first has in some form been recognised to be an integral element in the life of the Church, namely, the expression of helpful solidarity in face of the external needs of human society. This, too, is part of man's response to God. When and because it is the response of real man, necessarily in terms of Mt. 5[14] it is a shining light to people among whom alone man is real man. If God exists for man, as the Church's prayer, praise and confession declare in answer to the proclamation heard, then this man as the man for whom God exists must also exist for his fellow-men with whom alone he is real man. Yet the special utterance about God which consists in the action of this man is primarily and properly directed to God and not to men. It can neither try to enter into quite superfluous competition with society's necessary efforts at self-help in its straits, nor can it seek, as the demonstration of distinctively Christian action, to proclaim how God helps. "That they may see your good works, and glorify your Father which is in heaven," that they may be a commentary on the proclamation of God's help, is, of course, freely promised, but cannot be its set intention. Like prayer, praise and confession, especially in cases like Francis of Assisi and Bodelschwingh, it has always been spontaneous, unpremeditated, and in the final and best sense unpractical talk about God. Then and in this way its light has shone out.

This was surely overlooked in H. Bär's work, *Weniger Predigt!*, 1930, in which it is recommended that to-day we should not make preaching so much as service in moral and social reform our mode of proclamation.

If the social work of the Church as such were to try to be proclamation, it could only become propaganda, and not very worthy propaganda at that. Genuine Christian love must always start back at the thought of pretending to be a proclamation of the love of Christ with its only too human action.

Again, the Church's education of youth cannot as such seek to be proclamation.

In this respect G. Bohne's book, *Das Wort Gottes und der Unterricht*, 1929, seems to me to [051]
lack a certain necessary sobriety. Similarly, T. Heckel in his *Zur Methodik des evangelischen Religionsunterrichts*, 1928, surely goes too far when on p. 33 he claims the evangelical teacher as "witness, priest and herald."

In this field talk about God, as a preparation or a kind of technical substructure for the understanding of proclamation, means quite simply instruction or teaching about what the Church thus far, up to the appearance of the new generation of those called to it, has recognised and confessed as the right faith. It is the making known of the most important elements in the tradition with which proclamation must to-day be linked. To be sure, the education of youth will necessarily have to pass over at a definite point, though one which it is not so easy to define outwardly, into the divine service of youth. Yet this must never in any circumstances be to the detriment of what it has to effect as compared with this. The education of youth has to teach and not to convert, not to bring to a decision, and to this extent not to proclaim.

Finally, according to our understanding of the matter, neither can theology as such claim to be proclamation. It, too, is talk about God to men. Proclamation, however, is its presupposition, its material and its practical goal, not its content or task. Theology reflects upon proclamation. It confronts it as a court of criticism. It is Church instruction of youth on a higher grade and with the special purpose of testing the coherence of modern proclamation by the original and dominant being of the Church, and of giving directions for its correct and relevant continuation. Here too, and in every branch of theology, there will unavoidably be invasions of the sphere of proclamation, and they will often be highly appropriate as reminders of the theme. But here, too, the exceptions prove the rule, namely, that theology as such is not proclamation, but science, instruction and investigation. In a rather wider sense, we may thus reckon the Church's instruction of youth and theology among the elements in the Church's life in which man answers the proclamation heard, in which he attempts to take up a position in relation to it. All the functions here enumerated have this in common, that they have as a presupposition the proclamation which has already taken place or is to take place.

The talk about God to be found in the Church, however, is meant to be proclamation when it is directed to men with the definitive claim and expectation that it has to declare the Word of God to them. We at once see that the concept "talk about God" is set here in quite a new light, and indeed acquires a content which threatens to burst it wide open. All that we have hitherto touched on as the talk about God which takes place in the Church has it in common with this particular talk, that, whether it is addressed exclusively to
[052] God Himself or also to men, it is unequivocally talk about God which has God as its theme. In the Church's proclamation, however, this unequivocal nature of the concept rather than the concept itself is shattered. Proclamation, too, implies speaking about God. But here, in what is said about God, there lies concealed as the meaning and purpose of the action the intention to speak the Word of God Himself.

Παραλαβόντες λόγον ἀκοῆς παρ᾽ ἡμῶν τοῦ θεοῦ ἐδέξασθε οὐ λόγου ἀνθρώπων ἀλλὰ καθὼς ἀληθῶς ἐστιν λόγον θεοῦ[EN4] (1 Thess. 2[13]). *Ὡς ἐκ θεοῦ κατέναντι θεοῦ ἐν Χριστῷ λαλοῦμεν*[EN5] (2 Cor. 2[17]). *Εἴ τις λαλεῖ ὡς λόγια τοῦ θεοῦ*[EN6] (1 Pet. 4[11]). *Praedicatio verbi Dei est verbum Dei*[EN7] (*Conf. Helv. post.*, 1562, *Art.* I, 2. According to the translation: "Therefore when even to-day the Word of God is proclaimed in the churches by duly called preachers, we believe that the Word of God is proclaimed and accepted by the faith-

---

[EN4] when you received the word of God which you heard from us, you accepted it not as the word of men but as it really is, the word of God

[EN5] As commissioned by God, in the sight of God we speak in Christ

[EN6] whoever speaks, as one who utters oracles of God

[EN7] The preaching of God's word is God's word.

ful"). *Idem verbum est, quod et homo praedicat et Spiritus sanctus cordi inscribit: Una proprie vocatio, sed cuius causa et medium duplex, organicum: homo verbum extus praedicans principale: Spiritus sanctus intus illud cordi inscribens*[EN8] (H. Heidegger, *Corp. Theol.*, 1700, XXI, 22, quoted from H. Heppe, *Die Dogmatik der ev.-ref. Kirche*, 1861, 379).

Proclamation is human speech in and by which God Himself speaks like a king through the mouth of his herald, and which is meant to be heard and accepted as speech in and by which God Himself speaks, and therefore heard and accepted in faith as divine decision concerning life and death, as divine judgment and pardon, eternal Law and eternal Gospel both together.

Where human talk about God is proclamation, it raises this claim and lives in the atmosphere of this expectation. By what right? Certainly not by that of the logical form or material content, of the religious profundity or personal power, which might pertain to this human talk about God in itself. In and with all that it is in itself, it can only serve God's own Word. Nor does God's own Word cease to be itself when it allows itself to be served by human utterance. But as it allows itself to be served by it, it is itself this human utterance, and as this human utterance serves it, it is itself God's own Word.

For a proper explanation of this "is" we should have to refer even at this early stage to the christological doctrine of the two natures.

If, then, human talk about God aims to be proclamation, this can only mean that it wills to serve the Word of God and thus to point to its prior utterance by God Himself. It cannot assume that it is the Word of God, that God sanctifies the human pointer to be His own witness. The human will in question can only be the will to accept a task. It is a decisive part of the insight of all true prophecy that man as such has no possibility of uttering the Word of God. What human utterance concerning God aims to be when it is intended as proclamation is not grace, but service of grace or means of grace. If the will in question were man's will to reach out beyond himself, to put himself with his word about God in the place of God, it would be blasphemous rebellion. But there [053]
can no question of this in its claim and expectation. What is at issue is that the Church has a commission in relation to service of the Word of God, and that there must always be within it, therefore, the will to accept this commission. Thus proclamation is not asked concerning its formal or material perfection, since even the highest possible perfection would not make human utterance proclamation, nor could the least imposing prevent it from being proclamation. It is simply asked whether it is service, whether it is commissioned.

We might also say that it is asked whether it is διακονία τοῦ λόγου (Ac. 6[4]), *ministerium verbi divini*[EN9]. *Potes facere, quicquid infra te est: Quicquid autem toucheth dei cultum, nihil fac, nihil*

[EN8] It is the same word which human beings preach and the Holy Spirit inscribes on the heart: strictly speaking, it is one single vocation, but with a twofold cause and medium: the human person preaching the word externally as the executing organ, the Holy Spirit inscribing it inwardly on the heart as the primary agent

[EN9] ministry of the word

loquere, nisi certus sis habere dei verbum et opus ... quando autem verbum Dei runneth, tum opera omnia bona sunt[EN10] (Luther, *Pred. a. 2. Advent,* 1523, *W.A.* 11, 209, 22). "Tarry, beloved, until God bid thee, until thou hast certainty and boldness of heart. Yea, wert thou wiser and cleverer than Solomon and Daniel, thou shouldest flee as from hell from speaking a single word, except thou shouldest be bidden and called thereto. If God need thee. He will surely call thee. If He call thee not, beloved, let not thy skill tear open thy belly. Thou thinkest foolishly of the good and piety ... thou wouldest achieve. Believe me, none will do any good by preaching except he who is bidden and forced to preach without his own will or desire. For we have but one Master, our Lord Jesus Christ, who alone teacheth and bringeth forth fruit through His servants, whom He hath called thereto. But whoso teacheth uncalled, teacheth not without harm, both to himself and the hearers, for that Christ is not with him" (*Festpostille,* 1527, *W.A.* 17[11], 258, 38).

The will which does not say No but Yes, not so much to the venture of authoritative talk about God as to this commission that is to be accepted, is the will for proclamation in the Church. Its inner problem, insoluble because answered only in the divine predestination and in faith, is that of decision whether in this respect it is an obedient will.

But what is the function of proclamation in the Church among and alongside its other functions? We have seen that not all the talk about God that is to be found in the Church is meant to be proclamation. Obviously, however, this does not mean that it might not still be so, and be so indeed to a much higher degree than that which seeks to be such. Real proclamation of the Word of God cannot be conditioned by our intention to speak the Word of God. Why should not praise and active love, instruction and theology, sometimes and perhaps much more genuinely be proclamation? Given the validity of the *ubi et quando visutn est Deo*[EN11], as this ought to be valid for us, obviously it is fundamentally impossible to say that it cannot. Nor is it a trivial truth, but a trivial question, whether the sacrificial part of public worship is not in fact much more genuinely proclamation than the other part which in claim and expectation is dedicated to proclamation, and whether the existence of a Bodelschwingh has not been proclamation to a far higher degree than the
[054] deliberate proclamation of a thousand preaching parsons. The same question should also be raised, of course, in relation to Church instruction and theology. We must also bear it in mind that there can be nothing to prevent God from turning even such utterance concerning Him into proclamation of His Word to us which, in its character as sanctified utterance within the Church, is at first partially or even totally concealed from us. If the Church is visible, this need not imply that we actually see it in its full compass, that the dimensions of its sphere might not be very different from what we think we know them to be. God may suddenly be pleased to have Abraham blessed by Melchizedek, or Israel blessed by Balaam or helped by Cyrus. Moreover, it could hardly be

---

EN10 You can do whatever is below you; in whatever touches the worship of God, however, neither do nor say anything, unless you are certain that you have God's word and work ... for where the word of God runneth, there all works will be good

EN11 where and when God pleases

denied that God can speak His Word to man quite otherwise than through the talk about Himself that is to be found in the Church as known or as yet to be discovered, and therefore quite otherwise than through proclamation. He can establish the Church anew and directly when and where and how it pleases Him.

Modus vocationis opposite consideratus in externum et internum distinguitur. Ille foris per verbi et sacramentorum administrationem, hic intus per operationem Spiritus sancti peragitur. Non semper Deus utrumque vocationis modum ad hominum conversionem sibi possibilem adhibet, sed quosdam interno tantum Spiritus sancti lumine ac numine absque externo verbi sui ministerio ad se vocat. Qui vocationis modus per se quidem est ad salutem sufficiens, sed rarus admodum, extraordinarius. nobisque incognitus[EN12] (*Syn. pur. Theol.*, Leiden, 1624, *Disp.* 30, 32–33). This doctrine is to be confused neither with the doctrine of the *ideae Dei potentia semper inexistentes*[EN13] represented by A. Heidan (*Corp. Th. chr.*, 1686, *Loc*, I, 8 f.) under the influence of Descartes, nor with the Quaker doctrine of the *lumen internum*[EN14] attacked, e.g., by Hollaz (*Ex. Th. acr.*, 1707, I, 1, 9). It, too, has faith in view, but it emphasises that God is not to be thought of as tied to the way of *vocatio ordinaria*[EN15], of proclamation, as the basis of faith.

Hence it can never be the case that the Word of God is confined to the proclamation of the existing Church, or to the proclamation of the Church as known to us, or to the talk about God in this known Church which specially claims to be proclamation. Church proclamation itself, in fact, regards itself only as service of the Word of God, as a means of grace in God's free hand. Hence it cannot be master of the Word, nor try to regard the Word as confined within its own borders. Nevertheless, even when we have calmly recognised as such all the divine possibilities which may be reasonably expected at this point, and even when we are as open as possible in our expectation of their realisation at any time, we have still to remember that the question what God can do is a very different one from that of the commission laid on us by the promise given to the Church.

Non pas que Dieu soit attaché à telles aides ou moyens inferieurs, mais pource qu'il luy plaist nous entretenir soubz telle charge et bride[EN16] (*Conf. Gall.*, 1559, *art.* 35). The distinctiveness of the teaching of Paul Tillich, which ultimately makes it irrelevant as a contribution to the work of [055]
theology, seems to me to lie in the confusion of these two questions. If the first presupposition of thought is that we suppose we can think and speak about the Church equally well, if not better, from outside than from inside, without recognising the binding nature of its

EN12 The mode of proclamation, considered in its opposing forms, is differentiated according to whether it is external or internal. The former is accomplished outwardly through the preaching of the word and the administration of the sacraments; the latter inwardly through the operation of the Holy Spirit. God does not always use both modes for the conversion of people which is possible for him, but calls some to Himself solely by the internal light and divinity of the Spirit without the external ministry of his word. This mode of vocation is in itself fully sufficient for salvation, but it is extremely rare, most unusual, and cannot be known by us

EN13 ideas always inherent in us through God's power

EN14 inner light

EN15 ordinary vocation

EN16 It is not that God is bound to such inferior props or means, but that he prefers to lead us by this bit and bridle

commission as those who are also bound by it, then to be sure the door is open for the "radicalism" which "on the basis of the unconditioned" can handle the Church and culture, the sacral sphere and the secular, sacrament and nature. Protestantism and proletariat, possession and exorcism, and indeed the symbol of the Word and all other symbols, with the same sovereignty, independence and consistency as we exercise towards things which are beneath us and not above us. But if "on the basis of the unconditioned" is supposed to mean the same thing as "on the basis of God," it cannot imply "on the basis of the infinite potentiality of God," but only "on the basis of the concrete behest of God," which cannot without violating the omnipotence of God either require of us the superior position of God nor allow us to choose our own possibility, but which, as a command that either finds or does not find concrete obedience, decides concerning our reality. The connexion of the Church with this command, and with this command alone, is the subject of theological reflection. A philosophy of culture may very well reflect upon other things, including an "unconditioned" or a "far side of being" discerned elsewhere than in the command. But it must not imagine than in so doing it has even touched the task of theology. In this sense we must apply to Tillich the continuation of the passage quoted from the *Conf. Gall.*: *En quoi nous détestons tous fantastiques qui voudroyent bien. entant qu'en eux est, anéantir le ministère et prédication de la parole de Dieu et de ses Sacrements*[EN17].

If the question what God can do forces theology to be humble, the question what is commanded of us forces it to concrete obedience. God may speak to us through Russian Communism, a flute concerto, a blossoming shrub, or a dead dog. We do well to listen to Him if He really does. But, unless we regard ourselves as the prophets and founders of a new Church, we cannot say that we are commissioned to pass on what we have heard as independent proclamation. God may speak to us through a pagan or an atheist, and thus give us to understand that the boundary between the Church and the secular world can still take at any time a different course from that which we think we discern. Yet this does not mean, unless we are prophets, that we ourselves have to proclaim the pagan or atheistic thing which we have heard. Finally, we may truly and rightly think that we have heard the Word of God in the worship and active love and youth education and theology of the Church known to us. This does not mean, however, that we have received a commission to pursue these things as proclamation. However it may stand with the undoubted possibilities of God outside the Church or in a new Church; however it may stand with the greater sphere, perhaps unknown to us, of the visible Church, or even with the real, if involuntary, proclamation by other elements of Church life within the Church perceived by us, there can be no doubt that, together with the commission which it may seek to obey by listening and responding in these other functions, the Church known to us has a special commission of proclamation, and there-
[056] fore not merely of listening and response but decisively of talk about God both to men and for them, and that it neglects this commission if it seeks to proclaim what it has no commission to do or where it has no commission to do so.

[EN17] For this reason we detest all fanatics who would seek, so far as it lies within their power, to abolish the ministry and preaching of God's word and Sacraments

But what is this specially commissioned proclamation of the Church which it must accept as a commission to and for men? Our initial answer is purely descriptive.

1. This proclamation is preaching, i.e., the attempt by someone called thereto in the Church, in the form of an exposition of some portion of the biblical witness to revelation, to express in his own words and to make intelligible to the men of his own generation the promise of the revelation, reconciliation and vocation of God as they are to be expected here and now.

It might be instructive to compare this with the definition given by Karl Fezer (*Das Wort Gottes und die Predigt*, 1925, 77; cf. the review by Eduard Thurneysen, *Theol. Bl.*, 1925, 197 f.): "Preaching is man's attempt by free speech to co-operate in securing that the God who grants us His fellowship in the Word of Scripture should be corporately present to a group of other men by the Holy Spirit." (I hear that the formula has taken a different form in the oral instruction given by Fezer. I do not quote it for polemical reasons, but with a view to indicating the problems to be considered at this point.)

2. This proclamation is the sacrament, i.e., the symbolical act which is carried through in the Church as directed by the biblical witness of revelation in accompaniment and confirmation of preaching and which is designed as such to attest the event of divine revelation, reconciliation and vocation which does not merely fulfil but underlies the promise.

Cf. the unusually clear and exhaustive definition of the term "sacrament" in the *Heidelberg Catechism*, 1563, *Qu.* 66: "What are the sacraments?—They are visible, sacred signs and seals appointed by God, so that through the use of the same He may the better give us to understand the promise of the Gospel, and seal the same, namely, that for the sake of the one sacrifice of Christ accomplished on the cross He graciously grants us remission of sins and eternal life."

This is what the talk about God that is to be found in the Church seeks to be when it is meant to be proclamation and is thus directed to men with the claim and expectation that it has to declare to them the Word of God. It can and should aim to be proclamation as preaching and sacrament because the Church has a commission to make such proclamation.

In attempting to interpret what we have described in this way, our primary task must be to make it clear that, when man cannot regard himself as the one who gives the commission but only as the one who is commissioned, there are only two ways of establishing the factuality and meaning of a commission. Either the order must be repeated as it is thought to have been received and heard, or a fact must be created by the mere attempt to obey it. In both cases the answer given to those who ask concerning its basis is indirect. In both cases [057]
it can thus be regarded only as most unsatisfactory. In both cases the answer constitutes indeed a counter-question, and it is left to the enquirer whether, in the handing on of what has been heard as an order or in the attempt to obey the order, he perceives or recognises the will of the one who has given the commission, the meaning of his will, and therefore the existence of a true and meaningful commission. If, then, we ask why the Church's talk about God

seeks to be proclamation in the specific form of preaching and sacrament, or to what extent it thinks it has its particular commission to proclaim in this action, we can only give a twofold and either way a very simple answer. First, we can only reply that we learn from the biblical witness to revelation that Jesus Christ has given His Church not only the commandment of faith and love and hope, nor merely the commandment to call upon His name in concert and to show brotherly love, etc., but also the commission of proclamation, and indeed of proclamation by preaching and sacrament. Does He expect of His own only that they should take up their cross and follow Him? Does He desire as witness of this following only those other functions of His Church? Or does He not rather will these two things as He also and specifically and supremely wills that God's own Word should be proclaimed in and through His Church? And if so, is not the saying in Mt. 28[19 f.]: "Make disciples of all nations, baptising them—teaching them," a genuine summary of what we are told by the biblical documents with regard to this will of His, and has it not therefore to stand as His command to us? But secondly we cannot prove the existence and content of this order by referring to the convincing excellence of our obedience to it, as though the former could speak for itself in the latter. For again the question whether our act is obedience to this command is not decided by the person commissioned but by the Giver of the commission. Our talk about God may intend to be proclamation in terms of our commission. It may intend to be preaching and sacrament according to the will and command of the Lord of the Church. But we shall not find comfort in our obedience or in the uprightness of our intention to obey. We shall find it only in the actual command that we have heard—a command which must in fact speak for itself if it is to be recognisable to others as such. Once again, then, we can only ask, timidly and reluctantly enough, whether, in spite of all the concurrent disobedience, the Lord's command may not also speak, and speak for itself, in what the Church does.

Hence it is only subsequently, *a posteriori*[EN18], exegetically and not in the sense of demonstrating the Church's commission, that we may rightly consider whether even the thought of God's Word being revealed outside the known
[058] existing Church is possible for one who has not previously come to be acquainted with real proclamation within the Church; whether we can appeal to real parallel experiences, such as having heard the Word of God through Communism or some other reality that is thought to have existential application to us, unless we have brought a criterion to this hearing, and applied it either well or badly, on the basis of previous experience of the reality of the Word of God reaching us somehow as commissioned proclamation; above all—and this is the real point in the present context—whether the life of the Church would not lack its decisive centre, the reference point of all its other functions, without this function, the function of proclamation. We have seen

[EN18] afterward

indeed that all these other elements are in some sense an answer to the Word of God heard. Certainly preaching and sacrament may also be put in the same category. They, too, are an answer to what man has heard. And the other elements can undoubtedly be proclamation too, and have actually been so again and again. But just as the answering elements, as we have seen, cannot try to be proclamation as such, so there must stand opposed to them an element which, while it may also be interpreted, of course, as an answer, nevertheless not only can be and time and again is proclamation as distinct from them, but also seeks to be this, and does so because it ought to do so. In this element the proclamation presupposed in the others has its proper place and distinctive position. To be sure this centre, this point of reference to which all the Church's life, including the elements of proclamation, is orientated, can only be the Word of God Himself, and proclamation will as little try to push into the place of this Word as this would be fitting for any other of the Church's functions. The question arises, however, whether the Word of God does not want representatives within the realm of man's willingness to obey, whether it does not demand a specific function in the Church, whether the Church's proclamation is not thereby made at least as much of a task as the Church's responding to God's Word, as this might take place in worship and Church nurture, in instruction and theology. Whether the answer to this question is yes is not a matter to be inferred; it is decided by the commission which must be the source of all real proclamation.

Let us assume that this commission has been issued and accepted; the next thing to be made clear will be that proclamation consists significantly and precisely in preaching and sacrament. That which in the form of proclamation should confront listening and answering in the Church as a representation of God's Word demands in some sense a setting apart, a special, imperious calling of the man who is to function here. Furthermore, what this man can try to say as God's Word in the discharge of preaching cannot be God's own Word as such but only the repetition of His promise, repetition of the promise: "Lo, I am with you alway!" (Mt. 28^{20}). Proclamation must mean announcement— [059]
announcement as distinct from the real "I am with you" as future fulfilment. Again, if this announcement is to be the legitimate repetition of not just any promise, but of the promise given to the Church by God Himself, then it cannot be arbitrary religious discourse. It must be homily, i.e., discourse which as the exposition of Scripture is controlled and guided. But if it is to be real repetition of this promise, it cannot consist in the mere reading of Scripture or in repeating and paraphrasing the actual wording of the biblical witness. This can be only its presupposition. The concrete encounter of God and man to-day, whose actuality, of course, can be created only by the Word of God Himself, must find a counterpart in the human event of proclamation, i.e., the person called must be ready to make the promise given to the Church intelligible in his own words to the men of his own time. Calling, promise, exposition of Scripture, actuality—these are the decisive definitions of the concept of

preaching. If proclamation is by commission preaching—the fact that it is so need not be proved since it cannot be proved—then these concepts are a supplementary explanation of the meaning of preaching. Obviously, however, proclamation would suffer from a palpable weakness if understood solely as preaching. Preaching is human speech in the form of words thought and expressed by men. The promise as merely preached is thus a human work both on the preacher's lips and in the hearer's ear. At best it is an "existential" decision first made by the preacher and then to be made by the hearer. Were it no more than this, how could it be a pointer to the very Word of God? Does not man's word spoken and received, the more earnestly it is spoken and received, necessarily imply as such a total eclipse of the Word of God which it seeks to serve? The promise given to the Church and attested in Holy Scripture is itself obviously no such work of man, in contrast to the promise preached. It is the Word as the enacted divine event, as the accomplished divine action of judging and reconciling grace in which a decision is made about man prior to all his own decisions, from which alone his own decisions can be characterised as decisions of faith, from which alone, then, what the preacher and his hearer may do in human fashion can become a pointer to God's own Word. If this event is not also proclaimed, how far is the promise given to the Church really proclaimed, how far is the Church's proclamation, not a *ministerium verbi divini*[EN19], but an insuperable obstacle placed in the path of God's own Word? Yet how is this event to be proclaimed too? How can it come about that proclamation proclaims not only truth but truth as actuality, i.e., as God's work, and thereby for the first time unequivocally grace as grace? How is this to happen inasmuch as proclamation must be unambiguously identical
[060] with preaching? We are faced here with the fundamental difficulty in the task of preaching beside which one may with a good conscience describe all others as child's play. From this standpoint it is easy enough to understand that in practice little importance is attached in the Church to the claim and expectation that preaching should speak the Word of God. It is easy to understand that on the one hand Roman Catholic preaching seems to be largely content with the level of higher instruction in religion and morals while on the other hand typical Neo-Protestant preaching does not claim to be more than the most authentic and lively possible expression of the personal piety of the speaker concerned. We shall have to say more about these two aberrations. In face of the difficulty which is at the root of both, and in answer to the question how God's Word can be proclaimed as God's work, we cannot have recourse at once to what is, of course, the very true and valid reference to God Himself, to the Holy Spirit, who will confirm as His own work the work of the faith which is proclaimed in words of human thought and expression on the lips of the preacher and in the ears of the hearer, thus turning the preached promise into the event of the real promise that is given to the Church. This reference to the

EN19 ministry of the divine word

native power of God's own Word in and in spite of the darkness of the human word that serves it is, of course, the Alpha and Omega, the *ultima ratio*[EN20], apart from which not only the concept of preaching but also that of Church proclamation generally is quite impossible. The only question is whether, in the concept of the proclamation enjoined on the Church, this reference is not represented by a second element which is not identical with preaching as such and in which proclamation might be precisely what it cannot be as preaching alone, namely, the proclamation of reality, of the promise as God's work, of the grace of the faith preached and received, of the decision taken before and beyond all our decisions, which distinguishes human speaking and hearing as worship of God in spirit and in truth. Naturally, this second element in proclamation can also be no more than human talk about God. It can seek to be no more than preaching to the degree that it, too, can only announce, i.e., announce the future revelation, reconciliation and calling, and thus be repetition of the promise, a means of grace. Nor can it seek to be independent proclamation alongside preaching. It can only seek to be its confirmation, as the seal beneath a letter confirms its authenticity but adds nothing to its contents, making no statement except under the letter and in a sense standing apart. It must be co-ordinated with preaching in the sense that, as preaching represents the promise as such, it represents the character of the promise as event and grace in contrast to all man's work on the level of human occurrence. To represent this basis of the promise it must not consist in further words; it has to be action. But to be proclamation, it cannot be arbitrarily selected action any [061]
more than preaching can. It has to be the action demanded and controlled by the biblical witness. Again, like preaching, it cannot seek to replace the Word of God itself. As preaching is a strictly representative word, so it can be only a strictly representative action. Like preaching it can only be a serving of God's Word. What in either case is more than representation, service and symbol, is the event whose subject is not the Church but God Himself. And the object which it has to represent must be the presupposition of preaching which preaching as such, as word in human thought and expression, cannot represent, for which the human word as such cannot be the symbol, namely, revelation, reconciliation and calling, which the Church can only believe, hope and proclaim that it has before it when it has it behind it as the act of divine grace, which it can only truly expect when it already owes its origin to it (as enacted once and for all in the epiphany of Jesus Christ). Promise in the form of an adjunct to preaching, action in distinction from mere word, conformity to Scripture, representative symbolical connexion with the "once-for-all" of revelation—these are the decisive definitions of the concept of sacrament. We have not postulated this concept either, but exegeted it on the presupposition that its content is a reality in the life of the Church on the basis of God's commission, and that to this extent it is before us as a text which can be exegeted.

[EN20] final rationale

There can be as little question of a free establishing of the necessity of sacrament as there can of a necessity of preaching or of proclamation generally. Hence in retrospect of what has been said and in answer to the question of its final proof we should not omit to point away from the exegesis and back to the actual text before us.

In conclusion, however, this exegesis of the terms proclamation, preaching and sacrament requires an express declaration: As has been done, Evangelical dogmatics exegetes these concepts.

We may ignore at this point the fact that it is specifically Evangelical Reformed dogmatics which has done this in detail.

As regards the main concept of proclamation this exegesis stands first in antithesis to Modernist dogmatics. This, too, is acquainted with the function specified but it is not aware of its essential distinctiveness as compared with other functions in the Church—a distinctiveness which accrues to it when it rests on a commission to and for men, when as man's talk about God it has to serve God's own Word spoken from an ineffaceable antithesis to all humanity. Modernist dogmatics is finally unaware of the fact that in relation to God man has constantly to let something be said to him, has constantly to listen to something, which he constantly does not know and which in no circumstances and
[062] in no sense can he say to himself. Modernist dogmatics hears man answer when no one has called him. It hears him speak with himself. For it, therefore, proclamation is a necessary expression of the life of the human community known as the "Church," an expression in which one man, in the name and for the spiritual advancement of a number of others, drawing from a treasure common to him and to them, offers, for the enrichment of this treasure, an interpretation of his own past and present as a witness to the reality alive in this group of men.

Even Schleiermacher's *Christian Faith* is not without a section on ministry of God's Word (§ 133 f.). But we are told at once that the "divine Word" is simply "the spirit in all men," i.e., in all those united in the Church (§ 134, 3). Thus ministry of God's Word is the "act of the community as such" (§ 135, 2), or, concretely, the "relation of the active toward the receptive" (§ 133, 1), or the "influence of the stronger on the weaker" (§ 113, 2) through the medium of self-impartation, i.e., a "self-display with a stimulating effect, in which the emotion of the displayer, taken up by imitation, becomes in the receptively stimulated person who takes it up a power which calls forth the same emotion" (§ 133, 1). It embraces the "whole Christian life" and only needs special "management" for the sake of good order and preservation of the common consciousness (§ 134, 3; 135). We are only at the other, realistic end of the same path which Schleiemacher entered upon idealistically when, a century later, P. Tillich argues that "a new sacramental situation" will have to be "created" to save Protestantism (*Relig. Verwirkl.*, 1930, 166) by our "successfully reaching the depths of our own undivided, pre-objective being" (*op. cit.*, p. 154) and thus gaining an understanding of the fact that there is a mastery over natural things and situations, and hence over the Word among other things, that this is experienced in the "historical destiny" of reciprocal apprehending and being apprehended, and that in virtue of it these things can become the vehicles of "sacramental mastery" for believers (p. 176). If by "sacramental situation" Tillich means the same as what we call proclamation, and if the way to this "sacramental situation," i.e., the historical destiny by which it is created, is really the relation between a deepened understanding of self and a deepened understanding of the world, and *vice versa*, then we are forced to conjecture that here too man is finally conceived of as conversing only with himself. And indeed "religious symbols are created in the process of religious history" (p. 206). "One has a right to say that, e.g., Christ and Buddha are symbols in so far as the unconditionally transcendent can be viewed in them" (p. 104). "God as Object is a representation of what is ultimately intended in the religious act" (p. 103). "The unconditionally transcendent goes beyond any positing of an essence, even a supreme essence. In so far as such is posited, it is also abrogated again in the religious act. This abrogation, the atheism immanent in the religious act, is the depth of the religious act" (p. 102). "The truth of a symbol rests upon its inner necessity for the symbol-creating consciousness" (p. 103). "At the point where—apart from all material connexions—the spiritual expresses itself, it expresses itself religiously" (p. 94).

On this view the ideas of speech, word, proclamation and preaching, which in themselves might all still point to the juxtaposition of God and man, must obviously disappear in the general concept of operation or movement or into the notion of a general dynamic or even meaning which embraces God and man, which is in some way the vehicle of the existence of each and all of us, and which somehow—this is where proclamation is needed—is to be articu- [063] lated by us. But then Logos in its isolation as word spoken back and forth necessarily becomes one symbol among many others. "I cannot possibly rate the word so highly," i.e., as an expression of that dynamic or meaning. The question now becomes in all seriousness: Why do I choose precisely these symbols, talk about God and this form of it, namely, actual exposition of the Bible, along with these two or seven sacraments? Are these really the truest symbols when my spiritual nature should and would express itself? Might there not be truer ones than these?

That it should be said of the Word of God!—"in the choice (!) of this symbol lies the spiritual character of the self-impartation of transcendent being .... But it is quite wrong to equate the Word as a symbol of the self-impartation of transcendent being with the Word as the physical medium of the self-comprehension and self-impartation of the human spirit, and in this way to mix up God's Word and the word of Scripture or the word of preaching" (P. Tillich, *Rel. Verwirkl*, 1930, 48 f.; cf. p. 60). "Word is not only present when it is spoken and conceived but Word is also present when it is made present and actualised in powerful symbols. *Verbum*[EN21] is more than *oratio*[EN22]. Protestantism has largely forgotten this. *Verbum*, the Word of revelation, may (!) be in everything in which spirit expresses itself, even in the silent symbols of art, even in the works of society and law. And therefore a church must be able to speak in all these forms. They must all become symbols for the Word of revelation. And that means that nothing less than the whole life of society in every aspect is ordained to be symbolically powerful for God" (*Kirche u. Kultur*, 1924, 19 f.). Which of the various expressions that one might choose has the most "symbolical power" to-day? This is now the solemn question of the Berneuchener, and a "fountain" which is to be set up in the church "with running water as an allegory of God's creative life-stream" (*Berneuchener Buch*, 1926,

[EN21] Word
[EN22] speech

112), coloured window-panes as symbols of the "light from uncreated light," and various cheerful things of a similar nature, now have a chance of entering into not wholly purposeless rivalry with preaching, which has become less relevant ever since, long ago now, the organ was raised (by Julius Smend) to the dignity of a "second pulpit" that must proclaim to us in other tongues, above all in sacred tones, the element of the transcendent and ineffable in religion "(quoted according to Herbert Birtner, *Die Probleme der Orgelbewegung, Theol. Rundschau*, 1932, 66). For the sigh has become general and can no longer be ignored: "Preaching, pedestalled (!) on the person of the preacher, stands now too much in the foreground" (O. Dibelius, *Das Jahrhundert der Kirche*, 5th edn., 1928, 252). Therefore: "Less preaching! More action and more of other forms of proclamation!" "The competition of other intellectual performances" has now become far too great." More and more persons to-day have inadequate time to prepare their sermons." "Inspiration is needed in poets and in religious speakers. But few mortals can be inspired to order." Perhaps even Jesus would have been "increasingly dissatisfied with speaking had He been tied down to public work and public speaking for decades instead of a single year'' (!!) (H. Bär, *Weniger Predigt!*, 1930, 8 f., 12 f.). And so on!

And over and above all this the ultimate question may and must arise: Why proclamation at all? Why symbols at all? Why not better be silent? Why not, as the truest word we can utter, renounce all special talk about God, all use of symbols whatsoever?

[064] "Undoubtedly the supreme aim of a theological work would be to discover the point at which reality itself speaks unsymbolically both of itself and also of the unconditioned, to discover the point at which reality itself without a symbol becomes a symbol, at which the antithesis between reality and symbol is removed." Would it not be the most powerful expression of what is in us if we were to omit all expression in favour of "immediate talk about things so far as they impinge on us unconditionally, so far as they stand in the transcendent" (P. Tillich, *Rel. Verwirkl.*, 208)?

What needs to be said in criticism of this teaching is said clearly enough by the teaching itself. Understanding of the concept of proclamation along these lines can end only with its dissolution. Proclamation as self-exposition must in the long run turn out to be a superfluous and impossible undertaking. To a large degree it has obviously turned out this way already. The distinction between such proclamation and the other functions of the Church cannot be shown to be essential. But if it is not, do not these other functions also become inessential as answers (answers to what?)? What is the Church, what is it meant to be, if it has no centre, if man is not really addressed in it? Can the truth of its being really be that man is alone in and with his world? Is it not plain that there is here a fateful confusion between the man of the present, the man of the *regnum gratiae*[EN23], and the man of eternal glory, who, as we saw at the outset, neither needs nor will need any special talk about God, and consequently any being addressed by God, and consequently any Church? If we are not this man, whence does the Modernist doctrine get its legal ground?

All that Evangelical faith cannot understand about this alien belief on the left may be

[EN23] kingdom of grace

summed up in the questions of Rom. 10[14]: *Πῶς οὖν ἐπικαλέσονται εἰς ὅν οὐκ ἐπίστευσαν; πῶς δὲ πιστεύσωσιν οὗ οὐκ ἤκουσαν; πῶς δὲ ἀκούσωσιν χωρὶς κηρύσσοντος; πῶς δὲ κηρύξωσιν ἐὰν μὴ ἀποσταλῶσιν; ... ἄρα ἡ πίστις ἐξ ἀκοῆς, ἡ δὲ ἀκοὴ διὰ ῥήματος Χριστοῦ*[EN24].

The other no less serious difference that requires treatment here separates us from Roman Catholic dogmatics. In the first place, but only in the first place, it does not concern the main concept of proclamation but the mutual relations of the concepts of preaching and sacrament. The Roman Catholic Church is expressly and consciously the church of the sacrament. Its dogmatics cannot emphasise strongly enough that the Church lives by and in this means of grace.

The sacraments are the *canales gratiae*[EN25], the *vasa medicinae*[EN26] against sin and death, the *fundamenta et cardines vitae christianae*[EN27], the river which flows out of Eden according to Gen. 2[10], the seven pillars on which wisdom has built her house according to Prov. 9[1], the bond of peace of Eph. 4[16] (H. Hurter, S.J., *Theol. dogm. compend.*, 12th edn., 1908, Vol. III, p, 214). "The Church's work in performing them is the truest revelation and the outer confirmation of its mysterious life; they are the essential content of the Church's cultus and therefore the most excellent means of preserving the visible Church in unity and making it [065]
recognisable and distinguishable. Reception of them is the most essential mark of the Church's fellowship, their administration the most excellent and sublime activity of its priests ..." They are "the most concentrated expression and the inmost kernel of the Church's faith and life" (Scheeben-Atzberger, *Handb. d. kath. Dogm.*, Vol. IV, 1903, 463). Cf. also Bartmann, *Lehrb. d. Dogm.*, 7th edn., Vol. 2, 1929, 207.

But one might ask quite seriously whether the superlatives we have just heard do not always say too little when one realises that in this dogmatics preaching is not only assigned less importance, but virtually no importance at all compared to the sacrament which is received and celebrated so zealously. Nor is it merely that Roman Catholicism overemphasises the sacrament in the same way as Protestantism does oral preaching.

This schematism becomes pure nonsense when Klaus Harms (in his 95 theses of 1817) advances the exaggerated view that the Roman Church inclines to cling to the sacrament and build its life around this, that the Reformed Church does the same with the Word, but that the Lutheran Church "more splendidly than either" honours both sacrament and Word (briefly reproduced by Max Geiger, *Unsere Taufe*, 1931, 4). For one thing, Lutheran Protestantism, if it stays to any degree at all in Luther's footsteps, cannot wish to take middle ground and to break solidarity with Reformed Protestantism in respect of the greater emphasis on preaching and its higher ranking as compared with the sacrament. Again, for all the greater emphasis on preaching and its higher ranking, the importance which is assigned to the sacrament in the practice of the Reformed Church, and the care with which

---

EN24 But how are they to call upon him in whom they have not believed? And how are they to believe in him of whom they never heard? And how are they to hear without a preacher? And how can they preach unless they are sent? ... So faith comes from what is heard, and what is heard comes by the preaching of Christ [Rom. 10:14-17]

EN25 channels of grace

EN26 vessels containing the medicine

EN27 the foundations and linchpins of the Christian life

the problem of the sacrament has been and is treated in Reformed dogmatics, cannot possibly be regarded as parallel to what happens to preaching in Roman Catholic dogmatics. One would have to say the same even about Modernist dogmatics. Neither Schleiermacher's nor Troeltsch's estimation of the sacraments—judge them materially as one may—can be compared with what happens to preaching on principle and without exception, so far as I can see, in Roman Catholic dogmatics.

The fate of preaching here is quite simple: *Silentium altissimum*[EN28]. Roman Catholic dogmaticians pass on from the treatise on grace or from that on the Church to the treatise on the sacraments. They develop the doctrine of the sacrament of the priestly *ordo*[EN29]. They consistently speak of the teaching office of the Church as though preaching did not even exist as an indispensable means of grace that claims serious attention. The only points of interest in preaching, and naturally these have only passing interest, are legal questions like those about primary and secondary bearers of legitimate Church doctrine, the necessity of a special *missio canonica*[EN30] for preaching, etc.

Even in the articles on the "teaching office" in Josef Braun, *Handlexikon d. kath. Dogm.*, 1926, 185 f., there is complete silence about preaching, proclamation, etc. Cf. *C. jur. can. c.* 1327/28.

It should be noted that in practical writings Roman Catholic theology can incidentally find lofty and what seem to be dogmatically relevant things to say about preaching.

[066] Through "Word and sacrament" the priest builds up the mystical body of the Lord, the Church. "Through this word of preaching and in it Christ lives on mystically, edifies, extends, enlightens, comforts and blesses His Church continually, pursues His work of redemption through every century, feeds our souls on the bread of truth, just as He incorporates the whole man into Himself through the eucharistic bread. And preaching has no other task than to translate this Word of God into human speech, to expound and apply it." It works by itself becoming God's Word (Franz Hettinger, *Timotheus. Briefe an einen jungen Theologen*, 3rd edn., 1909, 45, 48). One would like to know whether such statements are to be regarded as merely *pia opinio*[EN31] (or perhaps *propositio temeraria*[EN32]?) of an individual—or why, if not, they find no parallels in the manuals of Roman Catholic dogmatics. There is a homiletics by the same author under the title *Aphorismen über Predigt und Prediger*, 1888, but here again we seek in vain any dogmatic basis for the necessity of preaching.

The occasional affirmation does not alter in the slightest the fact that Roman Catholic dogmatics itself, and the standard dogmatic utterances of the teaching office, which are neither of them wont to be sparing in words on matters of importance to them, shroud themselves in almost complete obscurity on this point.

The strongest plea for preaching in Denzinger's collection (No. 426) is a concessive state-

EN28 most profound silence
EN29 order
EN30 canonically valid mission
EN31 pious opinion
EN32 ill-advised proposal

ment in the *professio fidei Waldensibus praescripta*[EN33] of 1208. Here preaching is actually described as *valde necessaria et laudabilis*[EN34]. There is also a comparatively noteworthy estimation of preaching in the *Praefatio* to the *Catech. Roman*, of 1566. But this seems to coincide very closely with the contemporary need for active measures against Protestantism (Qu. 5–7) and the dogmatic content in this text is not very considerable, at least in regard to the connection between preaching, faith and grace.

Again, the fact that a weekly Sunday sermon is prescribed for the Roman Catholic parish priest, and that the Roman Catholic Church has produced more than one outstanding preacher both past and present, cannot alter in the least the way in which this function is obviously forced into a backwater even in its exercise, as shown externally by the ruling that the Mass may be complete without it.

The liturgical place of preaching is in the so-called pre-Mass (the ancient *missa catechumenorum*[EN35]). To-day the (Latin) reading of the Gospel constitutes the organic centre of this. Pius Bihlmeyer O.S.B. makes the following notes at the passage in question (*Das vollständige römische Messbuch*, 3rd edn., 1930, 533): "Now Christ speaks to us through His Word or through His miracles and redemptive acts. The same loving, wonder-working Saviour will appear Himself at the holy sacrifice, to accomplish mysteriously in us (!) what according to the Gospel narrative He has wrought in others (!). In this faith and hope we listen to the Gospel .... To the Gospel there is often (!) appended by ancient usage (!) a sermon in which the holy words of God are more closely explained and expounded as the rule for our lives." Note that the approach to this action is constituted by 1, the *Introitus* with the *Kyrie*, 2. the christological *Gloria*. 3. an *Oratio* for the day in question, 4. the reading of the Epistle, 5. the *Graduale* with or without the Tractus and Sequence, 6. the beautiful prayers: *Munda cor meum ac labia mea, omnipotens Deus, qui labia Isaiae prophetae calculo mundasti ignito: ita me tua grata miseratione dignare mundare, ut sanctum Evangelium tuum digne valeam nuntiare.* [067] *Per Jesum Christum Dominum nostrum. Amen. Jube, Domine, benedicere. Dominus sit in corde meo et in labiis meis: ut digne et competenter annuntiem Evangeliunt suum. Amen*[EN36]. And upon that reading with or without sermon there then follows (obviously saying more than Bihlmeyer): *Per evangelica dicta deleanur nostra delicta*[EN37], and then in conclusion the Niceno-Constantinopolitan Creed. One cannot avoid the impression that this mighty structure stands in no relation to the poverty of its centre to-day (e.g., is it worthwhile to appeal to Is. 6 for the sake of a mere lesson?). Is there not absent the very thing to which everything seems to point, namely, the sermon as the true and necessary *annuntiatio*[EN38] (beyond the mere lesson)? Even the present-day Benedictine reform of the liturgy does not seem to counteract at all the liturgically anomalous and non-necessary status of the sermon.

[EN33] profession of faith prescribed for Waldensians

[EN34] very necessary and praiseworthy

[EN35] mass of the catechumens

[EN36] Cleanse my heart and my lips, almighty God. As you once cleansed the lips of the prophet Isaiah with a burning coal, so by your gracious mercy hold me worthy of cleansing, so that I might have the strength to proclaim your holy Gospel in a worthy manner. Through Jesus Christ, our Lord. Amen. Lord, give your blessing. May the Lord be in my heart and on my lips, that I might proclaim His Gospel truly and rightly. Amen

[EN37] Through these words of the Gospel may our transgressions be cancelled

[EN38] proclamation

Inwardly the incidental place of the sermon is shown by the fact that it hardly seems to want to rise in principle above the level of apologetic instruction and moral exhortation. It does not appear in the main to claim the character of true proclamation which is equal in seriousness to the celebration of the sacrament.

Cf. the words quoted from Bihlmeyer. As regards the content of preaching *C. jur. can. c.* 1347, I reads as follows: *In sacris concionibus exponenda inprimis sunt, quae fideles credere et facere ad salutem oportet*[EN39].

In sharp distinction from the sacrament, preaching is not a constitutive element in the Roman Catholic concept of the priesthood.

Except in case of special dispensation, every priest has to celebrate his Mass daily, but according to *Trid. Sess. XXIII De sacr. ordinis, can.* 1, a man may be a priest without ever preaching.

This is something that cannot possibly be said of the position of the sacraments in the theory and practice of the Evangelical Churches except perhaps for certain sects.

If we are to understand this peculiar situation on the Roman Catholic side and then the meaning and significance of the opposing Evangelical thesis, we have to realise above all else that Roman Catholicism—not unlike Modernism in this respect—sees something quite different from proclamation take place at that centre of the Church's life which we have described as proclamation. Proclamation must mean repetition of the divine promise. On the basis of the Word which God has spoken to His Church attention is drawn in His Church, through men, to the Word which He wishes to speak to His Church. The presence of God is thus the grace of God, i.e., His unfathomably free act at a given time in which He recognises the attention drawn and therewith fulfils the promise in a twofold sense: by making the repetition effected by men a true one, and by corresponding to the proclaimed promise by a real new coming of His Word. The grace of this twofold fulfilment meets man, then, quite simply in his hearing of the promise and his obedience to it. It meets him only in faith. This is how the Reformers understood that event at the heart of the
[068] Church's life. They understood it in terms of proclamation, i.e., of the *promissio*[EN40] repeated by man's act, because they thought they could understand the presence of the holy God among unholy men only as the grace of the strictly personal free Word of God which reaches its goal in the equally personal free hearing of men, the hearing of faith, which for its part, too, can be understood only as grace. This presupposition is missing in Roman Catholic dogmatics. It, too, describes the event at the heart of the Church's life as grace. But it understands by grace, not the connexion between the Word and faith,

[EN39] In sacred sermons chiefly those things ought to be expounded which it is necessary for the faithful to believe and to do to obtain salvation

[EN40] promise

but the connexion between a divine being as cause and a divine-creaturely being as effect. With due reservations one might even say that it understands it as a physical, not a historical, event. It sees the presence of Jesus Christ in His Church, the mystical unity of the Head with the whole body, in the fact that under certain conditions there flows forth from Jesus Christ a steady and unbroken stream or influence of divine-human being on His people.

At this particular point one can scarcely fail to see the inner connexion between the Roman Catholic view and the Modernist view. The assertion of fellowship between God and man in the form of an operation beyond the juxtaposition of the divine and human persons, beyond the act of divine and human decision, is at least common to both even if one has to remember that this synthetic operation is regarded as man's work on the side of Modernism and as God's on that of Roman Catholicism. But of what importance here (and not only here) is the distinction between "anthropocentric" and "theocentric" theology? Both agree in the unwillingness to recognise the ultimate necessity of proclamation.

Proclamation obviously cannot be the term for this event. Grace here neither is (and remains) God's free and personal Word nor is (and remains) hearing faith. It neither has to be just Word from God nor faith in man. Man neither needs to listen to a Word of God already spoken nor to wait for a Word of God yet to be spoken. Faith neither has to grasp the promise made as made by God nor to wait for a fulfilment still to come. Blessedness is not seen in this grasping and waiting nor judgment discerned in a situation other than this grasping and waiting. All this can obviously be regarded only as partly inadequate, partly superfluous, and partly distorted if both from the standpoint of the divine Giver and also from that of the human recipient grace is an operation, an influence, an action and passion which takes place, not essentially and ultimately between person and person, but materially between God as author on the one hand and the ground of being in the human person on the other.

Protestant polemics is urgently recommended not to use the word "magical" in this connexion. The authentic Roman Catholic view of this material process cannot be brought under any meaningful definition of the term "magic". Cf. on this whole subject Damasus Winzen O.S.B. *Die Sakramentenlehre der Kirche in ihrem Verhältnis zur dialektischen Theologie, Catholica,* 1932, 19 f.

We are faced with a basic decision at this point. For the man who can interpret an operation or influence of an impersonal kind as the grace of Jesus Christ, the rest follows self-evidently. On this view the sacrament has to become the one and all. As act in distinction from spoken Word it is well adapted, if influence be the thing that takes place between God and man in the Church, to be the medium and channel of this influence. [069]

Naturally the significance of the sacrament has then to be described as a *causare, continere el conferre gratiam*[EN41] (*Conc. Florent.* 1438 *Decr. pro. Arm.* Denzinger No. 695) and its power as

[EN41] causing, containing, and conferring grace

effective *ex opere operato*[EN42], i.e., independently of divine decision and human faith—*Si quis dixerit, non dari gratiam per hujus modi sacramenta semper et omnibus, quantum est ex parte Dei, etiam si rite ea suscipiant, sed aliquando et aliquibus: A.S.*[EN43] (*Trid. Sess.* VII *Can. de sacr. in genere can.* 7) *S.q.d., per ipsa novae legis sacramenta ex opere operato non conferre gratiam, sed solam fidem divinae promissionis ad gratiam consequendam sufficere: A.S.*[EN44] (*ib., can.* 8).

And naturally preaching has to be forced into that particular backwater. It is in fact unnecessary here. It can continue alongside what is essential only as its preliminary and ancillary exposition and inculcation.

Certainly the Roman Catholic Church knows and stresses the fact (e.g., *Cat. Rom., Praef. qu.* 2) that *fides*[EN45] comes *ex auditu*[EN46] (Rom. 10^{17}). But it regards the faith which comes from hearing the Word only as preparatory to receiving righteousness before God. *Disponuntur autem ad ipsam justitiam dum excitati divina gratia et adiuti, fidem ex auditu concipientes, libere moventur in Deum, credentes, vera esse, quae divinitus revelata et promissa sunt*[EN47] (*Trid. Sess.* VI, cap. 6).

It cannot be a means of true sanctifying grace, *gratia gratum faciens*[EN48], only a means of preparatory grace.

If in the doctrine of what is called "actual" grace dogmaticians do talk about hearing too at a certain point, what is portrayed from this standpoint is only the very preliminary grace of *illustratio intellectus*[EN49] (M. J. Scheeben, *Handb. der kath. Dogm*, Vol. 3, 1882, new edn., 1925, 666; B. Bartmann, *Lehrb. der Dogm.*, 7th edn., Vol. 2, 1929, 15).

Any other view would in fact mean reviving the partly inadequate, partly superfluous and partly distorted situation which inevitably arises when it is a matter of the Word and hearing it. But Roman Catholic dogmatics does not want to see and understand the event at the heart of the Church's life in this problematic way. For it, then, preaching can have a place only on the extreme margin of the Church's action. In Roman Catholic practice it cannot seek to be more than instruction and exhortation. When the grace of Jesus Christ can be understood as a *causare gratiam ex opere operato*[EN50], all is in order, and this is the only possible order.

The Reformers, however, did not see themselves as in a position to construe

---

EN42 by the performance of the rite itself

EN43 If anyone should say that, as far as God's part is concerned, grace is not given through these sacraments always and to all, even if they receive them rightly, but only sometimes and to some, let him be anathema

EN44 If anyone should say that the sacraments of the new law do not confer grace by the performance of the rite itself, but that faith alone in the divine promise suffices for obtaining grace: let him be anathema

EN45 faith

EN46 from hearing

EN47 [People] are disposed to this righteousness when, aroused and aided by divine grace, and conceiving faith by hearing, they are freely moved toward God, believing those things to be true which have been divinely revealed and promised

EN48 grace which makes one acceptable

EN49 enlightenment of the intellect

EN50 causing grace by virtue of an act being performed

the grace of Jesus Christ in this way. They thought it should be understood, not as cause and effect, but as Word and faith. For this reason, they regarded the representative event at the centre of the Church's life as proclamation, as an act concerned with speaking and hearing, indicative of the fact that what is at issue in the thing proclaimed too is not a material connexion but a personal encounter. In this light they had to regulate the mutual relations of preaching and sacrament in a very definite way. To be sure, they could not and would not assign to the sacrament the place which falls to preaching according to Roman Catholic dogmatics. Proclamation of the basis of the promise which has been laid once and for all, and therefore proclamation in the form of symbolic action, had to be and to remain essential for them. But this proclamation presupposes that the other, namely, repetition of the biblical promise, is taking place. The former must exist for the sake of the latter, and therefore the sacrament for the sake of preaching, not *vice versa.* Hence not the sacrament alone nor preaching alone, nor yet, to speak meticulously, preaching and the sacrament in double track, but preaching with the sacrament, with the visible act that confirms human speech as God's act, is the constitutive element, the perspicuous centre of the Church's life. Understood *a parte potiori*[EN51], but only *a parte potiori,* the Evangelical Churches, Lutheran as well as Reformed, can and must be termed the churches of preaching. [070]

"To achieve such faith God has instituted preaching, given the Gospel and sacraments" (*Conf. Aug.* art. 5). "Then the Word brings Christ to the folk and makes Him known in their hearts, a thing they never knew from the sacraments. Therefore 'tis a hard thing for our times that people are all for holding masses and hasten only to found masses, and unfortunately the foremost thing for which masses are instituted is left out, that is, preaching "(Luther, *Ausleg. deutsch d. Vaterunsers,* 1519, *W.A.* Vol. 2, 112, 15). "Now to do away with this misuse, the first thing to know is that the Christian community should never come together, except there God's very Word be preached and prayer made .... Therefore where God's Word is not preached, 'tis better people should neither sing nor read, nor come together .... 'Tis better to leave out all, save the Word. And nought is better pursued than the Word. For all Scripture showeth that the same should be in full swing among Christians, and Christ also saith Himself, Lk. 10[42] 'One thing is needful.' For that Mary should sit at Christ's feet and hear His Word daily is the best part to choose, and is never taken away. It is an eternal saying that all else must pass away, however much there is for Martha to do" (*Von Ordnung Gottesdiensts,* 1523, *W.A.* 12, 35, 19 and 37, 29). *Primum vero et summum omnium, in quo omnia pendent alia, est docere verbum Dei. Nam verbo docemus, verbo consecramus, verbo ligamus et solvimus, verbo baptisamus, verbo sacrificamus, per verbum de omnibus iudicamus, ut cuicunque verbum cesserimus, huic plane nihil negare possumus, quod ad sacerdotem pertinet*[EN52] (*De instit. ministris Ecclesiae,* 1523, *W.A.* 12, 180, 5). " ... Where the preaching chair lies and snores, so that it does not wake up nor expound the words, one may well sing and read in it, but without any

EN51 with respect to the more important part

EN52 But the first and highest point of all, on which all other things depend, is to teach the word of God. For we teach with the word, we consecrate with the word, we bind and loose with the word, we baptise with the word, we offer sacrifice with the word, we judge all things by the word, so that if we grant the word to anyone, we evidently cannot deny him anything which pertains to a priest

understanding" (*E.A.* 1, 229 between 1530–34). "Therefore we should know that God hath so ordained that none should come to knowledge of Christ or acquire forgiveness through [071] Him or receive the Holy Ghost without external public means, but hath put such treasure in the oral word or preaching office, and will not establish it in a corner or secretly in the heart, but will have it cried aloud and imparted openly among the people, as Christ enjoined: 'Go ye into all the world and preach the Gospel to every creature'" (*Sermon on Matt.* $9^{1f.}$, *W.A.* 29, 579, 1.25). *Est itaque Benedicere: praedicare et docere verbum Evangelii confiteri Christum et cognitionem ipsius propagare in alios. Et hoc sacerdotale officium est et juge sacrificium Ecclesiae in novo Testamento, quae benedictionem illam distribuit praedicando, administrando sacramenta, absolvendo, consolando et tractando verbum gratiae*[EN53] (*Comm. on Gal.* 3^{9}, 1535, *W.A.* 40^{1}, 387, 21). *Ecclesia nihil facere debet, quam recte et pure docere Evangelium atque ita generare liberos*[EN54] (*on Gal.* 4^{27}, 664, 27). "For the very greatest, holiest, most needful, highest service of God, which God has demanded in the first and second commandment as the greatest, is to preach God's Word, for the preacher's office is the highest office in the churches, where then the service of God is omitted, how can there be knowledge of God, the teaching of Christ, or the Gospel?" (Melanchthon, *Apologie*, *C.R.* 28, 220). Calvin called preaching (*doctrina*) the *anima ecclesiae*[EN55] (*Instit.* IV, 12, 1, cf. *Suppl. Exhort.* 1543, *C.R.* 6, 459), or the *mater ex qua nos Deus generat*[EN56] (*Comm. Gal.* 4^{24}, *C.R.* 50, 237), and in his great letter to the Duke of Somerset (Oct. 1548, *C.R.* 13, 70 f.) he expressly declared that mere readings are no substitute for *prédication vive*[EN57] and that the possibility of excesses on the preacher's part, which at all events, have to be reckoned with, should not be an obstacle: *Tous les dangers quon peult craindre ne doibvent empescher que l'Esprit de Dieu nayt sa liberte et son cours en ceulx ausquelz il a distribue de ses graces pour edifier l'Eglise*[EN58]. For: ... *de dire que nous puissions avoir dévotion, soit à prière, soit à cérémonie sans y rien entendre c'est une grand moqiterie: combien qu'il se dict communement. Ce n'est pas une chose morte ne brutifve, que bonne affection envers Dieu: mais est un mouvement vif, procedant du sainct Esprit quand le coeur est droictement touché, et l'enlendement illuminé ... il n'y a nulle edification: sinon où il y a doctrine*[EN59] (*Forme des Prières* 1542, *Epistre au Lecteur, C.R.* 165 f.). In face of this one can only describe it as theological thoughtlessness and caprice that certain 19th century Lutherans (Klaus Harms, Vilmar, Löhe), more or less plainly discrediting preaching, thought they could again proclaim the "altar" and the "sacrament of the altar" as the centre of the Church's action. In contrast, listen to the verdict of the unobjectionably Lutheran Hermann Bezzel: "How are Word and sacrament related to one another? ... The Word has been the first and will remain the first. We do not read: Heaven

---

[EN53] So this is what it means to bless: to preach and teach the word of the Gospel, to confess Christ, and to spread knowledge of Him to others. And according to the New Testament this is the priestly office and the continual sacrifice of the Church which distributes that blessing by preaching, administering the sacrament, absolving, consoling, and expounding the word of grace

[EN54] The church ought to do nothing other than teach the Gospel rightly and purely, and thereby give birth to children who are free

[EN55] soul of the church

[EN56] the mother from whom God begets us

[EN57] live preaching

[EN58] No danger that one might fear must be allowed to prevent God's Spirit from having His liberty and His way in those on whom He has poured out His graces for the upbuilding of the Church

[EN59] to say that we can have true devotion, whether in private prayer or public worship, without understanding anything of it is a great mockery, as often as people generally repeat it. Genuine love for God is not something lifeless or thoughtless, but an active movement initiated by the Holy Spirit when the heart is properly touched and the understanding illumined ... there is no edification except where there is doctrine

and earth shall pass away but my sacraments shall not pass away; we read: But my words shall not pass away. And just because it is easy for an over-valuation of the sacraments to enter in among us, since one expects a magical effect from them, it is essential that one consider the sober Evangelical concept as between them. The Word is the primary thing. The Word existed before the sacrament was. The Word stands alone, the sacrament cannot stand alone. The Word is God's original essence, the sacrament is first aroused by our need. The Word will remain after our need, the sacrament will disappear after our need. This presupposed, I must say that the Word is the audible sacrament and the sacrament is the visible Word. The Word was before the sacrament and exists without the sacrament and will also still exist afterwards'' (Johannes Rupprecht, *Hermann Bezzel als Theologe*, 1925, 369).

2. DOGMATICS AND CHURCH PROCLAMATION

The claim with which Church proclamation steps forward and the expectation with which it is surrounded should not mislead us; it is always and always [072] will be man's word. It is also something more than this and quite different. When and where it pleases God, it is God's own Word. Upon the promise of this divine good-pleasure it is ventured in obedience. On this promise depend the claim and the expectation. But proclamation both as preaching and sacrament does not cease to be representation, human service.

"Therefore we also confess that the servants of the Church are God's fellow-workers, as St. Paul calls them ... yet with this addition and understanding that in all this we ascribe all effect and power to the Lord God alone, to whom servants render this service; for 'tis sure that this power and effect never should or could be attached to any creature, but to God, who imparts it of His own free will to whom He will" (*Conf. Helv. prior* 1536, *art.* 15).

To the degree that it is this, it is not an unassailable action whose authenticity is assured. Like all human action it is exposed to the question of its responsibility. This question can, of course, be put in such a way that it must be dismissed. For instance, Church proclamation, as regards its content, cannot let itself be questioned as to whether it is in harmony with the distinctive features and interests of a race, people, nation, or state. It cannot let itself be questioned as to its agreement with the demands of this or that scientific or aesthetic culture. It cannot let itself be questioned as to whether it is contributing what is needed to maintain or perhaps even to overthrow this or that form of society or economy. A proclamation which accepts responsibilities along these or similar lines spells treachery to the Church and to Christ Himself. It only gets its due if sooner or later its mouth is stopped by some refined or brutal ungodliness. Far better no proclamation at all than this kind. Just because of its real responsibility Church proclamation must be unconditionally free in every other area. Its real responsibility arises out of its intention to be proclamation of the Word of God. The very claim with which it steps forward and the expectation with which it is surrounded also point towards the critical authority by which it must let itself be questioned and in terms of which its legitimacy must always be decided. And because in proclamation the centre of the Church's life is at issue to the degree that it seeks to be the representation of the divine summons to which all other elements in the life of the Church must answer, we have to state that with and in proclamation the Church itself is generally questioned by that critical authority regarding the authenticity of its existence as the Church.

Est autem ecclesia congregatio sanctorum, in qua Evangelium recte docetur et recte administrantur sacramenta[EN60] (*Conf. Aug. art.* 7). Thus *docere Evangelium*[EN61] and *administrare sacramenta*[EN62] take place on the assumption of a *puritas*[EN63] and *rectitudo*[EN64] which is presupposed and sought in this action, of a norm that decides as to the rightness of the action. And this *rectitudo* of teaching and sacrament also decides whether the Church really is here and now the Church, the *ecclesia*[EN65], the *congregatio sanctorum*[EN66].

[073] Thus it is precisely in terms of its origin and basis, of the being of the Church, that Church proclamation, and with it the Church itself, is assailed and called in question. No other attack that may arise can even remotely harass the Church in the same way as this one. To the degree that it is really harassed here it can and should be of good courage in face of all other assaults. But the harassment in this question will always have two aspects, the one relating to the past and the other to the future. What was it that sought to be Christian proclamation yesterday? And what will it be that steps forward anew to-morrow with this claim and surrounded with this expectation? Between the yesterday and the to-morrow, applying to both, attacking yesterday's effort in retrospect and to-morrow's in advance, censuring the one in order to correct the other, there arises the question of the responsibility which is our present concern. Because it is God's service that Church proclamation seeks to be, it is God Himself and God alone who asks here and to whom response must be made here. But for this very reason and in this very way the Church is seriously and concretely burdened with this responsibility. As it can and should evade all other responsibilities, this becomes a burning one. If it does not, if the Church with its proclamation can feel secure before God, then the other responsibilities will become burning ones, and it can and must happen that all the opposition to Church proclamation from the standpoint of the state, society, culture and the like, though not intrinsically justifiable, will be legitimate in relation to the Church, and will become very necessary criticism of the Church in its whole failure to be the Church.

The *Ad fontes!*[EN67] of the Humanists at the beginning of the 16th century was in itself simply a matter of a historicism which is easily seen through theologically and is definitely to

---

EN60 The church is the congregation of saints where the Gospel is rightly taught and the sacraments are rightly administered
EN61 teaching the Gospel
EN62 administering the sacraments
EN63 purity
EN64 rightness
EN65 gathered community
EN66 assembly of saints
EN67 To the sources

be rejected. The discovery of the free creative individual which invaded every sphere with increasing force from the middle of the same century was intrinsically no more than a bit of reviving paganism. The rationality with which the 18th century thought it could master the problems of life better than the Church was sufficiently sharply distinct to be an obvious theological aberration. The eudaemonistic rationalist ideas in which modern Socialism had its origins and from which it derives its spiritual outlook even to this day can certainly have no place in the Church's proclamation. The new Humanism which is preached in America to-day, and which has some prospects of becoming the world-view of the immediate future, betrays already by its utter fatuousness that it is in a very inferior position *vis-à-vis* the Church. Nor can one see in the Asiatic crudities of Bolshevic ideology a rival which inwardly is even remotely a match for the Church's proclamation. But this is all true, and can still be true to-day, only if by "Church" we everywhere mean the Church which is conscious of its own responsibility regarding its proclamation, which is sorely pressed by it and seriously concerned about it. For an unconcerned and self-assured Church which is not assailed at its own centre, these opponents are all serious opponents.

The Church should fear God and not fear the world. But only if and as it fears God need it cease to fear the world. If it does not fear God, then it is not [074] helped at all but genuinely endangered if it fears the world, listens to its opposition, considers its attitude, and accepts all kinds of responsibilities towards it, no matter how necessary and justified may be the criticism it receives from this quarter.

It was the prophetic thinker and preacher Hermann Kutter (1863–1931) who in the last generation, with a force unequalled by any of his contemporaries, represented the insight that the sphere of God's power is greater than the sphere of the Church, and that from time to time it has pleased and pleases God to visit His Church with warning and comfort precisely in the figures and events of secular world history. Especially in his older books *Sie müssen* (1903), *Gerechtigkeit* (1905) and *Wir Pfarrer* (1907) Kutter says this with particular reference to the Social Democracy of the era before the First World War. What Kutter meant, not as a programme, but as an actual scanning and interpretation of the signs of the times, was first developed by Leonhard Ragaz into the theory that the Church must take up a position towards Socialism as a pioneer manifestation of the kingdom of God, and hence into a true system of religious Socialism. After the war P. Tillich, an incomparably more bloodless and abstract thinker than Kutter or Ragaz, replaced this Socialism by secular culture in general, and established and defended this secularism against the Church as a systematic principle, tricking it out with the insignia of prophetic significance. In relation to all this our comment in the present context is as follows. If we grant that there is truth in it, that the modern world, and perhaps Socialism in particular, has something decisive to say to the Church, then, if the most necessary criticism is not to be the most hopeless temptation, the only result of the encounter must be that the Church, recognising God's voice in this alien voice from without, lets itself be called to itself thereby, lets itself be reminded of the burden of its particular ministry with all its promise. Even the greatest and humblest and most open readiness of the Church to be told something by the world might mean that now for the first time it is not really thinking of taking its own responsibility more seriously but letting its energies be dissipated afresh, fondly imagining that it has only been wanting in relevance, openness and activity, and that, e.g., a sense of social need, a capacity for radical social insights and aims, and a will for social action can be a substitute for the required concentration on its own business which it has hitherto neglected. If there is really a prophetic view and interpretation of the opposition which the Church needs directly or indirectly from the

world, if it is really God's "diction" which the Church thinks it sees in this "contradiction," then in any circumstances what it has to glean from it can only be a demand for this conscientious concentration on its own business, for renewed uneasiness about its faithfulness to its commission, and not an invitation to the scattered assumption of alien responsibilities. It is not just an adequate outcome of this encounter between the Church and the world, but the only possible outcome for it, that the Church should take more seriously than before the simple question: What is meant by *pure docere Evangelium, recte administrare sacramenta*[EN68]? In distinction from that of Ragaz and Tillich, Kutter's teaching pointed in this direction. More cannot be said even of him in this connexion. It might have been a salutary prophetic concentration and impatience, but it might also have been a backward looking rather than forward looking philosophy of immediacy that caused him to see in all theology only an attempt to theorise and secularise the divine rather than to live steadfastly in it. Of Ragaz one may say, without getting to closer grips with him, that he has never wrestled carefully or profoundly with the attempt to take seriously the Church's encounter with Socialism along
[075] these lines, and that he is not perhaps in a position to understand it with detachment. For all the respect we cannot withhold from him, he can hardly expect his fevered attacks (latterly in the work edited by Georg Wünsch, *Reich Gottes, Marxismus, Nationalsozialismus*, 1931, pp. 1–65) to make any serious impression on us. But Tillich has on the one side remained too incorrigible a historian of thought, too much an heir of liberal theological resentment against the Church (and, as it would seem, increasingly so), while on the other side he has let himself be too moulded and set systematically by the pseudo-eschatological "situation" of the immediate post-war years, for his protests against "the final supranaturalistic stage of the dialectical movement in Barth's dogmatics" (*Rel. Verwirkl.*, 1930, 20) to arouse my interest. Both Ragaz (*op. cit.*, p. 53) and Tillich (*op. cit.*, p, 21) regard their own activity as dynamic and mine as static .... What am I to say to that?

Now according to the teaching of the parable of the talents the fear of God which the Church needs cannot be inactive, nor can its awareness of the responsibility of its proclamation be a theoretical proviso. God's assault demands something corresponding on man's side, i.e., man's reflection and investigation. Did the Church's proclamation measure up to its responsibility yesterday? Will it do so to-morrow? If the question of the Church is really put by God, then it must meet the Church, press it, and stimulate it in the sphere of human possibilities. The prayer that must be the ultimate answer to this attack has to be accompanied by work as a penultimate answer: critical, corrective, investigative work at Church proclamation in the light of the divine verdict to which it appeals as that which it seeks to be. In that which the Church can and should do here there can be no question at all of its coming forward with its own verdict side by side with the divine verdict, or of its thinking it can carry out this divine verdict. It would not be taking seriously the judgment of God in which it stands if it thought it could carry it out even on itself with any act of its own.

The delimitation necessary here is obvious. Roman Catholic dogmatics speaks of an infallibility of the Church, of the teaching office of the Church specifically, and very specifically of the Pope, *in definienda doctrina de fide vel moribus*[EN69] (*Conc. Vatic.* I, *sess.* IV, *Constit. dogm. de*

[EN68] teaching the Gospel purely, administering the sacraments rightly
[EN69] in defining a doctrine of faith or morals

Eccl. Christi cap. 4). This permits and commands it to treat the *doctrina* (*propositio*) *ecclesiae*[EN70] (cf. Bartmann, *Lehrbuch der Dogm.* 7th edn., Vol. I, 1928, 33 f.) as an *infallibilis el divina regula*[EN71] (Thomas Aquinas, *S. Theol.* II[1], *qu.* 6, *art.* 3). But can one equate *doctrina ecclesiae*[EN72] and *divina regula*[EN73]? Does not this imply that the Church is to judge itself with divine judgment? We can only repeat here the question already put: On this presupposition how far will serious work be done on Church proclamation? On this presupposition how far can concern for it be distinguished from the expository transmission of findings definitively known from of old? And, if this question is not settled, how far is a serious challenge to Church proclamation as a human work recognised? Or if it is not to be recognised, with what right and with what spirit?

The Church can neither question its proclamation absolutely nor correct it absolutely. It can only exert itself to see how far it is questioned and how far it [076] ought to be corrected. On its human work it can only do again a human work of criticising and correcting. And because this is so, it will be far from thinking that it either wants or is able to rid itself of the attack on its proclamation, the uneasiness which God Himself has prepared for it. This work of criticising and correcting its proclamation can be undertaken by the Church in the right sense only if it realises that the uneasiness prepared for it cannot be removed, and its success, if it is well done, will always be that of making it much more clearly aware of the uneasiness prepared for it. But this human work is obviously enjoined upon it with proclamation itself. Church proclamation has to be accompanied and confronted by Church theology, especially dogmatics. In distinction from all scattered answers to irrelevant questions, theology, and especially dogmatics, is the concentrated care and concern of the Church for its own most proper responsibility. In making its proclamation the raw material of dogmatics, it does the one thing it really needs apart from proclamation itself and the prayer that it may be right, the one and only thing it can do as the Church in relation to the obvious centre of its life. For how should not this be the one thing needful when it is not just a matter of right answers to the divine call as with its other functions (and this is certainly to be taken seriously too), but also of the correct representation of the divine call itself, and therefore of the service of God in the supreme sense of the term? And how should not serious reflection on the background of biblical exegesis and with reference to the practice of preaching be the only thing that has to be done, and can in fact be done, about this one thing (always apart from prayer)?

How disastrously the Church must misunderstand itself if, on whatever pretext, it can dream of being able to undertake and achieve anything serious in what are undoubtedly the important fields of liturgical reform or social work or Christian education or the ordering of its relation to state and society or ecumenical understanding, without at the same time doing what is necessary and possible with reference to the obvious centre of its life, as though it were self-evident, as though we could confidently count on it, that *evangelium pure docetur et*

EN70 doctrine (proposition) of the church
EN71 infallible and divine rule
EN72 doctrine of the church
EN73 divine rule

recte administrantur sacramenta[EN74]! as though we could confidently leave this to God and in the meantime busy ourselves with the periphery of the Church circle, which has perhaps been rotating for long enough around a false centre! as though we could put ourselves in God's hands without a care in the world for what happens at this decisive point! Again, how disastrously the Church must misunderstand itself if it can imagine that theology is the business of a few theoreticians who are specially appointed for the purpose, to whom the rest, as hearty practical men, may sometimes listen with half an ear, though for their own part they boast of living "quite untheologically" for the demands of the day ("love"). As though these practical men were not continually preaching and speaking and writing, and were not genuinely questioned as to the rightness of their activity in this regard! As though there were anything more practical than giving this question its head, which means doing the work of theology and dogmatics ! Again, how disastrously the Church must misunderstand itself if it
[077] can imagine that theological reflection is a matter for quiet situations and periods that suit and invite contemplation, a kind of peace-time luxury for which we are not only permitted but even commanded to find no time should things become really serious and exciting! As though there could be any more urgent task for a Church under assault from without than that of consolidating itself within, which means doing theological work! As though the venture of proclamation did not mean that the Church permanently finds itself in an emergency! As though theology could be done properly without reference to this constant emergency! Let there be no mistake. Because of these distorted ideas about theology, and dogmatics in particular, there arises and persists in the life of the Church a lasting and growing deficit for which we cannot expect those particularly active in this function to supply the needed balance. The whole Church must seriously want a serious theology if it is to have a serious theology.

We must now consider the relation between dogmatics and proclamation from the other side. When we call Church proclamation the raw material of dogmatics, what is meant is that Church proclamation is at all events man's talk about God as well. And precisely as man's talk it is the concrete problem of dogmatics, the *factum*[EN75] and *faciendum*[EN76] to which dogmatics relates as a science. Starting with the question how the Church talked about God yesterday, dogmatics asks how this should be done to-morrow. The question is aimed first and directly at those entrusted with the task of proclamation and then indirectly, though not on that account with any less weight, at the Church in general, which as a totality bears corporate responsibility for the proper discharge of this function as of all others. Only as a matter of order, but not in principle, and hence not without the possibility of exceptions, is the function of preaching and administering the sacraments linked to the class of theologians according to the Evangelical concept. This means, however, that in matters of the dogmatic question there can be no dispensation in principle for non-theologians either.

The luxury of "quite untheological" thought and talk which has no part in the dogmatic question, a luxury in which theologians of all people are also prone to indulge very gladly and not without being vain of their freedom, can strictly be achieved only by secretly leaving

EN74 sacraments are rightly administered
EN75 statement of what is the case
EN76 statement of what must be done

the Church either temporarily or permanently. The freedom claimed when men think they can and should theologise "quite untheologically" is the freedom to prattle heretically or in a way that makes for heresy. There is no room in the Church for this freedom.

The possibility of the dogmatic question, of dogmatic criticism and correction, arises out of the claim with which talk about God steps forth in the Church and out of the expectation with which it is surrounded there. One would have to deny this claim and this expectation, and therewith the Church itself, if one were seriously to disavow any interest in face of the dogmatic question. What is said about God in the Church seeks, as proclamation, to be God's Word. It is measured by its own specific criterion in dogmatics. In the raw material of dogmatics we first have a set of words which usually constitute the material of proclamation more or less constantly and emphatically in the [078] Church and irrespective of its divisions. Here as elsewhere these words acquire their meanings through the associations and connexions in which they are used. In virtue of these meanings, talk about God becomes in every age specific and distinctive talk. It is in a plenitude of such specific usages that it exists at any given time for dogmatics, and in general the dogmatic question will be whether and how far this talk, i.e., the sense in which the words are employed in it, is adapted or not to its purpose of serving God's Word. Yesterday's proclamation, with criticism of which dogmatics methodologically begins, is in principle, then, the sum of earlier efforts at Church proclamation as variously determined by the meanings attached to these words. In fact it is only a very small fraction of the whole which, when dogmatic work is done, can be assumed to be known and thus made the object of investigation. Even within this known fraction there may be again only a few elements which stand out representatively from the rest and with which this work can concern itself. Finally it might be neither pertinent nor profitable for dogmatics to try to relate itself to Church preaching as delivered yesterday, the day before, or before that. Genuinely to promote the self-examination of the Church in respect of this central function it will rather turn to that form of yesterday's proclamation in which the latter is already tested, criticised and corrected, i.e., the results of the history of dogmatics. In earlier dogmatics the Church has already stated authoritatively how far it thought it could regard as proclamation the talk about God found within it when this was measured by the standard of the Word of God. The result is—and we must see this as a necessity without sentimentalities—that dogmatics is at the decisive point a debate of dogmaticians among themselves; by dogmaticians, of course, we do not mean only dogmatic teachers and authors, but simply and generally all those both to-day and yesterday who are concerned about the dogmatic question. The essentially "gymnastic" character of dogmatics is shown already by these restrictions regarding the presupposed *factum*[EN77]. As a critical survey of the past dogmatics can work only through examples and not comprehensively or

[EN77] statement of what is the case

exhaustively. But the same character is also revealed in relation to the sought after *faciendum*[EN78]. Here again we have a set of words which constitute the material of all Christian proclamation. But now, so far as this is thought to be necessary, and on the basis of earlier criticism, these words are to be put in different associations and connexions, and they are thus to be used in new and, it is hoped, better senses. But as this correction of talk about God can deal with only a portion of what was said previously, so only a portion of what will be said about God in the Church to-morrow can be directly corrected, and even
[079] this portion can be regarded as only primarily and provisionally corrected. The self-examination of the Church in respect of its proclamation will have to continue to-morrow with the proclamation itself. On this side too, then, dogmatic work cannot claim more than a gymnastic character. It is *pars pro toto*[EN79]. As may be stated already, it cannot aim to be a system of Christian truth. Apart from all else, this would mean that it could criticise the totality of the past proclamation of the Church and definitively set forth the totality of its corrected proclamation. But it cannot do this. In relation to to-morrow, too, it can only take examples, and it can only take certain examples, pending better instruction, and in no sense conclusively. In dogmatics criticism and correction of talk about God can be practised only on a specific section of the whole world of past and future Church proclamation. We have to learn, and in dogmatics, too, this can be done only for the needs of the next day. In this regard dogmatics shows plainly that its business is that of the school, whose instruction cannot anticipate in any sense the reality of life, but only give the most immediate and most necessary guidance for meeting this reality. Church proclamation is the raw material of dogmatics. But it would be a fatal confusion to try to reverse this and say that dogmatics is the raw material of proclamation.

It is a familiar and perhaps unavoidable beginner's mistake of students and assistants, when preaching, to think that they can and should confidently take the content of their preaching from their treasured college notebooks and textbooks of dogmatics. On the other hand, older preachers are usually far too confident in removing themselves from the jurisdiction of this critical authority.

One cannot and should not expect to hear the content of proclamation from dogmatics. This content must be found each time in the middle space between the particular text in the context of the whole Bible and the particular situation of the changing moment. Dogmatics can only be a guide to the right mastery and the right adaptability, to the right boldness and the right caution, for the given moment when this space has to be found. It can only be a guide to orientation between the two poles of saying what has to be said in all circumstances and not saying what must not be said in any circumstances. In short, it can only be a guide to the act of choosing between various possibilities which is characteristic of this human action (as human action) in the same way

EN78 statement of what must be done
EN79 a part standing for the whole

as it is of all other human action. It can only be a guide from the standpoint that what is at issue in this action is proclamation of the Word of God, and that in this sense it must be given a form commensurate with human knowledge and conscience at its very best.

The direct connexion between theology, i.e., dogmatics, and the task of Church proclamation has been expressly stated already in Augustine: *ut non solum legendo alios ... sed et aliis ipsi aperiendo proficiant*[EN80] (*De doctr. chr. Prol.* 1, cf. I, 1). For the instruction of Church teachers the Reformation period yields not only Luther's *Larger Catechism* of 1529 but also the [080] *Berne Synod* of 1532 and the *Catechismus Romanus* of 1566. That the aim of dogmatics is to make the theologian *aptum reddere ad instituendum hominem ad salutem*[EN81] is notably asserted in older Protestantism by the Lutherans J. Gerhard (*Loci theol.* 1610, *Prooem.* 26 and 31), Quenstedt (*Theol. did. pol.* 1685, P. I, *cap.* 1, *sect.* 2, *qu.* 2, *ekth.* 15), Baier (*Comp. Theol. pos.* 1686, *Prol.* 1, 1) and Buddaeus (*Instit, theol. dogm.* 1724, I, 1, 28). Moreover, as is well known, it is none other than Schleiermacher who exalts the practical task of Church guidance to the status of a constitutive principle for theological science (*Kurze Darstellung*, 1830, § 1–13). He is vigorously followed by Vilmar of Marburg: "According as dogmatics removes itself from the sphere of the Church, it no longer serves salvation but panders to the intellectual vanity of the individual. Dogmatics has to realise that as a subject of preparation for spiritual office it stands in the relation of a school to real life, and to it, too, it is said: *Non scholae sed vitae discimus*[EN82]. The life of the Church stands above dogmatics." We find in Vilmar the expression which characterises the view set forth here, namely, that dogmatics "properly contains *gymnasmata*[EN83] for the Church office and its holders" (*Dogmatik* I. Teil. 1874, 59). Sound words against the idea that dogmatics has to provide the practising theologian with material for his sermons and catechisings are to be found in Schleiermacher's pupil August Twesten (*Vorlesungen über die Dogm. d. ev. -luth. Kirche*, Vol. I, 1838, 82 f.): Dogmatics does not yield him direct profit but the indirect and for that very reason all the more important profit that it impresses on all his activity the "character of a loftier circumspection." "But as concerns his teaching vocation, quite apart from its beneficent influence on the depth and breadth of his religious thinking, it accustoms him to a criticism which does not apply only to the form, as is usually the case, but also to the Christian content of his discourses and their relation to the highest tasks of practical theology in general" (*op. cit.*, p. 85). Finally the understanding of dogmatics in terms of a school and its relation to the "conduct of Christian instruction" is also a feature in the theological work of Albrecht Ritschl (*Unterricht i. d. christl. Rel.* 3rd edn., 1886, § 87; *Rechtfertigung und Versöhnung*, Vol. II, 4th edn., 1900, 3 and 13).

In all this what we are to understand by "proclamation of the Word of God" is primarily and decisively preaching and the sacraments, though with regard to the latter, which as *verba visibilia*[EN84] in actions belong to a special order, the thing which counts is simply the oral proclamation which accompanies them, the doctrine of the sacraments which is significant for the particular meaning of their administration. We have seen, however, that the task but not the reality of proclamation may be reduced and restricted to these two categories of

[EN80] that [students] may make progress not only by reading others ... but also by themselves opening to others [what they have read]

[EN81] suited to undertake the training up of a person to salvation

[EN82] We do not learn for school but for life

[EN83] training exercises

[EN84] visible words

preaching and sacrament. The other, sacrificial and generally responsive elements in the Church's life may also be proclamation. And to the degree that in these other functions of the Church there is talk about God by men, they, too, are subject to the question how far this talk is correct. That the *factum*[EN85] and *faciendum*[EN86] of the Church's education of youth must come in the sphere of dogmatics follows at once from the ineluctability with which it must continually move on from teaching to proclamation. Even in theology itself the exegete on the one side and the practical theologian on the other cannot evade the dogmatic question. The exegete cannot do so because his exposition of
[081] the Bible, however faithful to the text, is invariably a tissue of biblical material with a wrapping of imported personal associations and consequently of possible meanings, so that if this exposition is to be advanced as authentic proclamation in the Church it cannot avoid the query as to the legitimacy of the imported element. Again, the dogmatic question has to be put to the practical theologian too, because even the most external question regarding the conduct of worship to-day can be given very different answers according to the insight into what is proper proclamation and what is not. Furthermore the prayers and praises of the Church cannot be regarded as of no dogmatic importance at all; the liturgy and hymnal must be taken seriously from the standpoint that their substance consists of human words and can thus be effective as proclamation, perhaps as very distorted proclamation.

It is a strange thing that when there are revisions of books of order and hymn-books in the Evangelical churches every possible authority is usually consulted as a standard but not dogmatic science. The results naturally correspond.

Again in social work, which is much to the fore to-day, there is a variety of talk as well as action, and much of this talk claims to be proclamation. But things will be very different when theological reflection stands behind it and when it does not. We have stated too that the possibility has to be taken into account that God may also speak from outside the Church as we now know it or as it really is, and to this extent the attention of dogmatics must not let itself be limited by the walls of the Church. It will always be a venture, a departure from its true line, when dogmatics thinks it should devote itself to this proclamation of God's Word outside the Church, or when, conversely, it thinks it should also speak to the world and not to the known visible Church, which is its normal office.

It would make no sense to try to lay this down as a rule. Dogmatics is not by nature a general *gnosis*[EN87] of God and the world.

The individual dogmatician assumes the responsibility of the prophet when

---

[EN85] statement of what is the case
[EN86] statement of what must be done
[EN87] esoteric knowledge

he does this. One cannot deny that he may sometimes have to do it. But the normal and central *factum*[EN88] on which dogmatics focuses will always be quite simply the Church's Sunday sermon of yesterday and to-morrow. The Church stands or falls with this function enjoined upon it. It has every cause to take dogmatic work very seriously as the criticism and correction of this its decisive function.

In accordance with this statement of the problem we have now to interpret or correct what has been said about the raw material of dogmatics in both ancient and more recent times. In all kinds of variations, Roman Catholics and Protestants, ancients and moderns, have presented, as the raw material of dogmatics, God and the things of God, or man in his relation to God, or God's [082] revelation in Christ, or the Christian faith, or more recently the Christian principle, or the nature of Christianity, in short, the theme of Christian discourse, the subject-matter of Christianity.

Now obviously one cannot object to this in so far as Christian discourse is naturally the raw material of dogmatics as discourse about the subject-matter of Christianity, and so the subject-matter itself is indirectly the raw material too. But it is worth while not to lose sight of the indirectness with which alone this can happen. The three aspects which follow should be noted.

1. The necessity of dogmatics is different from that of Church proclamation. Proclamation is required as the execution of God's command to the Church. Dogmatics is required because proclamation is a fallible human work. These are two different things. The relation of proclamation to the theme of Christianity is obviously primary, that of dogmatics secondary. The datum from which dogmatics begins is neither God nor revelation nor faith. This is the datum from which proclamation starts. Certainly dogmatics can and should be proclamation too, and to this extent it, too, starts from this datum. But it also has its own function which is not the same as that of proclamation. Hence its datum is different, namely, the questionable fact that in proclamation God, revelation and faith are talked about by men in human terms—questionable because it is by no means self-evident that this is done in truth and purity, and because the Church cannot shirk the responsibility that it ought to be done in truth and purity. Dogmatics serves preaching by raising this question. It tests the orthodoxy of the contemporary kerygma. Concrete dogma, indeed, is simply the kerygma tested, provisionally purified, and reduced to a correct formula by the Church. One should not expect more of dogmatics than it can achieve *qua*[EN89] dogmatics. And we should not take exception to much in dogmatics that is peculiar to it *qua* dogmatics.

An example is the *rabies theologorum*[EN90], which Melanchthon was so glad he would no longer encounter in heaven.

[EN88] statement of what is the case

[EN89] as

[EN90] frenzy of theologians

Dogmatics does not seek to give a positive, stimulating and edifying presentation. It does not even try to give an instructive exposition in the same sense as preaching. It deals with God, revelation and faith only in respect of their reflection in proclamation. Even as presentation it is also investigation and polemic, criticism and correction.

Its task is ἐπικόψαι τὰς τῆς πλάνης ὁδούς, ἵνα μίαν ὁδὸν βασιλικὴν ὁδεύσωμεν[EN91] (Cyril of Jerusalem, *Catech.* 16, 5). "The Church's definitions of doctrine are only the railings which guard against falling into the abyss on both sides; they are like the buoys which mark off the proper channel" (F. A. Philippi, *Kirchl. Glaubenslehre*, 1854 f., Vol. 2, 150).

[083] We shall spare ourselves many unnecessary disappointments over both the form and also the results of dogmatics if we keep this soberly in view.

2. Dogmatics serves Church proclamation. Its relation to this should be seen as parallel to what was called *pistis*[EN92] and *gnosis*[EN93] in the early Church and what has been called *credere*[EN94] and *intelligere*[EN95] since Augustine, *pistis* or *credere* being understood as the simple reproduction and propagation of the content of the message in a way which unreflectingly corresponds to what has been heard, *gnosis* or *intelligere* as the scientific investigation of this correspondence. But in this juxtaposition we must insist upon three provisos which were not always observed in the early Church and non-observance of which can lead us into error even to-day.

(*a*) As compared with proclamation dogmatics involves a different mode and function but in no sense a higher stage of faith or the knowledge of faith.

It was clearly one of the results of the struggle with ancient Gnosticism that the Church rejected an aristocracy of scientific theologians in its midst. But the idea is a natural one, and in practice it can always be a temptation.

We must be very clear that the simplest proclamation of the Gospel can be proclamation of the truth in the most unlimited sense and can validly communicate the truth to the most unsophisticated hearer if God so will. Dogmatics is not the technique of certain people who are better placed spiritually. It is not the privilege of an esoteric Christianity whereby the truth is enjoyed in a better form than that in which God has it proclaimed to all people in the Church. Striving to improve what man does here, the dogmatician is not better in faith or knowledge than any other member of the Church with respect to what God does here.

(*b*) As compared with Church proclamation dogmatics does not have access to a higher or better source of knowledge which is to be sought in the fact that only here does Christian thought begin, or that thought is here more exact,

---

[EN91] to cut out the ways of error, so that we might follow the one royal highway
[EN92] faith
[EN93] esoteric knowledge
[EN94] believing
[EN95] understanding

comprehensive and profound than in simple preaching. It is not true that the attempt to think in human terms about God, revelation and faith first began in dogmatics. This attempt is already made in proclamation itself inasmuch as it is undoubtedly human speech, and also in listening to proclamation inasmuch as this is human listening. Nor is there any reason why it should not and could not be undertaken here too in the form of exact, comprehensive and profound thought.

Paul Althaus writes: "Theology means performing the act of faith in the sphere of thought. Faith is to overcome the world. Theology is the struggle to overcome the world of spirits and of thoughts. Theologians thereby practise deliberation ... as a service to the whole community and therefore, as it were, in representative thinking" (*Evangelium und Leben*, 1927, 26 f.). In spite of and in face of this definition are we not ascribing too much to theology if we make the goal of its "struggle" something that is promised only to faith as such (which may also be the faith of a "layman")? [084]

And certainly the introduction of critical reflection which distinguishes dogmatics from proclamation does not mean that a higher norm of knowledge is substituted for the norm of proclamation. Naturally there is the constant threat here that some philosophy will rush in and then raise the claim *in concreto*[EN96] that it represents this higher source of knowledge. For where can this critically reflective thought find its style and norm except in human reason and therefore *in concreto* in a philosophy? Here, then, we always need the insight that critically reflective thought, even though it be that of human reason, and no matter what philosophical tints it has, must still be set in relation to the theme of the Church's proclamation, and its execution must be governed, not by its human origin and nature, but by its divine object.

The *credo ut intelligam*[EN97] of Anselm (*Prosl.*, 1) certainly does not imply transition from faith to another genus but an *αἰχμαλωτίζειν πᾶν νόημα εἰς τὴν ὑπακοὴν τοῦ Χριστοῦ*[EN98] (2 Cor. 10[5]).

In practice it is not in our power to check that incursion of philosophy into dogmatics. Nor is it in our power actually to give to critically reflective human thought that relation to the divine object and control by it. But it is in our power to keep before us the need for that relation and control and hence to refuse to philosophy that right of usurpation and to give the final word, not to the immanent orders of critically reflective thought, not to the demands of the need of human thought, but only to the requirement of the object here in question. We can at least realise that only on one side should dogmatics be unconditionally open and obedient, and that it has this side in common, not with any philosophy, but with the Church's proclamation.

(*c*) As compared with Church proclamation, then, dogmatics cannot wish to be an end in itself. The situation is not that God, revelation and faith are given

---

EN96 concretely
EN97 I believe that I might understand
EN98 bringing into captivity every thought to the obedience of Christ

to proclamation and then independently and in some way differently to dogmatics too. They are all given to the Church, and they are not given for contemplation but for proclamation, and only to this extent are they also given to dogmatics as the presupposition of its testing of the human work of proclamation. They are given to the Church, namely, as its being, as the principle of life which creates and establishes it, and for that very reason not as a mere existent
[085] which might become the object of independent theory, gnosis, or speculation remote from its action, but as the divine activity with which the Church itself must actively come to terms. This human activity of the Church, however, is primarily proclamation, and the aim of dogmatics cannot be more than its correct performance. It has place and justification as a critical theory, gnosis or speculation only to the extent that it serves this purpose.

In the debate between Thomas Aquinas and Duns Scotus as to whether theology is a *scientia speculativa* or *practica*[EN99] older Protestant dogmatics with increasing definiteness came down on the side of Duns Scotus. The process, to which we shall return, is equivocal. It certainly had its origin on the one side in the rising religionism of the day and its lack of concern for God's objectivity. Yet on the other side it arose out of a healthy revulsion against an abstract and basically unchurchly contemplation and discussion of God, against the pure self-incurving theological speculation which achieved classical form in the celebrated writings of Pseudo-Dionysius, which exerted a powerful influence on the monastic scholarship of the Middle Ages and indeed on the Protestant orthodox themselves, and which may still be found to-day in certain sections of Roman Catholic dogmatics. It is in recognition of the danger which threatens Roman Catholic dogmatics from this angle that B. Bartmann in his manual appends to many (though by no means all) of his *loci*[EN100] a final special section under the title "practical values" (namely, of this specific dogmatic theme), though after all the problem can hardly be solved as easily as that. Speaking of the practical character of theology could mean an acknowledgement that the Church is not an academy and that there is also no academic corner within it. *Semper cogitandum est, Filium Dei non ob eam causam prodidisse ex arcana sede aeterni Patris, et revelasse doctrinam coelestem, ut seminaria spargeret disputationum, quibus ostendandi ingenii causa luderetur, sed potius ut homines de vera Dei agnitione et omnibus iis quae ad aeternam salutem consequendam necessaria sunt, erudirentur*[EN101] (M. Chemnitz, *Loci theol. ed.*, 1590, *Hypomnemata* 9).

In sum, since dogmatics does not imply a higher possibility of Christian life, since it may not advance an independent source of knowledge and since it cannot claim as theory an autonomous role and significance, therefore the subject-matter of Christianity does not exist for it in any other way than as it is found in Christian proclamation.

3. The theme of Church proclamation or subject-matter of Christianity demands dogmatics to the extent that its proclamation is a responsible act and

---

EN 99 speculative or practical science

EN100 topical sections

EN101 We must always keep in mind that the reason the Son of God came down from the hidden throne of the eternal Father and revealed heavenly doctrine was not to furnish material for seminary debates, in which the display of ingenuity might be the game, but rather so that human beings should be instructed concerning true knowledge of God and of all those things which are necessary to the pursuit of eternal salvation

to the extent that dogmatics is the effort to meet this responsibility towards the theme of proclamation. Yet it is by no means the case that in dogmatics the Church becomes as it were the lord and judge of the subject-matter, so that the current results of dogmatics are to be accepted as a law imposed as it were on God, revelation and faith. Dogmatics has to investigate and say at each given point how we may best speak of God, revelation and faith to the extent that human talk about these things is to count as Church proclamation. It should not think that it can lay down what God, revelation and faith are in themselves. In both its investigations and its conclusions it must keep in view that God is in heaven and it on earth, and that God, His revelation and faith always live their [086]
own free life over against all human talk, including that of the best dogmatics. Even if we have again weighed everything and corrected everything and formulated everything better, as is our duty to the subject-matter of Christianity in respect of human talk about it, and even if our findings have been given the status of Church confession and dogma, we have still to say: We are unprofitable servants, and in no sense are we to imagine that we have become in the very least masters of the subject.

In the well-known introductory words to the so-called Athanasian Creed dogmatics, or dogma, comes forward with the following claim: *quicunque vult salvus esse, ante omnia opus est, ut teneat catholicam fidem, quam nisi quisque integram inviolatamque servaverit, absque dubio in aeternum peribit*[EN102]. This is going too far. Such fixing of saving faith by a human and to that extent disputable theologoumenon has nothing whatever to do with the binding and loosing on earth which according to the Gospel (Mt. 16^{19}; 18^{18}) corresponds to being bound and loosed in heaven, for the judicial force which in the Gospel is ascribed to the act of obedience to apostolic proclamation is now transferred to a formula abstracted from this act, to a sequence of words as such, which in distinction from the act of obedience is an instrument whereby man masters God, revelation and faith. We ask to what degree this mastery does not take place in the Roman Catholic understanding of dogmatics and dogma. Nevertheless, since dogma on this view is only partly known and proclaimed, since dogmatics, then, cannot be complete, and since on the other hand distinction is made between an explicit and an implicit *fides catholica*[EN103], Roman Catholicism, too, acknowledges that revelation and saving faith live their own life as distinct from the law of faith, a life which is richer on the one side though more restricted on the other. From the opposite angle the theology of Wilhelm Herrmann also calls for consideration here. No feature in it is more distinctive than his unwearying battle against the idea of a dogmatic law imposed on faith. This is what gave Herrmann's life work a pronouncedly anti-Catholic impress. What was he fighting for in this battle? The independent life of the subject-matter of Christianity against all human pinning-down, against every attempt to make the "on earth" into an "in heaven," against all intellectual righteousness of works? Or simply the human right of a Romantic anti-intellectualism, individualism, and fanaticism for truth? One must admit that the latter is the answer in the foreground, the former the answer in the background. If with a certain exegetical daring one can include the former, then Herrmann's protest may be regarded as a

EN102 whoever wishes to be saved must above all else hold to the catholic faith; for whoever does not keep it whole and inviolate will without doubt perish eternally

EN103 catholic faith

necessary one against the *Quicunque vult salvus esse*[EN104]. In so far as the latter is the answer, Protestantism is well advised not to identify itself with Herrmann.

We are also not to understand the task of dogmatics in relation to proclamation as though it had to offer God, revelation and faith to this as the content of preaching. We have seen already that what dogmatics has to give does not consist of contents but of guidelines, directions, insights, principles and limits for correct speech by human estimate. It can be called doctrinal law in this sense. But its presupposition is that preaching acquires its content elsewhere. For that reason it cannot be lord and judge here either. It can and should give
[087] counsel in all seriousness but it neither can nor should seek to give orders in the Church.

Here we may apply 2 Cor. 1[24]: *οὐχ ὅτι κυριεύομεν ὑμῶν τῆς πίστεως, ἀλλὰ συνεργοί ἐσμεν τῆς χαρᾶς ὑμῶν*[EN105].

Like the subject-matter of Christianity, Church proclamation must also remain free in the last resort, free to receive the command which it must always receive afresh from that free life of the subject-matter of Christianity. Church proclamation and not dogmatics is immediate to God in the Church. Proclamation is essential, dogmatics is needed only for the sake of it. Dogmatics lives by it to the extent that it lives only in the Church. In proclamation, and in God, revelation and faith only to the degree that these are its objects, dogmatics is to seek its material.

What Ambrose (*De fide ad Grat.*, 1, 5, 42) wrote against a heretical theology really applies to all theology: *Non in dialectica complacuit Deo salvum facere populum suum. Regnum enim Dei in simplicitate fidei est, non in contentione sermonis*[EN106].

EN104 Whoever wishes to be saved

EN105 Not for that we have dominion over your faith, but are helpers of your joy

EN106 God has no desire to save His people through argument. The kingdom of God is found in simple faith and not in verbal disputes

§ 4 [088]

THE WORD OF GOD IN ITS THREEFOLD FORM

The presupposition which makes proclamation proclamation and therewith makes the Church the Church is the Word of God. This attests itself in Holy Scripture in the word of the prophets and apostles to whom it was originally and once and for all spoken by God's revelation.

1. THE WORD OF GOD PREACHED

We have to speak about the presupposition which makes proclamation proclamation and therewith makes the Church the Church. Proclamation must ever and again become proclamation. From being an action which, coming forward with the corresponding claim and surrounded with the corresponding expectation, wants to be and should be proclamation, it must become an action which is proclamation. And because the event of real proclamation is the function of the Church's life which governs all others, we have to say that in this event the Church itself must ever and again become the Church. Proclamation and the Church are, of course, simply and visibly there just as the bread and wine of Communion are simply and visibly there and the distributing, eating and drinking of the bread and wine in Communion take place simply and visibly. They are not simply and visibly there, however, as that which they want to be and should be, as theologically relevant entities, as realities of revelation and faith. They have ever and again to come into being as this.

The connexion with the Lord's Supper is not to be regarded as just incidental. What applies to proclamation and the Church generally cannot be better illustrated than by the sacrament. Calvin says of the tree of life in Paradise and of Noah's rainbow: *Non quod arbor praestaret illis immortalitatem ... aut arcus coercendis aquis foret efficax ... sed quia notam a verbo Dei insculptam habebant, ut documenta essent testamentorum eius ac sigilla. Et antea quidem arbor erat arbor, arcus arcus; ubi inscripta fuerunt verbo Dei, indita est nova forma, ut inciperent esse quod prius non erant*[EN1] (*Instit.* IV, 14, 18). And H. Bullinger says of the earthly elements in the sacrament: *Verbo Dei fiunt, quae antea non fuerunt, sacramenta. Consecrantur enim verbo et sanctificata esse ostenduntur ab eo qui instituit*[EN2]. For this reason and to this degree they are not called mere water, bread and wine but, without any change of nature, the bath of regeneration and

---

EN1 Not that the tree itself guaranteed them immortality ... or that the rainbow was the means of restraining the waters ... but they had a mark inscribed by the word of God, so that they were documents or seals of his promises. And, indeed, beforehand the tree was a tree, the rainbow a rainbow; but when they were inscribed with the word of God, a new form was prescribed for them, so that they might begin to be what they were not before

EN2 By God's word they become sacraments, which they were not before. For they are consecrated by the word and thus shown to be sanctified by Him who instituted them

the body and blood of the Lord (*Conf. Helvet. post.*, 1562, art. 19 in K. Müller, 207, 11 f. and 34 f.). It would be very out of place to recoil from terms like *fieri*[EN3] and *nova forma*[EN4] as used here by Reformed authors just because they bring to light a problem which cannot be
[089] easily dismissed, namely, that of the Roman Catholic doctrine of change. In the sacrament and in preaching and in the whole life of the Church it is always true that the existence of the earthly body acquires a new form from the heavenly Head, that it becomes the actuality of revelation and faith. Again, it would be very out of place to regard it as a nominalistic softening of this becoming when, e.g., Bullinger so plainly rejects the doctrine of transubstantiation here and so firmly regards the new designation of the elements as just a designation. This designation is not an arbitrarily imported meaning but the *nota a verbo Dei insculpta*[EN5]. We only show our failure to understand what it means that the earthly reality acquires this new *nota* by the Word of God if we regard this view of the new becoming as less realistic than that expressed in the Roman Catholic doctrine of transubstantiation or the Lutheran doctrine of consubstantiation.

The presupposition of this event is the Word of God. Between this central concept of our prolegomena and dogmatics generally on the one side and the concept of proclamation on the other there are four decisive connexions whose mutual relation may be compared to that of four concentric circles. These we must now analyse.

I. The Word of God is the commission upon whose givenness proclamation must rest if it is to be real proclamation. The necessity of proclamation does not find an objective foundation in the fact that certain circumstances and scales of value immanent in the existence of man and things crave to be known and declared. The answer to this craving is not proclamation but fundamentally secular science, and there can be no question but that all the circumstances and scales of value which might be regarded as possible objects of Church proclamation belong to the sphere of secular science and stand in no need of proclamation by preaching and sacrament. Again, the necessity of proclamation does not find a subjective basis in the fact that certain personal convictions of certain men call for this particular articulation. For in so far as these convictions are capable of rational presentation, the persons concerned should be referred again to the way of scientific exposition, and in so far as they are wholly or predominantly irrational they should be referred to the possibility of musical, poetic or artistic expression. In relation to all such objective or subjective motives, and the more so the more seriousness and worth they claim, one might well ask whether, quite apart from any scientific or artistic presentation, they might not be brought to primary expression in a practical moral and political attitude appropriate to them. However that may be, in presupposing such motives we lose all insight into the necessity of proclamation. Naturally such motives too will necessarily come into play, as everywhere, so also in the Church, even when it is a matter of proclamation. To speak even more plainly, these are the human motives of all alleged proclam-

---

[EN3] to become
[EN4] new form
[EN5] mark inscribed by the word of God

ation, and we cannot intrinsically have any others. It is not the case that we are able to reach above them and grasp and establish something higher, a motive which will be the necessary basis and actualisation of alleged proclamation. What more could we establish than circumstances and scales of value on the [090]
one side and convictions on the other? The fact that we are unable to indicate or establish a higher motive than these, and hence a real necessity of Church proclamation, and hence proclamation as real proclamation, is the very thing we acknowledge and confirm when we describe the commission to which it may be traced back as the Word of God. Certainly in so doing we are by implication speaking objectively of a circumstance and scale of values and subjectively of a personal conviction. This human motivation is the medium above which we can as little rise as we can cast off our shadows. But it is also the medium above which we will not want to rise because it is the place where we are to expect the divine commission. God's Word means in this context God's positive command: *God's* positive command, and hence a motive which acts according to its own absolutely superior principle even though present and at work within the whole unavoidable world of human motivations; God's *positive command*, and hence a motive which in its divinity is not present and at work in the way that circumstances and scales of value are over us and convictions in us, i.e., which we are not able to establish because we cannot grasp at it, but rather which is present and at work when and where it wills to be present and to be at work. No proclamation does not also rest on those human motives which are there and which have to be established. But no proclamation is real proclamation to the degree that over and above all this it does not rest on the commission which we cannot in any way take to ourselves, which we cannot in any way take for granted, which we can only receive and have in the act of receiving, which comes upon us and the whole world of our motivations absolutely from without, which lifts us up and controls us as a command that goes forth in a way we cannot foresee, and to which, as stated earlier, we can only take up an attitude by repeating it as we think we have heard it and by trying to conform to it as well or badly as we can. Real proclamation, then, means the Word of God preached and the Word of God preached means in this first and outermost circle man's talk about God on the basis of God's own direction, which fundamentally transcends all human causation, which cannot, then, be put on a human basis, but which simply takes place, and has to be acknowledged, as a fact.

"So say ye now: 'whom God hath sent.' That is, God's Word is not named unless it is sent. That is, let none think that God's Word cometh to earth of man's device. If it is to be God's Word, it must be sent. Otherwise it is impossible that Holy Writ could be understood or expounded by any arbitrary device. It availeth not that one should speak and he is not called, for God's Word cometh alone because He sendeth it. Where not, the whole world cannot utter what could redeem from sins and comfort the consciences. If He had not sent the Word and the office, we had nought. Therefore we should neither utter nor hear aught save [091]
only God's Word. If it is invented by man's choice and device, avoid it. It cometh not except

it be sent from heaven. And let him that hath dealings with monks ask whether their thing is God's Word. Then wilt thou hear them allege it is done of good intent to honour God. Hence 'tis service of God and God's Word. But there is more to it than good intent to do God service and pay for sins. From thy heart floweth the device, the opinion. But say thou whether God hath sent it from heaven, also whether He hath commanded it. Yea, is it done to God's honour? The wickeder it is, and a double blasphemy, that thou calledst that God's Word and service of God which thou thyself hast invented. Thus hath the Pope led the world astray under the name and title of the Church. But without God's sending cometh no Word into the world. Hath it grown out of my heart, cling I to Chrysostom, Augustine and Ambrose, 'tis not then God's Word. For there is a vast difference 'twixt the Word that is sent from heaven and that which of my own choice and device I invent. Holy Writ, so it be grown on earth, thus saith John: He that is of the earth speaketh earthly things. Thus we must learn to set our blessedness soundly on the power of God's Word and not on our own device or opinion" (Luther, *Ausl. des 3. und 4. Kap. Joh.*, 1538 f., *W.A.* 47, 193, 10).

2. The Word of God is the theme which must be given to proclamation as such if it is to be real proclamation. Proclamation is asked how far it is proclamation of something, objective proclamation, proclamation of a real theme. Again we must assert that in so far as this theme belongs to the sphere of objects of human apprehension and thought, to the sphere of objects of external or internal contemplation, it is hard to see to what extent it should be proclaimed by preaching and sacrament. Would not scientific, artistic, or even ethico-political presentation and publication be incomparably more appropriate to themes of this class? Again we must admit, of course, that we have no objects but those of outer and inner perception. This must be said even of the object of proclamation. If we have it as an object at all, it is as an object of outer or inner perception, of experience and thought. If we did not have it thus, we should not have it at all. But to the extent that we only have it thus, we do not have it as a possible object of proclamation. Metaphysics or psychology could then take charge of it, and indeed would have to do so. But these are the very sciences that cannot take charge of a theme that is worth proclaiming. In calling the object or theme of proclamation God's Word we mean that it is not merely or even primarily the object of human perception. It must become the object of human perception to be capable of being proclaimed. But to the extent that it is really proclaimed it is not at all the object of human perception. It is proclaimed to the degree that it presents and places itself as an object over against us and the whole world of all our objects, certainly in the unavoidable medium of perceptual objectivity, but in this medium as the object which can never in any sense be our possession, to which we can never point back as to a datum, which is a presupposition in the sense and only in the sense that it
[092] sets itself where we cannot possibly set it. We have it as it gives itself to us if we have it. In this way, in contrast to all the objects of metaphysics or psychology, it is the object of proclamation. Between this object and preaching and sacrament as the means to present and impart it there should be an inner connexion. Preaching and sacrament are, as we have seen, the promise of future revelation on the basis of the revelation that has already occurred. How, then,

can one speak of this object except in the form of this promise, which is quite distinct from that of science, art, or politics? Real proclamation, then, means God's Word preached, and in this second circle God's Word preached means human talk about God on the basis of the self-objectification of God which is not just there, which cannot be predicted, which does not fit into any plan, which is real only in the freedom of His grace, and in virtue of which He wills at specific times to be the object of this talk, and is so according to His good-pleasure.

There are some excellent delimitations on this point in H. M. Müller, *Glaube und Erfahrung bei Luther*, 1929: "The concrete, contingent givenness of faith, and to that extent the gift itself, is still something that can only be declared in the proclamation of the Gospel; it remains declaration" (p. 95). "Preaching as impartation of the promise is precisely not the transmission of revelation; it is an indication of the occurrence of revelation" (p. 119, cf. also 41, 149, 150, 162, 196, etc.).

3. The Word of God is the judgment in virtue of which alone proclamation can be real proclamation. Proclamation is also asked whether it is true. What is to decide this? What is the criterion here? One usually judges the truth of human speech by the nature of its theme on the one side and by the situation and concern of the speaker on the other. Naturally this may and must apply to Church proclamation too. It lies within the realm of human speech. The one who proclaims must submit to the question: What do you know of the thing you speak of? And: What is your concern in speaking of it? He has to let his work be judged by these questions. The only point is that what he says is not affected as proclamation by such judgments. What is assessed by them is its scientific or ethico-political or aesthetic character. Intrinsically proclamation as it takes place in preaching and sacrament presupposes that neither the nature of its object nor the situation or concern of the speaker is or can be so clear to any man as to put him in a position to pronounce on its truth. If there is to be any assessment at all of Church proclamation as such it must be from another angle. It is this fundamentally different aspect of the judgment to be made on Church proclamation that we have in view and describe when we acknowledge it to be the Word of God. We are not denying thereby that proclamation is subject to other criteria too. We are simply affirming that in fact we only know these other criteria in judging it here and now, that we are in no position to pronounce upon its truth in any other way. But here and now we [093]
have 1. to recollect that, even though it is not known to anyone, a different criterion from these others has given itself to be known and 2. to expect that this criterion which we do not know now, or know only from this recollection, will give itself to be known again. This criterion which is recollected and expected, though not at our disposal in our own or any present, is the Word of God. We cannot "handle" this criterion. It is the criterion which handles itself and is in no other hands. We can handle the other criteria in recollection and expectation of this criterion. But its judgment alone is absolutely binding and inviolable. Proclamation becomes real proclamation when it is endorsed by

this judgment. Real proclamation, therefore, is the Word of God preached, and in this third inner circle the Word of God preached means human talk about God which by God's own judgment, that cannot be anticipated and never passes under our control, is true with reference both to the proclaimed object and also to the proclaiming subject, so that it is talk which has to be listened to and which rightly demands obedience.

4. Finally—and only here do we make the decisive point—the Word of God is the event itself in which proclamation becomes real proclamation. It is not just the commission that man must have received. It is not just the theme or object that must enter the field in contrast to human talk. It is not just the judgment by which it must be confirmed as true. From all these angles the actualisation of proclamation might still be understood as an external and accidental characterisation, as a kind of clothing or enlightening of an event which as such is ultimately still the event of the willing and doing of proclaiming man. And then, of course, one misunderstands the significance of the "garment" or "light" in question, what it means that proclamation becomes real as God commands, God comes on the scene, God judges. But in this case who will not constantly misunderstand? Understanding of the subject in this statement has to render quite impossible all nominalistic misunderstandings regarding the predicate. But it lies deeply in the nature of the case that the nominalistic misunderstanding cannot be rooted out unequivocally and definitively. It is the miracle of revelation and faith when the misunderstanding does not constantly recur, when proclamation is for us not just human willing and doing characterised in some way but also and primarily and decisively God's own act, when human talk about God is for us not just that, but also and primarily and decisively God's own speech. It is this miracle that in the fourth and innermost circle of our deliberations we have not so much to explain as rather to evaluate as this specific miracle. "Not only—but also and primarily and decisively" is how the formula must run. The "not only—but also" means first that human
[094] talk, with its motives and themes and the judgments among which it stands as human talk, is there even while God's Word is there. The miracle of real proclamation does not consist in the fact that the willing and doing of proclaiming man with all its conditioning and in all its problems is set aside, that in some way a disappearance takes place and a gap arises in the reality of nature, and that in some way there steps into this gap naked divine reality scarcely concealed by a mere remaining appearance of human reality.

The decisive principle in the Roman Catholic doctrine of change is that through priestly consecration there takes place a *conversio totius substantiae panis in substantiam corporis Christi Domini nostri et totius substantiae vini in substantiam sanguinis eius*[EN6] (*Trid. sess.* XIII, *Decr. de ss.*

[EN6] conversion of the whole substance of the bread into the substance of the body of Christ our Lord, and of the whole substance of the wine into the substance of his blood

Euch. cap., 4). and this in such a way that only the *accidentia*[EN7] of bread and wine remain *sine subjecto*[EN8] (*ib. can.* 2 and *Conc. Constantiense 1415 Errores Joannis Wicleff* 2, Denz., No. 582).

The willing and doing of proclaiming man, however, is not in any sense set aside in real proclamation. As Christ became true man and remains true man to all eternity, real proclamation becomes an event on the level of all other human events. It can be seen and heard on this level, and its being seen and heard thus is no mere appearance but must take place in full essentiality. Without the ambivalence, the liability to misunderstanding and the vulnerability with which this takes place, with which it is itself one event among many others, it could not be real proclamation. But as Christ is not just true man, so it is not just the willing and doing of proclaiming man. It is also and indeed it is primarily and decisively the divine willing and doing. Precisely for this reason the human element is not set aside. What seems to be the burning question of the nature of the co-existence and co-operation of the two factors is a highly irrelevant question. God and the human element are not two co-existing and co-operating factors. The human element is what God created. Only in the state of disobedience is it a factor standing over against God. In the state of obedience it is service of God. Between God and true service of God there can be no rivalry. Service of God does not have to be removed in order that God Himself may be honoured in it. Where God is truly served, there—with no removal of the human element, with the full and essential presence and operation of the human element in all its humanity—the willing and doing of God is not just present as a first or second co-operating factor; it is present as the first and decisive thing as befits God the Creator and Lord. Without depriving the human element of its freedom, its earthly substance, its humanity, without obliterating the human subject, or making its activity a purely mechanical event, God is the subject from whom human action must receive its new and true name: not just a title tacked on; no, the name which belongs to it as essentially and primarily as possible in the full supremacy of the will of its Creator and Lord. Where Church proclamation takes place according to this will of [095]
God, where it rests on the divine commission, where God Himself gives Himself to it as its theme, where it is true according to His judgment, where, in short, it is service of God, there on the one hand its character as an event that can be seen and heard on earth is not set aside.

Bread remains bread and wine wine, to put it in eucharistic terms. The realism of sacramental consecration does not imply destruction of the signs' own existence.

On the other hand, through the new robe of righteousness thrown over it, even in its earthly character it becomes a new event, the event of God's own speaking in the sphere of earthly events, the event of the authoritative vicariate of Jesus Christ. Real proclamation as this new event, in which the event of

---

[EN7] accidents
[EN8] without their corresponding substance

human talk is not set aside by God but exalted, is the Word of God. Again, then, real proclamation means the Word of God preached. Only now is it clear that "preached" belongs to the predicate, and to what degree. The Word of God preached means in this fourth and innermost circle man's talk about God in which and through which God speaks about Himself.

Adolf Harnack in a fine essay (*Christus praesens—Vicarius Christi, Sitz.-Berichte der preuss. Akad. d. Wiss.*, 1927, 415 f.) has shown how there could be and was a movement from the concept "Word of God" through the "adoption of the Church into the main theological equations" (God, Christ, Spirit, etc.) to the doctrine of the infallibility of the papacy. In fact we are confronted here not merely by the problem of the Roman Catholic doctrine of transubstantiation but also by the problem of the Roman Catholic view of all that may be summed up under the concept of ecclesiastical *potestas*[EN9].

In itself it might well be wholly in line with our concept of the Word of God preached when Gregory of Nyssa (in actual analogy to the new qualification of the elements in the sacraments) says of the priest that up to yesterday he was simply one of many, one of the people, but now in virtue of his consecration as a priest he has become a *καθηγεμών, προέδρος, διδάσκαλος εὐσεβείας, μυστηρίων λανθανόντων μυσταγωγός*[EN10] (*Or. in diem luminum*); or when Ambrose explains to baptismal candidates with reference to the Christian priest: *Vidisti illic levitam, vidisti summum sacerdotem. Noli considerari corporum figuras, sed mysteriorum gratiam ... Quid tradiderit considera*[EN11] (*De myst.* 2, 6). *Non merita personarum considere, sed officia sacerdotum*[EN12] (*ib.*, 5, 27); or when Augustine with special regard to the Christian preacher insists: *Boni fideles non quemlibet hominum, sed ipsum Dominum obedienter audiunt*[EN13]—the *locus superior sedis ecclesiasticae*[EN14] from which the speaker speaks, even though he be personally the very reverse of good, forces him of itself to say what is good (*De doctr. christ.* IV, 27); or when he describes the earthly utterance of God's voice as follows, *quod creaturae motus expressit eam, serviens aeternae voluntati tuae ipse temporalis*[EN15] (*Conf.* XI, 6, 8); or when he says of the *doctrina de superiore loco in conspectu omnium personante*[EN16] that is, it always entails the decision concerning the hearers that *et qui faciunt audiant ad praemium et qui non faciunt audiant ad judicium*[EN17] (*De civ. Dei* II, 28).

This absolute singling out of the function of Church proclamation is intrinsically something which is common in the Reformers too: "Now I and any man that speaketh Christ's
[096] Word may freely boast that his mouth is Christ's mouth. I am sure my word is not mine but Christ's Word and so my mouth must also be His whose Word it speaketh" (Luther, *Eine treue Vermahnung*, 1522, *W.A.* 8, 263, 13). "Hereby all men on earth are subject to the preaching office, as the apostles and their successors lead on God's behalf, so that they must be submissive to the same and follow it if they would have God's grace and be saved" (*Pred. über* Joh. $16^{5f.}$, 1533, *E.A.* 3, 434). "That is a power against which emperor and king are naught, that an apostle, yea every disciple of Christ, may pronounce a judgment on the whole world that

---

EN 9 power

EN10 guide, president, teacher of piety, mystagogue of hidden mysteries

EN11 You have seen the levite, you have seen the chief priest. Do not consider their bodily form, but the grace of the mysteries ... Consider what he has handed over

EN12 Do not consider the merits of the individuals, but the functions of the priests

EN13 The truly faithful listen obediently not to a human person, but to God Himself

EN14 higher position of ecclesiastical authority

EN15 the movement of a creature, itself in time, expressed it, serving your eternal will

EN16 teaching sounding forth from an elevated platform in the sight of all

EN17 those who do [what they heard] might listen to their reward and those who do not might listen to their condemnation

sin should go. And such judgment should be so powerful and certain as if Christ Himself had uttered it ...." (*Predigt über* Joh. 20^{19-31}, 1533, *W.A.* 52, 269, 18). "'Tis a right excellent thing that every honest pastor's and preacher's mouth is Christ's mouth and his word and forgiveness Christ's Word and forgiveness. If thou hast sin and dost confess the same and believest in Christ, the pastor and preacher shall forgive thee that same sin in Christ's name, and the words he saith to thee on God's behalf thou shalt receive, as if Christ Himself had said them to thee. We rightly call the pastor's or preacher's word God's Word. For his office is not his but God's, and the word he preacheth is not his but God's" (Sermon on the same text, 1534, *E.A.* 3, 376). "On the last day God will say to me: Hast thou also preached that? and I shall then say, Yea, then God shall say to thee, Hast thou also heard that? and thou shalt say, Yea, and He saith further, Why then hast thou not believed? and thou then sayest, Oh, I held it for a word of man since some poor chaplain or village parson said it. So then shall that same word which sticketh in thine heart accuse thee and be thine accuser and judge at the last day. For it is God's Word, 'tis God Himself thou hast heard, as Christ saith,'He that heareth you heareth me,' and I have satisfied mine office for the judgment and before God when I have shown thee thy sins and iniquities and chastised thee for them, and am clean of thy blood. See thou then to it how thou standest" (*Ausl. des dritten und vierten Kap. Joh., W.A.* 47, 120, 28). "Hence might I be glad and say, God who hath created heaven and earth, who is the divine majesty, hath spoken with me. How? Through my brother man. He doth it to us for good, namely, for love and friendship. But when a man seeth a preacher he thinketh. This is a poor wretched man, and none considereth that beneath lieth the divine majesty. An angel might make heaven full of fire that lightning and thunder should strike and heaven and earth become black and everything collapse. Why then wilt thou not hear God who maketh Himself like a weak man and hideth Himself and holdeth Himself like the dear apostles? Therefore it is not a preacher's word but God's Word. Since it is God's Word thou shouldest start back thereat or be glad" (*ib.*, 213, 26). "If thou hear me who am a preacher, and hear and believe me none otherwise than another man, thou art condemned with me .... Therefore thou shouldest not hear me as a man that preacheth man's word. If thou hearest me thus, 'twere much better thou heardest me not at all. Thus too thy pastor shouldest thou not hear as a man that speaketh and preacheth man's word, but shouldest hear him as Him that speaketh the Word out of the mouths of babes and sucklings ..." (Sermon delivered in Merseburg, 1545, *W.A.* 51, 15, 30, 36). *Repraesentant Christi personam propter vocationem ecclesiae, non repraesentant proprias personas ut testatur Christus: qui vos audit, me audit. Cum verbum Christi, cum sacramenta porrigunt, Christi vice et loco porrigunt*[EN18] (Melanchthon, *Apol. De ecclesia, C.R.* 27, 529). Calvin, too declares most emphatically that God is certainly not bound to the human word about Him and can draw His own to Himself by some direct way. Nevertheless it has obviously pleased Him to let us ripen into the manhood of Christ *educatione ecclesiae*[EN19] and thus, without ceasing Himself and alone to rule in the Church, without abdicating His rights and honour to a man, to avail Himself of man's word as a *vicaria opera*[EN20]. It may thus [097]
be said of Christian preaching: *Deus ipse in medium prodit, et quatenus huius ordinis autor est, vult se praesentem in sua institutione agnosci*[EN21]. This is a proof that man can actually become God's temple. It is also a decisive test of our humility before God that we learn to render obedience to His Word not as one spoken directly from heaven but just as it meets us on the lips of a

[EN18] They represent the person of Christ on account of the church's calling, but they do not represent themselves, as Christ bears witness: "The one who hears you hears me." When they offer the word of Christ or the sacraments, they act in the name and place of Christ

[EN19] through the instruction of the church

[EN20] vicarious activity

[EN21] God Himself appears in its midst, and insofar as He is the author of this ministry, He wishes to be acknowledged as present in his institution *homuncio quispiam ex pulvere emersus*[EN22] who is in no connexion better than ourselves. Finally it is the strongest bond of the mutual love in which God wants to bind us together that in preaching He sets His Word on the lips of a fellow-man and thereby forbids us to try to satisfy ourselves (*Sermon on Lk.* 1[16f.], *C.R.* 46, 39; *Instit.* IV, 1, 5 and 3, 1; cf. E. Brunner, *Gott und Mensch*, 1930, 65). The relation between the order that in preaching *homines*[EN23] are to be instructed *per homines*[EN24] and Christian *charitas*[EN25] is already an insight of Augustine's (*De doctr. christ., Prol.* 6).

In the light of this concept of the Word of God preached, the familiar singling out of the bishop's office as first espoused especially by Ignatius of Antioch, then by Irenaeus, Tertullian and Cyprian, cannot be called intrinsically impossible. One can neither estimate the Roman Catholic position correctly nor take up the correct Evangelical position if (with Harnack, *op. cit.*, p. 446) one takes offence already at the idea of vicariate or succession. One would have to deny *Christus praesens*[EN26] to deny in principle the *vicarius Christi*[EN27]. The difference between Roman Catholic dogmatics and ourselves, which, of course, we must always keep in view, cannot refer to the fact of this vicariate or succession, but only to its manner. The three questions which follow are decisive in this regard, 1. How does a man become *vicarius Christi* and *successor Petri*[EN28]? According to Roman Catholic teaching he does so through his place at the bottom of a list of bishops that goes back without a break to an apostle, finally to Peter, and last of all to Christ as the Founder of the Church. We ask how the secular, historico-juridical fact of such a list can come to vouch for the regularity of ecclesiastical office. What does this documentary succession have to do with real, i.e., spiritual succession? 2. How does this vicariate or succession arise? According to Roman Catholic teaching it consists in a character which by ordination a bishop or priest receives for life in addition to his humanity. We ask how there can be a character for life if ordination can relate only to the official acts of the person ordained and even in respect of these acts cannot try to mean more than the proclamation of a promise? 3. In what consists this vicariate or succession? According to Roman Catholic teaching it consists in the permanent authority of the teaching office to establish and proclaim irreformable definitions in matters of faith and morals. We ask how far the exercise of this permanent authority of a human court to speak irreformably can still be understood as service of God. How far does one have here only a representation and not rather a supplanting of Christ? To summarise all three questions: Is not vicariate in the Roman Catholic sense one in which only the accidents of vicariate are retained while in substance it is simply the rule of Christ equated with that of the Church? We realise that this whole doctrine is a genuinely significant attempt to come to terms with the problem of real proclamation. But does not this solution mean that proclamation is dehumanised through the ideas of historical succession, *character indelebilis*[EN29] and the possibility of irreformable definitions, i.e., that it is set in a sphere in which it can only in appearance imply human action that is vulnerable, responsible, surpassable, and consequently serviceable? It is a consistent but still an incomprehensible fact that on the day of his consecration Innocent III simply preached about himself (Harnack, *op. cit.*, p. 441). Roman Catholic dogmatics is naturally aware of the lordship of Christ as a lordship not only in His Church but also over His Church. But where can this lordship of Christ over His Church take

---

EN22 some little human sprung from the dust
EN23 humans
EN24 by humans
EN25 charity
EN26 Christ as present
EN27 vicar of Christ
EN28 Peter's successor
EN29 indelible character

concrete shape in this system, where can it come into proper play, when all its power has already been fully transferred to the Church, when its power is simply present in the Church? And if it has no play of its own, is it distinguished in any way but name only from the power that is exercised in the Church by men without break, hindrance, or limit? Certainly a Roman Catholic could approve of Luther's interpretation of the metaphor of the Good Shepherd in Jn. 10: "Thus He refers the right shepherd's office, which is to help the rule of consciences and souls, to His own person alone, when He who alone hath done and accomplished it, the work of our redemption, who hath laid down His body and life for His sheep and founded the office, plies and upholds it, that through it He brings them to Himself and rules and sustains them. And thus the whole preaching of the Gospel is included where and when and by whom it is preached, who after Christ are also called shepherds, not on account of their own persons (for such can no one be save Christ Himself), but because they are in the office that is proper to Christ alone, and He exercises it through them and works in the same" (*Crucigers Sommerpostille,* 1543, *W.A.* 21, 323, 3). But on the question as to what "person" means here there is an inexorable parting of the ways. According to the Evangelical view one can no longer speak of an action of Christ's person in and over the Church when human authorities in the Church are deprived of their humanity in the way described and when Christ's own decisions are swallowed up in the decisions of these authorities. What can become, as shown, the endowment, quality, power and dignity of other persons ceases to this degree to be itself active person. Personal presence implies the possibility of absence as well. A personal gift implies the possibility of its refusal. This limitation of the power of the Church by the person of Christ is needed to prove that the Church is the true Church which serves Christ and which thus has a share in the benefits of His lordship, presence and gifts. But this limitation is ruled out by the doctrines of historical succession, indelible character, and the possibility of irreformable definitions. Hence we must reject these doctrines. In the sermon just quoted Luther continues: "Therefore 'tis thus also in this spiritual rule of consciences, where Christ doth not Himself through His shepherd's office guard, lead and guide, no other preaching helpeth or availeth aught, no matter if it be otherwise good and right. For it cannot stand in straits against the devil when he opens wide hell's vengeance through fear of sins and eternal death. For if it comes to that the poor sheep standeth alone and forsaken, all by itself; and its act, directed by the doctrine of the law and our works, hath neither help nor stay more with which to comfort itself and find rescue" (*ib.*, 324, 17). Then in a later sermon on the same text he says more belligerently: "That such preaching be used aright and be good and profitable, they must not enter into the sheepfold themselves like the others, nor imagine themselves to be shepherds, but only doorkeepers and servants of the true Shepherd Christ, who keep the sheep in watch and ward that naught strange break in on them. And they make way for the Shepherd and give place to Him who Himself leadeth them out and in to pasture. Therefore let such office be ordered not to point to self but to open up to the Shepherd that the sheep may hear Him and be pastured by Him" (*ib.*, 501, 8). In the Confession of the Synod of Strassburg in 1533 (cf. *Reformierte Kirchenzeitung,* 1931, No. 27, p. 211) Article 6 reads: "Faith cometh from hearing. Yet neither is he that planteth aught nor he that watereth, but God who giveth the increase is all. Hence injury is done to the divine grace and work if to the words and acts of evangelical preaching and sacraments they would ascribe some power to cleanse us from sins, which power they have in themselves be they but preached and administered by men, while those to whom they impart the Word and sacrament may believe as they like ..." And again Calvin has finely said what needs to be said about the Evangelical view of the relation (excluding any *opus operatum*[EN30]) [098]

[EN30] action valid by virtue of its being performed

[099] between God and man in the ecclesiastical office: *Et certe quum nobis constet Dei negotium hic nos et curare et agere, ipsum sibi operique suo minime defuturum confidimus. Caeterum qualiscunque exitus erit, nunquam nos coepisse, aut huc usque progressos esse poenitebit. Nobis Spiritus sanctus doctrinae nostrae fidelis est ac certus testis. Scimus, inquam, esse aeternam Dei veritatem quam praedicamus. Ministerium nostrum ut mundo sit salutare, optamus quidem, sicut par est: verum ut id consequamur, Dei est praestare, non nostrum*[EN31] (*Suppl. Exhort.*, 1543, *C.R.* 6, 534). But we can also sum up our objection to the Roman Catholic doctrine in the direction given to the preacher by the greatest Catholic theologian, Augustine: *Oret, ut Dominus sermonem bonum det in os eius*[EN32] (*De doctr. chr.* IV, 15). What does it mean if this *oret* is taken not merely as an ascetic and homiletic suggestion but more seriously in its material content, much more strictly than it need be even according to Augustine's own view? Must we really pray for the *sermo bonus*[EN33]? Can we only pray for it? Is Christ's action, real proclamation, the Word of God preached, tied to the ecclesiastical office and consequently to a human act, or conversely, as one might conclude from this *oret*[EN34], are the office and act tied to the action of Christ, to the actualising of proclamation by God, to the Word of God preached? From the standpoint of our theses this question is the puzzling cleft which has cut right across the church during the last 400 years.

2. THE WORD OF GOD WRITTEN

We have said that Church proclamation must be ventured in recollection of past revelation and in expectation of coming revelation. The basis of expectation is obviously identical here with the object of recollection. Hoping for what we cannot see, what we cannot assume to be present, we speak of an actualised proclamation, of a Word of God preached in the Church, on the basis that God's Word has already been spoken, that revelation has already taken place. We speak in recollection.

What is the meaning of this recollection of past revelation? Recollection of God's enacted revelation might mean the actualisation of a revelation of God originally immanent in the existence of every man, i.e., of man's own original awareness of God. In this case recollection of God's enacted revelation would be identical with the discovery and fresh appropriation of a long hidden, forgotten and unused part, and indeed the most central and significant part, of the timeless essential constitution of man himself, namely, his relation to the eternal or absolute.

EN31 Certainly, since there is no doubt in our mind that we take care of and conduct God's business here, we are confident that He will not in any way abandon Himself or his work. In any case, whatever the result, we should never repent of having undertaken it, or having pursued it to the present point. The Holy Spirit is the faithful and steadfast witness of our doctrine. We know, I say, that it is God's eternal truth which we preach. Certainly we wish that our ministry should benefit the world, as is proper, but that we are successful in this effort is up to God to grant, not to us.

EN32 Let him pray that the Lord will put a good word into his mouth

EN33 good word

EN34 let him pray

Augustine, following Plato's doctrine of *anamnesis*[EN35], understood *memoria*[EN36] along these lines. *Unde adest nisi ex memoria? Nam et cum ab alio commoniti recognoscimus, inde adest. Non enim quasi novum credimus, sed recordantes approbamus hoc esse quod dictum est. Si autem penitus aboleatur ex anima, nec admoniti reminiscimur. Neque enim omni modo adhuc obliti sumus, quod vel iam oblitos nos esse meminimus*[EN37] (*Conf.* X, 19, 28). According to Augustine God is what we all seek as we all seek a *vita beata*[EN38]. How is it that we want to be happy, that we love this *vita beata*? We obviously know it already. *Nimirum habemus eam nescio quomodo .... Neque enim amaremus eam nisi nossemus*[EN39] (*ib.*, 28, 29). Knowledge of God, therefore, can only be a confirmation of this that is already known before about God: *Neque enim aliquid de te inveni,* [100] *quod non meminissem ex quo didici te. Nam ex quo didici te, non sum oblitus tui. Ubi enim inveni veritatem, ibi inveni Deum meum ipsam veritatem, quam, ex quo didici, non sum oblitus*[EN40] (*ib.*, 24, 35). Much later we find a very similar line of argument when it is a matter of introducing Cartesianism into theology. What is the use of instruction or teaching, thought A. Heidan (*Corp. theol. Christ.*, 1686, *Loc.* I, 9), *nisi ex nobis ideam Dei formare possimus*[EN41]. The *idea Dei* does not come to us from without (*aliunde*). It is *potentia nobis semper inexistens*[EN42]. Along these lines, as Augustine already brought out quite clearly, recollection means inwardness, man's return from the distractions of the outside world and re-entry into himself to find God there. *Sero te amavi, pulchritudo tam antiqua et tam nova! Sero te amavi! Et ecce intus eras et ego foris et ibi te quaerebam ... mecum eras et tecum non eram*[EN43] (*Conf.* X, 27, 38).

Is the recollection of God's revelation on which the venture of Church proclamation is ventured this kind of recollection? One cannot prove *a priori* that this is impossible. Why could it not have pleased God to be immanent to His Church as the foundation which was hidden for a time, but which steadily endured because it had been timelessly laid, so that standing on it need be only a matter of profound self-reflection? Why should not God have let the Church be grounded upon itself as the Church, so that it could continually ground itself upon itself by continually returning to itself as such, this being recollection of God's past revelation? Why not?

The Neo-Platonist and the Catholic churchman could obviously exist quite well in personal union in Augustine. Why should not both have been right?

EN35 remembering

EN36 memory

EN37 Whence is [a name, forgotten but then remembered,] present except from memory? For even if we recognize it at someone else's prompting, it comes from memory. We do not believe it as something new, but when we recall it, we confirm that this indeed was that name. If the name were totally erased from the soul, we do not remember it even when prompted. However, we have not completely forgotten something if we remember having forgotten it.

EN38 blessed life

EN39 Without question we know it, though I know not how .... For we could not love it unless we knew it

EN40 Nor have I discovered anything about You, which I had not remembered from what I learned of You. For insofar as I had learned of You, I had not forgotten You. For wherever I found the truth, there I found my God, who is truth itself which I have not forgotten insofar as I learned of it

EN41 unless we are able to construct an idea of God out of ourselves

EN42 an inherent capacity always within us

EN43 Too late have I loved You, O Beauty so old, and yet so new! Too late I have loved you! Behold, You were within and I without, and I sought You there ... you were with me, but I was not with you

The concept of the divine freedom or potency provides no reason why this should be impossible. The real reason is that God did not make this specific use of His freedom or potency. The reason is thus a fact which points in a very different direction.

Here, too, we must begin exegetically, conscious that what we pursue is Evangelical and Reformation exegesis of the reality of the Church. The Church is not alone in relation to God's Word. It is not referred to itself or consequently to self-reflection. It has not the confidence to appeal to itself as the source of the divine Word in support of the venture of proclamation. It does not seek in the hidden depths of its own existence the commission, the object, the judgment and the event in recollection of which it is validated in its proclamation and believes it is summoned to proclamation. The return to its own being on the basis of which alone it may actually venture its proclamation does indeed mean for it a return to its own being, but to its self-transcendent being, to Jesus Christ as the heavenly Head to whom it, the earthly body, is attached as such, but in relation to whom it is also distinct as such, who has the Church within Himself but whom the Church does not have within itself, between whom and it there is no reversible or alternating relation, just as the relation between master and servant is not reversible. He is immanent in it
[101] only as He is transcendent to it. This is the fact which makes the recollection of God's past revelation different from reflection on its own timeless ground of being. It has pleased God to be its God in another way than that of pure immanence.

But this fact must be described more precisely. The distinction of the Head from the body and the superiority of the Head over the body find concrete expression in the fact that proclamation in the Church is confronted by a factor which is very like it as a phenomenon, which is temporal as it is, and yet which is different from it and in order superior to it. This factor is Holy Scripture. Holy Scripture is the concrete form of the reason why the recollection on the basis of which we expect God's revelation cannot be recollection of a timeless being of the Church. It is the bolt which in fact shuts out Platonic *anamnesis*[EN44] here. It does so in the first instance simply because it is there and tells us what is the past revelation of God that we have to recollect. It does so in the first instance simply by the fact that it is the Canon.

Κανών means rod, then ruler, standard, model, assigned district. In the ecclesiastical vocabulary of the first three hundred years it was used for that which stands fast as normative, i.e., apostolic, in the Church, the *regula fidei*[EN45], i.e., the norm of faith, or the Church's doctrine of faith. From this (only apparently) wider concept of the *κανὼν τῆς ἀληθείας* or *τῆς πίστεως*[EN46] there then develops from the 4th century onwards the more specialised idea of the Canon of Holy Scripture, i.e., the list of biblical books which are recognised as normative, because apostolic.

[EN44] remembrance
[EN45] rule of faith
[EN46] rule of truth or of faith

2. *The Word of God Written*

With its acknowledgment of the presence of the Canon the Church expresses the fact that it is not left to itself in its proclamation, that the commission on the ground of which it proclaims, the object which it proclaims, the judgment under which its proclamation stands and the event of real proclamation must all come from elsewhere, from without, and very concretely from without, in all the externality of the concrete Canon as a categorical imperative which is also historical, which speaks in time. And with its acknowledgement that this Canon is in fact identical with the Bible of the Old and New Testaments, with the word of the prophets and apostles, it expresses the truth that this reference of its proclamation to something that is concretely external is not a general principle, nor a mere determination of form whose content might be this or might be quite different, but that this reference is wholly determined in content, that it is a received direction and effected connexion, that this part of past history consisting of specific texts constitutes the working instructions or marching orders by which not just the Church's proclamation but the very Church itself stands or falls, which are not in any circumstances, not even hypothetically, to be lost to view, and which are not in any circumstances, not even hypothetically, to be regarded as replaced by others, if proc- [102]
lamation and the Church itself are not to be lost to view.

For a better understanding one should note first what we have called the similarity as phenomena between Church proclamation and this second entity which confronts it in the Church, namely, the Canon of Holy Scripture. This consists in the fact that in Holy Scripture, too, the writing is obviously not primary, but secondary. It is itself the deposit of what was once proclamation by human lips. In its form as Scripture, however, it does not seek to be a historical monument but rather a Church document, written proclamation. The two entities may thus be set initially under a single genus, Scripture as the commencement and present-day preaching as the continuation of one and the same event, Jeremiah and Paul at the beginning and the modern preacher of the Gospel at the end of one and the same series.

Luther had a good grasp of this relationship. On the one hand: "The Gospel simply means a preaching and crying out loud of God's grace and mercy merited and won by the Lord Christ with His death. And it is properly not what stands in books or is made up of letters, but rather an oral preaching and lively word and a voice that rings out in the whole world and is publicly cried out loud that it may be everywhere heard" (*Ep. S. Petri gepredigt und ausgelegt*, 1523, *W.A.* 12, 259, 8). On the other hand: "For we have John Baptist's word and spirit, and we parsons and preachers are in our time what John Baptist was in his time. We let John Baptist's finger point and his voice sound: 'Behold, the Lamb of God that taketh away the sin of the world'; we deliver John Baptist's sermon, point to Christ and say: This is the one true Saviour whom you should worship and to whom you should cleave. Such preaching must endure to the last day, even though it abide not in all places, all the time, alike, yet must it abide" (*Sermon on* Mt. 11$^{2f.}$, *E.A.* 1, 159).

In this similarity as phenomena, however, there is also to be found between Holy Scripture and present-day proclamation a dissimilarity in order, namely the supremacy, the absolutely constitutive significance of the former for the latter, the determination of the reality of present-day proclamation by its foundation upon Holy Scripture and its relation to this, the basic singling out of the written word of the prophets and apostles over all the later words of men which have been spoken and are to be spoken to-day in the Church. If what we have said is true, if the Church is not alone in respect of its proclamation but finds itself in a concrete confrontation in which it is mindful of the past revelation of God, and if the concrete form of its opposite is really the biblical word of the prophets and apostles, then obviously the latter must have fundamental distinction in relation to it. If the vicariate of Church proclamation is authentic, i.e., if the Church in its proclamation does not find its basis secretly in itself but in the Other who is its Lord without the Church ever becoming His lord, then the concrete form of vicariate must be succession.

[103] This concept from the Roman Catholic definition of the ecclesiastical office is also one which intrinsically need not give rise to any objection. The series God, Christ, apostle, bishop, community as it begins to appear in Church writings at the beginning of the 2nd century (e.g., Clement of Rome *ad Cor.*, 42 and 44) becomes a criterion which is applied almost formally by Irenaeus: Where there is *traditio* or *successio apostolorum*[EN47], there is the Church (e.g., *C. o. haer.* III, 2, 2; 3, 1; 4, 1; IV, 26, 2, 5; 33, 8; V, 20), and it is used in fighting heretics from the standpoint of the question of their relation to the apostolic origin of the Church: *Edant ergo origines ecclesiarum suarum, evolvant ordinem episcoporum suorum ita per successionem ab initio decurrentem, ut primus ille episcopus aliquem ex apostolis ... habuerit auctorem et antecessorem ... exhibent quos ab apostolis in episcopatum constitutos apostolici seminis traduces habeant*[EN48] (Tertullian, *De praescr. haer.*, 32). In itself all this can have its proper place as an expression of awareness of the concreteness of the form in which Christ and His Church are combined and yet contrasted. Apostolicity is in fact one of the decisive notes of the true Church (*credo unam sanctam catholicam et apostolicam ecclesiam*[EN49]). In virtue of its direct relation to the transcendent character of what is Christian it is also the decisive mark of true Church proclamation. The Evangelical Church says and confesses the same with its Scripture principle: "Now when He says, Ye also shall bear witness, for ye have been with me from the beginning, He thereby specially depicts the apostles for all preachers and confirms their preaching so that all the world should be bound to their word, and believe the same without any contradiction and be certain that all they preach and teach is right doctrine and the Holy Ghost's preaching which they have heard and received from Him. As I Jn. 1 adduces such witness and says: 'That which we have heard, that which we have seen with our eyes, that which we have beheld ... of the Word of life, that declare we unto you.' Such witness have no preachers on earth save the apostles only, for the others are hereby commanded that they should all follow in the apostles' footsteps, abide by the same doctrine and preach nothing more nor otherwise. And moreover the right sign is shown by which one may know and test such preaching of the Holy Ghost, for He saith: 'The Holy Ghost shall testify of me'" etc.

[EN47] tradition or apostolic succession

[EN48] Therefore let them relate the origins of their churches, and let them unroll the list of their bishops running straight down by succession from the beginning, so that the first bishop had one of the apostles ... as ordainer and predecessor ... for [orthodox churches] show those whom the apostles established in the episcopate and whom they have as sowers of the apostolic seed

[EN49] I believe one holy, catholic and apostolic church

(Luther, *Crucigers Sommerpostille, W.A.* 21, 426, 2). Here again, then, the difference between the Evangelical view and the Roman Catholic view is not in respect of the That but the How. And even in respect of the How no objection in principle can be raised on our part against the concentration of the apostolate in Peter or the possibility of a primacy in the Church which might be that of the Roman community. The protest of Protestantism in this question of succession is directed solely and simply against the fact that the *Tu es Petrus*[EN50], etc., is mechanically transferred over Peter's head to every succeeding Roman bishop as a second, third and hundredth Peter, as if the succession and tradition of the Peter of Mt. 16, to whom flesh and blood had not revealed such things, could be related to any succession but a spiritual one, or as if, being spiritual, it could be tied to the secular circumstance of a list of bishops of this kind. "The visibility and the related stability of the Church demand, then, an ecclesiastical ordination which begins with Christ, the starting point, and continues in unbroken sequence, so that, as the apostles were sent by the Saviour, they in turn appointed bishops, these again gave themselves successors, and so on to our own day. By this succession of bishops which began with the Saviour and has continued without a break it may be pre-eminently seen as by a sign which is the true Church founded by Him" (J. A. Möhler, *Symbolik*, 3rd edn., 1834, 396). It is to this that we can only say No. *Est enim ecclesia coetus non alligatus ad ordinariam successionem, sed ad verbum Dei. Ibi renascitur ecclesia, ubi Deus restituit doctrinam et dat Spiritum sanctum*[EN51] (Melanchthon, *De ecclesia et de auctoritate verbi Dei*, 1539, *C.R.* 22, 598). And the reason for the protest is that in these circumstances apostolicity [104] necessarily ceases to be a divine gift and human task and becomes an assured human possession, that it is "pre-eminently" understood in a mechanically historical and legal way, that it can no longer be a norm which confronts the Church with direction and judgment, that in contrast it falls completely under the *judicium ecclesiae*[EN52], the control of the second or third or hundredth Peter. Spiritual succession obviously presupposes that the *successor*[EN53] is spiritually but not mechanically identical with the *antecessor*[EN54], so that the *antecessor* still has elbow-room of his own as distinct from the *successor*. Such elbow-room, however, is not given to Peter in the Roman Catholic system. Here the *antecessor* is taken up and absorbed in the *successor*. What constitutes the apostolicity of proclamation here is the watch at Peter's grave. On this presupposition neither Peter, the apostolate, nor the Holy Spirit is any longer a free power in the Church and over against the Church. On this presupposition the Church is again left to itself and referred to itself and its self-reflection. This is why we cannot endorse the Roman Catholic doctrine of succession. Nor especially can we endorse the form in which it is presented and espoused by Friedrich Heiler, *Im Ringen um die Kirche*, 1931, 479 (cf. esp. the "four grounds", p. 506 f.); theologically this form can only be called dilettante whether from the Roman Catholic or the Evangelical standpoint.

The apostolic succession of the Church must mean that it is guided by the Canon, that is, by the prophetic and apostolic word as the necessary rule of every word that is valid in the Church. It must mean that the Church enters into the succession of the prophets and apostles in their office of proclamation, and does so in such a way that their proclamation freely and independently precedes, while that of the Church is related to it, is ventured in

---

[EN50] You are Peter

[EN51] For the church is a gathering not tied to a succession of ordinations, but to the word of God. The church is reborn wherever God restores true doctrine and gives the Holy Spirit

[EN52] judgment of the church

[EN53] successor

[EN54] predecessor

obedience on the basis of it, is measured by it, and replaces it only as and to the extent that it conforms to it. It must mean that the Church always admits the free power of their proclamation over it. As far as the idea of a living succession is concerned everything depends on the *antecessor* being regarded as alive and having free power over against the *successor.* But if, as here, the *antecessor* has long since died, this can happen only if his proclamation has been fixed in writing and if it is acknowledged that he still has life and free power over the Church to-day in this written word of his. On the written nature of the Canon, on its character as *scriptura sacra*[EN55], hangs his autonomy and independence, and consequently his free power over against the Church and the living nature of the succession. Naturally it might also have pleased God to give His Church the Canon in the form of an unwritten prophetic and apostolic tradition propagating itself from spirit to spirit and mouth to mouth.

In this case it might be legitimate and it might make sense that the grave of Peter should be the central shrine of the Church. Canon might be the event of tradition, i.e., "the distinctive Christian meaning present in the Church and propagating itself by Church education ... the living word continually alive in the hearts of believers" (J. A. Möhler, *Symbolik,* 3rd edn., 1834, 371).

[105] Now one cannot wish to contest the fact that there is something of this kind in the Church apart from the real Canon. But one must also say that if it had pleased God to make this unwritten spiritual-oral tradition the Canon of His Church, the Canon would be as little distinguishable from the life of the Church as the blood of our fathers coursing through our veins is distinguishable from our own blood. In other words, the Church would again be left alone and referred to itself, to its own vitality. Whatever there may be of such spiritual-oral tradition in the Church, since it does not have written form it obviously cannot have the character of an authority irremovably confronting the Church. In unwritten tradition the Church is not addressed; it is engaged in dialogue with itself.

The saying of Papias: *οὐ γὰρ τὰ ἐκ τῶν βιβλίων τοσοῦτόν με ὠφελεῖν ὑπελάμβανον ὅσον τὰ παρὰ ζώσης φωνῆς καὶ μενούσης*[EN56] (Euseb, *H.E.* III, 39, 4), is an indication of the change which came already at the beginning of the 2nd century and which was so disastrous in its effects. Living quality was now no longer sought and found in the written word of the apostles themselves but in the "voice" of those contemporaries who had known the apostles and preference was given to this "living and lasting voice" over the books, i.e., the apostolic writings. We are at the end of the same development—the living quality has now completely passed from *antecessor* to *successor*—when Karl Adam (*Das Wesen des Katholizismus,* 4th edn., 1927, 162) can speak of the "dead word" of the Bible in contrast to the "vitality" of Church tradition. But are we on another path, and not still in the middle of the same one, when Lessing refuses to suspend "no less than all eternity" "on a spider's thread," i.e., the word of the first witnesses (*Eine Duplik, Lessings Theol. Schr.,* ed. C. Gross, II, 2, 34)? For here

---

EN55 Holy Scripture

EN56 for I do not suppose that I profit from books as much as from a living and lasting voice

again the *regula fidei*[EN57] is not identical with Scripture (*Nötige Antwort, ib.*, II, 2, 215 f.). Only the enduring miracle of religion and not Scripture is the decisive proof of Christianity (*Eine Duplik, ib.*, II, 2, 33). "It must surely be possible that everything written by the apostles should be lost again and the religion taught by them would still persist" (*Fragm. eines Unbekannten, ib.*, II, 1, 262). Really? his opponent M. Goeze asked and Lessing answered defiantly: "God preserve me from thinking so poorly of Christ's teaching as to dare to answer this question with an outright negative. No, I will not utter this negative even though an angel from heaven dictated it to me. Even less when a mere Lutheran parson wants to put it on my lips" (*Axiomata, ib.*, II, 2, 118). With more right than the first words of John's Gospel, so Lessing thought, the Testament of John: "Little children, love one another," ought to be there in golden letters for all to read in the most visible place in all churches (*Das Test. Joh., ib.*, II, 2, 19). "It is, of course, apocryphal, this testament, but no less divine for that" (*Über den Beweis. ..., ib.*, II, 2, 14). Who does not feel reminded by this last statement that with Holy Scripture the Council of Trent too *nec non traditiones ipsas, tum ad fidem, tum ad mores pertinentes, tanquam vel oretenus a Christo vel a Spiritu sancto dictatas et continua successione in Ecclesia catholica conservatas, pari pietatis affectu et reverentia suscipit et veneratur*[EN58] (*Trid. sess.* IV *Recipiuntur libri ...*). Was Lessing guilty of catholicising or was the Council of Trent guilty of modernising (which began, of course, with Papias)? How are these two trends related to one another? One thing is certain; they agree in their effect, the granting of relative independence to the Church *vis-à-vis* the Canon of Holy Scripture, i.e., relative devaluation of this Canon.

If, then, apart from the undeniable vitality of the Church itself there stands confronting it a concrete authority with its own vitality, an authority whose pronouncement is not the Church's dialogue with itself but an address to the Church, and which can have *vis-à-vis* the Church the position of a free power and therefore of a criterion, then obviously in its writtenness as "Bible" it must be distinguished from and given precedence over the purely spiritual and oral life of ecclesiastical tradition. It is true that this real, biblical Canon is constantly exposed to absorption into the life, thought and utterance of the Church inasmuch as it continually seeks to be understood afresh and hence expounded and interpreted. Exegesis is always a combination of taking and giving, of reading out and reading in. Thus exegesis, without which the norm cannot assert itself as a norm, entails the constant danger that the Bible will be taken prisoner by the Church, that its own life will be absorbed into the life of the Church, that its free power will be transformed into the authority of the Church, in short, that it will lose its character as a norm magisterially confronting the Church. All exegesis can become predominantly interposition rather than exposition and to that degree it can fall back into the Church's dialogue with itself. Nor will one banish the danger, but only conjure it up properly and make it acute, by making correct exposition dependent on the judgment of a definitive and decisive teaching office in the Church or on the judgment of a historico-critical scholarship which comports itself with equal infallibility. If we [106]

EN57 rule of faith

EN58 also accepts and venerates with an equal feeling of piety and reverence traditions pertaining to faith and morals as having been received orally from Christ or dictated by the Holy Spirit and conserved in the Catholic Church by a continuous succession.

assume that one or other of these authorities is worthy of the Church's highest confidence, then either way the Church goes astray in respect of the Bible by thinking that in one way or the other it can and should control correct exposition, and thereby set up a norm over the norm, and thereby capture the true norm for itself. The exegesis of the Bible should rather be left open on all sides, not for the sake of free thought, as Liberalism would demand, but for the sake of a free Bible. Here as everywhere the defence against possible violence to the text must be left to the text itself, which in fact has always succeeded in doing something a purely spiritual and oral tradition cannot do, namely, maintaining its own life against the encroachments of individual or total periods and tendencies in the Church, victoriously asserting this life in ever new developments, and thus creating recognition for itself as a norm.

"Inward truth," in spite of Lessing's protest (*Axiomata, op. cit.*, II, 2, 127), is "a wax nose that any knave can mould as he will to suit his own face," and if Counter-Reformation polemics did apply the same excellent metaphor to the Bible (*scriptura est tanquam nasus cereus; quia flecti potest hinc inde*[EN59], quoted by Calvin, *Articuli Fac. Paris. cum Antidoto*, 1544, *C.R.* 7, 31), this simply proves to us how right it is to demand free exegesis for the sake of a free Bible.

[107] Already as a text the canonical text has the character of a free power. All the Church need do is just this: After any exegesis propounded in it, even the very best, it has to realise afresh the distinction between text and commentary and to let the text speak again without let or hindrance, so that it will experience the lordship of this free power and find in the Bible the partner or counterpart which the Church must find in it if it is to take the living *successio apostolorum*[EN60] seriously.

Now we must also ask, of course, how it comes about that the prophetic and apostolic word in particular takes up this normative position over against the Church and its proclamation. We have tried to make it clear that it must be a written word, a text, to be a true Canon as distinct from the Church's own life. But obviously the fact that it is written does not alone make it the norm. There are other texts about which much the same might be said regarding their exegesis or the free power residing within them. And finally a large part of the non-canonical tradition is also present as text, e.g., in so far as it has been given fixed form in dogma. What is it that makes the Bible of the Old and New Testaments the Canon? Why must the Church's recollection of God's past revelation always have the Bible as its concrete object? It is no evasion of this question, which we are always right to raise afresh, if in the first instance we reply at once that the Bible constitutes itself the Canon. It is the Canon because it imposed itself upon the Church as such, and continually does so. The Church's recollection of God's past revelation has the Bible specifically as its object because in fact this object and no other is the promise of future divine revelation which can make proclamation a duty for the Church and

---

[EN59] Scripture is like a wax nose, because it can be turned this way and that
[EN60] succession of the apostles

which can give it joy and courage for this duty. If we thought we could say why this is so, we should again be acting as if we had in our hands a measure by which we could measure the Bible and on this basis assign it its distinctive position. Our ultimate and decisive wisdom would then be once again the wisdom of a self-dialogue, even if a self-dialogue about the Bible. No, the Bible is the Canon just because it is so. It is so by imposing itself as such. And if we can only register this event (as such) as the reality in which the Church is the Church, nevertheless, when this is done, it is not impossible afterwards, exegetically, to state in what this self-imposing consists and how far it sets a limit to the wisdom of our dialogue with ourselves. At this point we should already refer in advance to the content of Holy Scripture. The prophetic and apostolic word is the word, witness, proclamation and preaching of Jesus Christ. The promise given to the Church in this Word is the promise of God's mercy which is uttered in the person of Him who is very God and very Man and which takes up our cause when we could not help ourselves at all because of our enmity against God. The promise of this Word is thus Immanuel, God [108] with us—with us who have brought ourselves, and continually bring ourselves again, into the dire straits of not being able to be with God. Holy Scripture is the word of men who yearned, waited and hoped for this Immanuel and who finally saw, heard and handled it in Jesus Christ. Holy Scripture declares, attests and proclaims it. And by its declaration, attestation and proclamation it promises that it applies to us also and to us specifically. The man who so hears their word that he grasps and accepts its promise, believes. And this grasping and accepting of the promise: Immanuel with us sinners, in the word of the prophets and apostles, this is the faith of the Church. In this faith it recollects the past revelation of God and in this faith it expects the future revelation that has yet to come. It recollects the incarnation of the eternal Word and the reconciliation accomplished in Him, and it expects the future of Jesus Christ and its own redemption from the power of evil. Thus Scripture imposes itself in virtue of this its content. In distinction from all other scripture the Scripture with this content—really this!—is Holy Scripture. When the Church heard this word—and it heard it only in the prophets and apostles and nowhere else—it heard a magisterial and ultimate word which it could not ever again confuse or place on a level with any other word. The Scripture with this content sets a natural limit for recollection in the form of self-dialogue. If "Immanuel, with us sinners" is true, then our own deepest ground of being, whatever we think concerning it, cannot be the past revelation of God, and the return to ourselves, however significant it may be in other ways, has nothing whatever to do with the return to God's revelation. The Scripture with this content must confront the life of the Church, which can be life only in this relation, as an entity full of its own vitality and free power, as a criterion which cannot be dissolved into the historical life of the Church. Finally, the Scripture with this content must always become again and again the thing we started with, the object of authentic recollection in which the Church with its proclamation looks and moves forward to the future. "I believe, therefore do I speak" (Ps. 116[10]). Hearing this word with faith in its promise demands proclamation and makes it possible.

The great historical example of this discovery of the Canon that is given to the Church in the Bible in virtue of its content is the early period of the Reformation. What took place in Wittenberg and Zurich in the twenties of the 16th century and in Geneva in the thirties is like a book of illustrations of what has just been said. The Church perceives again that it does not have Christ with His gifts in itself; it must be found by His Word which comes to it from without ("Salvation has come to us of grace and pure goodness ..."). But it perceives this because His Word, and in this He Himself, has already found it, because it is no longer left to itself, because He has already come on the scene to comfort and to judge as its partner and
[109] counterpart in the biblical word, because, concretely, the Old and New Testaments have already spoken to it and already forced themselves on it as the "canon of truth." Its proclamation is again placed under the necessity of becoming a succession, an obedient following of the prophetic and apostolic word. Hence the Bible is now important to it again as a book, in its supremacy and freedom over against the Church itself, above everything, even its own exegesis of the book, and in its singularity, which consists in and is established by the fact that it is the book of Christ, of the promise of grace, which is not to be heard anywhere else and which puts an end to the distress and pride of the man who stands on himself and takes counsel with himself. And because this book is there as the Canon, it must be preached, as in that age it was preached, with a volume and intensity that surprises us to-day. Because it is there as the Canon, with the Bible and in the Bible and through the Bible the Church discovers in a completely new way what Church proclamation really is.

All that remains now is to add a final word. Presupposing that we are right about the fact described, that by Holy Scripture the Church is summoned and directed to its proclamation and empowered for it, this implies that Holy Scripture, too, is the Word of God. It is so in exactly the same sense in which we have said this of the event of real proclamation. Recollection of God's past revelation, discovery of the Canon, faith in the promise of the prophetic and apostolic word, or better, the self-imposing of the Bible in virtue of its content, and therefore the existence of real apostolic succession, is also an event, and is to be understood only as an event. In this event the Bible is God's Word. That is to say, in this event the human prophetic and apostolic word is a representative of God's Word in the same way as the word of the modern preacher is to be in the event of real proclamation : a human word which has God's commission to us behind it, a human word to which God has given Himself as object, a human word which is recognised and accepted by God as good, a human word in which God's own address to us is an event. The fact that God's own address becomes an event in the human word of the Bible is, however, God's affair and not ours. This is what we mean when we call the Bible God's Word. We confess and acknowledge therewith that the recollection of God's past revelation, without which the enterprise of Church proclamation would be impossible, is just as much God's grace and gift as is the actualisation our own proclamation needs. It is not in our own power to make this recollection, not even in the form of our grasping at the Bible. Only when and as the Bible grasps at us, when we are thus reminded, is this recollection achieved. If this takes place, if the Bible speaks to us thus of the promise, if the prophets and apostles tell us what they have to tell us, if their word imposes itself on us and if the Church in its confrontation with the Bible thus becomes again and again what it is, all this is God's decision and not ours, all this is grace and not our work. The Bible is God's Word to the extent that God causes it to be His Word, to the extent that He speaks through it. In this second equation no less than the first (namely, that Church proclamation is God's Word) we cannot abstract from the free [110] action of God in and by which He causes it to be true to us and for us here and now that the biblical word of man is His own Word. The statement that the Bible is God's Word is a confession of faith, a statement of the faith which hears God Himself speak through the biblical word of man. To be sure it is a statement which, when venturing it in faith, we accept as true even apart from our faith and beyond all our faith and even in face of our lack of faith. We do not accept it as a description of our experience of the Bible. We accept it as a description of God's action in the Bible, whatever may be the experiences we have or do not have in this connexion. But this is precisely the faith which in this way sees and reaches beyond itself and all related or unrelated experiences to God's action, namely, to the fact that God's action on man has become an event, and not therefore that man has grasped at the Bible but that the Bible has grasped at man. The Bible, then, becomes God's Word in this event, and in the statement that the Bible is God's Word the little word "is" refers to its being in this becoming. It does not become God's Word because we accord it faith but in the fact that it becomes revelation to us. But the fact that it becomes revelation to us beyond all our faith, that it is God's Word even in spite of our lack of faith, is something we can accept and confess as true to us and for us only in faith, in faith as opposed to unbelief, in the faith in which we look away from our faith and unbelief to the act of God, but in faith and not in unbelief, and therefore precisely not in abstraction from the act of God in virtue of which the Bible must become again and again His Word to us.

In the struggle against Calvinists, Schwenckfeldians, Quakers, etc., Lutheran orthodoxy developed a doctrine of the *efficacia Verbi divini etiam ante et extra usum*[EN61]. The Word of God preached and written has its own divine power no matter what may be its effect on those who hear or read. In the Bible and preaching there takes place a divine *actus purus*[EN62] no matter how it stands with the *actus secundus*[EN63] in the hearts of men (Quenstedt, *Theol. did. pol.*, 1685, I, *cap*. 4, *sect*. 2. *qu*. 16; Hollaz, *Ex. theol. acroam.*, 1707, III, 2, 1, *qu*. 4). Now in so far as the concern of this doctrine is to prove the truth of the statement of faith that the Bible and preaching are God's Word in its full compass as independent of subjective experience and superior to it, we must certainly concur. But the doctrine was trying to do more than this, and here we cannot accept it. Quenstedt even denied that the Bible is an *instrumentum*[EN64] which requires *novo motu et elevatione nova ad effectum novum ultra propriam suam naturalem*

EN61 efficacy of the divine Word both prior to and apart from its use
EN62 pure act
EN63 act that follows
EN64 instrument

virtutem producendum[EN65]. The Bible and preaching are rather *media* in which *summa vis et efficacia*[EN66] intrinsically and permanently reside (*ib.*, *ekth.* 7). The Bible, so Hollaz thinks, is God's saving Word in the same way as the sun gives warmth even behind clouds, or as a seed of grain has force even in the unfruitful earth, or as the hand of a sleeping man is a living hand. Hollaz also declares in blunt terms that the Word of God is not an *actio*[EN67] but a *vis*[EN68], a *potentia*[EN69], which as such has *efficacia*[EN70] even *extra usum*[EN71], in other words a *vis hyperphysica analoga efficaciae physicae i.e. vera et realis*[EN72]. As though the theological criterion
[111] of truth and reality could and should be the analogy to the physical! A force comparable to sunshine or the thrust of a seed certainly needs no *nova elevatio*[EN73]. It is there as natural forces are there. But is God's Word there in that way? If it is really Word? And if it is the Word of the God who is person? One surely has to choose between the terms Word of God and *vis hyperphysica*[EN74], and in Evangelical theology there should not really be any doubt about the choice.

3. THE WORD OF GOD REVEALED

The Bible is the concrete means by which the Church recollects God's past revelation, is called to expectation of His future revelation, and is thus summoned and guided to proclamation and empowered for it. The Bible, then, is not in itself and as such God's past revelation, just as Church proclamation is not in itself and as such the expected future revelation. The Bible, speaking to us and heard by us as God's Word, bears witness to past revelation. Proclamation, speaking to us and heard by us as God's Word, promises future revelation. The Bible is God's Word as it really bears witness to revelation, and proclamation is God's Word as it really promises revelation. The promise in proclamation, however, rests on the attestation in the Bible. The hope of future revelation rests on faith in that which has taken place once and for all. Thus the decisive relation of the Church to revelation is its attestation by the Bible. Its attestation! Once again, the Bible is not in itself and as such God's past revelation. As it is God's Word it bears witness to God's past revelation, and it is God's past revelation in the form of attestation. When the Canon, the staff which commands and sets moving and points the way, is moved by a living stretched-out hand, just as the water was moved in the Pool of Bethesda that it might thereby becomes a means of healing, then it bears witness, and by this act of witness it establishes the relation of the Church to revelation, and there-

---

EN65 a new motion and a new elevation in order to produce a new effect beyond its own natural power
EN66 the highest force and efficacy
EN67 action
EN68 force
EN69 power
EN70 efficacy
EN71 apart from its use
EN72 a supernatural force which is analogous to physical (i.e., true and real) efficacy
EN73 new elevation
EN74 supernatural force

with establishes the Church itself as the true Church, and therewith its proclamation as true proclamation. By its witness! Witnessing means pointing in a specific direction beyond the self and on to another. Witnessing is thus service to this other in which the witness vouches for the truth of the other, the service which consists in referring to this other. This service is constitutive for the concept of the prophet and also for that of the apostle; the time has not yet come to speak of the difference between them.

When Paul writes of himself in 1 Cor. 9^{16}: *ἐὰν γὰρ εὐαγγελίζωμαι, οὐκ ἔστιν μοι καύχημα· ἀνάγκη γάρ μοι ἐπίκειται· οὐαὶ γάρ μοί ἐστιν ἐὰν μὴ εὐαγγελίσωμαι*[EN75], he is hereby describing (cf., e.g., Jer. $20^{7f.}$) the situation that is common to both the prophet and the apostle.

Standing in this service, the biblical witnesses point beyond themselves. If we understand them as witnesses, and only as such do we authentically understand them, i.e., as they understand themselves, then their self, which in its inner and outer determination and movement constitutes as it were the matter of their service, must be decisively understood by us from the standpoint of its form as a reference away from themselves. They do not speak and write for their own sakes, nor for the sake of their deepest inner possession or need; they speak and write, as ordered, about that other. They do not try to push themselves, not even as the champions or advocates of the cause they represent; beyond all immanent teleology they are forced to speak and write about that other. They do not want to offer and commend themselves to the Church, and especially not their own particular experience of God and relationship to God, but through themselves that other. And not even "through themselves" in the sense that man himself must be a more or less perfect organ for the revelation of objective facts and values or subjective stimulations (as is true enough in the achievements of science, politics and art), but through themselves in such a way that what makes man a witness is solely and exclusively that other, the thing attested, which constrains and limits the perfect or imperfect human organ from without. [112]

At this point we cannot reflect assiduously enough "on the difference between an apostle and a genius" (Kierkegaard, 1847). The model of the biblical witness in his unity of form is John the Baptist, who stands so notably at midpoint between the Old Testament and the New, between the prophets and the apostles: *Ἐγένετο ἄνθρωπος, ἀπεσταλμένος παρὰ θεοῦ, ὄνομα αὐτῷ Ἰωάννης. οὗτος ἦλθεν εἰς μαρτυρίαν, ἵνα μαρτυρήσῃ περὶ τοῦ φωτός, ἵνα πάντες πιστεύσωσιν δἰ αὐτοῦ. οὐκ ἦν ἐκεῖνος τὸ φῶς, ἀλλ' ἵνα μαρτυρήσῃ περὶ τοῦ φωτός*[EN76] (Jn. $1^{6f.}$, cf. $3^{27f.}$). In this connexion one might recall John the Baptist in Grünewald's Crucifixion, especially his prodigious index finger. Could anyone point away from himself more impressively and completely (*illum oportet crescere me autem minui*[EN77])?

[EN75] For if I preach the gospel, that gives me no ground for boasting. For necessity is laid upon me. Woe to me if I do not preach the gospel!

[EN76] There was a man sent from God, whose name was John. He came for testimony, to bear witness to the light, that all might believe through him. He was not the light, but came to bear witness to the light.

[EN77] he must increase, but I must decrease

And could anyone point more impressively and realistically than here to what is indicated? This is what the Fourth Evangelist wanted to say about this John, and therefore about another John, and therefore quite unmistakably about every "John."

Why and in what respect does the biblical witness have authority? Because and in the fact that he claims no authority for himself, that his witness amounts to letting that other itself be its own authority. We thus do the Bible poor and unwelcome honour if we equate it directly with this other, with revelation itself.

This may happen when we seek and think we find revelation in the heroic religious personality of the biblical witness. But it may also happen in the form of a general, uniform and permanent inspiredness of the Bible, which we shall have to speak about later. In the work already mentioned (*Der Begriff des Auserwählten*, ed. T. Haecker, 1917, 314), Kierkegaard very rightly says that mistaking an apostle for a genius is to be seen not only on the side of heterodoxy but also on that of hyperorthodoxy, and on that of thoughtlessness in general. We
[113] should not in fact forget that the historical view of the Bible with its cult of heroes and the doctrine of mechanical inspiration are both products of the same age and spirit. A common feature is that they both represent means whereby Renaissance man tried to control the Bible and also tried to set up obstacles to stop it controlling him, as indeed it ought to do.

The direct identification between revelation and the Bible which is in fact at issue is not one that we can presuppose or anticipate. It takes place as an event when and where the biblical word becomes God's Word, i.e., when and where the biblical word comes into play as a word of witness, when and where John's finger does not point in vain but really indicates, when and where we are enabled by means of his word to see and hear what he saw and heard. Thus in the event of God's Word revelation and the Bible are indeed one, and literally so.

"For this preaching means: 'Fear not, for unto you is born this day the Saviour, which is Christ the Lord.' Men's words which have grown up in the hearts of men are not like that. For the wisest folk on earth know naught thereof. But this preaching rang down from heaven, of which same, God be praised for ever, we are become partakers. For 'tis all the same if thou hearest or readest this preaching as if thou hadst heard it from the angel himself. For the shepherds too saw not the angels, they saw but the light and the glory. But the words of the angels they heard, which we still hear in preaching, may still be read in the Book, if we will but open our eyes and our ears and learn and use aright such preaching" (Luther, *Predigt von der Engel Lobgesang*, 1544, *W.A.* 52, 50. 13).

But for this very reason one needs to see that they are not always the same and also to what extent they are not always the same, to what extent their union is really an event. Purely formally, the revelation to which the biblical witnesses direct their gaze as they look and point away from themselves is to be distinguished from the word of the witnesses in exactly the same way as an event itself is to be distinguished from even the best and most faithful account of it. But this distinction is trifling compared with the fact, for which there is no analogy, that in revelation our concern is with the coming Jesus Christ and finally, when the time was fulfilled, the Jesus Christ who has come. Literally, and this time really directly, we are thus concerned with God's own Word spoken by God Himself. What we have in the Bible are in any case human attempts to repeat and reproduce this Word of God in human words and thoughts and in specific human situations, e.g., with reference to the complications of the political position of Israel as a buffer between Egypt and Babylon, or with reference to the errors and confusions in the Christian Church at Corinth between A.D. 50 and 60. On the one hand *Deus dixit*[EN78], on the other *Paulus dixit*[EN79]. These are two different things. And precisely because they are not two things but become one and the same thing in the event of the Word of God, we must maintain that it is by no means self-evident or intrinsically one that revelation should be understood primarily as the superior principle and [114] the Bible primarily as the subordinate principle.

As early as the epistles of Ignatius of Antioch (e.g., *Ad Magn.* 13, 2) a model is found for the hierarchical church bishop relation in the apostle Christ relation. Augustine in his first homily on John's Gospel compares the biblical witnesses to the hills from which help comes according to Ps. 121: Yet not from the hills themselves but from the Lord who made heaven and earth and who is over these hills. For: *Audeo dicere fratres mei, forsitan nec ipse Joannes dixit ut est, sed et ipse ut potuit; quia de Deo homo dixit: Et quidem inspiratus a Deo sed tamen homo. Quia inspiratus, dixit aliquid; si non inspiratus esset, dixisset nihil: Quia vero homo inspiratus, non totum quod est dixit, sed quod potuit homo dixit*[EN80]. One has to distinguish, says Augustine in another passage, between what *veritas incommutabilis per se ipsam ineffabiliter loquitur rationalis creaturae mentibus*[EN81] and its expression *per mutabilem creaturam*[EN82] by means of spiritual images and a physical voice (*De civ. Dei* XVI, 6, 1). Anselm distinguishes in the same way between the directly (*sine humana doctrina*[EN83]) enacted divine sowing in the hearts of the prophets and apostles and the increase from the resultant harvest with which we now work (*De concordia qu.*, III, 6). Holy Scripture is *super solidam veritatem … velut super firmum fundamentum fundata*[EN84] (*Cur Deus homo?* II, 19); it is not, then, just identical with it. Luther speaks of the same direct revelation when he distinguishes between the prophets on the one side and the wise men and scribes on the other: "They are prophets which preach out of the mere inspiration of the Holy Ghost, which have not drawn it from Scripture or through men, as Moses and Amos were. And these are the highest and best which are wise and know how to make others wise, and to set out and expound Scripture; such were almost all the patriarchs before and with Moses, and after him many too, especially the apostles, who were laymen and sorely unlettered folk as Luke saith in Ac. 5, 'ignorant of Scripture'" (*Kirchenpostille*, 1522, *W.A.* 10^1, 271, 21). On the other hand wise men and scribes already presuppose the existence of prophetic Scripture. Even Calvin, who approximated revelation and Scripture much more closely than Augustine did, says in the very passage which is most frequently quoted, and

---

EN78 God said

EN79 Paul said

EN80 I dare to say, my brothers, perhaps not even John spoke of it as it is, … because a man spoke of God; and though inspired by God, still he is only a human being. Because he was inspired, he said something; if he had not been inspired, he would have said nothing; but because he was an inspired man, he did not say everything that is but [only] what a human being can say

EN81 the unchanging truth speaks through itself in an ineffable way to the minds of rational creatures

EN82 through a changeable creature

EN83 without human teaching

EN84 built upon solid truth … as on a firm foundation

with a plain reservation, that Holy Scripture has with believers the authority appropriate to it, *ubi statuunt e coelo fluxisse, acsi vivae ipsae Dei voces illic exaudirentur*[EN85] (*Instit.*, I, 7, 1), and in the decisive passage his formulation of the doctrine of Scripture is that *summa Scripturae probatio passim a Dei loquentis persona sumitur*[EN86] (*ib.*, 7, 4). Even in the orthodoxy of the following age with its fatal slide into the doctrine of inspiredness, recollection of a conscious distinction lives on in the most varied ways. According to Bullinger (*Comp. rel. christ.* 1598, 5, quoted according to A. Schweizer, *Glaubensl. d. ev. ref. Kirche*, Vol. I, 1844, 200) we must say: *Literae, verba caro sunt, sententiae vero Dei*[EN87]. According to W. Musculus (*Loci comm.*, 1564, 73, Schweizer, *op. cit.*, p. 199) Holy Scripture is called holy *quoniam de sacris rebus loquuntur*[EN88]. According to Peter Martyr (*Loci comm.*, 1580, 13, Schweizer, *op. cit.*, p. 200) Holy Scripture is an *expressio quaedam sapientiae Dei*[EN89]. According to J. Gerhard (*Loci theol.*, 1610, *Prooem.*, 18) the *verbum externum Dei*[EN90] goes forth one way *per inspirationem*[EN91] and another way *per sermonem externum*[EN92], i.e., through angels, men, or human writings. In the *Syn. pur. Theol. Leid.*, 1624, *Disp.* 1, 8 we read: *Sacrae Theologiae revelatio a Deo prophetis et Apostolis facta, est immediata, quae autem per hos Ecclesiae Dei manifestata est, mediata est*[EN93]. And frequently along the lines and even in the words of this very distinction the period of high orthodoxy (e.g., B. Bucan, *Instit. Theol.*, 1605, *Loc.* 4, 16), both Reformed (e.g., F. Turrettini, *Instit. theol. elenct.*, 1679, *Loc.*, 2, *qu.* 2, 5 f.) and Lutheran (Quenstedt, *Theol. did. pol.*, 1686, I,
[115] *cap.* 4, *sect.* 2, *qu.* 3, *ekth.* 3 and I, 7, 1, *thes.* 1, *n.* 2; Baier, *Comp, theol. pos.*, 1686, *Prol.*, 2, 1; Hollaz, *Ex theol. acroam.*, 1707, *Prol.*, 3, *qu.* 2), for all its concentration on Scripture as such, could still find a place for discussion of revelation itself as this is to be distinguished from Scripture because it alone is what establishes it as inspired Scripture.

Revelation engenders the Scripture which attests it: as the commission or burden laid on the prophets and apostles, as the object which introduces itself in distinction from them, as both the judge and the guarantor of the truth of what they say, and as the event of inspiration in which they become speakers and writers of the Word of God. Because revelation engenders the Bible that attests it, because Jesus Christ has called the Old and New Testaments into existence, because Holy Scripture is the record of a unique hearing of a unique call and a unique obedience to a unique command, therefore it could become the Canon, and again and again it can become the "living" Canon, the publisher of revelation, the summons and command of God, God's Word to us. If in the prophets and apostles the Church has a concrete counterpart by which it is reminded of God's past revelation, set in expectation of future revelation, and thus summoned to proclamation and empowered for it, this takes place because it really has in them the publishers of past revelation. But the

[EN85] when they declare them as having flowed from heaven, as if the living words of God themselves were heard there

[EN86] the highest authentication of Scripture is generally assumed to be the fact that God in person is speaking

[EN87] The writings are words become flesh, what they mean, however, is God's [message]

[EN88] because they speak of holy matters

[EN89] a kind of expression of the wisdom of God

[EN90] external word of God

[EN91] through inspiration

[EN92] through outward speech

[EN93] The revelation of sacred Theology, as granted by God to the Prophets and Apostles, is immediate; but that which is manifested through them to the Church of God is mediate prophets and apostles did not appoint themselves the publishers of revelation, nor are they ever this intrinsically or as a matter of course. What makes them this is the occurrence of God's revelation itself apart from their own existence. The occurrence, and so we must call this thing that happened to them: *Deus dixit*[EN94]. What has engendered Scripture and what Scripture for its part attests has happened truly and definitively, once and once-for-all. We have already discussed in outline what it was that happened: God was with us, with us His enemies, with us who were visited and smitten by His wrath. God was with us in all the reality and fulness with which He does what He does. He was with us as one of us. His Word became flesh of our flesh, blood of our blood. His glory was seen here in the depths of our situation, and the full depths of our situation were disclosed for the first time when illumined then and there by the Lord's glory, when in His Word He came down to the lowest parts of the earth (Eph. 4[9]), in order that there and in that way He might rob death of its power and bring life and immortality to light (2 Tim. 1[10]). This happened, and this is what the Old Testament as a word of prophecy and the New Testament as a word of fulfilment both proclaim as having happened, as having happened conclusively, totally, and sufficiently. This makes the biblical witnesses remarkable figures like John who cannot be brought under any morphology of genius. This is why it is true of them, though in different ways: "The zeal of thine house hath eaten me up" (Ps. 69[9]). This is why, although they seek no [116] authority, even with their fallible human word they can continually claim and enjoy the most unheard-of authority. This came upon them, and through them it constantly seeks to come afresh upon the Church and to be cried aloud as absolutely the most urgent thing that any age and any man in any age and any man in any respect can and must hear: This "God with us" has happened. It has happened in human history and as a part of human history. Yet it has not happened as other parts of this history usually happen. It does not need to be continued or completed. It does not point beyond itself or merely strive after a distant goal. It is incapable of any exegesis or of even the slightest addition or subtraction. Its form cannot be changed. It has happened as self-moved being in the stream of becoming. It has happened as completed event, fulfilled time, in the sea of the incomplete and changeable and self-changing.

A bit of apocryphal Christian legend from the 2nd century might be mentioned here because for all its historical foolishness it shows very clearly what fulfilled time would look like if we were able to view it. In the so-called *Protevangelium of James*, chap. 18, Joseph, the foster-parent of Jesus, tells us what he is supposed to have experienced in the environs of Bethlehem on the night of the Lord's nativity: "But I, Joseph, went about and went not about. And I looked up at the vault of heaven and saw it stand still, and I looked up into the air and saw it fixed, and I saw the birds of heaven immovable, and I looked on the ground and saw a dish standing there and labourers lying down and their hands in the dish, and the chewers chewed not, and those on the point of lifting out brought nothing up, and those who wanted to bring to their mouths brought nothing to their mouths, but all faces were

---

[EN94] God said

directed upwards, and lo, sheep were being driven and remained standing, and the shepherd raised his hand to smite them and his hand stayed up, and I looked at the water in the river and saw the mouths of the goats held down to it and they did not drink; and suddenly everything resumed its course" (*NT Apokryph*, ed. E. Hennecke, 2nd edn., 1924, 91). If in its perfect divine actuality fulfilled time is to be the one and only truly moved and moving time, then it does indeed mean suspension, the total relativising of all other time and of its apparently moved and moving content.

This fulfilled time which is identical with Jesus Christ, this absolute event in relation to which every other event is not yet event or has ceased to be so, this "It is finished," this *Deus dixit*[EN95] for which there are no analogies, is the revelation attested in the Bible. To understand the Bible from beginning to end, from verse to verse, is to understand how everything in it relates to this as its invisible-visible centre. But since this is so we have to say that we are in no position to understand the Bible ourselves. It can only be that the Bible gives itself to be understood by us, so that we come to hear the Bible as God's Word. To hear the Bible as God's Word means, therefore, that then and there, in the undoubtedly very modest, changing, perhaps increasing but possibly also decreasing compass in which it is true at any given time for an individual, we
[117] hear the human words of the Bible as the bearers of this eternal Word, based on this centre and having it in view again in everything they say. When the Bible itself is revelation in this way, it establishes the Church and makes its proclamation necessary and possible. The unity of revelation guarantees the unity of the biblical witness in and in spite of all its multiplicity and even contradictoriness. The unity of the Bible guarantees the unity of the Church in and in spite of the difference in the proportion of faith in which the Bible becomes revelation to this man and that man and to this man and that man to-day and to-morrow. On this basis the unity of the Church guarantees the unity of proclamation.

According to all that has been said revelation is originally and directly what the Bible and Church proclamation are derivatively and indirectly, i.e., God's Word. We have said of Church proclamation that it must continually become God's Word. And we have said the same of the Bible: It must continually become God's Word. The reference of this "continually," of course, is not to human experience, as though our reaction to this event or our attitude to it could be constitutive for its reality and content. The reference is to the freedom of God's Word. *Ubi et quando visum est Deo*[EN96], not intrinsically but in virtue of the divine decision taken ever and anon in the Bible and proclamation as the free God uses them, the Bible and proclamation are God's Word. But this cannot be said about revelation. When we speak about revelation we are confronted by the divine act itself and as such, which we have already had to bear in mind as the basis and boundary, the presupposition and proviso, of what had to be said about the Bible and proclamation. For (1) proclamation is

[EN95] God said
[EN96] Where and when it pleased God

real proclamation, i.e., the promise of future revelation, only as the repetition of the biblical witness to past revelation, and (2) the Bible is real witness, i.e., the factual recollection of past revelation, only in its relation to this past revelation attested in it. This being so, the freedom of God's grace is the basis and boundary, the presupposition and proviso, of the statements according to which the Bible and proclamation are the Word of God. The decisive content of these statements, the positive thing they state and the evident negations by which this is surrounded, the relation in which the statements are true, is their relation to revelation. But revelation is simply the freedom of God's grace. It is naturally not the principle of this freedom. This principle is only the obviously necessary product of human reflection on this freedom. It is rather the event in which the free God causes His free grace to rule and work. In this event of God's grace proclamation and the Bible are "held" in the three senses of the term: (1) "held up on high," singled out, made visible and familiar, to the degree that the Bible seeks to bear witness to this event and proclamation seeks to repeat this attestation, to the degree that in the Bible and proclamation this event is what is really meant in the human talk; (2) "held in place," [118] relativised, limited, to the degree that this event is also the boundary of what proclamation and the Bible can try to accomplish in and of themselves, the boundary which we obviously cannot think is set aside by what men wanted and want to say; and (3) "held in store," preserved, secured, to the degree that this event is the confirmation and ratification, the fulfilment of what proclamation and the Bible achieve in and of themselves, the presence of what is meant in the human word of the Bible and proclamation. Precisely in view of revelation, or on the basis of it, one may thus say of proclamation and the Bible that they are God's Word, that they continually become God's Word. But for this very reason one cannot say the same of revelation. One has to say the exact opposite, namely, that revelation becomes God's Word, i.e., in the Bible and proclamation, because it is this Word in itself. It is this that "holds" the Bible and proclamation in that threefold sense. Revelation is itself the divine decision which is taken in the Bible and proclamation, which makes use of them, which thus confirms, ratifies and fulfils them. It is itself the Word of God which the Bible and proclamation are as they become it.

ὅν γὰρ ἀπέστειλεν ὁ θεὸς τὰ ῥήματα τοῦ θεοῦ λαλεῖ οὐ γὰρ ἐκ μέτρου δίδωσιν τὸ πνεῦμα. ὁ πατὴρ ἀγαπᾷ τὸν υἱόν, καὶ πάντα δέδωκεν ἐν τῇ χειρὶ αὐτοῦ. ὁ πιστεύων εἰς τὸν υἱὸν ἔχει ζωὴν αἰώνιον· ὁ δὲ ἀπειθῶν τῷ υἱῷ οὐκ ὄψεται ζωήν, ἀλλ' ἡ ἀργὴ τοῦ θεοῦ μένει ἐπ' αὐτόν[EN97] (Jn. 3^{34-36}).

It does not stand, therefore, under any condition—one can say this only of our knowledge of revelation—but is itself the condition. Of it one may say, not

---

[EN97] For he whom God has sent utters the words of God, for it is not by measure that he gives the Spirit; the Father loves the Son, and has given all things into his hand. He who believes in the Son has eternal life; he who does not obey the Son shall not see life, but the wrath of God rests upon him.

ubi et quando[EN98], but *illic et tunc visum est Deo.* The reference here is not to a possibility still to be realised but to the reality of the Word of God as the basis of all possible self-realisations. *Ubi et quando* can and must be said because ultimately or primarily we have to say *illic et tunc.* Because there is a moving hand there is also a moved and moving Canon and a commissioned, objective, true and actual proclamation in obedience to this Canon. When we say "Word of God revealed," then in distinction from the "written" and "preached" of the two other forms of the Word of God, "revealed" does not belong to the predicate. It is simply a paraphrase, a second designation of the subject. If "written" and "preached" denote the twofold concrete relation in which the Word of God is spoken to us, revelation denotes the Word of God itself in the act of its being spoken in time. Above this act there is nothing other or higher on which it might be based or from which it might be derived unless it was from the transcendence of the eternal Word of God that it came forth in revelation. It is the condition which conditions all things without itself being conditioned. This is what we are saying when we call it revelation. Revelation, *revelatio,*
[119] ἀποκάλυψις, means the unveiling of what is veiled. If this is meant strictly and properly, then all that is distinct from revelation is concealment, the hiddenness of the veiled.

The revealed Word of God is the mystery not made known to the aeons but veiled, Rom. 16^{25}; Col. 1^{26}; Eph. 3^{9}. But this means that no other reason is to be sought or suggested for its disclosure than the actual disclosing itself. It is in the νῦν[EN99] qualified by ἀποκάλυψις[EN100] or φανέρωσις[EN101] that the witness of revelation speaks as such. In this alone can it be understood as unveiled. The final word on the qualification is simply a reference to the will of God: κατ᾽ ἐπιταγὴν τοῦ αἰωνίου θεοῦ[EN102] (Rom. 16^{25}), οἷς ἠθέλησεν ὁ θεὸς γνωρίσαι[EN103] ... (Col. 1^{26}). "Christian faith and Christian life stand in the one little word revelation by God, for where this is not present, no heart can ever be rightly aware of this mystery, which was hidden from the world. Now God revealeth it only to His eternally elected saints, to whom He will have it made known, otherwise it is hidden from everyone and remaineth a proper mystery. What good can the free or enslaved and captive will say or do about that? How will it come in its own might to this light and mystery? If the almighty strong God hide it from it, by no preparation or good work will it ever reach thereto. No creature can come to this knowledge. Christ alone revealeth it to it in the heart. There all merit falleth to the ground, all the powers and abilities of reason, and count for nought with God. Christ alone must give it" (Luther, *Sermon on* Mt. 11^{25-30}, 1527, *W.A.* 23, 689, 4).

All revelation, then, must be thought of as revealing, i.e., as conditioned by the act of revelation. The event in which revelation occurs must be seen in connexion with what has happened once and for all in this act. All fulfilled time must be seen as filled with the fulness of this time. Revelation itself, how-

---

EN 98 where and when, but there and then it pleased God
EN 99 now
EN100 revelation
EN101 disclosure
EN102 according to the commandment of the everlasting God
EN103 to whom God would make known

ever, is not referred to anything other, higher, or earlier. Revelation as such is not relative. Revelation in fact does not differ from the person of Jesus Christ nor from the reconciliation accomplished in Him. To say revelation is to say "The Word became flesh." To be sure, one can say something quite different by revelation, something purely formal, and relative as such. But to say this is not to say what the Bible means by the word or what Church proclamation is referring to when it refers to the Bible or what must be called revelation in Christian dogmatics if this is to take itself seriously as such. When in the word revelation we say "The Word was made flesh and dwelt among us," then we are saying something which can have only an intertrinitarian basis in the will of the Father and the sending of the Son and the Holy Spirit, in the eternal decree of the triune God, so that it can be established only as knowledge of God from God, of light in light. The same applies if instead of Jesus Christ we say concretely "God with us." It is true that in the term revelation we might have something relative rather than this absolute in view, but the Bible is thinking only of this absolute, and in the knowledge of this absolute the Church with the help of the Bible recalls past revelation, and a dogmatics that works in the sphere of the Church and not in a vacuum has also to cling to it. But to say "God with us" is to say something which has no basis or possibility outside itself, which can in [120]
no sense be explained in terms of man and man's situation, but only as knowledge of God from God, as free and unmerited grace. As the Bible bears witness to God's revelation and as Church proclamation takes up this witness in obedience, both renounce any foundation apart from that which God has given once and for all by speaking. The Bible and proclamation both appeal to this fact that has been given here and now. They cannot reproduce it as a given fact. They cannot bring it on the scene themselves. They can only attest and proclaim it. To bring it about that the *Deus dixit*[EN104] is present with the Church in its various times and situations is not in the power of the Bible or proclamation. The *Deus dixit* is true—now the *ubi et quando*[EN105] must come into force again—where it *is* true, i.e., where and when God, in speaking once and for all, wills according to His eternal counsel that it be true, where and when God by His activating, ratifying and fulfilling of the word of the Bible and preaching lets it become true. This being and becoming true of revelation consists, then, in the fact that the Church really recollects past revelation, and in faith receives, grasps and really proclaims the biblical witness of it as the real promise of future revelation, future revelation here being simply that which has taken place once and for all but is now directed to us too, just as the Christ who comes again is no other than the Christ who has come, but this Christ as the One who now comes also to us. The "God with us" becomes actual for us *hic et nunc*[EN106] as the promise received and grasped in faith because it is *illic et*

[EN104] God said
[EN105] where and when
[EN106] here and now

tunc[EN107] a divine act. It is thus that which is true in and for itself, and it becomes true for us as recollection and also as promise, as recollection of Christ come in the flesh and as hope of Christ coming again in glory. It is Jesus Christ Himself who here speaks for Himself and needs no witness apart from His Holy Spirit and the faith that rejoices in His promise received and grasped. This independent and unsurpassable origin of the Word of God that comes to us is what we have in view when we speak of its third form, or materially we should rather say its first form, i.e., its form as the Word of God revealed.

4. THE UNITY OF THE WORD OF GOD

We have been speaking of three different forms of the Word of God and not of three different Words of God. In this threefold form and not otherwise—but also as the one Word only in this threefold form—the Word of God is given to us and we must try to understand it conceptually. It is one and the same whether we understand it as revelation, Bible, or proclamation. There is no distinction of degree or value between the three forms. For to the extent that
[121] proclamation really rests on recollection of the revelation attested in the Bible and is thus obedient repetition of the biblical witness, it is no less the Word of God than the Bible. And to the extent that the Bible really attests revelation it is no less the Word of God than revelation itself. As the Bible and proclamation become God's Word in virtue of the actuality of revelation they are God's Word: the one Word of God within which there can be neither a more nor a less. Nor should we ever try to understand the three forms of God's Word in isolation. The first, revelation, is the form that underlies the other two. But it is the very one that never meets us anywhere in abstract form. We know it only indirectly, from Scripture and proclamation. The direct Word of God meets us only in this twofold mediacy. But Scripture too, to become God's Word for us, must be proclaimed in the Church. So, to give a survey of the whole, the following brief schedule of mutual relations may be drawn up.

The revealed Word of God we know only from the Scripture adopted by Church proclamation or the proclamation of the Church based on Scripture.

The written Word of God we know only through the revelation which fulfils proclamation or through the proclamation fulfilled by revelation.

The preached Word of God we know only through the revelation attested in Scripture or the Scripture which attests revelation.

There is only one analogy to this doctrine of the Word of God. Or, more accurately, the doctrine of the Word of God is itself the only analogy to the doctrine which will be our fundamental concern as we develop the concept of revelation. This is the doctrine of the triunity of God. In the fact that we can

---

[EN107] there and then

substitute for revelation, Scripture and proclamation the names of the divine persons Father, Son and Holy Spirit and *vice versa*, that in the one case as in the other we shall encounter the same basic determinations and mutual relationships, and that the decisive difficulty and also the decisive clarity is the same in both—in all this one may see specific support for the inner necessity and correctness of our present exposition of the Word of God.

The doctrine of the three forms of the Word of God in the sketch attempted here is not new. We have seen in detail how revelation, Scripture and proclamation have from the very first stamped themselves on Christian thought as special forms of God's Word. Some passages in Luther are especially relevant here. Already in the *Dictata super Psalterium* (1513–16) Luther says (on Ps. 45[1]): *Quod verbum Dei triplici modo dicitur*[EN108]: 1. There is a speaking by God *per verbum externum et linguam ad aures hominum*[EN109], whose model Luther sees in the word of the Old Testament patriarchs and prophets under the veil of the mere letter. 2. There is a Word of God which He now speaks through His Spirit to His saints on earth, namely, in His Son, this being a *verbum consummans et abbreviatum*[EN110] compared to the prophetic Word, but still wrapped in manifold veils. 3. There is a Word that God the Father [122] speaks in Himself and to the saints in eternal glory. So we shall hear it one day, *cum nobis verbum suum ipse sine ullo medio revelabit. Unico et simplicissimo verbo suo*[EN111] will He then satisfy us, and the Spirit Himself will then be the one sacrament in place of all signs (*W.A.* 3, 262, 5). That scant justice is done here to the first form, *the verbum externum*[EN112] of preaching, and that its significance is not understood, may be seen already from the fact that Luther saw no way to carry out the Trinitarian articulation which he obviously had in mind in relation to the second and third forms, because he could not very well relate to the Holy Spirit what he then regarded as a *verbum externum*. How he conceived of the advance from the first to the second form is also not clear in detail. Furthermore the separation between the Word that the Father speaks *in se ipso*[EN113] in the third form and *in filio*[EN114] in the second should not be made in the way it is. On the whole, however, the three forms, up to and including the eschatologically characterised third form, are very accurately perceived and described. There is an interesting variation on the theme in the already quoted sermon on Mt. 23[34f.] (*Kirchenpostille*, 1522, *W.A.* 10[1], 272, 17), which refers to "the three ways in which the truth may be revealed: Scripture, word, thought; Scripture by books, word by the mouth, thought by the heart. One cannot conceive the doctrine in any way save heart, mouth, and Scripture." The last form here, called thought, is simply our "revelation" in virtue of which Scripture and preaching reach man and touch his heart. More important is a passage in a sermon on the wise men (from the same *Kirchenpostille* of 1522). This surprises us especially by the completely new and one might almost say exaggerated value that the *verbum externum* or proclamation now has in Luther. "The oral and public sermon ... the voice or word cried forth by the mouth" is now for him the light referred to in 2 Cor. 4[6]; 2 Pet. 1[19]. "Now Scripture is not understood until the light ariseth." Scripture here is primarily the prophetic word to be found in the Old Testament. At first Luther simply contrasts the New Testament with this as living, i.e., oral proclamation whose task is to open up the prophetic word which is

---

EN108 That the word of God may be described in three ways

EN109 through the external word by way of human tongues and ears

EN110 word that fulfils and is abbreviated

EN111 when He Himself will reveal His word to us without any medium. With His word in its single and simplest form

EN112 external word

EN113 in Himself

EN114 in the Son

closed in its written form. "For through the Gospel the prophets are opened up, therefore the star must first rise and be seen. For in the New Testament preaching should be done publicly with a living voice and should bring forth to speech and hearing what was hitherto hidden in letters and secret guise. For the New Testament is nought other than an opening and revealing of the Old Testament, as is shown in Rev. 5, where the Lamb of God openeth the book with seven seals. We also see in the apostles how all their preaching was nought but bringing forth Scripture and building thereon." And now Luther has the astonishing continuation: "Therefore even Christ Himself wrote not down His teaching, as Moses did his, but did it orally and gave no command to write it. The apostles, too, wrote little, and not all of them that .... Even those who did write no more than point us to the ancient Scripture, as the angel pointed the shepherds to the manger and the swaddling clothes. And the star pointed the magi to Bethlehem. Therefore 'tis not like the New Testament to write books about Christian doctrine, but without books there should be in all places good, learned, spiritual, diligent preachers who draw the living word out of ancient writ and unceasingly din it into the people as the apostles did. For ere they wrote they first had preached to the people and converted them by the living voice, which was their proper apostolic and New Testament work. This is likewise the right star which sheweth Christ's birth and the angelic message telling of the swaddling bands and the crib. But man's need to write books is a great injury and it is a violation of the Spirit that the need hath compelled it and is not the way of the New Testament ..." New Testament Scripture as an adjunct or interpretation of the Old Testament is regarded as a defensive measure against corruption in the Church. "There
[123] finally had to be resort to that, and need was that some sheep should be saved from the wolves: so men began to write, and yet through writing, so far as possible, to bring Christ's little sheep into Scripture, and they prepared thereby that the sheep should be able to pasture themselves and guard themselves against the wolves when their shepherds would not pasture them or turned wolves." But it would have been better if other books had not been written in the Church. And the star of Bethlehem, the star of the wise men, should be in every case "the lively preaching and simple revelation of Christ as the same is hid and promised in Scripture; therefore he that seeth the star knoweth assuredly the King of the Jews, the newborn Christ; for the Gospel teacheth nought but Christ, and Scripture likewise hath nought but Christ. But whoso knoweth not Christ may hear the Gospel or hold the book right in his hands, but understanding of it he hath not yet, for to have the Gospel without understanding is to have no Gospel. And to have Scripture without the knowledge of Christ is to have no Scripture, and is none other than to let this star shine and yet not perceive it" (*W.A.* 10^1, 625–28). This exaggerated thought is by no means an isolated one in Luther at this period. For him the Old and the New Testament are related as the written word on the one side and the word preached on the other. "Thus the books of Moses and the prophets are also Gospel, since they have preached and described beforehand the same thing about Christ as the apostles have preached and written after. Yet there is a difference between them. For if both are written on paper as regards the letter, the Gospel or the New Testament should not really be written but put in the living voice, which then soundeth forth and is heard everywhere in the world. That it is also written is surplus. But the Old Testament is put only in writing and is thus called 'a letter,' and so the apostles call it 'writ,' for it hath pointed only to the coming Christ. But the Gospel is a living sermon about Christ already come" (*Ep. S. Petri.*, 1523, *W.A.* 12, 275, 5; cf. also 259, 8; 556, 9). It need hardly be shown, of course, that in other passages Luther attached supreme importance to the written New Testament, that he did not treat it as a necessary evil, and that it is thus quite wrong to hold him systematically to this distinction. But one may still learn from the distinction how he viewed the relation between Scripture and preaching generally. Both have the same theme and content, and this in such a way that preaching takes it first from Scripture and can thus be no other

than scriptural exposition, but also in such a way that it always draws from Scripture in the form of living proclamation and has thus to become God's Word to us. Allegorising on Lk. 2^{12} at the same period, Luther summed up his view as follows: "Christ is completely wrapped in Scripture as the body in the swaddling clothes. Preaching is the crib in which he lies and is set, and from it we get food and provender" (*Sermon on* Lk. 2, 1523, *W.A.* 12, 418, 24). Protestant orthodoxy, which at the peak of its development had no liking for talk about the distinction between the forms of the Word of God and the fluidity of their mutual relations, emphasised the more zealously something which is equally true and instructive in itself, namely, their unity. With reference to the unity of the Word of God to the biblical witnesses and through them: *hae distinctiones non faciunt essentialem aliquam differentiam inter verbum Dei hominibus communicatum, sed tantum distinctos communicationis et revelationis modos exprimunt*[EN115] (J. Gerhard, *Loci theol.*, 1610, *Prooem.*, 18), *Distinctio Verbi in ἄγραφον et ἔγγραφον non est divisio generis in species ... quasi alius esset Verbum non scriptum a scripto; sed est distinctio subjecti in sua accidentia, quia eidem Verbo accidit, ut fuerit non scriptum olim et nunc sit scriptum*[EN116] (F. Turrettini, *Instit. theol. el.*, 1679, *Loc.* 2, *qu.* 2.4). *Nec vero aliud est verbum Dei quod a Deo vel quod inspiratum viris Dei, quam quod in scriptura traditur, aut praedicatur, vel mente humana reconditur*[EN117] (Hollaz, *Ex. theol. acrom.*, 1707, III, 2, 1). All this is true. Yet in the statements of this period of transition one misses painfully the Reformers' insight into the [124]
dynamics of the mutual relationships of the three forms. Its absence comes to light in the theory of inspiration, which implies a freezing, as if were, of the relation between Scripture and revelation. But it may be seen especially in the fact that the theologians of this period hardly seem to have any more a true and essential awareness of the third form of the Word of God, proclamation. Preaching is called "God's Word" in them too, but the real connecting point between revelation and Scripture in the present is increasingly something far different from the act of Church proclamation; it is the knowledge, faith, sanctification and blessedness of the individual. But this means that the unity of revelation and Scripture, however stiff the objectivity in which it is arrayed, takes on more and more the aspect, not of God's dealings with His Church, but rather of a private divine institution for so many private persons, preaching and the sacraments being adequate instruments of this as the so-called *media salutis*[EN118]. Forgetting that the correlate of revelation and Scripture is not in the first instance the saving or amending of the individual but (on the same level as revelation and Scripture) proclamation as the service of God, the Church forgot nothing less than itself. From being a place for the service of God, through which as such men are also helped, it now made itself a place for the finest service of men in which God will finally have to figure as the supremely objective and supremely miraculous means, yet only as a means. Boasting of the objectivity with which the Word of God was invested, especially in its biblical form, was only the expression of a bad conscience. It helped to conceal the fact that the men of this age no longer knew what they were really saying when they said "Word of God," that they no longer knew that they were talking about the present-day action, not of man in his relation to God, but of God in His relation to man, and therefore about the Church. When they no longer knew this, was it surprising that the rising Modernism of the new age discovered that

---

[EN115] these distinctions do not introduce any essential differentiation in the word of God communicated to humans, but only describe distinct modes of communication and revelation

[EN116] The distinction between the unwritten and the written Word is not a difference between genus and species ... as though the unwritten word were another kind of thing than the written; but it is a distinction of the subject and its accidents, because it happens to the same Word that at one point had not been written and that now it has

[EN117] Nor is the word of God that is from God or has inspired men of God, other than that which is handed down in Scripture, or which is preached, or which is stored in the human mind

[EN118] means of salvation

the goal of the finest service of man could be reached by a simpler and less miraculous way than that which orthodoxy still espoused with great external but not so great internal fidelity? Was it surprising if the objectivity which orthodoxy still claimed for revelation and Scripture, and theoretically for preaching and the sacraments too, struck one bright mind and thousands of bright minds and even pious hearts as more and more a superfluous idol which it could only seem to them a good work, well-pleasing to God, to smash in pieces? The catastrophic crash of orthodoxy in the 18th century, the consequences of which we still have to carry to this day, is no more puzzling than the collapse of a house whose foundations are giving way. Responsibility for the disaster must be borne, not by the philosophy of the world which had become critical, but by the theology of the Church which had become too uncritical, which no longer understood itself at the centre. For all our great respect for the work done by orthodoxy, and for all our understanding of the ultimate intentions of this work, our task to-day must be the different one of re-adopting Luther's concepts and taking proclamation seriously again as the work of the Church in and through which God is to be served and not man, and God is to speak. On that basis we must then try to understand once again in what sense first the Bible, and even before that revelation, is really the Word of God. It was here that forgetfulness set in before the disaster of the 18th century. It is here obviously that new reflection must begin. Hence the direct object of dogmatics to-day must be Church proclamation.

§ 5 [125]

THE NATURE OF THE WORD OF GOD

The Word of God in all its three forms is God's speech to man. For this reason it occurs, applies and works in God's act on man. But as such it occurs in God's way which differs from all other occurrence, i.e., in the mystery of God.

1. THE QUESTION OF THE NATURE OF THE WORD OF GOD

At this point we have to deviate in two ways especially from the first edition of this book. We refer first to the discussions in the original § 5, 1. There, after establishing the concept of the Word of God in its threefold form by means of an analysis of Church proclamation, we made a transition from a phenomenological treatment to an existential treatment, i.e., from thinking in terms of an outward observer to thinking in terms of an existential participant. Objection was rightly raised against this section from various quarters (cf. F. Gogarten, "*Karl Barths Dogmatik*," *Theol. Rundschau*, 1929, 70 f.; T. Siegfried, *Das Wort und die Existenz*, I, 1930, 35 f., 250 f.). It might be asked whether the concepts of phenomenological and existential thought are properly specified and distinguished in this way. It might also be asked whether existential thinking is more than a particular form of phenomenological thinking or whether there is not even some point where the two coincide. It might thus be asked whether the idea of transition from the one to the other is not in any case impossible. But these are philosophical rather than theological questions. The objection that I have since made against myself is that these concepts, whatever their content and mutual relation may be, cannot in any way constitute or signify decisive turning-points on the way of dogmatic thought as seemed there to be presupposed. No matter how philosophers may or may not reach an understanding on these matters, they will do so as philosophers and not as theologians. That is, they will not do so out of any responsible regard for the theme of theology. Hence theology cannot learn anything from them and ought not to do so, unless it is ready to let them intrude a philosophical theme instead of its own, as has always happened when it has accepted material instruction from any philosophy. Now at this point in the first edition it was not my purpose to take up a philosophical theme in this way. When I spoke of "transition" this was meant to be much more innocuous and incidental than it has been taken to be. It is obvious that in dogmatics as in any science, while we do not have to use a specifically philosophical or any other vocabulary, we may do so when it lends itself to the incidental illustration or bringing into focus of what is said with theological intent, when the meaning and purpose of the linguistic borrowing is fixed with relative certainty by the context, and when there is comparatively little danger of the misunderstanding that theological statements are being supported by a reference to philosophical statements, or that a philosophical theme is being substituted for the theological. In the section at issue, however, this misunderstanding was relatively close, and it arose immediately. To my horror T. Siegfried

[126] (*op. cit.*, p. 36) interpreted the passage as follows: "On this foundation (i.e., the existential thinking introduced) he proposes to build his dogmatics." This was not really my intention. But I ought to have had the better judgment to see that to drag in those concepts at that point in relation to what I wanted to say there was a superfluous and dangerous game: superfluous because it was not in any case followed by any attempt to prove the doctrine of the Word of God by showing it to be posited by existential thinking or by advancing an existential philosophy as its background and justification; and dangerous because all that does follow on the basis of the passage can be regarded as a kind of grounding of theology in existentialist philosophy, though in obscure combination with the intentions of Roman Catholic and older Protestant theology. Moreover, there could and can be no way of developing seriously what I then understood by that transition. It would be quite fatal if in all that has been said thus far we have not been thinking and speaking as participators in these things at the level of existence. But if this has not been so thus far, it is not in our power to make a transition and to undertake to think and speak as participants now. On the other hand, neither before nor after can we ever fail, when thinking and speaking of these things, to regard them from without, however much we might participate in them. Again, it should be said of this contemplation from without that it is not in our power to regard the things of which we speak here exclusively from without. No matter how we analyse and relate philosophically the two approaches which I tried to distinguish there, they are more or less intrinsic to all human thought and speech. And a theological train of thought as such cannot be rendered correct or incorrect, important or unimportant, by reason of this "more or less." No serious theological decision is taken in the actual transitions from more to less and *vice versa* as they can naturally take place in theological trains of thought too. This leads us to the second point. In the first edition the doctrine of the Word of God is developed at this juncture as follows. In §§ 5 and 6 two analyses are given of man's situation first as preacher and then as hearer of the Word of God. In § 7 there is then an analysis of the distinctive knowledge of the Word of God generally. In the last sub-sections of the three sections there are then annexed to the three analyses as their ostensible results three more precise definitions of the Word of God which together represent what is here to be developed as the doctrine of the nature of the Word of God. That arrangement in the first edition had three faults. 1. The more precise definitions of the Word of God, being scattered over three sections and appearing almost in the form of appendices, were by this external placing isolated from the readers' attention in a way that was fatal to a proper understanding of the whole. It might easily happen, and did in fact happen, that these conclusions to §§ 5, 6, 7 could be regarded as a mere response to the analyses which might easily have been omitted, since the analyses themselves constituted the true and to some extent provocative part of the sections. 2. I did not succeed (and happily could not succeed) in making these conclusions on the concept of the Word of God, as I had proposed, illuminating and credible as results of the three analyses. There were certain associations of thought between the analyses and the more precise definitions, but fundamentally and comprehensively the latter are grounded elsewhere, they are not necessary at this point, and therefore they cannot be as impressive or catch attention in the same way as the actual analyses. 3. The (necessarily) unsuccessful attempt to deduce the doctrine of the Word of God from an analysis of the concrete situation of the preacher or hearer, or the man who knows God's Word generally, involved following a "false tendency" in the same sense and the same direction as the introduction and use of the concepts of phenomenological and existential thought already criticised. In fact the more precise definitions were not at all deduced from the analyses. But I proceeded as though they could and
[127] should be. An anthropology, albeit a Church anthropology, was thus being advanced as the supposed basis on which we know decisive statements about God's Word. In this regard, along with the general declaration that from now on, and especially in §§ 5, 6, 7, we should

be concerned with existential thinking, I was paying homage to false gods, even if only after the manner of the *libellatici*[EN1] of the Decian persecution. If there is one thing the Word of God certainly is not, it is not a predicate of man, even of the man who receives it, and therefore not of the man who speaks, hears and knows it in the sphere of the Church. But it has to be this if the more precise definitions of its nature are really deduced from an analysis of the concrete situation of this man, as was my intention and claim there, even if it did not actually happen.

F. Gogarten in the review of the first edition already quoted had in the main two objections to its contents: 1. that it has no "true anthropology" (p. 66) and 2. that in some parts at least "it now speaks of a God isolated in and for Himself over against man and now of man isolated in and for himself over against God" (p. 72) instead of speaking always about both God and man in their interconnexion (cf. also "The Problem of a Theological Anthropology" in *Z.d.Z.*, 1929, 493 f.). A special response will be made to the second objection in the course of this section. As regards the first, I have already stated my position in the preceding self-criticism and it remains only to make this explicit in relation to Gogarten. I might sum up all that has been said against myself by expressing regret to-day that five years ago I was at least on the way to a "true anthropology." Gogarten ought really to have acknowledged this from his own standpoint. The fact that he could not, but spoke of a lack of true anthropology in spite of my obvious tendency in this direction, is very comforting to me to-day, since it proves that the damage has not been so great as it might well have been. For I can only regard it as doing great harm to do what happily Gogarten has not found me doing but would like me to have done, namely, setting up a "true anthropology" as "the central task" and "real problem of theology" (*Z.d.Z.*, 1929, 505), as "the hardest bit of work" that theologians have to do to-day (*Theol. Rundschau*, 1929, 67), and that means, of course, as the source and criterion of all further theological propositions. Gogarten finds two bases for the concern behind his demand for a true anthropology. The first is historical (*Z.d.Z.*, 1929, 502 f.). As a result of his modern knowledge of nature and the world man has been externally pushed out of the central position that was so obviously his in the Middle Ages and he has thus been led to a discovery and inner awareness of himself and his historicity. The "humanising of life" was what bound Luther already to the humanists of his age and especially to the Renaissance, and for all the reservations we have to make Schleiermacher's theology is to be estimated as the first great attempt to make this feature of Lutheran teaching the feature of a theology planned and executed on a big scale. Since the thinking of the new age is more strongly affected by the problem of man himself, anthropology must be regarded as the real problem of a modern theology. Now let us assume that the historical background of this analysis of our age is right—though perhaps not all Lutherans would be pleased by this sketch—and let us also assume that the analysis itself is materially right—though this was probably more true before the First World War than in our own time, which has become much more realistic again and in which it can hardly be said of a large and especially a younger group of our contemporaries that the "humanising of life" is a significant concept in their life-consciousness. Even if we assume all this, however, the question always remains whether in face of the alleged anthropologising of the modern (or once modern) life-consciousness it is wise to follow in the steps of Schleiermacher and to orientate oneself to his life-consciousness even though under another sign. Theology has all too often tried to seek out and conquer the consciousness of an age on its own ground. We have protested [128]
already against theology allowing adversaries to dictate its action, since this can only mean conceding to them half or more than half of what should not be conceded, namely, the

[EN1] Christians who purchased documents certifying that they had apostatized, but in fact remained Christians

Church's lack of independence of life and thought over against the world and the primacy of the questions the world has to put to the Church over the questions the Church has to put to itself. Might it not be to-day that a theology which refuses even in method to make common cause with the aforesaid "humanising of life" will be more relevant—if this is the point—than one which admits at the very outset that it can speak only a second word, a word on the situation (the situation outside the Church)? Gogarten's second concern seems to emanate from Christology. "Must not thought start out," he says (*Theol. Rundschau,* 1929, 73), "from the man God became? Can there be any other starting-point than the God who is not isolated *vis-à-vis* man, and does not that mean that thought must start out from man?" I could understand this if he had said "to man" instead of "from man." In fact theological statements are distinguished from those of metaphysics or morality to the degree that in conformity with the Immanuel that is the content of revelation, they take the reality and truth of which they purport to speak and make it intelligible as reality and truth from God to man. But is it really a consequence of Christology, of the incarnation of the Word, that *post Christum*[EN2] thought can and even should start out from man—and for Gogarten this does not mean from Jesus, from the one God-man, but from that other man who has ceased to be isolated *vis-à-vis* God and yet is not identical with the God-man? Is it really a consequence that this must be the very centre of theology? Does the man who is no longer isolated from God, apart from the one God-man, really exist in such a way that he can and should be the starting-point of thought? At any rate the older Lutheran dogmaticians did not draw this deduction even though their Christology might have suggested it. The first to do so was Schleiermacher, and then, with malicious intent, Feuerbach. Hence this second strictly theological concern of Gogarten's seems to me not merely unconvincing but materially dubious.—Yet I must still regard the anthropology which Gogarten fails to find in me as harmful because with it I see no way of avoiding the danger of a fresh betrayal of theology to some philosophy and therewith the loss of theology's real theme. I am not unaware that Gogarten (expressly in the essay in *Z.d.Z.* and also inferentially in the review in *Theol. Rundschau,* e.g., 68, 73) has declared quite clearly that the theme of his "true anthropology" is "man who cannot be thought of apart from the God who has united Himself with man in revelation," so that its content can be derived only from the Gospel itself or from the context of theology as a whole (*Z.d.Z.,* 1929, 494 f.). Gogarten's purpose here seems to be along the lines of what I called "Church anthropology" in my draft of 1927. But what I presented there, namely, an analysis of the self-understanding of the man who preaches and hears God's Word and knows it in this concrete situation, did not seem to satisfy Gogarten as being true anthropology; indeed, he regarded it as so inadequate that he could not even recognise or praise what ought to have been from his standpoint my good intentions in this direction. Why was he not satisfied? At the time Gogarten wrote that my undervaluation of anthropology was "very closely" connected with my failure to supply "a basic investigation of the question of the scientific nature of theology, i.e., the question of the relationship between theology and philosophy and all that this involves" (*Theol. Rundschau,* 1929, 66 f.). May one not assume—and does not his declaration of solidarity with Bultmann in this regard support the assumption—that Gogarten's own high estimate of anthropology is "very closely" connected with this investigation? But if it is the purpose of anthropology to clarify the relation between theology and philosophy—and in Bultmann's proximity this certainly means to derive the
[129] possibility of theology from the relation perceived—then the question arises how one can take seriously the theological independence of the anthropology desired by Gogarten or its derivation from the Gospel and the Gospel alone. The decisive statements in Gogarten's programme are to the effect that there is a circle between the doctrine of man on the one

[EN2] after Christ

side and the doctrine of God on the other: "There is no understanding of man without understanding of God, but ... again I cannot understand this God without already understanding man" (*Z.d.Z.*, 1929, 496). If in the last clause Gogarten had written "also" instead of "already" no objection could be taken. The thought would then be that understanding man presupposes understanding God and understanding God always includes understanding man also. But this does not seem to be Gogarten's thought. It is indeed hard to see how one could move on from this to the primacy of anthropology, the elucidating of the relation between theology and philosophy, and the establishing of the scientific nature of theology. And Gogarten does in fact write "already." This "already" seems to give the understanding of man priority over the understanding of God, a priority which for its part seems unthinkable unless one presupposes a "pre-understanding" with regard to man, as Bultmann actually does. But such a pre-understanding, by means of which one can as it were leap into the aforementioned circle of the understanding of God and man in their mutual relationship, seems again not to be in harmony with Gogarten's unequivocal declaration that man may not be regarded primarily as one "who also exists outside revelation, who may thus be thought of without thinking also of God's revelation" (*op. cit.*, p. 497). God's revelation! What does Gogarten mean by this in this context? He interprets the expression in the same passage by adding: (the revelation) "in which God has bound Himself to man from creation as his God and Lord," and even more clearly a little later: "the revelation which is the creation and preservation of man from the beginning of the world" (*op. cit.*, p. 498). And this sets us a final puzzle. What are we to understand by the revelation which takes place from creation or which is man's creation and preservation? It might mean (along the lines of *Qu.* 19 of the *Heidelberg Catechism*) the Gospel which has constantly been published to man since creation. But why should Gogarten lay explanatory stress on this in the present context? And how can one deduce the primacy of anthropology, for which Gogarten is arguing, from the fact that the one Gospel is the Gospel for all ages from the foundation of the world? The only other possibility is to assume, as the second formula suggests, that "from creation" means the revelation of God which is given in and with creation and preservation and which is present and known to us as such (i.e., apart from God's second revelation as distinct from creation) in the orders of the reality of our creatureliness, of our creaturely existence. The connexion and relationship between God and man on which Gogarten would erect his anthropology is in this case posited in the relation between God as Creator and man as creature. If this is so, then at a stroke everything is clear. On the one hand Gogarten can rightly say that his concern is solely and exclusively with the man who is to be found only in revelation, and on the other hand he can also quite rightly give to the understanding of man (with his "already") priority over the understanding of God, i.e., the God who is to be understood in terms of His revelation in the Gospel. But there still remains the slight linguistic difficulty that Gogarten frequently speaks of the man who is to be understood in the light of the "Gospel" (and not just revelation). Gospel here, however, is this revelation which is given with creation and which precedes the proclaimed revelation, or perhaps it is the confirmation of this revelation of creation implicitly given in the Gospel. If this is so, then the primacy of anthropology, Bultmann's pre-understanding, the remarkable "already" and the even more remarkable "from man," not to forget finally the possibility of elucidating the relation of philosophy and theology and of establishing the scientific nature of theology, are all assured. [130]
If revelation in this context means a manifestation of God which precedes revelation in the more precise and proper sense, and which is posited with our creaturely existence as such, then an analysis of this creaturely existence, i.e., of God's manifestation in it as the "pre-understanding" of proper, special revelation, must really be the first step of theological reflection with which we leap into the circle of the understanding of God and the understanding of man from an outer and enclosing circle. In this case we cannot understand God,

namely, the God of proclaimed revelation, "without already (i.e., first) understanding man," namely, the man to whom God is originally manifest as his Creator. Primarily, i.e., in the leap into the inner circle, our thought must start out "from man," i.e., from this man who is bound to God by the fact that he is created. And this man, who in the outer circle of his creatureliness is already bound in this way to God, can really be regarded as the common theme or as it were the turntable between philosophy and theology, and anthropology can be used to elucidate the relation between these two sciences or to establish theology as a science. If the revelation from creation to which Gogarten refers means this, then I can at least see some sense in the "true anthropology" which he does not find in me but so obviously represents himself. But I fail to see what difference there is between this intrinsically coherent scheme and everyday natural theology. To analyse man in the light of a divine revelation from creation as the *introitus*[EN3] to the inner circle of true theology grounded in a *revelatio specialis*[EN3] has always been the nature and purpose of all natural theology. And this is the urgent twofold question which confronts me: After all that has been said, to what extent can one say that the nature and purpose of Gogarten's "true anthropology" is not identical with the nature and purpose of all natural theology? And: How can it be that Friedrich Gogarten of all men really wants to be understood in this way? How can this be reconciled with the sharp declarations which Gogarten has made against natural theology even and precisely in this context (p. 495 f.)? What are we to take seriously in Gogarten: his anthropological programme or his energetic renunciation of natural theology? Or how far are we to take both seriously? How is the one related to the other and *vice versa*? However that may be, I can only say that I am unable to supply what he misses in me because I fail to see how anything other than a new (or rather the old) natural theology can result therefrom. But natural theology in the sense described is an enterprise that is possible only in the realm of Roman Catholicism, since this presupposes that God's manifestation in our creatureliness, the creation of man which is also the revelation of God, is in some place and in some sense, e.g., as confirmed by the Gospel. directly discernible by us. This direct discernment of the original relation of God to man, the discernment of the creation of man which is also the revelation of God, has, however, been taken from us by the fall, at least according to Reformation ideas of the extent of sin, and it is restored to us only in the Gospel, in *revelatio specialis*. But this means that it is restored to us in such a way that, while we must certainly understand God's Word in revelation, Scripture and proclamation to be God's Word to man, to man as God's creature, we cannot view it in such a way that propositions may be taken from it which, isolated from the giving of God's Word in revelation, Scripture and proclamation, can be known as general truths by man, i.e., by the man who now understands himself as God's creature on the basis of the Word of God heard, so that they for their part can then be made—and this is the decisive point—the presupposition of an understanding of God's Word or the basis of theology. There is, of course, a theological anthropology, but this will consist neither in an explication and application of christological statements such as Gogarten had perhaps originally in view nor in an analysis that can now
[131] be made again of the created state of pre-fallen man, which is also God's revelation. It will consist simply in a depiction first of the original *status integritatis*[EN4] which is indicated in the Word of God itself and manifested in Jesus Christ and then of the *status corruptionis*[EN5] which now obtains. This depiction certainly cannot serve to explain how there are any possibilities of moving from man to God. Its content is rather the isolation of man from God, concerning

[EN3] introit
[EN4] special revelation
[EN5] state of innocence
[EN6] fallen state

which there is as little chance of reaching agreement with any philosopher as there is in relation to any other locus of dogmatics. It is thus quite impossible to use it in the way Gogarten does to introduce his "true anthropology." The circle between the understanding of God and man of which Gogarten speaks so impressively, the circle in which man's relationship to God is known, is thus in truth only a single circle, and it is a tightly closed circle. Gogarten, too, speaks of only one circle, and a tightly closed one at that. But it is not clear to me that it remains either. If it is only one, tightly closed circle, then it is impossible even in terms of the concept of creation to leap into it from without, i.e., to advance a common platform on which to agree with the philosopher, be it Grisebach or Heidegger, as to how far movement is possible at all in this circle even as seen from without. For we do not even know we are created merely from being created but only from the Word of God, from which we cannot deduce any independent, generally true insights that are different from God's Word and hence lead up to it. Knowledge in this circle is irreversible. Movement in it is not automatically from above to below and below to above. It cannot be replaced by the religio-psychological circle of Wobbermin. We cannot according to our own caprice try now to understand man on the basis of understanding God and now to understand God on the basis of understanding man. Even on the basis of understanding man in the light of God, understanding God is always a new thing in itself. Or rather it is an understanding grounded in God's Word and not in the preceding understanding of man. "From man" can only mean from man of the lost *status integritatis* and hence from man of the present *status corruptionis*. Thus to understand God from man is either an impossibility or something one can do only in the form of Christology and not of anthropology (not even a Christology translated into anthropology). There is a way from Christology to anthropology, but there is no way from anthropology to Christology. On the basis of all these considerations I must not only decline Gogarten's invitation to improve my dogmatics by introducing a true anthropology. I must also eliminate all that might seem to be a concession in that direction in my draft of five years ago.

In the first place it must no longer seem as if the doctrine of the Word of God is either based upon or subsequently supported by the fact that it is a result of existential thought. And then secondly there must not even be the appearance of an anthropology serving as the basis of the understanding of God's Word. §§ 5–6 of the first edition, which dealt with man as the preacher and hearer of God's Word, may be dropped out altogether, partly because its essential content is already anticipated by §§ 3–4 of the new edition, partly because it belongs to the question of the knowledge of the Word of God, and partly because its real home is in homiletics rather than dogmatics. The fact that God's Word is His Word to man, and the extent to which this is so, will be shown in our discussion of the epistemological question, i.e., the question as to the truth of God's Word. But the answer to the question: What is the Word of God?, the doctrine of its nature, must no longer seem to be governed by this enquiry. It must not arise in the proximity of a "true anthropology." It must be developed before this and independently.

We have spoken of the forms of the Word of God. Obviously form is always the form of a nature. But can one also speak of a nature of the Word of God? [132]
Can one answer the very natural and popular question, also found not infrequently on the lips of theologians: What is the Word of God? Confronted by this question as to the nature of the Word of God we find ourselves in the same difficulty as we shall be later on in dogmatics when we face the question of God's nature. God and His Word are not given to us in the same way as natural and historical entities. What God and His Word are, we can never establish by

looking back and therewith by anticipating. This is something God Himself must constantly tell us afresh. But there is no human knowing that corresponds to this divine telling. In this divine telling there is an encounter and fellowship between His nature and man but not an assuming of God's nature into man's knowing, only a fresh divine telling. In this divine telling knowledge of God and His Word is actualised with the God with us. Only thus, i.e., in faith in God's Word, can we say who God is: He is the one God, Father, Son and Holy Spirit. And only thus, i.e., having regard to the reality of the Church in whose sphere we think, can we say what God's Word is that we recollect and expect here, the one Word of God: proclamation, Scripture and revelation. But of course, as in faith we who know *who* God is we can and must say *how* He is, how there is on the basis of the doctrine of the Trinity a doctrine of attributes in which is manifested the nature of God that is hidden from us, that cannot be anticipated or repeated in any human word, that cannot be adequately rendered in any human word, so, as we know *what* God's Word is, namely, as we know its three forms, we can also say *how* it is, in what sequence of determinations it is this Word, God's Word, spoken to us in these three forms. Thus we can certainly say what God's Word is, but we must say it indirectly. We must remember the forms in which it is real for us and learn from these forms *how* it is. This How is the attainable human reflection of the unattainable divine What. Our concern here must be with this reflection.

2. THE WORD OF GOD AS THE SPEECH OF GOD

Church proclamation is talk, speech. So is Holy Scripture. So is even revelation in itself and as such. If we stay with God's Word in the three forms in which it is actually heard in the Church, if we do not go outside the Church and think of things God might have willed and done but has not done and so not willed in the Church, we have no reason not to take the concept of God's Word primarily in its literal sense. God's Word means that God speaks. Speaking is not a "symbol" (as P. Tillich, *Rel. Verwirkl.*, 1930, 48 thinks). It is not a designation and description which on the basis of his own assessment of its
[133] symbolic force man has chosen for something very different from and quite alien to this expression. For all its human inadequacy, for all the brokenness with which alone human statements can correspond to the nature of the Word of God, this statement does correspond to the possibility which God has chosen and actualised at all events in His Church. We are not absolutising the human possibilities of the intellect. We might well be of the opinion that it would have been finer and better if God had not spoken and did not speak with such "intellectualism," and that it would be more appropriate to God if God's Word meant all kinds of other things apart from the fact that God speaks. But is this private opinion of ours so important, resting as it does on a

philosophy? If perhaps not, then let us simply stick to the fact, and not try to think beyond it, that in this form in which the Church knows God's Word—the one and only form which necessarily, because imperiously, affects us—in this form God's Word means that "God speaks," and all else that is to be said about it must be regarded as exegesis and not as a restriction or negation of this statement. We shall have to regard God's speech as also God's act, and God's act as also God's mystery. But as only God's act is really God's mystery (and not any other mystery), so only God's speech is really God's act (and not any other act). Hence the concepts of act and mystery, exegetically necessary though they be, cannot point us away from the concept of speech. Being explanations, they can only point us back repeatedly to this as the original text. If they are true exegesis, then in their own way, of course, they say no less than everything, no less than the one and total thing, that has to be said here, like the original text itself. What the Word of God is can be said very well and without danger by the concepts of act and mystery too if our purpose in using them, unlike that of Faust who was merely seeking the proper symbol, is not to give a translation of Logos differing from that of speech but rather to explain the only possible translation in terms of the concept of speech. We shall first attempt without exegesis to understand the text itself in the only translation possible. What does it imply for the concept of the Word of God if the Word of God means originally and irrevocably that God speaks?

1. It implies first of all the spiritual nature of the Word of God as distinct from naturalness, corporeality, or any physical event. We hasten to add that there is no Word of God without a physical event. The fact that preaching and sacrament belong to it is also a reminder of this. So, too, is the letter of Holy Scripture. So finally and supremely is the corporeality of the man Jesus Christ. But all this does not justify us in saying that the Word of God is equally and in the same sense both spiritual and also natural or physical. There is here in all forms of the Word of God an upper and lower aspect, a first and second, which in all its relativity is not to be effaced or reversed. The Word of God is also [134]
natural and physical because without this it would not be the Word of God that is directed to us men as spiritual-natural beings, really to us as we really are. This is why the sacrament must stand alongside preaching. This is why preaching itself is also a physical event. This is why the letter of Scripture is the very reverse of a *pudendum* or *negligendum*[EN7]. This is why the Church (though its relation of subordination is clearly shown therein) is called the body of Christ. The Word of God is also natural and physical because in the creaturely realm in which it comes to us men as Word there is nothing spiritual that is not also natural and physical. Nevertheless, the fact that the Word of God binds itself not only to the spirituality but also to the corporeality of the creature should not prevent us from seeing that it is in no sense neutrally above or in both, and that above all it is not primarily or pre-eminently nature.

[EN7] ground for shame or indifference

At this point we should not let ourselves be disconcerted by the current wave of realism and antispiritualism. Reference is often made to the statement of F. C. Oetinger that corporeality is the end of all the ways of God. This was a sound if exaggerated expression of very necessary opposition to the flight of the Enlightenment spirit from nature, but it is not really suited for conversion into a dogma. And if Erich Przywara (*Stimmen der Zeit*, 1929, 231 f.) once levelled against me the criticism that I have a notable penchant for the two terms Word and Spirit, that I betray therewith a concealed spiritualism, and hence the ultimate immanence of what is supposed to be my very transcendent concept of God, whereas God is not bound to one realm of creation more than the other but is free in relation to both, the question arises whether, without prejudice to His freedom, God has not within creation bound Himself to spirit differently and more fully and closely than He has to nature; whether the uniform anthropology of the Bible, which is really not to be changed, does not teach that man is to be considered first and especially with reference to the invisible quality of life breathed into him by God; whether it is a mere accident that speaking about God is commanded hundreds of times in the Bible but setting up images of God is forbidden and barred *expressis verbis*[EN8]; whether it is just accidental that the terms Word and Spirit play this special role even in relation to God in both the Old and New Testament; whether words from the other sphere of creation might be used just as well as *Logos*[EN9] and *Pneuma*[EN10] in the doctrine of the Trinity. It is an excellent thing that we are ready to hear again, as most of those immediately before us were not, what the New Testament has to say about the bodily resurrection of Christ and also about the resurrection of our own bodies. It is an excellent thing that we are being reminded again of a long neglected New Testament truth by the favourite doctrine of Eastern orthodoxy, namely, that eschatological redemption includes within it in the most comprehensive sense the cosmos, the creature, as well. But it would not be a good thing to try to overlook the fact that in the Old and New Testaments, while man is certainly addressed as a natural being, he is addressed as this particular natural being, the natural being characterised by spirit, or, as we might simply say, that he is *addressed*, that address and not a natural event, or address even in a natural event, is the way in which God visits him. A certain relative "canonisation of spirit against nature" (Przywara)—more ought not to be asserted—we surely find it impossible not to assert for all our recognition of the realistic concern.

[135] The Word of God is primarily spiritual and then, in this form, in this spirituality, for the sake of it and without prejudice to it, it is also a physical and natural event. This particularly is what is meant when in accordance with the three forms in which we hear this Word we call it the speech of God. Speech, including God's speech, is the form in which reason communicates with reason and person with person. To be sure it is the divine reason communicating with the human reason and the divine person with the human person. The utter inconceivability of this event is obvious. But reason with reason, person with person, is primarily analogous to what happens in the spiritual realm of creation, not the natural and physical realm. The Word of God—and at this point we should not evade a term so much tabooed to-day—is a rational and not an irrational event.

The reminder of supposedly "deeper" layers of anthropological being beyond the rational

EN 8 explicitly
EN 9 Word
EN10 Spirit

rests on a philosophical construction and a philosophcal value-judgment on which philosophers themselves must find agreement. Our only comment on this is that according to what we know of it in the Church the encounter of God and man takes place primarily, pre-eminently and characteristically in this sphere of *ratio*, no matter how "deep" or less "deep" this may be by philosophical evaluation. " ... the king of whom the psalm speaketh here, although of course He hath His kingdom on earth, yet so ruleth the spiritual world and pointeth to the heavenly that, though we see not His kingdom as a wordly realm, nevertheless we hear it. But how? 'Out of the mouths of babes and sucklings thou hast ordained strength.' And Christ's kingdom is a kingdom of hearing, not a kingdom of seeing. For the eyes lead and guide us not thither where we find Christ and get to know Him, but the ears must do this ..." (Luther, *Sermon delivered in Merseburg*, 1545, *W.A.* 51, 11, 25). "As when thou seest and hearest a preacher preach the Word of God by which at Christ's command he proclaimeth repentance and remission of sins, thou seest there no plough or barrow but seest and hearest that the preacher taketh up only the tongue and the word .... Hence also when we see the holy sacraments extend ... deliverance and liberation from sins and death, that thou shouldest no longer be holden fast in the devil's kingdom, thou seest not but only hearest what is announced and granted to thee with the tongue of the preacher by the word" (*ib.*, 12, 9).

Speaking stands in correlation to hearing, understanding and obeying. Whatever problems may arise with regard to these terms through the fact that our concern here is with God's speaking, and hence with the hearing, understanding and obeying correlative to this speaking—it is faith that hears, understands and obeys God's speech—we must certainly not leave the level of these concepts of speaking, hearing, understanding and obeying if we are not to set ourselves at some other place than where God's Word is heard.

Whatever "the holy" of Rudolf Otto may be, it certainly cannot be understood as the Word of God, for it is the numinous, and the numinous is the irrational, and the irrational can no longer be differentiated from an absolutised natural force. But everything depends on this differentiation if we are to understand the concept of the Word of God.

The Word of God has natural force too. But primarily and pre-eminently [136] and decisively it has the simple spiritual power of truth. What we are saying here about God's Word does not apply equally to every word. Of no other word can it be said that this word has decisively the power of truth. For every other word *physis*[EN11] means a limit at which the impotence of its spirituality is also unmasked. Every other word lacks either truth or reality or both. Typical of every other word is a uncertain oscillation between a spasmodic idealism and an equally spasmodic realism. The naturalness and spirituality of every other word are those of fallen man. Only in God's Word do we find the normal order of the natural and the spiritual. But in God's Word we do find it, and we should not allow the aberrations of human spirituality in its flight from nature to lead us into an attempt to level up or even reverse the order. In theological and ministerial utterance we have to be clear, then, what it means to employ naturalistic terms. In view of the language of the Bible itself we cannot lay an

[EN11] nature

absolute embargo on talking about life, light, fire, source, river, or storm, about irruptions, shatterings, overpowerings and experiences. But one must remember in so doing that in the Bible, to be precise, all this takes place within that definite order, so that in naturalistic speech the Word of God is not denoted in its primary sense, and while it certainly is also what is said, it certainly is not this in the first instance. One has thus to remember how easily there is here in either hearer or speaker a slipping into the natural sphere where it is no longer a matter of speech and answer, of perception and decision, but only of movement, pressure and impact, where it is no longer a matter of truth but only of reality. To be sure, this is always a concern too, and for this reason naturalism is not to be banished even from theological utterance. But this is not the first or proper concern in the Word of God. The moment, then, it becomes the only thing that matters in what we say, then by human judgment, by what we know about the Word of God through the Word of God itself, there can be no service of God in theology or proclamation. Awareness of the fact that the Word of God is primarily spiritual is an admonition to concentrate on the spiritual sphere and to beware of straying into the natural sphere.

2. God's Word means that God speaks. This implies secondly its personal quality. God's Word is not a thing to be described nor a term to be defined. It is neither a matter nor an idea. It is not "a truth," not even the very highest truth. It is *the* truth as it is God's speaking person, *Dei loquentis persona.* It is not an objective reality. It is *the* objective reality, in that it is also subjective, the subjective that is God. God's Word means the speaking God. Certainly God's Word is not just the formal possibility of divine speech. It is the fulfilled reality. It always
[137] has a very specific objective content. God always speaks a *concretissimum*[EN12]. But this divine *concretissimum* cannot as such be either anticipated or repeated. What God speaks is never known or true anywhere in abstraction from God Himself. It is known and true in and through the fact that He Himself says it, that He is present in person in and with what is said by Him.

Non satis est habere donum, nisi sit et donator presens, sicut petivit et Moses exo. 33: "*Si non tu ipse precedas nos, ne educas nos de loco ipso*[EN13]" etc. (Luther, *Romans*, 1515–1516, *Fi. Schol.* 140, 15). *A Deo enim vivo disceditur dum a verbo eius disceditur, quod est vivum et omnia vivificans, imo Deus ipse*[EN14] (*Hebrews*, 1513, *Fi. Schol.* 42, 2). According to another saying of Luther Christ's Word is Christ's mouth: "That it ever proceedeth out of Christ's mouth from one mouth to another, and yet remaineth Christ's mouth" (*Sermon on John* 14[23f.] *Cruc. Sommerpostille*, 1543, *W.A.* 21, 469, 3).

The underlying and basic third form of the Word of God, which we have tried to pin down in the concept of revelation, is what has forced us constantly to keep this proviso in mind in our analysis of the concepts of proclamation

---

[EN12] something utterly concrete

[EN13] It is not enough to have the gift, if the giver is not also present, as Moses prayed in Exodus 33: "If your presence will not got with me, do not carry us up from here"

[EN14] For one departs from the living God when one departs from his Word, which is living and the source of all life, truly God Himself

and Scripture. Understanding the Word of God not as proclamation and Scripture alone but as God's revelation in proclamation and Scripture, we must understand it in its identity with God Himself. God's revelation is Jesus Christ, the Son of God.

In the vocabulary of Trinitarian doctrine God's Son cannot be differentiated from God's Word. If Jn. $1^{1f.}$ reads: *Ἐν ἀρχῇ ἦν ὁ λόγος, καὶ ὁ λόγος ἦν πρὸς τὸν θεὸν, καὶ θεὸς ἦν ὁ λόγος. οὗτος ἦν ἐν ἀρχῇ πρὸς τὸν θεόν*[EN15], the fourth statement is only a meaningless repetition of the second unless the *οὗτος*[EN16], though to be filled out in the first instance by *λόγος*[EN17], does not also in this emphatic use point forward beyond what immediately follows to the proper name mentioned for the first time only in v. 18, namely, *Ἰησοῦς Χριστός*[EN18], with whose bearer the Logos in the prologue of this Gospel is to be regarded as identical. And in Rev. 19^{12-13} the returning Christ, the rider on the white horse, is described as the wearer of a tiara *ἔχων ὄνομα γεγραμμένον ὃ οὐδεὶς οἶδεν εἰ μὴ αὐτός*[EN19], i.e., whose wording is obviously known to anyone who sees it but whose meaning—the being to which the name points—is known only to Himself. *Καὶ κέκληται τὸ ὄνομα αὐτοῦ* (the wording of this name): *ὁ λόγος τοῦ θεοῦ*[EN20]. Here again, then, what the Word of God is cannot be stated directly. It is the name of revelation, i.e., of the Revealer. He is the Word of God. From Him alone it may and will be experienced what the Word of God is. Of ourselves we can only say how it is, i.e., how He is.

The equation of God's Word and God's Son makes it radically impossible to say anything doctrinaire in understanding the Word of God. In this equation, and in it alone, a real and effective barrier is set up against what is made of proclamation according to the Roman Catholic view and of Holy Scripture according to the later form of older Protestantism, namely, a fixed sum of revealed propositions which can be systematised like the sections of a corpus of law. The only system in Holy Scripture and proclamation is revelation, i.e., Jesus Christ. Now the converse is also true, of course, namely that God's Son is God's Word. Thus God does reveal Himself in statements, through the
medium of speech, and indeed of human speech. His word is always this or [138]
that word spoken by the prophets and apostles and proclaimed in the Church. The personal character of God's Word is not, then, to be played off against its verbal or spiritual character. It is not at all true that this second aspect under which we must understand it implies its irrationality and thus cancels out the first aspect under which we must understand it.

This is obviously the view of P. Tillich, in whom we find the following rather naive polemic: "But it is quite wrong to equate the Word as a symbol for the self-impartation of beyond being with the word as a physical medium of self-understanding and self-impartation on the part of the human spirit, and in this way to confound God's Word and the word of Scripture or the word of preaching. In reply to this one may simply (!) point out that for Christian

---

EN15 In the beginning was the Word, and the Word was with God, and the Word was God. The same was in the beginning with God

EN16 the same

EN17 Word

EN18 Jesus Christ

EN19 he has a name inscribed which no one knows but himself

EN20 the Word of God

theology Jesus Christ is the Word, not His words but His being, which finds expression equally in His words and also in His action and passion" (*Rel. Verwirkl.*, 1930, 49). On this one may comment that the words, action and passion of Jesus Christ and His being certainly cannot be separated from one another in such a way that the words, action and passion are only an expression of His being, as though His being stood behind the words, action and passion. The being of this person is identical with His speech, action and passion. But this being of Jesus Christ is not directly present to us. It must be present to us and can be present to us only indirectly, namely, through the proclaiming of the Word first by Holy Scripture and then also by the Church. If the being of Jesus Christ is present to us, this occurs altogether in such a way that it is equated with the word as a physical medium of self-understanding and self-impartation on the part of the human spirit, the word of Scripture and the word of preaching becoming the Word of God. "For where My Word is, there also am I" (Luther, *Sermon on Mt.* 22, 1544, *W.A.* 52, 509, 26) " ... God could not otherwise send forth Christ into the world, He had to fashion Him into the Word and so spread Him abroad and bear Him to every man. Otherwise Christ would have remained for Himself alone and unknown to us, and thus He would have died for Himself alone. But because the Word beareth Christ to us, so it beareth us to Him who hath overcome death, sin and the devil" (*Sermon on Jn.* 8^{46-59}, 1525, *W.A.* 17^{11}, 234, 11).

The personalising of the concept of the Word of God, which we cannot avoid when we remember that Jesus Christ is the Word of God, does not mean its deverbalising. But it (naturally) means awareness of the fact that it is person rather than thing or object even if and in so far as it is word, word of Scripture and word of preaching. To be person means to be subject, not merely in the logical sense, but also in the ethical sense: to be free subject, a subject which is free even in respect of the specific limitations connected with its individuality, able to control its own existence and nature both as particular form and also as living development, and also able to select new possibilities of existence and nature. If we consider what this implies, it will not occur to us to see in this personalising of the concept of God's Word a case of anthropomorphism. The doubtful thing is not whether God is person, but whether we are. Can we find
[139] among us even one man whom we can call this in the full and proper sense of the term? But God is real person, really free subject. And if it is true that this brings us up against His inconceivability, because we cannot think through this thought to a finish, it is also true that on hearing His Word we should not refuse to think this initial thought, to see Him as person precisely in His Word. What we are saying is that not just anything, not a *θεῖον*[EN21], but He Himself comes to us in His Word. Precisely in His Word God is person. But this then means concretely that He is Lord of the wording of His Word. He is not bound to it but it to Him. He has free control over the wording of Holy Scripture. He can use it or not use it. He can use it in this way or in that way. He can choose a new wording beyond that of Holy Scripture. What Holy Scripture proclaims as His Word can be proclaimed in a new wording as His Word so long as it is He Himself who speaks in this wording. Furthermore, the personal character of God's Word means, not its deverbalising, but the posing of an absolute barrier

[EN21] something divine

against reducing its wording to a human system or using its wording to establish and construct a human system. It would not be God's faithfulness but His unfaithfulness to us if He allowed us to use His Word in this way. This would mean His allowing us to gain control over His Word, to fit it in with our own designs, and thus to shut up ourselves against Him to our own ruin. God's faithfulness to His Church consists in His availing Himself of His freedom to come to us Himself in His Word and in His reserving to Himself the freedom to do this again and again.

3. God's Word means that God speaks. But this implies thirdly what one might call the purposive character of the Word of God. This might also be called its relatedness or pertinence, its character as address. In its form neither as proclamation, Holy Scripture, nor revelation do we know God's Word as an entity that exists or could exist merely in and for itself. We know it only as a Word that is directed to us and applies to us. The fact that it is this is not, of course, self-evident. It is not something one might deduce from a general concept of speech. It is so in fact, but it might not be. In the intertrinitarian life of God the eternal generation of the Son or Logos is, of course, the expression of God's love, of His will not to be alone. But it does not follow from this that God could not be God without speaking to us. We undoubtedly understand God's love for man, or in the first instance for any reality distinct from Himself, only when we understand it as free and unmerited love not resting on any need. God would be no less God if He had created no world and no man. The existence of the world and our own existence are in no sense vital to God, not even as the object of His love. The eternal generation of the Son by the Father tells us first and supremely that God is not at all lonely even without the world and us. His love has its object in Himself. And so one cannot say that our existence [140]
as that of the recipients of God's Word is constitutive for the concept of the Word. It could be no less what it is even without us. God could satisfy His love in Himself. For He is already an object to Himself and He is an object truly worthy of His love. God did not need to speak to us. What He says by Himself and to Himself from eternity to eternity would really be said just as well and even better without our being there, as speech which for us would be eternal silence. Only when we are clear about this can we estimate what it means that God has actually, though not necessarily, created a world and us, that His love actually, though not necessarily, applies to us, that His Word has actually, though not necessarily, been spoken to us. The purposiveness we find in proclamation, the Bible and revelation is thus a free and actual purposiveness by no means essential to God Himself. We evaluate this purposiveness correctly only if we understand it as the reality of the love of the God who does not need us but who does not will to be without us, who has directed His regard specifically on us.

In this connexion it is appropriate and necessary for once to consider not what God has actually done but what He might have done, since it is only in this antithesis that we can really understand what He has done. In this light one can also see how dubious it is to set the doctrine of the Word of God in the framework of an anthropology. In that case the freedom of the divine purpose for man can be asserted only at a later stage, while it is really denied by the starting-point.

Hearing man, as the object of the purpose of the speaking God, is thus included in the concept of the Word of God as a factual necessity, but he is not essential to it. He is not, as I most astonishingly stated on p. 111 of the first edition, "co-posited" in it in the way Schleiermacher's God is in the feeling of absolute dependence. If he is co-posited in it with factual necessity, this is God's free grace. If we think that in this sense we must see in purposiveness or relation to us a third quality of the Word of God, and if we go on to investigate the content of this purpose, the implication of this relatedness or pertinence of God's Word for its understanding, we must remember that wherever and whenever God speaks to man its content is a *concretissimum*[EN22]. God always has something specific to say to each man, something that applies to him and to him alone. The real content of God's speech or the real will of the speaking person of God is not in any sense, then, to be construed and reproduced by us as a general truth. As readers of Scripture and hearers of proclamation we can and must, of course, work with certain general conceptual materials, apparently repeating or anticipating what God has said to this or that man or will say to this or that man. There is obviously no other way in which we can remind
[141] ourselves or others of the Word of God that came then and will one day come again. We may do this in words of our own coining or in Scripture quotations. But in so doing we have always to bear in mind that these materials are our own work and are not to be confused with the concrete fulness of the Word of God itself which we recall and for which we wait, but only point to it. What God said and what God will say is always quite different from what we can and must say to ourselves and others about its content. Not only the word of preaching heard as God's Word but even the word of Scripture through which God speaks to us becomes in fact quite different when it passes from God's lips to our ears and our lips. It becomes the Word of God recollected and expected by us in faith, and the Word which was spoken and will be spoken again by God stands over against it afresh in strict sovereignty. But even in this strict sovereignty in which its true content remains inconceivable to us, it retains its purposiveness, it is the Word that comes to us, that is aimed at us, and as such it is a definite Word determined not by us but by God Himself as the One who aims it at us. We are not anticipating its actual content but simply noting the aspects under which we shall have to consider its actual content if we make the following points in relation to its purposiveness, in relation to the fact that it is an address to us.

(1) First, the Word of God as directed to us is a Word which we do not say to ourselves and which we could not in any circumstances say to ourselves. Every human word, including that of proclamation and even the Bible, we could and

[EN22] something utterly concrete

can perhaps say to ourselves as such. Encounter with the human word as such is never genuine, irrevocable encounter, nor can it be. Encounter with the Word of God is genuine, irrevocable encounter, i.e., encounter that can never be dissolved in union. The Word of God always tells us something fresh that we had never heard before from anyone. The rock of a Thou which never becomes an I is thrown in our path here. This otherness which is yet related to us and made known to us, though only in this way, stamps it fundamentally and comprehensively as the Word of God, the Word of the Lord, compared to which all other words, however profound or new or arresting, are not words of the Lord. Whatever God may say to us will at all events be said in this way; it will be said as the Word of the Lord.

(2) Secondly, the Word of God as this Word of the Lord directed to us is the Word which aims at us and smites us in our existence. No human word has the competence to aim at us in our existence and no human word has the power to smite us in our existence. The only word that may aim at us in our existence and can smite us in our existence is one which questions and answers us in just the same way as death might question and answer us at the end of our existence. But death is dumb. It neither questions nor answers. It is only the end. It is not really a thing outside and above our existence which can aim at our [142] existence and smite it. The Word of God is the Word of the Lord because it comes from the point outside and above us from which death itself would not speak to us even if it could speak at all. The Word of God applies to us as no human word as such can do, and as death does not do, because this Word is the Word of our Creator, of the One who encompasses our existence and the end of our existence, by whom it is affirmed and negated, because everything has come into being and is preserved by this Word, and without it would not exist. He who makes Himself heard here is the One to whom we belong. Whatever He may say, it will be said in this relation of the Creator to His creature.

(3) Thirdly, the Word of God as the Word of the Creator directed to us is the Word which has obviously become necessary and is necessary as a renewal of the original relation between us and Him. The fact that God speaks to us, that He reveals Himself to us, i.e., that He turns to us in a wholly new way, that as the Unknown He makes Himself known—even after creating us and although we belong to Him—all this implies on the one side a criticism of the reality of the present relation between Him and us and on the other side a declaration on His part to uphold and re-establish the relation in and spite of this criticism of His. Neither of these could be the content of a human word. Only the One who has instituted the relation can confirm and renew it when it is disrupted or destroyed. Only God can pronounce the verdict and give the promise and raise the claim which all lie equally in the concept of revelation. Under this third aspect of its purposiveness the Word of God is the Word of reconciliation, i.e., the Word of the Reconciler, of the God who effects a new creation, who sets up His covenant with us afresh in judgment and grace. Whatever God may say to us, it will at all events be said in this relationship of renewal.

(4) Fourthly and finally the Word of God as the Word of reconciliation directed to us is the Word by which God announces Himself to man, i.e., by which He promises Himself as the content of man's future, as the One who meets him on his way through time as the end of all time, as the hidden Lord of all times. His presence by the Word is His presence as the coming One, coming for the fulfilment and consummation of the relation established between Him and us in creation and renewed and confirmed in reconciliation. Again this final Word cannot be a word of man. Human words are never final words. They are never the promise of a specific and definitive coming of the Other. It is proper to God's Word and to God's Word alone to be also the full and authentic presence of the Speaker even if this be as the coming One. God's Word is the Word of our Redeemer, i.e., of the Lord who will be Lord as He was and is, who in His relation to us keeps faith both with Himself and us. In this way He is
[143] Lord indeed, the Lord of all lords. And whatever God may say to us, it will at all events be said always in this final, consummating, eschatological relation too.

Again, what God says to us specifically remains His secret which will be disclosed in the event of His actual speaking. The concrete fulness of what He has said and will say specifically to men is and remains in truth His own business. We can only cling to the fact—but we must cling to it—that when He spoke it was, and when He will speak it will be, the Word of the Lord, the Word of our Creator, our Reconciler, our Redeemer. Understanding it as directed and applying to us, we are well advised to keep what we think and say about it open in at least these four directions, to be ready and vigilant from these four standpoints.

3. THE SPEECH OF GOD AS THE ACT OF GOD

When God speaks, there is no point in looking about for a related act. The fear that talk might be "only" talk is, of course, only too apposite in relation to human speech. When man speaks, then his misery, the rift between truth and reality in which he lives, is plainly exposed, and the more so the better and more beautifully and truly he speaks. When man speaks, he involuntarily tries to protect himself against being unmasked in this way, perhaps by making it known through tone and gesture that he is not just talking but engaged in action too, perhaps in content by speaking as practically as possible, i.e., by talking as much as he can about his own deeds or those of others, whether past or future. The fear that he is just talking, the question of the related act, will arise all the same and will undoubtedly apply to him in some respect. When God speaks, however, the fear is groundless. The man who has heard God speak and might still ask about the related act is simply showing that he has not really heard God speak. We can hear Christian sermons and ask what really happens as they take place. What does actually correspond to all these words?

This is a question well worth putting. We can even hear Holy Scripture and simply hear words, human words, which we either understand or do not understand but along with which there is for us no corresponding event. But if so, then neither in proclamation nor Holy Scripture has it been the Word of God that we have heard. If it had been the Word of God, not for a moment could we have looked about for God's acts. The Word of God itself would then have been the act. The Word of God does not need to be supplemented by an act. The Word of God is itself the act of God. It is act to a degree that everything else that we usually call act, event, practice, life, etc., and that we usually miss and demand as a supplement to man's word, can only seem to be very questionable as real act in comparison with it. The Word of God makes history [144]
in the supreme sense.

"For he spake, and it was done; he commanded, and it stood fast," Ps. 33⁹. When God's Word comes to the prophets of the Old Testament, this is denoted by the verb *hayah* (happen), cf. Jer. 1. We may recall all the direct connexions between Word and creation, Word and calling, Word and remission of sins, Word and miracle, Word and blessing, Word and punishment, etc., in both the Old Testament and the New. But even when the connexion is indirect, e.g., when the prophets speak of future events or the apostles speak in retrospect of the acts of Jesus, these are not just references to remote events but an immediate introduction, through the Word, of things understood to have happened already or to be still happening. "Look at the creation of all creatures. 'In the beginning God created heaven and earth.' How? By His Word, as Moses writeth: 'God said, Let there be light, and there was light.' 'God said, Let there be a firmament between the waters' etc., 'and it was so'; 'God said, Let the waters under the heaven be gathered into places apart, that dry land may appear, and it was so.' The speaking doth it. When this Speaker saith something that He will have, it must be so. So then of naught, solely by His speaking, God hath created heaven and earth and all creatures. How then should He not be able by His Word and sacrament to do what He willeth, especially as His Word standeth fast and beareth witness thereto?" (Luther, *Sermon on the Sunday Cantate on 1 Cor.* 15 1544, *W.A.* 49, 405, 33). "And so ... we should hold His Word glorious and lofty as an almighty power. For whoso hath it hath all and can do all. Again, whoso hath it not, him naught else can or shall guard against sin, death and devil. For what our dear Lord Christ doth here with the nobleman's son, saving him from death by His almighty word and keeping him alive, that will He do for us all by His Word if we will but accept it ..." (*Sermon on Jn.* 4^{47-59}, *W.A.* 52, 515, 4). "'Tis for Christ but the matter of a little word, and it is forthwith yea. And so God ruleth His Christian Church, yea He so ruleth the whole world, that for Him 'tis no heavy task, but He effecteth all by a word. Thus should we learn to hold God's Word in honour and to believe the same. The same Word we have in the preaching of the Gospel, in baptism, in the sacrament, in absolution .... If we believe the Word it will happen to us as it happened to this nobleman, namely, that we obtain what is promised us in the Word" (*Sermon on Jn.* $4^{47, 54}$, 1534, *E.A.* 5, 215).

The distinction between word and act is that mere word is the mere self-expression of a person, while act is the resultant relative alteration in the world around. Mere word is passive, act is an active participation in history. But this kind of distinction does not apply to the Word of God. As mere Word it is act. As mere Word it is the divine person, the person of the Lord of history, whose self-expression is as such an alteration, and indeed an absolute alteration of the world, whose *passio*[EN23] in history is as such *actio*[EN24]. What God does when He speaks, in exactly the same way as what He says, cannot, of course, be generally defined either by way of anticipation or by that of reproduction. We can refer only to the *concretissima*[EN25] of the acts which are attested in the Bible and which are also to be expected from God in the future.

It always was and always will be the special thing ὅσα ἡτοίμασεν ὁ θεὸς τοῖς ἀγαπῶσιν αὐτόν[EN26] (1 Cor. 2^9).

[145] What we can and should consider is what it implies that God's speaking, and therefore the Word of God in all its forms, is in fact the act of God.

1. The fact that God's Word is God's act means first its contingent contemporaneity. What is meant by this is as follows. The time of the direct, original speech of God Himself in His revelation, the time of Jesus Christ (which was also and already that of Abraham according to Jn. 8^{56}), the time of that which the prophets and apostles heard so that they could bear witness to it—that is one time. But the time of this witness, the time of prophecy and the apostolate, the time of Peter on whom Christ builds His Church, the time of the rise of the Canon as a concrete counterpart in which the Church receives its norm for all times—this is another time. And the specific time of the Church itself, the time of derivative proclamation related to the words of the prophets and apostles and regulated by them—this is yet another time. These are different times distinguished not only by the difference in periods and contents, not only by the remoteness of centuries and the disparity in the men of different centuries and millennia, but distinguished by the different attitude of God to men. Jesus Christ was no less true man than the prophets and apostles. But in virtue of His unity with God He stood absolutely over against them as a master over against his slaves. As men, even religious men, the biblical witnesses were not singled out in principle from later Church teachers or from us or even from the teachers and leaders of other religions. Yet in their office as witnesses they were and are in an absolutely once-for-all and unique position compared to all the rest of us. Again, even though our human existence may be closely compared in principle with that of Christ and the apostles, yet in virtue of our relation to Scripture, and through Scripture to revelation, and also through the intervening experience of the Church in which we have an advantage over the prophets and apostles, or which does at least distinguish us from them, our own situation in the Church is a third and very distinctive situation. It is this difference of order, of first and second, of higher and lower, that makes the times of the Word of God so different. Three times there is a saying of the Word of God through human lips. But only twice, in the biblical witnesses and us, is there first a letting of it be said to us, and only once, in our case, an indirect letting of

---

EN23 passive (or passive experience)
EN24 action
EN25 utter concreteness
EN26 that God has prepared for those who love him

it be said to us mediated through the Bible. The different position in God's order differentiates these three times as human times are not differentiated elsewhere, as they are differentiated only here, as only the times of God's Word are differentiated. One can, of course, dissolve the difference in time by ignoring the differentiation of the times in God's order, by viewing and presenting them, not as times of God's Word but only immanently, i.e., by taking into account only the difference of the periods and their human contents as such. [146] Estimating the difference along these lines need then be no obstacle to a direct insight into the continuity and unity of the times, to an insight into our contemporaneity with Christ and all His saints. Indeed, it rather facilitates and establishes this insight by teaching us to see and understand the man of the past, be he Jeremiah or Jesus or Paul, or Luther, as a fellow-man, to criticise him as such, but also to respect and love him, in short, to treat him as companion of one and the same time.

This is the way that recent Protestant theology, after overcoming the great crisis of the non-historical thinking of the Enlightenment, has now taken in all its typical representatives. The revelation of God in history is something they think they have discovered afresh and for the first time properly in emancipation from the rigid antitheses of the older Church and theology. So far as I can see and understand the matter, the epoch-making name in this regard is that of Lessing. The "ugly, wide ditch" (between the Bible and us), of which he said in a well-known passage (*Der Beweis des Geistes und der Kraft, Theol. Schr.*, ed. Gross, II, 2, 13) that for all his good intentions he could not jump across it, was not, and for the author of the *Laokoon* could not be, the general problem of a historical understanding that leaps over the gap of the centuries and their different forms of human life. Lessing could make this jump. So could Herder and Schleiermacher after him, and others up to A. Ritschl and Harnack, Lagarde and Troeltsch, always with increased excellence and skill. Similarly we should not trivialise Lessing's other famous dictum that "the accidental truths of history can never be proof of the necessary truths of reason" (*op. cit.*, p. 12), as though the truth of history were simply the specific concrete empirical truth of a historical datum as such and the truth of reason were the timeless truth of mathematical and philosophical axioms. The religious philosophy of Kant still moves within this antithesis of the singular and the general, the empirical and the rational. But this is not true of Lessing, who is the more modern in this regard. Lessing is well acquainted with a proof of Christianity through history. But it must be "the proof of spirit and of power." That is, history does not prove any truth for us so long as it is the "contingent truth of history" merely reported to us by others and not truth "felt" and "experienced" by ourselves. It becomes the "necessary truth of reason," i.e., truth that is necessary and real for us, when and to the extent that it is thus felt and experienced by us, experienced in the way "the paralytic experiences the beneficent shock of the electric spark." ("Religion is not true because the evangelists and apostles taught it; they taught it because it is true. By its inner truth, scriptural traditions must be explained, and all the traditions in the world cannot give it inner truth if it does not have it," *Fragm. eines Ungen., op. cit.*, II, 1, 261; *Axiomata, op. cit.*, II, 2, 122; according to K. Aner, *Die Theologie der Lessingzeit*, 1929, 148 f., the apologetic use of experience may be found already in the sermons of Abbot J. F. W. Jerusalem from 1745.) And Lessing obviously regards this inner truth as something quite accessible to us and apprehensible by us. We can judge its presence in virtue of our own feeling and experience. This is why he appeals from Luther's writings to Luther's spirit (*Anti-Göze, op. cit.*, II, 2, 140), from the letter of the Bible to the spirit of the Bible (*Axiomata,*

op. cit., II, 2, p. 112), from the reported miracles to the "ever continuing miracle of religion itself" (*Eine Duplik, op. cit.*, II, 2, 33), and finally from the Christian religion to the religion of Christ (*Die Rel. Christi, op. cit.*, II, 3. 448 f.). "No one in Hamburg will ever again wish to
[147] dispute with me the utter difference between gross and net" (*Axiomata, op. cit.*, II, 2, 108). "Historical words are the vehicle of the prophetic word" (*op. cit.*, p. 112). This was Lessing's obstacle, and this was the way he overcame the obstacle. His problem was the lack of contemporaneity between Christ, the apostles, and us. This lack was one of order, and, as he rightly saw, it could not be overcome. He thus abandoned it for an immanent lack of contemporaneity that could be overcome by way of immanence. From now on all the more lively thinkers, in contrast to the Enlightenment and Kant, found no further difficulty or stumbling block in interpreting revelation as history and history as revelation.

But if we abandon the distinction of the three times in terms of order, then no matter how loudly or sincerely we may talk about revelation and its concreteness and historicity, and no matter how illuminating or practical may be the shape we give everything, we have really abandoned the concept of the Word of God itself. When we are able to eliminate our non-contemporaneity with Christ and the apostles by putting ourselves on the same soil as them or putting them on the same soil as us, so that, sharing the same prophetic Spirit and having the measure of inner truth in our own feeling, we can discuss with them the gross and net value of their words; when contemporaneity, therefore, rests on the hypothesis of a merely quantitative difference between them and us, then the concept of the Word of God is humanised in such a way that it is no wonder people prefer to use it comparatively rarely and in quotation marks; the surprising thing is that they have not preferred to drop it completely and unequivocally. Distinctions immanent in history, no matter how seriously they are taken as such, cannot justify a serious use of the concept of God's Word. For fundamentally the appreciation of these distinctions does not mean that we let something be said to us. There can be no serious saying of the Word of God in the realm of these distinctions. Within these distinctions there is only a togetherness with Christ and the apostles. For all our respect for the greatness and vitality of history, it is we the living who have right on our side and who thus finally fix and manipulate the norm and the conditions of this togetherness. The present Church, however historically it may feel and think, speaks the last word as the heir and interpreter of history. Not having God's Word in the serious sense of the term, it stands alone and is referred back to itself. If, however, we insist that the concept of God's Word means that the Church is not alone and is not referred back to itself, then we must accept the fact that the distinction of the times is one of order, and in no case can the contemporaneity of modern proclamation with Scripture and revelation be understood as one that we can bring about by eliminating the distinction, by incorporating Scripture and revelation into the life of humanity. It can be understood only as an expression of the fact that God's Word is itself God's act. It thus has nothing directly to do with the general problem of historical under-
[148] standing. Of course there is always some historical understanding when the Word of God is manifest to us in its contemporaneity. But this historical under-

standing as such does not mean hearing and does not establish proclamation of God's Word. When God's Word is heard and proclaimed, something takes place that for all our hermeneutical skill cannot be brought about by hermeneutical skill.

The biblical witnesses had also a specific relation of historical understanding to Jesus Christ (*ἐγνώκαμεν κατὰ σάρκα Χριστόν*[EN27], 2 Cor. 5[16]). But in this relation it did not come about through the immanent power of this relation that they saw in Jesus Christ the Son of God.

They did not do so, then, by the power of Lessing's feeling and experiencing: *σάρξ καὶ αἷμα οὐκ ἀπεκάλυψέν σοι*[EN28] (Mt. 16[17]). Those who receive the light that has come into the world, those who see the kingdom of God, do not do so in virtue of their earthly birth (Jn. 1[13]; 3[3f.]). The Father has hidden the secret of the Son from the wise and prudent, i.e., from the judgment of an inner truth already known to man (Mt. 11[25]).

In the Old and New Testaments this recognition is rather traced back to election, revelation, calling, separation, new birth—concepts which as it were shatter the immanence of the historical relation from within inasmuch as God is the Subject of the action denoted by them, inasmuch as it is God's good-pleasure (*εὐδοκία*, Mt. 11[26]; Gal. 1[15]; Eph. 1[9]) that as a purely external truth first creates and posits the inner truth as such in the free action denoted by these terms, quite apart from all the undeniable historical relations, in these relations but not through them. These concepts are not to be regarded as later explanations of an event that is properly and intrinsically immanent. They do not explain; they state how things are in the first instance. The immanent explanations of the terms are really the later interpretation. In the sense of the biblical authors one can only understand the concepts as terms for God's free acts, or else they are not understood at all. They tell us that without elimination of the distinction the time of Christ by God's free act becomes contemporaneous with the time of the prophets and apostles.

The prophets prophesy of Christ and the apostles proclaim Him, neither as reporters, but both as witnesses who speak not only about Christ but also in Christ, not because they have experienced Christ as one might experience Plato, but because it pleased God *ἀποκαλύψαι τὸν υἱὸν αὐτοῦ ἐν ἐμοί*[EN29] (Gal. 1[15]).

The Word of Scripture in its very different time and with its very different temporal content as compared with the Word of revelation is now put in its proper position. It is called the Word of the prophets and apostles, and as such, as witness of Christ and in subordination to the Word of Christ, it also speaks the Word of Christ.

The same step from one time to another, which can be understood only as God's act, is taken again when the proclamation of the Church becomes real

---

[EN27] we knew Christ according to the flesh
[EN28] flesh and blood has not revealed this to you
[EN29] to reveal his Son in me

[149] proclamation, i.e., God's Word, by reason of the fact that Holy Scripture comes to articulation in it, and the Word of Christ in Holy Scripture. Here again there is and has to be a specific relation of historical understanding with all the relevant components from philological analysis to the art of sympathetic identification. Proclamation is possible only in this relation of understanding, just as there could be prophecy and apostolate only in a specific relation of understanding. But in this relation proclamation of the Word of God does not come about through the individual or corporate components of the relation, e.g., through philological perspicacity or the most talented or refined identification. It comes about solely and simply through the power of the biblical Word itself, which now makes a place for itself in a very different time, and becomes the content of this place, as Paul steps forth in proclamation, not as a religious personality, but as an apostle of Jesus Christ, so that Jesus Himself is present in him. As the Word of God is this act, then in this step from revelation to Scripture and then to the proclamation of the Church, in a full and strict differentiation of the times, it is one, it is contemporaneous—*Ἰησοῦς Χριστὸς ἐχθὲς καὶ σήμερον ὁ αὐτός*[EN30] (Heb. 13^{8}).

We spoke of "contingent" contemporaneity to emphasise the fact that it has the character of an act, an event. Indeed, one might speak of a twofold contingency to the extent that in the relation between revelation and Holy Scripture and then again in the relation between Holy Scripture and proclamation there is always a contingent *illic et tunc*[EN31] from the standpoint of the speaking God and a contingent *hic et nunc*[EN32] from the standpoint of hearing man. We have spoken of a step from the one to the other in both relations. This step must not be volatilised into the general truth of a fixed or continuous relation between the three forms. It is really a step which has actuality only as this or that specific step, as a contingent act. The problem of God's Word is that this specific revelation of God is granted to this specific man to-day through the proclamation of this other specific man by means of this specific biblical text, so that a specific *illic et tunc* becomes a specific *hic et nunc*. The problem of the Word of God is always, then, a wholly specific, once-for-all and distinctive problem, and regarding this problem one can only say that it is solved by the Word of God itself as the Word of God spoken by the mouth of God is contemporaneous *illic et tunc* and also (i.e., as spoken *illic et tunc*) *hic et nunc*.

2. The fact that God's Word is God's act implies secondly its power to rule. God's speech is His action in relation to those to whom He speaks. But His action is divine. It is the action of the Lord. It is thus His ruling action. When and where Jesus Christ becomes contemporaneous through Scripture and proclamation, when and where the "God with us" is said to us by God Himself, we come under a lordship. The concepts election, revelation, separation, call-

[EN30] Jesus Christ the same yesterday and today
[EN31] there and then
[EN32] here and now

ing, and new birth which we touched on earlier all denote a promise, a judgment, a claim on man by which God binds man to Himself. Gospel and Law as the concrete content of God's Word imply always a seizure of man. No matter what God's Word says to man *in concretissimo*[EN33], it always tells him that he is not his own but God's. If in the light of its origin in revelation, in Jesus Christ, we understand the Word of God as the epitome of God's grace, grace means simply that man is no longer left to himself but is given into the hand of God. [150]

The Gospel or the Word of the cross is the *δύναμις θεοῦ*[EN34] to believers, or to them that are saved, we read in Rom. 1^{16} and 1 Cor. 1^{18}. The Word of God is called "living" in 1 Pet. 1^{23} and "quick and powerful" in Heb. 4^{12}. And Mt. 4^{4} says of man that he lives *παντὶ ῥήματι ἐκπορευμένῳ διὰ στόματος θεοῦ*[EN35].

If a man knew nothing of this power that both sustains and stimulates, both protects and punishes, both pacifies and disturbs, if he merely heard about it without knowing it as a power, he would only give evidence that he knew nothing of the Word of God. We are acquainted with the Word of God to the degree that we are acquainted with this power. We speak of God's Word when we speak in recollection and expectation of this power, and when we do so in such a way that we realise that this power of the Word of God is not one power among others, not even among other divine powers, but the one unique divine power which comes home to us, to which we are referred, in face of which we stand in decision between the obedience we owe it and the unfathomable inconceivability of disobedience, and consequently in the decision between bliss and perdition. The Holy Spirit, at least according to the Western understanding of the divine Triunity, cannot be separated from the Word, and His power is not a power different from that of the Word but the power that lives in and by the Word. Nor do we know anything about God's power in the creation and governance of the world except through the Word revealed, written and proclaimed. And when we know it through this Word we cannot possibly separate it from the power of the Word.

Ἐδόθη μοι πᾶσα ἐξουσία ἐν οὐρανῷ καὶ ἐπὶ γῆς[EN36] (Mt. 28^{18}). *Τὰ πάντα δι' αὐτοῦ καὶ εἰς αὐτὸν ἔκτισται· καὶ αὐτός ἐστιν πρὸ πάντων καὶ τὰ πάντα ἐν αὐτῷ συνέστηκεν*[EN37]. (Col. 1^{17}).

Where God has once spoken and is heard, i.e., in the Church, there is no escaping this power, no getting past it, no acknowledgment of divine powers that are not summed up in this power, that are not related to the manner of this power and active in its mode.

[EN33] in most concrete terms

[EN34] power of God

[EN35] by every word that proceeds from the mouth of God

[EN36] All authority in heaven and on earth has been given to me

[EN37] All things were created through him and for him; and he is before all things, and in him all things hold together

Καὶ αὐτός ἐστιν ἡ κεφαλὴ τοῦ σώματος, τῆς ἐκκλησίας[EN38] (Col. 1^{18}, cf. Eph. $1^{22f.}$). This is said of Christ. But Christ is the Word of God, contemporary in prophecy and the apostolate and contemporary in the proclamation of His Church. If He is contemporary here, if He makes that step, then we are necessarily faced with the recognition of the sover-
[151] eignty of God's Word in the Church which characterises the Reformation view of God and the Church. "The holy Christian Church whose sole Head is Christ is born of the Word of God, is incorporated in the same, and heareth not the voice of a stranger" (Zwingli, *Berne Theses* of 1528, *Art.* 1). "God's Word is a flowret, that is, the longer the dearer .... That is, whoso once graspeth God's Word aright, loveth it so dearly that he always desireth it more and more ..." (Luther, *Sermon on Lk.* 5^{1-11}, 1534, *E.A.* 4, 342). "... our preaching is this, that whoso heareth this preaching about Christ and believeth in Him, hath everlasting life. The Word of God is sent from heaven to be heard, that even if thou wert burnt to ashes, thou wouldst yet know the outcome" (*Exposition of Jn.* 3–4, 1538f., *W.A.* 47, 188, 28). "For 'tis certain we all have salvation through God's Word alone. What should we know else of God, the Lord Christ and His sacrifice, and the Holy Ghost?" (*Sermon on Mk.* 7^{31-37}, 1544, *W.A.* 52, 451, 39). "For God hath given us no other staircase and shewn us no other way up which we can go to heaven save His dear Word, the holy Gospel. Whoso heareth the same gladly, marketh it diligently and sheweth desire and love thereto, is helped" (*ib.*, 452, 16). "For God will not reveal Himself in thy heart without the Word. Wouldst thou see and know Him, it must befall solely through the Word and the outward sacraments" (*ib.*, 453, 31). "How doth the Father train us? Through Christ. How through Christ? By the Word. Thus he attracteth and charmeth thee; so an thy need driveth thee, go blithely to it, and boldly bring forth thine ill hap; but ever bring the Word withal" (*Sermon on Jn.* 8^{46-59}, *E.A.* 11, 130). "For the soul of man can be preserved by nought save the Word of God, that is its food and pasture, and so much as it availeth itself thereof, dependeth and believeth thereon, so far it is counselled and helped" (*Sermon on* Lk. 11, 1527, *W.A.* 17^{11}, 280, 30). According to Luther there corresponds to the ascension and session of Christ at God's right hand the *regnum Christi*[EN39] in the world, which is to be understood as a *doctrinale regnum*[EN40] equivalent to the *ministerium Verbi*[EN41] (*Enarr. ub. Cap. 53 Esaiae*, 1544, *E.A., Exeg. Op. lat.* 23, 448 f.). "For through the Word He shall rule and not otherwise" (*Passion, 5th Sermon*, 1534, *E.A.* 3, 268). "That is the New Testament and kingdom of Christ that cometh home with as little might, and yet with almighty power and might which none can withstand. It appeareth to be foolish that Christ doth set up the New Testament in this wise" (*Sermon on Acts* 2^{1-13}, 1534, *E.A.* 4, 86). "Yet there all is petty and naught to look at, both matter and instruments. The matter and preaching are petty; the instruments, i.e., the apostles and disciples whom Christ useth as tools for this preaching are much pettier. Yet through this petty preaching and these worthless tools goeth the New Testament and kingdom of Christ" (*ib.*, 87). "This preaching is not come from men, but Christ Himself hath brought it and put it thereafter into the hearts of the apostles and their successors, that they grasped it, and into their mouths, that they spake and preached it. That is His kingdom, therefore ruleth He so that all His power standeth and resteth on the Word of God, and the Word then becometh so mighty that it createth all that is needed by man, and bringeth all good things that men may have. For it is the power of God that can and may save all those who believe therein, as St. Paul saith in Rom. 1" (*Sermon on Jn.* $10^{12ff.}$, 1523, *W.A.* 12, 530, 24). "But He keepeth specially before Him two members, ears and tongue; for the kingdom of God is founded upon the Word which

[EN38] And he is the head of the body, the church
[EN39] kingdom of Christ
[EN40] kingdom of teaching
[EN41] ministry of the Word

one cannot grasp or conceive without these two members, ears and tongue, and ruleth alone through the Word and faith in the hearts of men. The ears grasp the Word and the heart believeth it: but the tongue uttereth or confesseth it as the heart believeth. So if we do away with the tongue and ears, there remaineth no marked difference betwixt the kingdom of Christ and the world" (*Sermon on Mk.* 7^{31-37}, *E.A.* 13, 308). " ... *la parole de Dieu seule doit estre suffisante pour nostre foy. Si on demande sur quoy nostre foy est fondee et comment elle vient à sa* [152]
perfection c'est par la parole de Dieu[EN42] (Calvin, *Sermon on Gal.* $1^{11f.}$, *C.R.* 51, 361. *Iterum hic memoria repetere convenit, qualis sit regni Christi natura. Ut enim ipse aureo diademata ornatus non est, vel instructus terrenis armis; ita non dominatur in mundo armorum potentia, nec sibi autoritatem conciliat pomparum splendore, vel terrore et metu populum suum cogit: sed evangelii doctrina regium eius insigne est, quo sub obsequium suum colligit fideles. Proinde ubicunque annunciatur pure evangelii doctrina, illic Christum regnare certum est: ubi vero reiicitur, simul etiam aboleri eius imperium*[EN43] (*Comm. on Is.* 11^4, *C.R.* 36, 240). *Car Dieu regne, quand il conduit tout par sa providence: mais cependant nous n'apercevons rien de son empire, quand nous luy sommes rebelles, que tout va pesle mesle et que sa parole n'est point escoutee, laquelle est le sceptre royal par lequel il domine sur nous: que son Esprit ne domine point pour nous conduire en son obéissance, et pour nous ranger tellement à luy, qu'il vive plustost en nous, que nous ne vivions à nos appetits, et selon nostre naturel. Dieu donc ne regne point en ceste facon sinon quand l'Evangile nous est presché et que nostre Seigneur Jesus Christ, qui a este constitué son lieutenant, nous gouverne tant par sa parole que par son S. Esprit .... Or il est bien certain que ... Dieu estant Createur de tout le monde, n'a iamais quitté son authorite. If faut donc que sa puissance ait son estendue par tout: mais c'est d'une facon qui nous est cachée et incompréhensible, quand Dieu gouverne, et que sa parole cependant n'est point preschee ... puis de là nous pouvons recueillir combien la doctrine de l'Evangile nous doit estre precieuse et amiable, veu que par icelle Dieu nous prend sous sa charge et nous recognoist et advoue pour son peuple ... qu'il veut habiter au milieu de nous*[EN44] (*Sermon on Mt.* 3^2, *C.R.* 46, 490 f.).

Recognition of the power of God's Word to rule has the following implication. We are speaking of God's Word. Therefore we have to speak of its

---

EN42 ... God's word alone ought to be sufficient for our faith. If one were to ask on what our faith is founded and how it is perfected, it is by God's Word

EN43 It is worthwhile at this point to review once more from memory what the nature of Christ's kingdom is. For just as He Himself is not adorned with a golden crown, or practised in the exercise of wordly weapons, so He does not rule in the world by the power of weaponry, nor does He acquire authority through splendor of royal processions, nor does He compel His people through terror and fear; rather, his royal banner is the teaching of the gospel, by which he gathers the faithful in allegiance to him. In the same way, wherever the teaching of the gospel is proclaimed purely, there it is certain that Christ reigns; but where it is rejected, it is equally certain that his rule is abolished as well

EN44 For God reigns, insofar as He guides everything by His providence: but we do not see anything of His rulership, when we rebel against Him, when everything is disordered and His word (which is the royal sceptre by which he exercises power over us) is not heard, when His Spirit does not prevail in us to guide us in obedience, and so to turn us to Him, that He lives in us, so that we do not live for our own satisfaction or according to our nature. Furthermore, God does not reign in this fashion except when the Gospel is preached to us and our Lord Jesus Christ, who has been appointed God's lieutenant, governs us equally by His word and by His Holy Spirit .... Now it may be taken as quite certain that, inasmuch as God is the Creator of the whole world, He has never abandoned His authority. It is therefore necessary that His power extend everywhere; but that God governs is hidden from and incomprehensible to us when His Word is not preached, and from this we can understand how precious and desirable the teaching of the Gospel ought to be to us, seeing that by it God takes us under His care, acknowledges and claims us as His people in the midst of whom He wishes to dwell

power, its might, its effects, the changes it brings about. Because the Word of God makes history, as Word it is also act.

"Is not my word like as a fire? saith the Lord; and like a hammer that breaketh the rock in pieces?" (Jer. 23^{29}). "For as the rain cometh down, and the snow from heaven, and returneth not thither, but watereth the earth, and maketh it bring forth and bud, that it may give seed to the sower and bread to the eater: So shall my word be that goeth forth out of my mouth; it shall not return unto me void, but it shall accomplish that which I please, and it shall prosper in the thing whereto I sent it" (Is. $55^{10f.}$). Cf. in the New Testament the basic connexion between *καλεῖν, κλῆσις, ἐκκλησία, κλητός*[EN45] and the totality of that which *ἐν Χριστῷ*[EN46] becomes radically different for man and in man.

The promise of the Word of God is not as such an empty pledge which always stands, as it were, confronting man. It is the transposing of man into the wholly new state of one who has accepted and appropriated the promise, so that irrespective of his attitude to it he no longer lives without this promise but with it. The claim of the Word of God is not as such a wish or command which remains outside the hearer without impinging on his existence. It is the claiming and commandeering of man. Whatever may be his attitude to God's claim, man as a hearer of His Word now finds himself in the sphere of the divine claim; he is claimed by God. Again, the judgment of the Word of God is not a
[153] mere aspect under which man himself remains untouched, just as the same man may seem to be a giant from the standpoint of the ant or a dwarf from the standpoint of the elephant without in fact being any different either way. The judgment of God as such creates not only a new light and therewith a new situation, but also with the new situation a new man who did not exist before but who exists now, being identical with the man who has heard the Word. Again, that would not be the blessing of God's Word which as *benedictio*[EN47] was not immediately and as such seen and understood to be *beneficium*[EN48] as well, a real placing under God's good-pleasure and protection.

We find all this expressed in the strongest imaginable way in Jas. 1^{18}, where (cf. also 1 Pet. 1^{23}) there is reference to the fact that the Christian is begotten of the *λόγος ἀληθείας*[EN49]. Then v. 21 goes on logically to speak of a *λόγος ἔμφυτος*[EN50], i.e., a *λόγος* which, so to speak, belongs to man himself, without which man would no longer be himself.

And because the word at issue is the Word of God, we must add explicitly that its efficacy, its power to change, is not just relative as in the case of other powers. It is not uncertain. It is not conditioned or restricted by the behaviour of other factors, e.g., man. All this may be true of what it effects in man, of what may be seen of its operation in the life of man. But it is not true of its operation

---

EN45 to call, calling, church, a person who has been called
EN46 in Christ
EN47 good-talk
EN48 good-deed
EN49 the word of truth
EN50 engrafted word

in itself and as such. The power of the Word of God in itself and as such is absolute power.

" All flesh is as grass, and all the glory of man as the flower of grass. The grass withereth, and the flower thereof falleth away τὸ δὲ ῥῆμα κυρίου μένει εἰς τὸν αἰῶνα[EN51] (1 Pet. 1[24f.]). The Word of God is not only the λόγος ζῶν[EN52]; it is also the λόγος μένων[EN53]. It is an incorruptible seed, v. 23: ὁ λόγος τοῦ θεοῦ ἐν ὑμῖν μένει[EN54] is said in 1 Jn. 2[14] to the "young men," i.e., to those not yet proved (cf. the anointing that abideth in v. 27).

All this must be said of the Word of God because the Word of God is Jesus Christ and because its efficacy is not distinct from the lordship of Jesus Christ. He who hears God's Word is drawn thereby into the sphere of the real power of this lordship. There applies to him and for him everything the Word of God says as promise, claim, judgment and blessing. Preaching does not put it into effect; preaching declares and confirms that it is in effect. It is proclamation of the Word of God when it proclaims it as something that is already in effect.

This is also and especially true of preaching among both coloured and white heathen. If this were not based on the axiomatic presupposition that its hearers are already set aside as heathen, that they are already drawn into Christ's sphere of power even as God's Word is proclaimed to them, in what way would this be any better than propaganda, in what sense would it be "mission," i.e., sending, in what way would it be the proclamation of the Word of God that takes place in faith? Though we may have all conceivable and even very accurate ideas as to the convictions and circumstances of the hearers, nevertheless, when we preach to them in faith in the promise of the presence and efficacy of the Word of God and the [154]
Gospel, only one thing concerns us in relation to them: "Thou hast borne all sin."

Nor is it faith that puts in effect all that the Word of God tells us. Faith too, and faith especially, is faith in Jesus Christ. It is thus the recognition and confirmation that God's Word was already in effect even before we believed and quite apart from our believing. Faith particularly—and this is the element of truth in the older Lutheran doctrine of the *efficacia verbi extra usum*[EN55]—lives by the power which is power before faith and without faith. It lives by the power which gives faith itself its object, and in virtue of this object its very existence. Baptism was instituted for this reason, as a sign of this true and supreme power of God's Word. As a real act on man, as an act of sovereign disposition, it proclaims for its part that man belongs to the sphere of Christ's lordship prior to all his experiences and decisions. Even before he can take up an attitude to God, God has taken up an attitude to him. Whatever attitude he may adopt, it will be done within and on the ground of the attitude that God has adopted to him. If he believes, this will be just a confirmation of the fact that he has God's promise and is claimed, judged and blessed by God. If he does not believe, this again will not be a possibility he can freely choose. He

EN51 but the Word of the Lord abides for ever
EN52 living word
EN53 abiding word
EN54 the Word of God abides in you
EN55 efficacy of the Word apart from its use

will sin against God's Word. He will not show himself to be free, but unfree. He will not choose, but will be rejected. He will grasp, not a possibility, but an impossibility. In a Word, in his very unbelief he will be measured by the Word of God and smitten by its power. The preceding attitude of God to him will make his unbelief unbelief, his sin sin. Only in the sphere of grace is there faith and unbelief, righteousness and sin. Only through the power of God's Word are there the two categories, those who are saved and those who are lost.

Ἰδοὺ οὗτος κεῖται εἰς πτῶσιν καὶ ἀνάστασιν πολλῶν ἐν τῷ Ἰσραήλ[EN56] (Lk. 2^{34}). The stone laid in Sion becomes a stumbling-block and rock of offence to some, "and whosoever believeth on him shall not be ashamed" (Rom. 9^{33}). And Paul calls his preaching of the Gospel a *Χριστοῦ εὐωδία τῷ θεῷ ἐν τοῖς σωζομένοις καὶ ἐν τοῖς ἀπολλομένοις, οἷς μὲν ὀσμὴ ἐκ θάνατου, εἰς θάνατον, οἷς δὲ ὀσμὴ ἐκ ζωῆς εἰς ζωήν*[EN57] (2 Cor. $2^{15f.}$).

This whole consideration should not be restricted to the relation of the Word of God to the isolated individual as such. All that has been said applies *mutatis mutandis*[EN58] to the relation of the Word of God to the human cosmos in general, or, concretely, to the relation of Church and history or Church and society. It is not the case that God has somewhere and somehow revealed Himself, that somewhere there is a Bible and somewhere a Church with its preaching and sacraments—but history and society stand apart from all this, unaffected, sovereign, following their own laws, and the Church must come as it were from outside, from a God who has remained alien to this cosmos, to
[155] represent and champion its cause, or the cause of its God, to this cosmos by attack or defence. It is not at all true that the Church is outside with God and the world is inside without God. Things can be seen thus only if the Bible and the Church are seen apart from the revelation that constitutes them or if the revelation itself is understood, with Schleiermacher, only as the distinctive beginning of the religion that is our own. But this is not recollecting the Word of God that has come and expecting the Word of God that will come. If by revelation we understand this Word of God, and if the Bible and the Church are understood in the light of this recollection and expectation, then as a totality, too, the world of men standing over against the Word of God must be considered as subject to a decisive alteration. But in this case the world cannot be held to its ungodliness by the Church; it cannot be taken seriously in its ungodliness. So long and so far as the Church holds it to this, it simply shows that it does not believe seriously in the Word of God. If it did, it would have to reckon concretely with its power. It is not, of course, that man is claimed for God on the basis of a relic of his relationship and commitment to God by creation, as though the fall had not been so radical in its consequences. It is

---

[EN56] Behold, this child is set for the fall and rising of many in Israel

[EN57] aroma of Christ to God among those who are being saved and among those who are perishing, to one a fragrance from death to death, to the other a fragrance from life to life.

[EN58] with the necessary changes having been made

not a question of natural theology but very much indeed of supernatural theology. But such a theology, bearing in mind the power of God's Word, will have to claim the world, history, and society as the world, history and society in the midst of which Christ was born and died and rose again. Not in the light of nature but in the light of grace, there is no self-enclosed and protected secular sphere, but only one which is called in question by God's Word, by the Gospel, by God's claim, judgment and blessing, and which is only provisionally and restrictedly abandoned to its own legalism and its own gods. What the Word says stands whatever the world's attitude to it and whether it redound to it for salvation or perdition.

Ἐγένετο ἡ βασιλεία τοῦ κόσμου τοῦ κυρίου ἡμῶν καὶ τοῦ Χριστοῦ αὐτοῦ καὶ βασιλεύσει εἰς τοὺς αἰῶνας τῶν αἰώνων[EN59] (Rev. 11^{15}). Just because it is eschatological this *ἐγένετο*[EN60] must be taken very literally and seriously. Christ does not have to become but already is *βασιλεὺς βασιλέων καὶ κύριος τῶν κυρίων*[EN61] (Rev. 19^{16}; cf. Phil. $2^{9f.}$; Col. 2^{15}; Eph. 1^{21}).

The world, then, cannot evolve into agreement with God's Word on its own initiative nor can the Church achieve this by its work in and on the world. The Church is the Church as it believes and proclaims that prior to all secular developments and prior to all its own work the decisive word has in fact been spoken already regarding both itself and also the world. The world no longer exists in isolation or neutrality *vis-à-vis* revelation, the Bible, and proclamation. Whether it believes or not, whether it develops in this way or that, whether the Church exerts greater influence or less, whether it consists of millions of con- [156]
fessors and proclaimers or whether only two or three are gathered together in Christ's name—whatever becomes of the Church and the world the only thing that can matter is the event that follows the decisive word already spoken.

Sermo enim Dei venit mutaturus orbem, quoties venit[EN62] (Luther, *De servo arb.*, 1525, *W.A.* 18, 626, 26).

If the Church believes what it says it believes, then it is the place where the victory of Jesus Christ is not the last word to be heard and passed on but the first. For this reason and in this sense it is the place of revelation, of mercy and of peace, the hill of Zion to which the heathen, wittingly and willingly or not, are on the way. The Church which is this place will have something to say to the world and will be taken seriously by the world. In relation to what has been said here it is as well to remember that the power at issue is the power of the Word, the power to rule, the power of God. All this distinguishes it from other powers, its efficacy from any other efficacy, its effect from any other effect. Precisely here it should not be forgotten that the Word of God is and remains the

---

[EN59] The kingdom of the world has become the kingdom of our Lord and of his Christ, and he shall reign for ever and ever

[EN60] has become

[EN61] King of kings and Lord of lords

[EN62] For the Word of God, as often as it comes, to change the world

speech of God, and its power, which is not to be confused with any other power, is thus the power of truth. The fact that the truth, which is directly associated with grace in Jn. 1 [14f.], is also power is something we can state without reservation in the present context.

3. The fact that the Word of God is the act of God means thirdly that it is decision. This is what distinguishes an act from a mere event. Considered in itself a mere event is an occurrence subject to some higher necessity. It is occasioned by a cause. Beside it all the other events in whose nexus it occurs help to condition it. It is a cause because it is caused and as other things cause and are caused along with it. This is true of events in nature and also of those in the individual and corporate life of man. It is a mere hypothesis to call an event a deed, a decision, an act of free choice. At all events this predicate is not intrinsic to the concept of event. This must be remembered when the concept of the Word of God is connected with that of history. No doubt this must be done. According to all that we have said about the contingent contemporaneity of the Word of God and its power of rule, the Word of God is also historical, temporal event. But if it were only event, its character as act or decision would be as hypothetical as is the case with all the other things we usually allege to be such. The Word of God is not to be understood as history first and then and as such as decision too. It is to be understood primarily and basically as decision and then and as such as history too. If we think in terms of an act that might be
[157] interpreted equally well or even better as a mere event, an act which takes place out of a higher necessity and which is conditioned by other acts on the right hand and the left, we are thinking of the ambivalent thing that is usually called an act in the human sphere; we are not thinking of the Word of God. If we let ourselves be blinded by the circumstance that the Word of God is also, of course, a human act in Jesus Christ, in the Bible and in proclamation, and conclude from this that it is only a human act and is thus implicated in the unavoidable dialectic of human act and mere event, if we see it in the half-light of this dialectic, then *eo ipso*[EN63] we are not thinking of the Word of God. The Word of God is first understood as decision or it is not understood at all. We might also say quite simply: as divine act. As divine act, even though it is a human act too, it is distinguished from all human acts by the fact that it is not affected by the *sic et non*[EN64] of that dialectic. It is also human act, and as such it is also event, but as act and event it is free, as free as God Himself, for indeed God Himself is in the act. God is the Lord. There is no one and nothing above Him and no one and nothing beside Him, either on the right hand or the left, to condition Him or to be in a nexus with Him. God is *a se*[EN65]. This is unreservedly true of His Word too. But God's aseity is not empty freedom. In God all potentiality is included in His actuality and therefore all freedom in His

---

[EN63] by definition
[EN64] yes and no
[EN65] of and from Himself

decision. Decision means choice, exercised freedom. We understand the Word of God very badly in isolation from the unconditional freedom in which it is spoken, but we also understand it very badly if we regard it as a mere possibility rather than freedom exercised, a decision made, a choice taking place. A choice taking place: In the humanity of Christ, in the Bible and in proclamation the Word of God is also a human act and it is thus a temporal event. But it is by choice that the Word of God is identical with the humanity of Christ, Holy Scripture, and proclamation, and is thus a temporal event. Both together, the choice and the event, make the Word of God the act of God as distinct from all other acts. The fact that the Word of God is the act of God and is thus a choice that takes place, a decision that is made, a freedom that is exercised, has the following concrete implications.

(*a*) The Word of God is not a reality in the way that a phenomenon is real if it is commensurate with our sense perceptions and our understanding. Nor is it a reality in the same way as the so-called laws of nature, which in a transformed perspective are also the laws of the spiritual world. Nor is it a reality in the sense of the axioms of mathematics and physics in so far as there are such. Nor is it a reality like the reality that I am I and not thou, or thou art thou and not I, or yesterday is not to-day and will never be to-morrow. It is not a reality in the sense that the structure of the so-called character and so-called destiny of each of us, down to the tiniest details, is probably a cosmically (yes, cosmic- [158]
ally!) predetermined reality which may perhaps be read on our palms, or perhaps in our features, or our handwriting, or the conjunction of the stars at our birth. In short, it is not a reality in the same way as the totality of what we otherwise call reality is real, even although it has a share in this reality and meets us precisely in this reality. It is not reality in this way because unlike all other reality it is not universally, i.e., always and everywhere present, and hence it is not universally, i.e., always and everywhere ascertainable. One cannot even say that at least it might be thus present and ascertainable *mutatis mutandis*[EN66]. The distinctive thing here is the absence of this "might," of the potentiality in virtue of which many comparable entities could be adduced. It is quite impossible to say that the Word of God "might" be universally present and ascertainable. This "might" always characterises a created reality distinct from God in His aseity and actuality. The Word of God is uncreated reality, identical with God Himself. Hence it is not universally present and ascertainable, not even potentially. Never in any circumstances can it be universally present and ascertainable. Always in all circumstances the Word of God is reality in our reality *suo modo, sua libertate, sua misericordia*[EN67]. Consequently it is present and ascertainable only contingently—again *suo modo*[EN68].

[EN66] with the necessary changes having been made
[EN67] in its own way, in its own freedom, in its own mercy
[EN68] in its own way

This is why there are times when a revelation from Yahweh is rare according to 1 Sam. 3^{1}. This is why we find such remarkable prophecies as Am. 8^{11}: "Behold, the days come, saith the Lord God, that I will send a famine and thirst in the land, so that all its inhabitants mourn, not a famine of bread, nor a thirst for water, but of hearing the words of the Lord, so that they shall wander from sea to sea, and from the north even to the east, they shall run to and fro to seek the word of the Lord, and shall not find it, "and Mic. 3^{6}:" Therefore night shall be unto you, that ye shall not have a vision; and it shall be dark unto you, that ye shall not divine; and the sun shall go down over the prophets, and the day shall be dark over them. Then shall the seers be ashamed, and the diviners confounded: yea, they shall all cover their lips; for there is no answer of God." For the prophets and others singled out by Yahweh, as for all Israel and the individual Israelite throughout the Old Testament (not excepting even Ps. 119 and the later canonical literature generally), the concept of the word or law or command or direction or order or claim of Yahweh thus implies an event that it is to be expected and besought from Yahweh and revealed by Him, not one that takes place by immanent necessity, and especially not a higher state of affairs that is universally present and ascertainable. And for the same reason the being of the true light in the world is described in the New Testament as an *ἔρχεσθαι εἰς τὸν κόσμον*[EN69] (Jn. 1^{9}), as an *ἀποκαλύπτεσθαι* or *φανεροῦσθαι*[EN70]. We again have in mind here the connexion between revelation and the divine *εὐδοκία*[EN71]. *Ὅπου θέλει πνεῖ*[EN72] (Jn. 3^{8}) applies indeed to God's Word as well as God's Spirit. All this plainly means that the Word of God is decision.

It is real, and can be understood as real, if and when it gives itself, and gives itself to be understood. The question: What is God's Word? is utterly hopeless
[159] if it is the question as to the category in which God's Word is to be put or the syllogism by which it might be proved. Questions of category and syllogism obviously presuppose that the Word of God is one of the realities that are universally present and ascertainable and therefore created. All concepts tending in this direction, even that of a supreme being, an *ens perfectissimum*[EN73] or an unconditioned being, even that of the breaking through and knowledge of such a supreme being, are not as such—as general concepts—the concept of the Word of God. As general concepts, they suppress the essential point that the Word of God is a reality only in its own decision. The fact that the Word of God is decision means that there is no concept of the Word of God apart from the name of God, which we love and fear and worship because it is identical with the Bearer of the name.

(*b*) Because the Word of God, unlike created realities, is not universally present and ascertainable, and cannot possibly be universally present and ascertainable, therefore, as decision, it always implies choice in relation to man. The Word of God is an act of God which takes place *specialissime*[EN74], in this way and not another, to this or that particular man.

"Before I formed thee in the belly I knew thee; and before thou camest forth out of the

---

[EN69] coming into the world
[EN70] being revealed or being disclosed
[EN71] good pleasure
[EN72] It blows where it wills
[EN73] most perfect being
[EN74] with maximum specificity

womb I sanctified thee, and I ordained thee a prophet unto the nations" (Jer. 1^{5}, cf. Is. 49^{1}). This is, of course, the concept of prophetic election, to which the only thing to correspond generally in the Old Testament is the election of Israel among the nations, which in Deutero-Isaiah is remarkably enough associated with the election of the individual prophet and Servant of the Lord. But in the New Testament the terms ἐκλέγεσθαι, ἐκλογή, ἐκλεκτός[EN75], undoubtedly in correspondence with καλεῖν[EN76] etc., are also used of individual believers as such, and this in such a way that ἐκλέγεσθαι or προορίζειν[EN77] is the presupposition of καλεῖν (Rom. 8^{30}), whereas not every καλεῖν has a corresponding ἐκλέγεσθαι.

This choice takes place as the Word is spoken and received: the choice of grace to faith and its righteousness or the choice of gracelessness to unbelief and its sin. The *vocatio*[EN78] can take place *efficaciter, efficacissime*[EN79], and yet the *electio*[EN80] effected therein may be *rejectio*[EN81], i.e., the Word may be spoken and received and yet the choice which takes place therein may be the choice of gracelessness.

Πολλοὶ γάρ εἰσιν κλητοί, ὀλίγοι δὲ εκλεκτοί[EN82] (Mt. 22^{14}). This critical relationship between κλῆσις and ἐκλογή[EN83] is undoubtedly in view when Mt. $24^{40f.}$ and Lk. $17^{34f.}$ refer to the two who are together in the field, or sleeping in one bed, or grinding at one mill, and it has then to be said of them: ὁ εἷς παραλημφθήσεται, καὶ ὁἕτερος ἀφεθήσεται[EN84]. We also recall the parable of the four different soils where the seed is expressly called the Word of God and the general exposition in Mk. 4^{11} says specifically: "Unto you it is given to know the mystery of the kingdom of God; but unto them that are without, all these things are done in parables, ἵνα βλέποντες βλέπωσιν καὶ μὴ ἴδωσιν, καὶ ἀκούοντες ἀκούωσιν καὶ μὴ συνιῶσιν, μήποτε ἐπιστρέψωσιν καὶ ἀφεθῇ αὐτοῖς[EN85]".

Under the heading of the power of God's Word to rule, we have referred [160]
already to the twofold possibility of its operation. The inner ground of this twofold possibility is that it is decision and therefore choice. Do we have to know an inner reason for the choice, a vindication of God for the freedom He takes and enjoys, when speaking to man, now to accept and now to reject him, to illumine one with His light and to blind the other with the same light, to treat the one as Peter and the other as Judas? By way of justification one need say no more than in the case of the general dogma of predestination disclosed here, namely, that the decision taken in the Word is God's decision and therefore it is a just and good decision. It is a decision to which the hidden reality of the relation existing between Jesus Christ and Peter or Jesus Christ and Judas

[EN75] to elect, election, an elect person
[EN76] to call
[EN77] to elect or to predestine
[EN78] calling
[EN79] effectively, with maximum effectiveness
[EN80] election
[EN81] rejection
[EN82] For many are called, but few are chosen
[EN83] calling and election
[EN84] the one shall be taken, and the other shall be left
[EN85] so that they may see but not perceive, and may hear but not understand; lest they should turn again, and be forgiven

certainly corresponds exactly, but the main point is that it is intrinsically justified as a divine decision. It is a fact that we may hear the Word of God and hear it again, and we may hear it correctly, accepting its promise as promise, obeying its claim as claim, submitting to its judgment, receiving its blessing, finding in it—in it and not in ourselves—the substance on which we feed and by which we live, or we may not hear it correctly, but only seem to accept, obey, submit and receive, so that we have to go on living without it as our sustenance. We may know the one or the other or both. But what we must know is that it is the Word of truth itself that decides as to the "correctly" or "not correctly," i.e., that we receive either grace or judgment as they come from God, and therefore come by right.

(*c*) As divine decision the Word of God works on and in a decision of the man to whom it is spoken. What does the revelation attested in Holy Scripture and proclaimed in preaching and sacrament say to me? What is revealed to me in it? "God with us" is how we stated generally the content of God's Word. But when this "God with us" is said to me and heard by me, without ceasing to be the content of the Word, without changing as such, as the living and inalterable content of the Word it must now reach its goal in my variously fashioned and conditioned situation over against it, in the qualification effected in me by the Word that God speaks to me. This new qualification of mine is the decision as to my faith or unbelief, my obedience or disobedience, i.e., the divine decision as to whether my act is faith or unbelief, obedience or disobedience, correct or incorrect hearing. This decision arises only in face of the Word of God spoken to me, only as the reply to it.

It is not a specific instance among the possibilities of human decision in general. Hence it cannot be pre-understood within the sphere of a general anthropology. Even the most radical crisis in which man may find himself as he views himself from the standpoint of general anthropology has nothing whatever to do with this crisis. For even in the most radical of
[161] general human crises man also discovers himself as the one who can select his own possibility. Decision does not come upon him; he himself makes a decision. And this individual behaviour of his is the true and primary revelation of God. (Cf. on this H. E. Eisenhuth, *Das Irrationale als philosophisches Problem*, 1931, especially the closing section pp. 260–67, which perhaps follows through to the end, i.e., reduces *ad absurdum*[EN86], a theological use of the philosophy of M. Heidegger.) From this standpoint there can be neither faith nor unbelief, neither obedience nor disobedience, nor decision between them. The very possibility of faith or unbelief, obedience or disobedience, in relation to God's Word can be dealt with only in the framework of a theological anthropology.

As God's Word itself is revelation, i.e., a new word for me, so the situation in which it sets me as it is spoken to me is an absolutely new situation which cannot be seen or understood in advance, which cannot be compared with any other, which is grounded in the Word of God and in this alone. It is, of course, a situation of decision. But this is not the decision of my own particular resolve and choice (though there is a place for these too). It is a decision of being

[EN86] to the point of absurdity

judged and accepted. And because the particular judgment and acceptance are God's, it is a decision of my particular reality, of the particular meaning of my resolve and choice. Just because the Word of God means "God with us," just because it is the Word of the Lord, of our Creator, Reconciler and Redeemer, it obviously pronounces our judgment to us. In it, it is decided who we are. We are what we are on the basis of this judgment, what we are as its hearers, i.e., we are believers or unbelievers, obedient or disobedient. Previously and *per se* we are neither the one nor the other. Previously and *per se* we do not even have the possibility of being either the one or the other. Faith and unbelief, obedience and disobedience, are possible only to the extent that, as our act, they are our particular reply to the judgment of God pronounced to us in His Word. In faith and obedience my resolve and choice is truly good before God. Whatever else may have to be said about me, I exist in correspondence to God's Word. I have received and accepted His grace. In unbelief and disobedience my own resolve and choice, whatever else may have to be said about me, is truly bad before God. I exist in contradiction to God's Word. I have not accepted His grace. Either way it is I—this is really my own supremely responsible decision. But it is not in my decision that it acquires the character of being a good choice on the one hand or a bad one on the other. The implication of this decision of mine taken with my own free will, namely, the step either to the right hand or to the left, the choice to believe and obey or the refusal to do either—this qualification of my decision is the truth within it of the divine decision concerning me. In speaking to me God has chosen me, as the man I am, to be the man I am. The new quality I acquire through the Word of God is my true and essential quality. I cannot give myself this true and essential quality. Only God [162]
can judge me. I am wholly and altogether the man I am in virtue of the divine decision. In virtue of the divine decision I am a believer or an unbeliever in my own decision. In this decision whereby it is decided who I am in my own decision and whereby it is decided what my own decision really means—in this realisation of my reality, this bringing of our works to light (Jn. $3^{20f.}$; Eph. $5^{12f.}$), the Word of God is consummated as the act of God. It is always the act of the inscrutable judgment of God.

4. THE SPEECH OF GOD AS THE MYSTERY OF GOD

In order to refer everything that has been said from the standpoint of "speech-act" to the truly decisive point, that in everything our concern is with God's speech and God's act, we must now speak of the Word of God in a third series of attributes. In what has been said already we have constantly sought to set forth delimitations along these lines. But when we consider all the concepts: spiritual, personal and purposive character, contemporaneity, power to rule and decision, the question can continually arise whether we might not be speaking of some other logos, whether we are really speaking of God's Logos.

Or there might be a continual temptation to think and speak of the Logos of God as thus described in the same way as we think and speak of some other spiritual factor that may be hard to grasp but can in fact be grasped, namely, in such a way that we think we know it—and the harder the work, the better and surer the knowledge—that we think we perceive its structure and understand its operation, so that in thought and speech at least we are its master, as well or as badly as man may become the master of any object of thought or speech.

At this point I should introduce a word of caution which can, of course, be given only a basis in experience, which can be understood only in terms of experience, and which it is thus easy to disregard. Continually raising it in relation to myself, I raise it to some degree in respect of all my older and younger theological contemporaries, especially in so far as they are engaged in what is called "systematic" theology. Serious theological work is an ideal on the lips of all of us. It seems that not only the Bible but also the fathers of Protestantism and the early Church are again speaking to us with greater emphasis. The great concepts of God, Word, Spirit, revelation, faith, church and sacrament, etc., have again come into our field of vision. We see again that great tasks are posed here for theology. Many of us already know how to speak of these things very cleverly, clearly and definitely. In many places theological dialogue has been initiated in a surprisingly intensive way. One can only rejoice at being a theologian in this time of ours. But it may be feared that we are all on the point of becoming much too positive. I am not thinking of the questionable and partisan meaning of the word, which is now obsolete, though something of the pathos of the earlier "positive" theology certainly lives on, or has come to life again, in what I am calling positive here. I am thinking
[163] rather of a certain assurance of voice, speech and attitude with which, it seems, we think we can work on the new or older field, a certain confidence with which we think we can take those great concepts on our lips and analyse them and interrelate them constructively or in other ways, a certain sprightliness with which we speak about the things denoted by them as though we were speaking about them because we know how to speak about them with comparatively so little freedom from restriction. And this assurance, confidence and sprightliness are perhaps all the greater because we are clever enough to include an element of uncertainty or comforted despair or even a line of death or the like in our more or less spiritual calculations. Is it clear to our generation in life as well as thought that the serious element in serious theological work is grounded in the fact that its object is never in any circumstances at our command, at the command of even the profoundest biblical or Reformation vision or knowledge, at the command of even the most delicate and careful construction? Absolutely any theological possibility can as such be pure threshing of straw and waste of energy, pure comedy and tragedy, pure deception and self-deception. Even the most zealous amassing of theological treasures is certainly mere folly without that being "rich toward God" (Lk. 12^{21}) which none can manufacture for himself and none maintain. A theology which is sure in faith, i.e., sure of its object, can as little be without awareness of this danger as clockwork without a pendulum. And this awareness needs to be perceptible. It needs to make theological thinking and utterance fruitful and full of content in a proper sense. To what extent may it be seen in the theological production of our day? To what extent is that assurance, confidence and sprightliness, that leaven of the positive and of positive theologians, compatible with this awareness? To what extent is our theological dialogue no real discourse? *C'est le ton qui fait la musique*[EN87]. One cannot discuss tone in general, nor yet the tone which can make discussion real discourse, and especially not with

[EN87] It is the tone that makes the music

those to whom we think ourselves closest at this point. I fancy I can hear already the lamentation and the jeering and the "certainly—but" with which these lines will be received. Nevertheless, must it not be said again and again: Beware of this leaven?

It would obviously confirm our question, and we should really be speaking of another logos than the Logos of God, if we thought that in face of this question we could and should prove that we have not deceived ourselves, that we have really been speaking of the Logos of God. Thinking we can prove this in some sense, we should really betray the cause, or rather betray the fact that we have confused this cause with some other. For if anything at all serious was intended in what we said previously, we must accept the fact that only the Logos of God Himself can provide the proof that we are really talking about Him when we are allegedly doing so. And we should have succumbed already to the afore-mentioned temptation if we were to look about for some means to ward it off, to secure ourselves against it, and to make ourselves immune to temptation. For it would be a highly refined way of becoming master of God's Word to think we could put ourselves in a position in which we have securely adopted the right attitude to it, that of servant and not master. Would not this be the loftiest triumph of human certainty? But would it not be a confirmation of the question and a fall into the temptation? For what would it imply if we had made, or were in process of making, that delimitation of the divine from [164]
the human? If we could do this, we should have said, or should be saying, what the Word of God is. The goal of all yearning in theology is to be able to do this, but this is the goal of an illegitimate yearning. The object of all pride in theology is to think one can really do this, but undoubtedly this is the object of an unhealthy pride. For according to all that we can know of the how of the Word of God, one thing is ruled out. It cannot be an entity which we can demarcate from other entities and thereby objectify, even though we do it with supreme humility and discretion. Certainly it is delimited from all other entities; it is objective and *sui generis*[EN88]. God's speech is different from all other speech and God's action is different from all other action. But do we not deny this very distinction if we think we can possess and apply a measure of this distinction? Is it not a property of the other entities which are not identical with God's Word that we can more or less clearly distinguish them from one another and objectify them? Is not this a sign that we can perceive and understand and ultimately master and control them, because finally we are on the same plane as they are? Would the Word of God be *sui generis* if we could describe *suum genus* and allot it a fixed place as very much the "wholly other"? Is not the Word of God *sui generis*, God's Word, just because we cannot do this, because it does it itself and it alone? This is why even in the delimitations already prescribed we cannot, as it were, give the Word of God its own sphere in the world which is known to us and which is to be conceptually classified by us. All our delimitations can only seek to be signals or alarms to draw attention

[EN88] of its own kind

to the fact that God's Word is and remains God's, not bound and not to be attached to this thesis or to that antithesis. A sketch of the concept such as the philosopher would like has not emerged and should not do so. Only God conceives of Himself, even in His Word. Our concept of God and His Word can only be an indication of the limits of our conceiving, an indication which must not be allowed to condense into a negative proof. This cannot be our concern even now when we must give added sharpness to the decisive point that the Word of God is God's Word. We can sharpen this here only by remembering again and explicitly our own limits, only by making it even clearer to ourselves that we cannot utter even a wretched syllable about the how of God's Word unless the Word of God is spoken to us as God's Word, which means spoken to us in such a way that all we think and say about its how has its substance not in itself but outside itself in the Word of God, so that what we think and say about this how can never become the secret system of a what. It is for this reason and in this sense that we finally speak of the Word of God as the mystery of God. The issue is not an ultimate "assuring" but always a penultimate "de-assuring"
[165] of theology, or, as one might put it, a theological warning against theology, a warning against the idea that its propositions or principles are certain in themselves like the supposed axioms of the mathematicians and physicists, and are not rather related to their theme and content, which alone are certain, which they cannot master, by which they must be mastered if they are not to be mere soap-bubbles.

In using the term mystery to sum up what we have to say here we have in view the meaning of the word "mystery" in the New Testament. Mystery does not just denote the hiddenness of God but His revelation in a hidden, i.e., a non-apparent way which intimates indirectly rather than directly. Mystery is the concealment of God in which He meets us precisely when He unveils Himself to us, because He will not and cannot unveil Himself except by veiling Himself. Mystery thus denotes the divine givenness of the Word of God which also fixes our own limits and by which it distinguishes itself from everything that is given otherwise. Distinguishes itself? This means that we cannot establish its distinction. Otherwise it would not be a mystery. It distinguishes itself by giving itself to us in this way and this alone; not in such a way that we can arrive at a triumphant distinction, but in such a way that there is reserved for it the right to distinguish itself.

1. The speech of God is and remains the mystery of God supremely in its secularity. When God speaks to man, this event never demarcates itself from other events in such a way that it might not be interpreted at once as part of these other events. The Church is also in fact a sociological entity with definite historical and structural features. Preaching is also in fact an address. The sacrament is also in fact a symbol in compromising proximity to all other possible symbols. The Bible is also in fact the historical record of a Near Eastern tribal religion and its Hellenistic offshoot. Jesus Christ is also in fact the Rabbi of Nazareth who is hard to know historically and whose work, when He is known, might seem to be a little commonplace compared to more than one of the other founders of religions and even compared to some of the later represen-

tatives of His own religion. Nor should we forget that theology also, in so far as it uses human speech, is in fact a philosophy or a conglomerate of all kinds of philosophies. Even the biblical miracles do not break through this wall of secularity. From the moment they took place they were interpreted otherwise than as proofs of God's Word, and obviously they can always be interpreted in a very different way. The veil is thick. We do not have the Word of God otherwise than in the mystery of its secularity.

This means, however, that we have it in a form which as such is not the Word of God and which as such does not even give evidence that it is the form of the Word of God. In other words the self-presentation of God in His Word is not direct, nor is it indirect in the way in which a man's face seen in a mirror can be called an indirect self-presentation of this man.

When Paul speaks of a *βλέπειν δἰ ἐσόπτρου*[EN89] in 1 Cor. 13[12] the addition *ἐν αἰνίγματι*[EN90] should be noted. He is pointing out that we have here a twofold indirectness of vision. First the Word of God meets us in a form that is to be distinguished from its content, and secondly the form as such is an enigma, a concealing of the Word of God. The relevant concept here is that of paradox. A paradox is a communication which is not only made by a *δόξα*, a phenomenon, but which must be understood, if it is to be understood at all, *παρὰ τὴν δόξαν*[EN91], i.e., in antithesis to what the phenomenon itself seems to be saying. Just because the Word of God alone fulfils the concept of paradox in full rigour, whereas in all other conceivable paradoxes the antithesis between communication and form is such that it can be dissolved from a superior point of vantage, it is to be recommended that theology make more sparing use of the term now that it has played its part, and also caused all manner of confusion. [166]

The self-presentation of God in His Word is not comparable with any other self-presentation, for every other self-presentation that meets us is either direct communication or, if indirect, it is characterised by a certain similarity and correspondence between matter and form, a feature which makes it possible, as when a face is seen in a mirror, to dissolve the indirect into direct communication or knowledge. This is the very thing that is ruled out in the case of God's Word. Its form is not a suitable but an unsuitable medium for God's self-presentation. It does not correspond to the matter but contradicts it. It does not unveil it but veils it. The secularity of the Word of God does not imply only that it meets us in the garment of creaturely reality. Because this creaturely reality is that of fallen man and because the Word of God meets us in this reality, we have to say that its form is not that of a pure nature which as such stands in immediate contrast with the distorted nature of its environment. Even our knowledge of the Word of God is not through a reason that has somehow remained pure and that can thus pierce the mystery of God in creaturely reality. It is wholly through our fallen reason. The place where God's Word is revealed is objectively and subjectively the cosmos in which sin reigns.

[EN89] seeing through a glass
[EN90] in an enigma
[EN91] against the phenomenon

The form of God's Word, then, is in fact the form of the cosmos which stands in contradiction to God. It has as little ability to reveal God to us as we have to see God in it. If God's Word is revealed in it, it is revealed "through it," of course, but in such a way that this "through it" means "in spite if it." The secularity proper to God's Word is not in itself and as such transparent or capable of being the translucent garment or mirror of God's Word. And in face of it there can never be any question of getting behind it by any effort or skill and of perceiving that the secularity is precisely that of God's Word. What can be brought to light by interpretation or exegesis of this part of the world will always be itself a hidden part of the world, since it is in our own interpretation and exegesis that we try to find aid, and this part in turn will need fresh interpretation and exegesis, will ultimately resist all solution, and will thus be a
[167] contradiction of God's Word and not a complement of God's Word and therefore its simple reflection. The real interpretation of its form can only be that which God's Word gives itself.

The passage which we can hardly take too seriously in this connexion is 1 Cor. 1^{18}–2^{10}. What Paul preaches is ὁ λόγος ὁ τοῦ σταυροῦ, Χριστὸς ἐσταυρωμένος[EN92], which is indeed the power and wisdom of God, by which God turns the wisdom of the world into folly, but which as such, from the world's standpoint, can only be μωρία[EN93], which stamps its proclaimers and hearers as foolish, weak and lowly, as nothings (μὴ ὄντα), which as σοφία ἐν μυστηρίῳ ἡ ἀποκεκρυμμένη[EN94] can enlighten only by divine election, by the ἀπόδειξις πνεύματος καὶ δυνάμεως[EN95], by ἀποκάλυψις[EN96], "that no flesh should glory in his presence,'' "that your faith should not stand in the wisdom of men but in the power of God." What God has prepared for those that love Him, no eye has seen, nor ear heard, nor has it entered the heart of any man. It is the Spirit given by God that knows it, no one and nothing else. *Quia mirandum est, idcirco non creditur. Qualia enim decet esse opera divina, nisi super omnem admirationem? Nos quoque ipsi miramur, sed quia credimus ... Nam si Deus et sapiens et potens ... merito in adversariis sapientiae potentiaeque id est in stultitia et impossibilitate materias operationis suae instituit; quoniam virtus omnis ex his causam accipit a quibus provocatur*[EN97] (Tertullian, *De bapt.*, 2). At issue is the insight which in the Heidelberg Disputation of 1518 (*W.A.* 1, 362 f.) Luther opposes as a *theologia crucis*[EN98] to a *theologia gloriae*[EN99], i.e., a direct or only relatively indirect desire for knowledge of God. W. von Loewenich (Luthers *Theologia crucis*, 1929, 7 and 12) has rightly concluded that we do not have here merely a special chapter in theology but a special form of theology, and not just a principle of the younger Luther but a principle of his whole theology. *Iam adhuc agimus cum Deo velato, in hac enim vita non possumus cum Deo agere facie ad faciem. Universa autem creatura est facies et larva Dei. Sed hic requiritur sapientia quae*

EN92 the word of the cross, Christ crucified
EN93 foolishness
EN94 wisdom hidden in a mystery
EN95 demonstration of the Spirit and of power
EN96 revelation
EN97 Because [what happens in baptism] is too wonderful, it is not believed. For what would one expect divine works to be, if not beyond all wonder? We ourselves also wonder, but we do so because we believe .... For if God is both wise and powerful ... it is appropriate that he should ground his working in that which is opposed to wisdom and power – that is, in foolishness and impossibility – because every strength has its cause in those things by which it is challenged
EN98 theology of the cross
EN99 theology of glory

*discernat Deum a larva. Hanc sapientiam mundus non habet, ideo non potest discernere Deum a larva*EN100 (*Comm. on Gal.* 2[6], 1535, *W.A.* 40[1], 174, 12). At a pinch a Roman Catholic theologian brought up on Plato or Aristotle might have said the same in an application of the doctrine of the *analogia entis*EN101. (There is thus no point in following K. Heim and his disciples, who out of such statements about the character of all creation as *larva Dei*EN102 concoct a new and particularly profound conception of the world on Luther's part.) The core of Luther's idea is that the *larva Dei,* the indirectness of His self-communication, is twofold, one due to the creatureliness and another due to the sinfulness of the creature: *ut ergo fidei locus sit, opus est, ut omnia quae creduntur, abscondantur. Non autem remotius absconduntur. quam sub contrario obiectu, sensu, experientia. Sic Deus dum vivificat, facit illud occidendo; dum iustificat, facit illud reos faciendo; dum in coelum vehit, facit id ad infernum ducendo*EN103 (*De serv. arb.*, 1525, *W.A.*, 18, 633, 7). "The Word I hear, and I see Paul, who is a poor man. But this salvation, grace, life and peace, these I see not; but rather their counterparts I must see daily, sin, terror, ill-luck, suffering and death; that it seemeth there are no men so abandoned by God as Christians, so they hear this Word" (*Sermon on Ac.* 13[26f.], *E.A.* 8, 191). And even more pointedly: *Nam fides ita dicit: Ego credo tibi Deo loquenti. Quid loquitur Deus? Impossibilia, mendatia, stulta, infirma, absurda, abominanda, haeretica et diabolica, si rationem consulas*EN104 (*on Gal.* 3[6], 1525, *W.A.* 40[1], 361, 14). And finally with almost unheard-of sharpness: "Therefore must God's faithfulness and truth even become first a great lie ere it become the truth. For to the world 'tis a heresy. So seemeth it ever to ourselves as if God would leave us and not keep His Word and in our heart He looketh to become a liar. And in fine God cannot be God, He must first become a devil, and we cannot come up to heaven, we [168] must first go down to hell, we cannot become God's children, we must first become the devil's children. For all that God saith and doth, the devil must have said and done" (Ps. 117 *expounded,* 1530, *W.A.* 31[1], 249, 21).

Thus in all applications of the proposition that proclamation, Scripture or revelation is God's Word we must have regard to the fact that this is true only in this twofold indirectness. In the speaking and receiving of God's Word what is involved is not just an act of God generally, and not just an act of God in creaturely reality as such, but an act of God in the reality which contradicts God, which conceals Him, and in which His revelation is not just His act but His miraculous act, the tearing of an untearably thick veil, i.e., His mystery.

This means that we are not to frame Church proclamation in such a way that within the cosmos it seems to be a necessary element in culture, education, national development, social progress, etc. We are not to try to show that the Bible is a credible and commendable

EN100 Now we still have to do with a God who is veiled, for in this life we cannot meet God face to face. At the same time, the whole creation is a kind of 'face' or mask of God. But here is required the wisdom that discerns God from the mask. The world does not have this wisdom, and so cannot discern God from the mask

EN101 analogy of being

EN102 mask of God

EN103 Therefore, so that a place might be preserved for faith, it is necessary for all things that are believed to be hidden. But they are not hidden farther away than by being associated with the contrary object, perception or experience. And so when God makes alive, He does it by killing; when He justifies, He does it by making guilty; when He brings to heaven, He does it by leading to hell

EN104 Now faith says this: I believe You – the God who speaks. What does God speak? If you judge according to reason, impossibilities, lies, things that are foolish, weak, absurd, blasphemous, heretical and diabolical

book from various human standpoints, as was usually done in the age of orthodoxy and the Enlightenment (unfortunately even Calvin did something of the same incidentally in *Instit.*, I, 8), and as has been attempted with all the tools of historical thinking from the days of Herder. Above all, we should on principle spare revelation itself, i.e., Jesus Christ, all our direct or relatively indirect desire to prove its superiority over all other religions (cf. K. Holl, "*Urchristentum und Religionsgeschichte*," 1925, in *Ges. Aufsätze zur Kirchengesch.*, II, 1 f.). In the long run a purely historical treatment of Christianity will always prove to be theologically more fruitful here than these attempts at penetration which purport to be historical but which ultimately rest on a confusion of categories.

One is not to think of the secularity of the Word of God as a kind of fatal accident or an inconvenience which will some day be set aside either totally or at least in part. This secularity, this twofold indirectness, is in fact an authentic and inalienable attribute of the Word of God itself. Revelation means the incarnation of the Word of God. But incarnation means entry into this secularity. We are in this world and are through and through secular. If God did not speak to us in secular form, He would not speak to us at all. To evade the secularity of His Word is to evade Christ. Even though it dawns on us for the first time what is meant by the fact that we are flesh and therefore not God, that we have no organ or capacity for God, that we are in enmity against Him and powerless to be obedient to Him, nevertheless, what seems in the first instance an absurd obstacle that God Himself has put in the way is in fact His real way to us, and consequently a necessary way and a good way. It is not as though we could see why it can and must be so. We are not above God or ourselves. Hence the only sentence we can pronounce on the necessity and goodness of the relation in which God has set Himself to us is one that seeks to reproduce the actuality of this relation. But we have nothing else to reproduce, and therefore we must repeat the fact that just as surely as God enters
[169] into relation with us through His Word, so surely His Word must be as it is, i.e., secular, a Word spoken in twofold indirectness. It is not, then, that God was concealed from us by some unfortunate disturbance and that He revealed Himself by removing the concealment. If this were so, the attempts of man to help God by forcing his own way into the mystery would be understandable and excusable if not actually necessary. The truth is, however, that God veils Himself and that in so doing—this is why we must not try to intrude into the mystery—He unveils Himself. It is good for us that God acts as He does and it could only be fatal for us if He did not, if He were manifest to us in the way we think right, directly and without veil, without secularity or only in the innocuous secularity that can be pierced by the *analogia entis*[EN105]. It would not be love and mercy but the end of us and all things if the Word were spoken to us thus. The fact that it is spoken as it is, revealing in its concealment, is a decisive indication of the truth that it has really come to us instead of our having to go to it, an attempt in which we could only fail. In its very secularity it is thus in every respect a Word of grace.

[EN105] analogy of being

Among other places in a powerful passage at the beginning of his *Commentary on Galatians* (*W.A.* 40^{1}, 75 ff.) Luther has made it clear that this must distinguish us from the papacy, Turks, Jews, and all *justitiarii, ut abstineamus a speculatione Maiestatis*[EN106], which can only be harmful to both body and soul; *scrutator enim Maiestatis opprimitur a gloria*[EN107]. To want to know God directly means righteousness by works, and righteousness by works means the fall of Lucifer and despair. We, on the contrary, must cleave to the true and actual Christ as He lies in the crib and in the Virgin's lap. Calvin spoke similarly: *Quand donc nous n'aurions sinon la maiesté de Dieu qui se présentera devant nos yeux, elle sera pour nous effrayer et n'y pourrons pas avoir aucun acces à cause que nous sommes creatures fragiles, et mesmes qu'il n'y en nous que peché: nous campons ici sur la terre: mais nous sommes dignes d'estre engloutis iusques au profond d'enfer*[EN108] (*Sermon on Gal.* $1^{3f.}$, *C.R.* 50, 289). *Magnifions la bonte de nostre Dieu, veu qu'il luy plaist d'avoir regard a nous et à nostre rudesse, et qu'il est content que sa gloire nous soit cachée, afin que nous n'en soyons point abysmez. Car ... nous ne la pouvons porter estans ainsi fragiles que nous sommes*[EN109] (*Sermon on Deut.* $5^{4f.}$, *C.R.* 26, 248). "Yea, if one feel it as actually 'tis in truth, man must straightway from that hour die. For man being flesh and blood cannot understand it, in life man's heart is much too strait to conceive of such ... (Luther, *Sermon on Mk.* 16^{1-8}, *Sommerpost*, 1526, *W.A.* 10^{1}, 2, 216, 19). "It is forbidden, I must not see, feel, know or see it, but only hear it, and with faith cleave to it, and stand on the mere Word of God. And it is with us as with one that hath dizziness in his head should he climb a high tower or come on to a bridge under which deep water floweth, so that he must be blinded and be led blindly and hang a cloak about his head, and be led and borne, else he falleth from the tower and breaketh his neck, or falleth into the water and drowneth. So, if we are to be saved, we must follow our guide, and then we are safe. We, too, must shut our eyes tight and follow our leader, the divine Word, and say: I will let myself be wound in swaddling clothes and a cloak be wrapped about my head, and let myself be led to that which I believe and see not, and will live and die thereon. Otherwise we shall not feel it even if we tear ourselves to pieces there- [170]
for. Many have troubled themselves sorely and would fain know where our dwelling or lodging is when we die, whither we are going, and many great people have become mad that they wot not where one goes on leaving this life, and have therefore coined this saying:

I live and know not how long,
I die and know not when,
I go and know not whither,
A wonder 'tis I'm glad.

And 'tis true a non-Christian cannot know, but a Christian must judge otherwise thereof, he hath a trusty conductor, he followeth his leader and guide. Christ, who telleth what a man should do, and saith: Hear what we speak, for we know what to say, our words are truth, trust me, give thyself over and lay thee in my cloak that I have wound about thy head, I will carry thee over. If thou doest thus, thou wilt not be misled by Him. But thou dost say, I know not whither I go, I feel nought, grope for and grasp nought. That is true, but thou must rely on God's Word and trust God who will uphold thee so that if thou fallest from the tower thou

---

[EN106] jurists, that we refrain from speculation about the divine Majesty

[EN107] for anyone who seeks to explore the divine Majesty is crushed by its glory

[EN108] Thus, if we were to have the majesty of God present itself to our eyes, it would only terrify us, and we could not have any access to it, inasmuch as we are fragile creatures, and also because there is nothing in us but sin: we sojourn here on the earth, but we are worthy of being plunged down to the depths of hell

[EN109] Let us magnify the goodness of our God, seeing that he has been pleased to have regard for us and our crudeness, and that He is happy to hide His glory from us, so that we should not be destroyed by it. Because ... we cannot bear it, being the fragile creatures that we are

wilt not break thy neck in twain or if thou shyest from the ship and art like to drown. But there is nought there to see, we know not where the ladder or the steps are or the cord on which the ladder hangs, we can see no way that leadeth to heaven. But in Christ the way to heaven is alone prepared for us, which is reserved for us through the divine Word, otherwise thou treadest upon air and so fallest ... This then is the difference between a Christian and a pagan, that a godless man and a pagan departeth like a cow, seeing, judging and feeling all things according to the old birth as what he feels and grasps. But a Christian followeth not as he seeth, but followeth what he seeth not nor feeleth, and abideth by the witness of Christ, heareth what Christ saith, whom he followeth right on into the darkness. Thus we stay fast in the bag and are wound in His cloak and He leadeth us where Himself is and in Christ we walk up to heaven that maketh him blessed" (*Exposition of Jn.* 3–4, *W.A.* 47, 33, 38). "Lo, 'tis this whereon St. John insisteth strongly in his Gospel, that we should simply let go of fair and lofty thoughts whereby reason and clever folk go about and seek God in majesty outside Christ. He is ready in Christ to lie in the cradle and in His mother's lap and to hang on the cross; they would mount up to heaven and find out how He sits and rules the world. These are vain and fearful thoughts when not guided aright. For they are all bound to this one spot where we should not grope or peer further. Wouldest thou seize and grasp all that God is and doth and hath in mind, then seek it nowhere save where He hath put and laid it. Thou nearest that in the saying, 'All that is thine is mine,' etc. Thus a Christian ought to know not to seek or find God otherwise save in the Virgin's lap and on the cross or as and where Christ sheweth Himself in His Word" (*Sermon on Jn.* 16^{20}, 1528–29, *W.A.* 28, 135, 38).

In direct connexion with these thoughts of Luther and Calvin we must now come back again to F. Gogarten. In the first edition of this book, apart from the absence of a "true anthropology," he has objected especially to the fact that in some parts at least "it now speaks of a God isolated in and for Himself over against man and now of a man isolated in and for himself over against God" (*Theol. Rundschau*, 1929, 72). This may be seen in the use of the terms "objective" and "subjective" in relation to God and man, and in the distinction between an "eternal history of God" and God's revelation as history or man addressed by God, between a "God in Himself" and a "God for us." But it is a mistake, he thinks, to presup-
[171] pose that in theology we should start our thinking "with the past incarnation of the Word." I can scarcely be wrong in assuming that in this attack Gogarten had in view Luther's polemic against *speculatio Maiestatis*[EN110], of which a few instances have just been given. True he does not actually accuse me of overlooking this warning of the Reformers. He rather quotes a series of passages from my own book in which I contradict myself by erasing the distinction. He even believes that the erasure of the distinction is my own true opinion and that I then contradict it by making the distinction. He claims "to see that Barth gets very close to these things. But in getting close to them, he already leaves them again" (p. 73). Gogarten advances two explanations for this error of mine. He suggests first that it is the result of working with untested and unpurified concepts instead of first reducing them to order in a true anthropology. These unpurified concepts progressively introduced alien problems into my thinking and thus spoiled the first draft (p. 78f.). But at the close of his essay Gogarten makes the rather different point that it is clear to him that in the very thing to which he has to take exception there is to be noted the "true theological concern" of the book, namely, the effort to put the stress on "God Himself" in all dogmatic questions, an intention in which he is in full agreement with me (p. 79f.). In reply, let me admit that he is right when he says that I make the alleged distinction only to abandon it again, or *vice versa* that I come very close to tilings (Gogarten obviously means the clear and definitive erasure of the distinction) and then leave them again. As regards "unpurified concepts," I again concede the fact,

---

[EN110] the attempt to speculate about the divine Majesty

but can only repeat that I reject the whole enterprise of an anticipatory purifying of concepts in an anthropology of theologically dubious character, and that for my own part I can expect results only from a purifying wluich takes place in the process of the dogmatic enquiry and exposition itself. As for the "theological concern" which Gogarten sees at work even in my alleged error, and in which he associates himself with me in spite of my error, it would have been instructive if he had stated to what degree he thinks the error is based not merely on certain mishaps with unpurified concepts, for which perhaps only formal regrets are in order, but upon certain material ineluctabilities. Does he perhaps think that what he censures cannot be avoided if thought is to start theologically, and not philosophically, with "the past incarnation of the Word"? On this basis theological thought is distinguished from philosophical thought by the fact that it does not regard the incarnation of the Word as the truth of a state, e.g., the truth of the unity of subject and object, of the man-relatedness of God or the God-relatedness of man, which is then an underlying principle of dogmatics that has to be exegeted—this is something Luther and the older Lutheran dogmaticians never did in spite of their rejection of *speculatio Maiestatis*—but regards it rather as the truth of a divine act. But if it is understood as an act, then the *terminus a quo*[EN111] ("God in Himself") and the *terminus ad quem*[EN112] ("man in himself") must be differentiated and then interrelated in the description of the act as such. What would "God for us" mean if it were not said against the background of "God in Himself"? To erase the distinction, i.e., in order to speak about this particular matter, there has also to be differentiation in this matter. If we are not prepared to say the latter here, we can obviously say nothing when we say the former. We recall what was said under the second sub-section about the purposiveness or pertinence of the Word of God. We tried to emphasise there that we properly understand God's love for us only when we regard it as unmerited and free, and similarly the Word of God is properly understood only as a word which has truth and glory in itself and not just as spoken to us. It would be no less God's eternal Word if it were not spoken to us, and what constitutes the mercy of its revelation, of its being spoken to us, is that it is spoken to us in virtue of the freedom in which God could be "God in Himself" and yet He does not will to be so and in fact is not so, but [172] wills to be and actually is "God for us." This freedom of God, without which one cannot understand His Word as grace, seems to me to be obscured if in too triumphant a victory over what is called Greek thought we abandon altogether the distinction between objective and subjective in the Word of God, as Gogarten obviously wishes to do.

At this stage I must recall another critical review of my book in which I am censured from the very opposite side. In *Stimmen der Zeit* (Nov. 1928, p. 105) Erich Przywara S.J. wrote that there is a sinister reduction running through my whole work. I am affirming the whole world of Christian revelation only to the extent that it is the one manifestation of the process of revelation as Kierkegaard conceived of it, namely, as God's address to man. With me the Trinity supposedly dissolves into that of revealer, revealing and being revealed, the incarnation is only a concretion of this process of revelation, and grace is simply the subjective possibility of revelation. All the fulness of the divine life is thus reduced to the one address, and in the last resort the final pantheistic correlation-theology of Protestant Liberalism is simply reversed in me. The "from below upwards" is changed into a "from above downwards." God is not now reduced to the nature of man but—and this obviously seems to be much worse in Przywara's opinion—man is exalted to the nature of God to the degree that the nature of God Himself is called the "address of revelation" ... Now this is certainly not a correct estimation of my intentions nor of what I actually said. But the fact that a clever and slightly malicious eye like that of Przywara could see and interpret me in this way I regard as a

EN111 starting point
EN112 ending point

warning not to go further in the direction desired by Gogarten. If we do not wish to be understood as Przywara (however wrongly) understands me here, we have to be very clear that we are not engaged in correlation-theology, i.e., in a theology in which God swings up or down in His relation to us, either from below upwards so that God becomes a predicate of man, or from above downwards so that man becomes a requisite in God's nature. In the thinking necessary in correlating God and man we must not think away the free basis that this correlation has in God, as Wobbermin and his disciple R. Winckler so obviously do, and as Bultmann in my view can hardly avoid doing. If we are not to do this, then it is not just good sense but absolutely essential that along with all older theology we make a deliberate and sharp distinction between the Trinity of God as we may know it in the Word of God revealed, written and proclaimed, and God's immanent Trinity, i.e., between "God in Himself" and "God for us," between the "eternal history of God" and His temporal acts. In so doing we must always bear in mind that the "God for us" does not arise as a matter of course out of the "God in Himself," that it is not true as a state of God which we can fix and assert on the basis of the concept of man participating in His revelation, but that it is true as an act of God, as a step which God takes towards man and by which man becomes the man that participates in His revelation. This becoming on man's part is conditioned from without, by God, whereas God in making the step by which the whole correlation is first fashioned is not conditioned from without, by man. For this reason—and we agree with Gogarten here—theology cannot speak of man in himself, in isolation from God. But as in the strict doctrine of the Trinity as the presupposition of Christology, it must speak of God in Himself, in isolation from man. We know ourselves only as those addressed by God's Word, but precisely as those addressed by God's Word we must know God as the One who addresses us in freedom, as the Lord, who does not exist only as He addresses us, but exists as the One who establishes and ratifies this relation and correlation, who is also God before it, in Himself, in His eternal history. If this principle, this recollection of the immanent objective God-ness of God in Himself in distinction from His God-ness for us, is already *speculatio Maiestatis*[EN113], then
[173] Luther himself engages in *speculatio Maiestatis* when he compares the Word that was in the beginning, that was with God and was God (Jn. 1[1]), to the way in which love or anger, even without being expressed or declared, can absolutely fill a man and constitute the entire nature of this man, and then continues: "According to this metaphor God in His majesty and nature is also pregnant with a word or utterance which God hath with Him in His divine nature and which is His heart's thought, which same is as complete and great and perfect as God Himself, none seeth, heareth nor conceiveth this utterance save God alone. He hath an invisible and inconceivable utterance which hath been word for all angels and for all creatures, for afterwards hath He through this utterance and word given their nature to all creatures; in utterance, word and thought God is indeed burning, He thinking nought else therefor" (*Exposition of Jn.* 1–2, 1537–38, *W.A.* 46, 545, 6). But what connexion is there between this and the *speculatio Maiestatis* which Luther attacks in the *Commentary on Galatians* and elsewhere? The attack is not on recognising and understanding the incarnate Word in all seriousness as God's Word. It is not on acknowledging its invisible majesty. It is not on the distinction between what we can see and feel and grasp by reason and what we must believe on the presupposition of this whole visible aspect. It is an attack on the attempt to evade the necessity of believing by trying to get a direct or only relatively indirect knowledge of God apart from the secularity and the resultant mystery of the incarnate Word. When Luther points to the crib of Bethlehem and the cross of Golgotha, he is not saying that direct knowledge of God is possible and actual here in this very secular phenomenon as such. He is not saying that there is no need here to distinguish between what we see and hear and appre-

---

[EN113] the attempt to speculate about the divine Majesty

hend and what we have to believe, between the true humanity and the true deity, between the *terminus ad quem*[EN114] and the *terminus a quo*[EN115]. What he is pointing to is the total secularity, i.e., the hiddenness of the Word, and therewith the sole reality of indirect knowledge, and therewith that distinction whose elimination can only be thought of as in process and never as completed, and therewith the immanent Trinity, the eternal essence and the eternal counsels of God. Here in the *humanitas Christi*[EN116] we are to seek and find everything. We seek and find this, but we seek and find; we do not see and have directly. And now conversely I fail to see how, if we take the course indicated by Gogarten and make a direct identification of "God in Himself" and "God for us," we can avoid trespassing into what Luther has repudiated as *speculatio Maiestatis*, into a denial of the indirectness of our knowledge of the Word of God. If we really say indirectness and do not mean an innocuous indirectness of low potency that can easily be changed into directness in virtue of the *analogia entis*[EN117], but the true, emphatic and indissoluble indirectness of the revelation and knowledge of God in the flesh, in the offence of the cradle and the cross, then we must make the second statement in order to make the first, the only first that comes into consideration here. Are we taking the secularity and hiddenness of God's Word seriously if we think we can say the one thing in one word instead of two? Naturally I am not claiming that Gogarten thinks this or that he wants to deny the indirectness of our knowledge of the Word of God. But I am again faced by a riddle: Since he obviously thinks the one and does not want to deny the other, what does he really have in mind and what is he really after in his criticism? Has he broken with the conceptions of A. Ritschl, of which his criticism uneasily reminds me, in the way that one ought to break with these conceptions, i.e., with those of Enlightenment theology? Be that as it may, Gogarten has not, strictly speaking, referred to actual mistakes of material importance in my presentation, but only to a source of possible material mishaps. In contrast, I learn from Przywara's review from the opposite corner how seriously advance in the direction desired by Gogarten would endanger material understanding in C.D.-G the very point which I regard as crucial. In this respect, then, it is unavoidable that I [174]
should speak even more sharply along the lines that Gogarten does not approve, or that I should preserve an even more eloquent silence, unable in either case to yield a single inch.

2. The speech of God is and remains the mystery of God in its one-sidedness. I have in mind here the relation of veiling and unveiling occasioned by the secularity of the Word. That God's Word is one-sided means that when spoken to us and received by us it does not meet us partly veiled and partly unveiled, but either veiled or unveiled, yet without being different in itself, without being spoken and received any the less truly either way. Its veiling can change for us absolutely into its unveiling and its unveiling can change absolutely into its veiling. Absolutely, for it is always unalterably the same in itself, always the one or the other for us. We can only grasp the other in the one, i.e., we can grasp the other only as we grasp the one; we can grasp it only in faith. We are set in the greatest clarity in relation to the one, in such clarity that we have very distinct and in themselves clear thoughts regarding what is said to us, and we can react thereto with the whole outer and inner attitude of our lives, with joy,

EN114 ending point
EN115 starting point
EN116 humanity of Christ
EN117 analogy of being

gratitude, confidence, zeal, seriousness, terror, confusion, anxiety, remorse. But this reaction is really reaction to the Word of God only when our clarity, our thought, our attitude, has a very definite limit in the other, the limit set by the very Word spoken to us, which will not let itself be made a whole, a synthesis or a system whether in theory or in practice, the limit beyond which the Word is a mystery, and really becomes a mystery again, for all the clarity with which it is spoken to us and received by us. To receive the Word of God does not mean on either side to be able to see and know and state the relation between the two sides, to be able to say why and how far the veiled Word now means unveiling or the unveiled Word means veiling. If we could know and state this, the Word of God would obviously cease to be a mystery, and would just be a paradox like others, a paradox behind whose supposed mystery one can more or less easily penetrate. The speech of God is and remains a mystery to the extent that its totality as such, and hence with all the weight and seriousness of God's Word, is always manifest to us only on one side and always remains hidden on the other side. Hidden, and not simply withheld: In what is manifest to us the hidden side is always contained, but as a hidden side, so that we can grasp and have it only as such, i.e., only in faith. In virtue of this one-sidedness what God says to us remains what it is. His ways remain higher than our ways and His thoughts higher than our thoughts (Is. $55^{8f.}$), not just in quantity but in manner and possibility. What remains hidden in what is made manifest to us remains in God's own hand. It is still to be sought and found [175] there, with Him. It cannot be translated into our own insight or the corresponding attitude. For the point of God's speech is not to occasion specific thoughts or a specific attitude but through the clarity which God gives us, and which induces both these in us, to bind us to Himself. This happens, however, as we are constantly set before our limit, i.e., before His mystery.

We must examine this more closely. When by the miraculous act of God His Word is spoken to us and received by us in its secularity, this may mean that we really hear the "God with us" that is spoken to us but we hear it only in the secular form in which it is said to us. But it may also mean that we do indeed hear it in its secular form but really hear it thus. From God's standpoint this is one and the same thing, but for us it is not the same; it is two things, or one only in faith. The one time God unveils Himself in His Word, but also veils Himself therewith. The other time He veils Himself, but also unveils Himself therewith. In both instances it is a matter of hearing the full and true Word of God, the unveiling of God in His veiling or the veiling of God in His unveiling. The secular form without the divine content is not the Word of God and the divine content without the secular form is also not the Word of God. We can neither stop at the secular form as such nor can we fly off beyond this and try to enjoy the divine content alone. The one would be realistic theology, the other idealistic theology, and both bad theology. In both cases, however, we hear only in faith the full and true Word of God. Erasure of the distinction and indeed of the antithesis of form and content we cannot achieve. The coinci-

dence of the two is clear to God but is not discernible by us. What is discernible by us is always form without content or content without form. Our thinking can be realistic or idealistic but it cannot be Christian. Obviously the concept of synthesis would be the least Christian of all, for it would mean no more and no less than trying to do God's miraculous act ourselves. In faith and in the thinking of faith there can be no thought of synthesis. Faith means recognising that synthesis cannot be attained and committing it to God and seeking and finding it in Him. Finding it in God, we acknowledge that we cannot find it ourselves, whether by achieving it in a specific attitude or by thinking it out systematically. Committing it to God and seeking it in God, we really do find it; we hear the full and true Word of God, whether it be the divine content in its secular form or in the secular form the divine content. To hear the full and true Word of God does not mean perceiving the unity of veiling and unveiling, of form and content, and thus achieving Christian thought by the detour of faith. No, the thinking of faith will always be quite honestly a realistic or idealistic thinking, i.e., a thinking that in and of itself is most unchristian. As such, and without becoming any different in itself and as such, the thinking of faith is justified and sanctified thinking. But justification and sanctification in faith [176]
mean justification and sanctification by the object of faith, by God, though the believer, and therefore his thinking, do not cease to be less needy on this account. And since we cannot give ourselves faith, we ourselves cannot fashion this justification and sanctification of our thinking, nor can we make our thinking Christian, nor even affirm that it is so in ourselves or others. We can only believe this as God's grace even in face of the fact that our thinking either on the one side or the other is confronted by a wall which we can neither overthrow nor make transparent, namely, in face of the fact that considered in and of itself our thinking is irrefutably non-christian. Hence believing means either hearing the divine content of God's Word even though nothing but the secular form is discernible by us or it means hearing the secular form of God's Word even though only its divine content is discernible by us.

At this point we may certainly recall the notable relation between the concepts "Father" and "Son" in their application to God as such and His incarnate Word as such in the Gospel of John. Both concepts are used there in such a way that the content of the one is presupposed to be discernible and then there follows the declaration that from knowledge of the content of the one there can and must and will be knowledge of the content of the other. Thus "that which the Father giveth me" (6^{37}), or "whom the Father draweth" (6^{44}) or "to whom it hath been given of the Father" (6^{45}) or "whoso is given to the Son by the Father" (10^{29}), this man comes to me, the Son. Or on the other hand "he that honoureth not the Son, honoureth not the Father" (5^{23}), or "if any man serve me, him will the Father honour" (12^{26}), or "no man cometh unto the Father but by me" (14^{6}), or "he that hath seen me has seen the Father" (14^{9}), or "that the Father may be glorified in the Son" (14^{13}). Then in almost direct contrast: "I honour my Father" (8^{49}), and: "My Father that honoureth me" (8^{54}). The statement that "I and the Father are one" (10^{30}), or " ... that they may be one even as we are" (the Father and the Son, 17^{11}), obviously does no more than underline the fact that in John believing is equally both coming from the known Father to the unknown Son and also coming from the known Son to the unknown Father. There can hardly be anything contrary to the sense of John if in this context we substitute for Father and Son the concepts of form and content in their distinction and unity.

Invariably, then, faith is acknowledgment of our limit and acknowledgment of the mystery of God's Word, acknowledgment of the fact that our hearing is bound to God Himself, who now leads us through form to content and now from content back to form, and either way to Himself, not giving Himself in either case into our hands but keeping us in His hands.

It might seem surprising that the movement of faith, or rather the movement of God's Word which faith can only follow, is described so explicitly and totally as twofold. This is not done in the interests of a scheme but because the matter described leaves us no option. It is especially true that what is at issue in faith is to pierce, or to see to be pierced, the concealment in which God speaks
[177] to us in proclamation, in the Bible and in Christ Himself, and thus to see and hear that the very concealment of God is his true and real revealing.

We have in mind here the familiar and remarkable sermon of Luther on the story of the Syro-Phoenician woman in Mt. 15[21f.]: "Believing steadfastly in the proclamation of Christ that she has heard (in 'such good crying abroad'), the woman comes to Him, but lo, He takes another tack as though He would cause her faith and good confidence to fail and falsify the report of Him, so that she might well think. Is this the kindly, friendly man? or are these the good words that I have heard tell of Him, wheron I have relied? It must be untrue. He is thine enemy and favoureth thee not. Surely He might speak a word and say to me, I will not. But He is as silent as a stock. Lo, this is a hard blow if God show Himself so stern and angry, and hide His grace so high and deep. ... Now what doth the woman thereupon? She putteth from her eyes such unkind and hard bearing in Christ, is not deceived by all that, taketh it not to heart, but abideth downright and firm in her confidence, holding on to the good report that she had heard and conceived of Him, and leaveth not off. So must we also do, and learn to cling fast to the Word alone, though God range Himself towards all creatures other than the Word saith of Him. But oh, how sad that is for nature and reason that they must strip themselves bare and let go all they feel and lean alone on the mere Word although they feel the opposite. God help us in straits and dying to such courage and faith. Even the intercession of Jesus' disciples leadeth but to the answer, 'I am not sent but to the lost sheep of the house of Israel.' Here must all saints and all intercession halt. Yea, here must the heart let even the Word go, when its feeling is to cling to it. But what doth the woman? She leaveth not off, cleaveth to the Word even though it be torn from His heart as it were by force, taketh no heed of such a stern answer, still trusteth firmly that His kindness yet lurketh beneath and will not yet judge that Christ is ungracious or might be. That is what it means to hold fast. And once more her own 'Help me, Lord' leadeth but to the reply, 'It is not meet to take the children's bread and cast it to the dogs.' What will she say here? He answereth her ill that she is one of the damned and lost that should not be reckoned with the elect. That is a right unanswerable reply that none can deal with. Yet she leaveth not off, but even agreeth with His judgment and granteth she is a dog, nor desireth more than a dog, namely, to eat the crumbs that fall from the master's table. Is not that a masterpiece? She taketh Christ at His own words. He likeneth her to a dog; that she granteth, and asketh no more than that He let her be a dog as Himself judgeth; what then? He was fairly taken. To a dog one indeed leaveth the crumbs beneath the table, that is its right. Therefore He openeth right up and yieldeth to her will, that she is not now a dog but even a child of Israel

... here thou seest, though Christ take a seeming hard stand, yet giveth He no final judgment that He should say nay, but all His answers sound like nay, yet are not nay but swing in suspense. For He saith not, I will not hear her, but is quite silent, and replieth not yet a nay. Likewise He saith not that she is not of the house of Israel, but that Himself was sent to the house of Israel only. He thus leaveth it to hang and swing in suspense 'twixt yea and nay. So he saith not, Thou art a dog and shalt not be given the children's bread, but, it is not meet etc. He thus leaveth it again in suspense whether she be a dog or no. Yet all three sayings ring a bit stronger to nay than yea, but there is still more in them than nay. In sooth simple yea is in them, but very deeply and secretly, and what appeareth is simple nay. Thereby is indicated how our heart standeth in trial. According as it feeleth, so taketh Christ here His stand. Its thought really is that simple nay is there, yet 'tis not true. Therefore must it turn from such feeling and grasp and hold the deep and secret yea beneath and above the nay with firm [178] faith in God's Word, as the woman doth, and concede God the tightness of His judgment on us. So have we won and captured Him in His own words, as when we feel in conscience God chideth us for sinners and judgeth us unworthy of the kingdom of heaven, then we feel hell and bethink us eternally lost. Whoso then learn here from this woman and capture God in His own judgment and say. Yea, Lord, 'tis true, I am a sinner and not worthy of Thy grace, yet Thou hast promised pardon to sinners and art not come to call the righteous, but, as St. Paul also saith, to save sinners, lo, so must God by His own judgment have mercy upon us" (*Fastenpostille*, 1525, *W.A.* 17^{II}, pp. 201–4).

But conversely in the unveiling of God there is to be seen and acknowledged His veiling, i.e., the close relation between the content and the form, the glory and the humility, the goodness and the severity of the Word of God. Only in the consummation when faith ceases altogether can we imagine man no longer needing but relieved of this reverse movement of faith, this recollection of the secularity of the Word of God. Even the faith that breaks through or is led through the visible to the invisible, the No to the Yes, is after all regarded as human experience, action and thought, the faith of the man who even and precisely in his triumph stands in need of correction and completion, and indeed of a wholly new relation to God. He must therefore retrace the way already traversed. Freed by the Word, he must be taken captive again by the same Word. He must be placed again before God, which means before the God who is concealed in His concealment. What could experience of God's unveiling be but *superbia*[EN118] if it were content therewith? And what could thought about this experience be but *theologia gloriae, speculatio Maiestatis*[EN119], if it were to stop there? Roman Catholic and Protestant *theologia gloriae* has constantly appealed to this experience, to triumphant faith, and has failed to see that in abandoning the indirectness of the knowledge of God it has immediately abandoned true faith and the real Word of God as well. In fact faith and the Word of God are no less needed for this return from finding to seeking, from being inside to being outside, from having to asking, from the triumph of experience and thought to honest and complete spiritual poverty. It is indeed no less hard and inconceivable for the victor that he too and he specifically

EN118 pride
EN119 theology of glory, the attempt to speculate about the divine Majesty

should see and confess that he is beaten than it is for the beaten man to know that as such he is the victor.

An important difference between faith and mysticism is that the mystic as such denies this reversal; in ecstasy before unveiled Deity he ceases to be aware of the veiling; he regards proclamation, Bible and Christ in their secularity as mere symbols of the Godhead now unveiled to him, which have now become dispensable and which he can basically discard; henceforth he sees his future only in ever fuller unveilings which lead him more and more into the depths or the heights. In contrast, the triumphant believer returns immediately as such to proclamation, the Bible, and Christ in their secularity; he sits down again, as it were,
[179] in the lowest room; he seeks his future only (and genuinely so) in the God who is totally concealed (not already revealed but totally concealed) from him as from every other sinner. It is in this very going and going back again that the believer as such, because both goings are at the command of the God who calls, has apart from all else an assurance that the mystic as such can never have.

Human experience and thought as such, if they were to follow their own bias, would proceed in a straight line from despair to even deeper despair, from solemnity to even greater solemnity (there is also a negative *theologia gloriae*), or from triumph to even higher triumph, from joy to even greater joy. To faith, however, this straight line movement is forbidden by the Word of God which calls us from despair to triumph, from solemnity to joy, but also from triumph to despair and from joy to solemnity. This is the *theologia crucis*[EN120]. So, in this discipline by His Word, which never leaves us alone whether in our humility or our pride, God is faithful to Himself and to us, always, then, in an unequivocal one-sided advance or retreat in which the other side remains unsaid and everything depends on our hearing it either way as said by God. How necessary it is to be clear about this twofold movement of the Word of God and the faith that follows it may be seen finally from the fact that one has only to extend the lines a little on both sides to move from the concepts of veiling and unveiling, or form and content, to other opposing concepts, namely, Law and Gospel, demand and promise, or in another direction letter and spirit, or in yet another God's wrath and judgment and God's grace. The Word of God in its veiling, its form, is the claiming of man by God. The Word of God in its unveiling, its content, is God's turning to man. The Word of God is one. In the claim there takes place the turning, and the turning does not take place without the claim. When man is truly and seriously put under the Law he comes to the Gospel, and when he comes to the Gospel by revelation and faith, he is truly and seriously put under the Law. God's wrath and judgment is only the hard shell, the *opus alienum*[EN121] of divine grace, but the man who knows grace, the *opus Dei proprium*[EN122], he and he alone knows what is God's wrath and judgment. The letter of proclamation and the Bible is the

---

[EN120] theology of the cross
[EN121] alien work
[EN122] God's proper work

bearer of the Spirit, but it is the Spirit that constantly brings us back to the letter. When we consider these pregnant concepts that develop out of the veiledness or unveiledness of God's Word, we shall not want to say—we could do so only by a hopeless weakening of all these serious concepts—that we simultaneously experience their content in its truth and that we can systematically interrelate them. One of them is always true in experience and thought, and we must always believe the other that we do not see.

In Ex. 19–20 we find the story of the concluding of the covenant between Yahweh and Israel at Sinai. The nature of the covenant is indicated by the reminder of the help Israel has [180] thus far received from its God and by the promise: "Ye shall be my peculiar treasure among all peoples." But this is not the crucial content of this chapter. The important thing is on the one hand (Ex. 19) the astonishingly direct and impressive warning in all circumstances to keep away from the place where this gracious and friendly God manifests Himself in order to avoid instant death, along with the description of the terrible event of His manifestation which is experienced at close quarters only by the one man Moses, and then on the other hand (Ex. 20) the account of the conditions that Yahweh imposes on Israel, i.e., the commandments of the covenant, to whose strict observance the promise is tied. In the same Old Testament Canon Jer. $31^{31f.}$ speaks again of a covenant of the same Yahweh with the same Israel. It is based on the presupposition that Israel broke the first covenant whose commandments it was supposed to keep. As if this did not signify the end of any possible covenant, as if God were unfaithful to Himself, a new covenant is now proclaimed. In it, too, there is to be a Law, but it is not now revealed from afar amid thunder and lightning. This Law—but what does Law mean in this case?—is to be written in the hearts of the Israelites, so much so, so truly in their hearts, that all instruction in the knowledge of Yahweh from man to man will be superfluous. This new revelation of the Law, this completely new position of Israel close to Yahweh, this new covenant which is utterly inconceivable from the standpoint of the first, is to rest on the forgiveness of sins, "and I will be their God, and they shall be my people" (v. 33). Now if we are to listen to both Ex. 19–20 and Jer. 31, we obviously cannot listen to both at the same time. A historical analysis of the two texts will in its own way show us at once that a systematic conspectus of both is impossible. Hence we can only listen either to the one or the other at the one time. Nor can it be a matter of harmonising exegesis but solely a matter of faith to see the validity of each covenant in the other, of the new in the old and the old in the new. There is a similar relation in the Old Testament between predictions of salvation and predictions of disaster by the prophets. The prophets admittedly surprise us by the abrupt one-sidedness with which at one moment they relentlessly speak only of judgment to come and at another they speak unrestrainedly only of coming redemption. There was a time when Old Testament scholarship thought it impossible that one and the same prophet should have spoken one way in one passage and the other in another. We are more cautious to-day. We would say that prophecies of salvation and disaster in the absolute sense in which they occur were naturally impossible at the same time or in any inner connexion. There can thus be no system of prophetic utterance. It was either threat or promise. In this very one-sidedness it sought to be God's Word. To understand it there was and is needed what is called faith in the New Testament, namely, the perception either way of what is not said. In the New Testament itself we may recall the relation between the Synoptic tradition and the Johannine tradition in respect of the humanity and deity of Jesus Christ. Both speak of both, but with such varying interests and emphases that we can only misunderstand both if, as the historico-critical school once did, we try to measure the one by the other or (in what was

once taken to be the positive method) we seek to balance the one by the other. That the Johannine view is actually directed against the Synoptic presentation is theologically a not too bad historical hypothesis favoured by many modern scholars. It is impossible to listen at one and the same time to the two statements that Jesus of Nazareth is the Son of God and that the Son of God is Jesus of Nazareth. One hears either the one or the other or one hears nothing. When the one is heard, the other can be heard only indirectly, in faith. I will adduce as a last example the relation between the cross or death of Christ and His resurrection in the preaching of Paul. Paul often used the two terms very close together, but they
[181] always point in very different directions whether with reference to Christ Himself or with reference to the reality of salvation for Christians. Paul undoubtedly has both in view when he simply says Ἰησοῦς Χριστός[EN123] or ἐν Χριστῷ[EN124], but it is worth noting that he can really say both only by this name. But this name is not a system representing a unified experience or a unified thought; it is the Word of God itself. In it the cross and resurrection are one, but they are not one—either for Paul, or his first readers, or us either—in what is said in explanation over and above this name. We can listen only to the one or the other, realising what is said by the one or the other, and then, in and in spite of the concealment, we can also in faith hear the other in the one. These are just some of the great one-sidednesses of the Bible written and received as God's Word. It is a characterisation of the Bible as a whole when the Word of God is described (Heb. 4^{12}) as "sharper than a two-edged sword" (cf. also Rev. 1^{16}) and when it is then said to pierce asunder soul and spirit, joints and marrow, and to become judge of the thoughts and intents of the heart, so that no creature can hide from it, but everything is laid bare and held before its eyes.

As we must say already at this juncture, it is this external one-sidedness of God's Word, resting on an inner one-sidedness not apparent to us, that makes faith faith, that makes it the apprehended apprehension—moving from the depths to the heights and the heights to the depths—of the ever invisible God who is beyond all experience and thought. From the Word of God faith has not only its existence but also this its nature.

Ὁ λόγον Ἰησοῦ κεκτημένος ἀληθῶς, δύναται καὶ τῆς ἡσυχίας αὐτοῦ ἀκούειν, ἵνα τέλειος ᾖ, ἵνα δι᾽ ὧν λαλεῖ πράσσῃ καὶ δι᾽ ὧν σιγᾷ γινώσκηται[EN125] (Ignatius of Antioch, ad *Eph.*, 15,2). Luther calls the *fides Christi a res arduissima. quia translatio et raptus est ab omnibus quae sentit intus et foris in ea quae nec intus nec foris sentit scilicet invisibilem, altissimum, incomprehensibilem Deum*[EN126] (*Hebr. Br.*, 1513, *Fi. Schol.* 39, 3). *Non enim habent nomen neque speciem ea, quae fides intelligit. Nam praesentium rerum prosperitas vel adversitas penitus subvertit omnem hominem, qui fide non intelligit invisibilia. Hic enim intellectus ex fide venit, iuxta illud 'Nisi credideritis, non intelligetis' et est ingressus ille caliginis, in qua absorbetur, quicquid sensus, ratio, mens intellectusque hominis comprehendere potest. Coniungit enim fides animam cum invisibili, ineffabili, innominabili, aeterno, incogitabili verbo Dei simulque separat ab omnibus visibilibus, et haec*

[EN123] Jesus Christ

[EN124] in Christ

[EN125] whoever has truly grasped the word of Jesus is able also to hear his silence, so that he may be perfect, that he may act through what he says, and may be known through that on which he is silent

[EN126] faith of a Christian a most arduous thing, because it entails being forcibly taken from everything which one perceives inside and out to that which is not perceived either inside or out, namely, the invisible, most high and incomprehensible God *est Crux et phase Domini*[EN127] (*Oper. in Ps.*, 1519 f., *W.A.* 5, 69, 24). More than once Luther described the situation of the believing man as a *pendere*[EN128] or *haerere*[EN129] between heaven and earth, drawn and held off on both sides, now held fast and now pushed away (e.g., *Hebr. Br., Fi. Schol.* 71, 11; *Lect. on Isa.*, 1527, *W.A.* 25, 328, 33). He did this classically in the words: "But to watch is to cling to the eternal good and to see and long for the same. But therein he is alone and none with him, for they are all asleep. And he saith. On the housetop, as though he said, the world is a house, inside they are all asleep and locked up, but I am outside the house, on the roof, not yet in heaven and not in the world, the world I have under me and heaven above me, thus 'twixt the world's life and eternal life swing I lonely in faith" (*Seven Pen. Pss.*, 1517, *W.A.* 1, 199, 1). This would all have to be termed madness if it did not have to be exactly thus and not otherwise on the basis of the "one-sidedness" of the Word of God.

3. The speech of God is and remains the mystery of God in its spirituality. With this statement, which must form the conclusion to our exposition of the [182] nature of God's Word, we expressly allude for the first time to the concept of the Holy Spirit. To say Holy Spirit in preaching or theology is always to say a final word. For when we do this, then whether we are aware of it or not, and it is best to be aware of it, we are always speaking of the event in which God's Word is not only revealed to man but also believed by him. We are always speaking of the way in which the Word of God is so said to this or that man that he must hear it, or of the way in which this or that man is so open and ready for the Word of God that he can hear it. To the extent that part of the nature of God's Word is that it may be perceived by man, we may say of it that it is spiritual, i.e., that where it is actual and where it is thus believed by man, it is itself finally and ultimately the ground of this event. The Bible and Church dogma and all older theology, whatever else they may say of this event when they come to speak of it, always refer to the Holy Spirit. All that has also to be said about man—and we have inevitably to speak about man here—all theological anthropology, i.e., all teaching about the man to whom God's Word is revealed and by whom it is received, must stand under this sign. The sign means that under this new aspect too, even when we take the concept of revelation (which is constitutive for that of Holy Scripture and Church proclamation) and try to grasp it from below as it were, in terms of ourselves, even then and then specifically it must be seen and said that God is the Lord in this event. The Lord of speech is also the Lord of our hearing. The Lord who gives the Word is also the Lord who gives faith. The Lord of our hearing, the Lord who gives faith, the Lord by whose act the openness and readiness of man for the Word are true

EN127 Now those things which faith understands have neither name nor classification. For the experience of prosperity or adversity completely destroys every person who does not understand the invisible things in faith. And this understanding comes from faith according to that verse, 'Unless you believe, you will not understand,' he enters a deep darkness where whatever the human senses, reason, mind and intellect can understand is submerged. For faith joins the soul to the invisible, ineffable, unnamable, eternal, unthinkable Word of God, and at the same time separates it from all visible things: and this is the Cross and Passover of the Lord

EN128 being suspended

EN129 being caught

and actual, not another God but the one God in this way, is the Holy Spirit. Quite apart from the place these things have in the actual Dogmatics, we shall return later in the Prolegomena to the whole aspect that opens up here and to the sign under which it is to be understood. For the moment we shall confine ourselves to the finding that even in reaching its goal in man, even in the event of human faith in the Word of God, the Word of God is God's miraculous act. We must believe in our faith no less than in the Word believed, i.e., even if we think we can and should regard our attitude to God's Word as positive, even if we thus confess our faith, we can regard it as positive only as it is made possible and actual by God, only as the miracle of the Holy Ghost and not as our own work.

Luther's well-known but insufficiently appreciated exposition of the Third Article is pertinent here: "I believe that of no reason or power of my own can I believe in Jesus Christ my Lord or come to Him; but the Holy Ghost hath called me through the Gospel, illumined me by His gifts, hallowed and maintained me in the right faith, even as He calleth the whole of Christendom on earth, gathereth and sanctifieth it, and in Jesus Christ maintaineth it in the right faith ... " (*Smaller Catech.*, 1531, *W.A.*, 30[1], 367, 4).

[183] Concretely this means that the hearing and receiving of the Word of God by a man can be known by him and others only in faith. We are saying the same thing when we say, in the Holy Spirit. Faith, of course, is also a human experience. A specific human attitude corresponds to this experience, and this human attitude finds its expression, too, in specific human thoughts. But whether or not this experience is the experience, this attitude the attitude, and these thoughts the thoughts of the faith that has heard the Word of God, is decided spiritually, i.e., not by faith, but by the Word believed. Hence one cannot lay down conditions which, if observed, guarantee hearing of the Word. There is no method by which revelation can be made revelation that is actually received, no method of scriptural exegesis which is truly pneumatic, i.e., which articulates the witness to revelation in the Bible and to that degree really introduces the Pneuma, and above all no method of living, rousing proclamation that truly comes home to the hearers in an ultimate sense. There is nothing of this kind because God's Word is a mystery in the sense that it truly strikes us spiritually, i.e., in all circumstances only through the Holy Spirit, in all its indirectness only directly from God. In its spirituality it is definitively distinguished from any mere idea or hypostasis to which, if it is to be discerned by us even as such, there must correspond with some certainty, however small or hard to grasp, an experience, attitude or concept on our side. One will seek in vain anything corresponding to God's Word on our side even though one would be content with ever so little and even though one would be ready to go to the ultimate depths and outermost bounds of human existence to find it. Naturally the Word of God is always actual in very specific human experiences, attitudes and thoughts, but in its own power and dignity and not in that of the human experiences, attitudes and thoughts, not, then, in such a way that their

existence can in any way guarantee the presence of the Word of God, nor in such a way that they are necessarily and unequivocally the signs of its reality.

As a modern instance of the way one can easily forget this spirituality of the Word of God I adduce what P. Tillich tells the Church about its task of proclamation to-day. He thinks he should advise it above all to refrain from any direct offering of the religious contents provided in the Bible and tradition. Instead the following rules are to be observed: "First it must insist on a radical experience of the borderline situation; it must take from modern man the secret reservations which prevent him from placing himself with unconditional resolution at the frontier of his human existence ... Secondly, it must speak of the Yes that comes to man in the borderline situation when taken with unconditional seriousness ... Thirdly, Protestantism must finally witness to the new being from which alone it is possible to speak that word with authority, i.e., so to speak it that it does not again become a ground of assurance" (*Rel. Verwirkl.*, 1930, 38 f.). According to Tillich the task of Evangelical religious instruction is also "to bring to light, in terms of the frontiers of the human, the situation of man in its secular and religious expressions so far as these are known to the pupil and may be under- [184]
stood by him" (*Zeitschrift für den ev. Religionsunterricht*, 1931, 290). We ask: What is a "radical experience of the borderline situation"? What is "unconditional resolution"? How does one take from a man the reservations that prevent him from placing himself at this spot with resolution? Does it go without saying that "in the borderline situation when taken with unconditional seriousness" a Yes comes to man, and what does it mean to speak about this Yes? What is meant by speaking "in terms of the frontiers of the human" or indeed of the new being, i.e., speaking in such a way that the human word cannot become again a ground of assurance for the hearer? Obviously Tillich thinks he can produce a new and better method with all this. A method for what? One must give him credit that in what he says he has in view proclamation of the Word of God. But if so, are not all his proposals mere naiveties compared to which it is perhaps much more realistic to stick now as always to the direct proclamation of the contents of the Bible and tradition? By means of the negations or delimitations of man which according to Tillich we can obviously carry out for ourselves we do not even remotely produce the Word of God for him or for ourselves. Precisely by proclaiming the contents of the Bible and tradition we bear witness to the fact that we are in no position at all to do so.

Naturally there can be no question of recommending as the true method the insight that no method is possible here at all. This insight is sound, but one can have and apply it just as well as any other without its having any bearing at all on the demonstration of the event of hearing the Word of God. It, too, is far from putting this handle in our hands. The search for the possibility of getting such a handle, the search for a receptacle of human experience, attitude and teaching which would be undoubtedly and unequivocally the receptacle of the divine content—this search is not one that should be pursued further and further into every new and hitherto unknown or even undreamed-of area of human reality, no matter whether it is a matter of new positions or merely of the possible limits of this or that or even all possible positions. The insight that is needed here is that this search is pointless.

H. M. Muller, in the book already quoted in which he follows E. Grisebach, introduces the concept of "experience" or "trial" into theological discussion in a new sense. But so far I am not clear how far this differs from a long sought and finally discovered frontier concept which is in no way adapted as such to denote unequivocally the real hearing of God's Word.

The only proper thing to do here is to renounce altogether the search for a method of hearing God's Word, for an unequivocally correct description of its entry into man, into the realm of his experiences, attitudes and thoughts. "Since the Word of God is not in man's power either to speak or touch on fruitfully, but only in God's hand, therefore 'tis needful that we pray to Him to give us Himself the Holy Word through itself or through a man" (Luther, *German Exposition of the Lord's Prayer*, 1519, *W.A.* 2, 108, 28). "No man can illumine another, but this word alone can lighten all of him, and preachers should just be forerunners and witnesses of this light to men, that all may believe in the light" (*Sermon on* Jn. 1^{1-14}, *Kirchenpostille*, 1522, *W.A.* 10^{1}, 223, 3). "Therefore 'tis always a wondrous realm; the word is there and no one aware that it is so active and achieveth such great things for them that believe in it; it must itself be felt and tasted in the heart. Therefore we preachers can do no
[185] more than be our Lord Christ's mouth and His tools by which He preacheth the Word bodily. He letteth the Word go forth publicly that every man may hear it. But that we may feel it inwardly in the heart is the work of faith and is a secret doing of Christ's where He seeth that it is to be done of His own divine foreknowledge and good-pleasure" (*Sermon on Jn.* $10^{12f.}$, 1523, *W.A.* 12, 531, 4). "Christian faith and Christian life stand in the one little word revealing by God, for where that is not to hand, no heart is ever right aware of this mystery that is hidden there from the world's standpoint. Now God alone revealeth it to His saints elect from eternity, to whom He will have it made known, otherwise it remaineth indeed hid from every man and a right mystery. What good will the free will or the slavish, captive will say or do about that? How of its own power will it attain to this light and mystery? If the almighty strong God hide it from it, 'twill ne'er arrive thereat by any preparation or good works. No creature can come to this knowledge. For Christ alone revealeth it to it in the heart itself. Thus falleth to the ground all merit, all powers and faculties of reason, and availeth naught for God. Christ alone must give it" (*Sermon on Mt.* 11^{25-30}, 1527, *W.A.* 23, 689, 4).

Only on the assumption of this renunciation, which must be explicitly stated, shall we be able to speak of the knowability of God's Word in the next section. We shall have to speak there of the fact that it can be an object of human experience. But we cannot speak of it in such a way as to give an account of how this object and this knowledge can be delimited with clarity and certainty from other objects and knowledge of them. This would be the method of hearing God's Word, which is impossible as such because hearing God's Word is faith, and faith is the work of the Holy Spirit. Naturally the human experiences, attitudes and thoughts which are bound up with any confession of faith, including the Christian, lie as such in the realm of humanity and can be defined as such and delimited from others. But they do not lie in the realm of humanity to the degree that Christian faith is hearing the Word of God. As hearing of God's Word they can be attested in the realm of humanity only by appeal to proclamation by the Church, to Holy Scripture and to revelation in the form of interpretation of this threefold form of God's Word. But as hearing of God's Word they cannot be the subject of what might be called controversies within this realm. That is to say, as hearing of God's Word they cannot be justified and delimited alongside and over against whatever else is heard in this realm, and hence they cannot be domesticated within it.

The nature of the renunciation demanded here can be seen with perfect clarity from the three "inalienable verities" which Eduard Spranger, undoubtedly a chosen mouthpiece of modern German spirituality, ventures to suggest to theology "for fresh consideration": 1. man's responsibility for the basis of his readiness to believe; 2. controversy with the known autonomies of the so-called course of this world; and 3. controversy with the existing multiplicity of religious convictions ("*Der Kampf gegen den Idealismus*," *Sitzungsberichte d. preuss. Akad. d. Wissenschaft*, 1931, XVII, 436). One might be surprised at the innocent way in which Spranger submits for "fresh consideration" what has been said profusely enough and adopted respectfully enough by Protestant theology for the last two hundred years. If he can [186] be satisfied with the applause that even to this day his inalienable verities are sure to find in wide circles in the Church and theology, he must also allow us to evaluate them as excellent formulations of the very thing that any theology worthy of the name must in all circumstances and without reservation renounce. Here to-day, as in the past, our only reply can be one of the sharpest opposition: 1. As regards the basis of man's readiness to believe, theology has no responsibility outwards. The responsibility of theology is simply to make it clear that the readiness to believe, seen from outside, has its basis within itself and thus bears no responsibility in respect of its basis. 2. Theology cannot be in controversy with the autonomies of the course of this world because it is itself inside and not outside the course of this world, and because, like the Church in general, it has to attest but not to put into effect in this world God's own controversy with its autonomies. 3. Theology cannot be in controversy with the existing multiplicity of religious convictions because, though it does in fact find this multiplicity in the sphere of human experiences, attitudes and thoughts, it has no interest in controversy with it in this sphere, while it does not find it in the sphere of faith and therefore cannot be in controversy with it there. The question whether this reply to Spranger will enlighten and impress Spranger himself and his associates in philosophy and theology is relatively less important than the question whether there will always be a remnant in the Church which can only give this or a similar answer regarding the work that theology has to do.

If in respect of the event of hearing God's Word we do not point to a datum in man's existence, nor to the limit of all the data of human existence, nor finally to the possibility of a contingent experience, but only to faith, and that means to the Holy Spirit, we are simply confirming what was said at the beginning of the section, namely, that the question "What is the Word of God?" can be answered only by indicating the How of God's Word in an interpretation of its threefold form. We thus ask: "How is the Word of God?" and the answer is: It is on our lips and in our hearts as the mystery of the Spirit who is the Lord.

[187] § 6

THE KNOWABILITY OF THE WORD OF GOD

The reality of the Word of God in all its three forms is grounded only in itself. So, too, the knowledge of it by men can consist only in its acknowledgment, and this acknowledgment can become real only through itself and can become intelligible only in terms of itself.

1. THE QUESTION OF THE KNOWABILITY OF THE WORD OF GOD

Our way thus far has been briefly this. In § 3 we found in the concept of the Word of God the mandated content of Church proclamation and hence also the criterion of dogmatics as the scientific testing of Church proclamation. In § 4 we noted the three forms, namely, proclamation, Scripture and revelation, in which the entity denoted by the concept is actual. Finally in § 5, with these three forms in view, we asked concerning the nature of this entity and we learned to know it as three distinct but not different determinations, the speech of God, the act of God and the mystery of God. Before we now go on to give a provisional definition of the concept of dogmatics on the basis of these findings, we must first give an explicit answer to the question as to the knowability of the Word of God.

In the concept of Church proclamation and hence also in that of dogmatics it is obviously taken for granted that it is possible for man to hear and even speak, and hence also to know, the Word of God. In these concepts this is assumed, of course, not for human existence generally, but for a specific sphere of human existence, namely, the sphere of the Church. But even within the limits of this sphere as they are known to us or as they actually are in God's eyes, it is at any rate men who are summoned to hear God's Word and speak it. If the Church, and in it Church proclamation, and in the service of Church proclamation dogmatics, can make appeal to the truth, this must imply that men—not all men but certain men, and even these men not always and everywhere but in certain situations—may know the Word of God. If this were not so, the whole concept of the Word of God would have to be called a figment of
[188] the imagination, and Church proclamation, including dogmatics, would have to be called a pointless and meaningless activity, and therefore the Church would have to be called a place of self-deceptions without parallel. For even though there were in this case some unknown entity corresponding to the concept of the Word of God, if we really had no knowledge of it, the thing denoted by the concept would have no reality for us despite its unknown cor-

relate, but would still be a figment of the imagination. In the concept of the Church as a place where the truth is spoken and heard, and in the concept of Church proclamation and dogmatics as a meaningful activity, it is presupposed that there can be knowledge of the Word of God by men.

By the knowledge of an object by men we understand confirmation of their acquaintance with its reality in respect of its existence and its nature. But confirmation of their acquaintance means that the reality of the object concerned, its existence and nature, being true in themselves, now become in some way, and with some degree of clarity and distinctness, true for men too. Their acquaintance with it, instead of being a contingent and outward determination of their own existence, now becomes a necessary and inward determination. Knowing, they are affected by the object known. They no longer exist without it, but with it. In so far as they think of it, with the same confidence with which they dare to think in general they must think of it as a true reality, as true in its existence and nature. Whatever else and however else they may think of it, they must begin by thinking of the truth of its reality. Face to face with this truth they can no longer withdraw into themselves in order to affirm, question or deny it thence. Its truth has come home to them, has become their own. And in the process they themselves have become the truth's. This event, this confirmation, in contrast to mere cognizance, we call knowledge. Cognizance becomes knowledge when man becomes a responsible witness to its content.

Knowledge of the Word of God in this sense is the presupposition of the Church. We may and must also reverse the statement and say that the Church is the presupposition of knowledge of the Word of God. Either way we are saying that the Word of God becomes knowable for men. In particular Church proclamation implies that God's Word can be heard by men and spoken by men themselves. If it were not knowable, if a self-confirming acquaintance with the Word of God were not possible, if it were not possible that its reality should affect men in such a way that they can no longer exist without it but only with it, that they can only think of its reality as true, that they can only start their existence with the truth of its existence and nature, if their freedom to retire into themselves in face of God's Word were infinite and inviolable—this would mean that any serious hearing and speaking of God's Word would be ruled out. Serious hearing and speaking rests on the possibility of knowledge. [189]
The presupposition of the Church is thus the possibility of this relation, the relation of knowledge between man and the Word of God. Or, conversely, the Church is the presupposition of the possibility of this relation of knowledge. On our path thus far we have tacitly counted on this presupposition, or one might also say that the question of its special nature and material correctness has already been implicitly raised and answered in the preceding section on the nature of the Word of God. But the question is important enough to demand independent and explicit treatment at this point. How can we men know the Word of God? This is how we must formulate the question.

A few preliminary observations on this way of putting it will lead on directly to the matter itself.

1. We do not say: How do men know the Word of God? This would mean asking about the reality of this knowledge. But after all that we have heard about its forms and nature, the reality of the knowledge of God can be the content of an answer that man must give to this question only in so far as this answer consists in the repetition of the biblical promise given to the Church and the reference to its coming fulfilment, and only in so far as the Word of God itself is added to this human repetition and reference and undertakes to give the real answer. In other words man's only answer to the question as put in this way is proclamation. But in order to be clear that this is so, our question must be: How can men know the Word of God? We must ask about the possibility of this event. The very significance of the insight that the Word of God alone answers the question of real knowledge of the Word of God demands that we consider whether it can only be thus or whether it might be otherwise.

2. We do not say: How can all men know the Word of God? or even: How can any man know the Word of God? We have already recalled that it is not an issue of men universally or of man in general but very concretely and specifically of man in the Church. Where the Word of God is known and therefore can be known, it must have been spoken and it must have come as a divine call to specific men. God knows them, these men, who on specific occasions know God's Word as real hearers and proclaimers, who are thus able to know it, and who thereby constitute the Church as living human members in the body of Christ. Our concern is with the possibility of knowledge of these men.

3. Just because God knows them, we prefer not to say: How do Christians know the Word of God? We might put it thus, but we should have to add: called and elect Christians, and this would be obscure, for the real issue is how men by knowing God's Word can become called and elect and therefore real Christians, hearers and proclaimers of the Word of God. God knows those who
[190] become this. But we know even Christians only as men who as such put to us the question how it is possible that they should know the Word of God.

4. When we ask about the possibility of knowledge of the Word of God, we are presupposing that the concept of knowledge is known. But as above we shall deliberately have to take it so generally, with such philosophical and epistemological imprecision, that the possibility is left open of correction, restriction or reversal in the light of the object concerned. When knowledge was defined earlier as acquaintance with the reality of an object which is self-confirmed in the subject, this was meant to be only a sketch of the problem of knowledge and not an anticipatory interpretation. Any interpretation at this stage would mean philosophical and epistemological definition. But the problem of knowledge cannot be presupposed with such distinctness here even as a problem if we are not to incur the most serious risk of anticipating the answer

in the presupposition in a very definite and perhaps most inappropriate way. What knowledge means as knowledge of God must in no case be introduced in a definitive form into investigation of this question.

As an example to the contrary I note a statement of F. Traub. In *Monatsschrift f. Past. Theol.*, 1928, p. 82 he brings against me the criticism that in my dogmatics no answer will be found to the question: "How can I succeed in affirming the Word of God, i.e., affirming it as the Word of God and as reality?" Here "to be able to know the Word of God" is interpreted in advance as "to be able to succeed in affirming it." This is the premature introduction into the investigation of a philosophical and epistemological definition of the problem which in certain circumstances might be calculated to compromise in advance the treatment of this problem of knowledge. Who tells us that the constitutive act of knowledge of God's Word consists in our affirmation of it? And above all who tells us that we can "succeed" in making such an affirmation? The answer to the question as thus posed would obviously have to be the statement of a way or method by means of which this "success" can be achieved. Who tells us whether this question may be put at all and therefore whether any meaningful answer can be found at all?

A result of the uniqueness of this object of knowledge might well be that the concept of its knowledge cannot be definitively measured by the concept of the knowledge of other objects or by a general concept of knowledge but that it can be defined at all only in terms of its own object.

2. THE WORD OF GOD AND MAN

How necessary is the reservation just made may be seen at once if we consider first what it means that it is man whom we are to understand here as the one who knows God's Word. It is part of the concept of the Church that this should be so. The Word of God which it hears and proclaims, and which makes [191] it the Church, is God's Word addressed to men. Preaching and sacrament are addressed to men. The word of the prophets and apostles is addressed to men. The revelation of God Himself in Jesus Christ is addressed to men. The Word of God whose three forms we have again denoted herewith is addressed to men. If it is addressed to men, it obviously seeks to be known and therefore heard by them, yet not only known and heard, but known in the sense already generally established. Mediated by their acquaintance with it, it seeks to confirm itself as a reality to them. It is addressed to them in order that they may let it be spoken to them and that they may no longer be what they are without it, but with it.

Consider here the connexion between grace (mercy) and truth in Ps. $89^{14.\ 24}$; 98^{3}; 117^{2} and the way in which this connexion is taken up in Jn. $1^{14\ 17}$. Consider the description of the Gospel as the λόγος τῆς ἀληθείας[EN1] in 2 Cor. 6^{7}; Eph. 1^{13}; Col. 1^{5}; 2 Tim. 2^{15}; Jas. 1^{18}. Consider finally the description of the decisive thing in being a Christian as ἐπίγνωσις τῆς ἀληθείας[EN2] in 1 Tim. 2^{3}; 4^{3}; 2 Tim. 2^{25}; 3^{7}; Titus 1^{1}.

EN1 word of truth
EN2 knowledge of truth

Primarily and originally the Word of God is undoubtedly the Word that God speaks by and to Himself in eternal concealment. We shall have to return to this great and inalienable truth when we develop the concept of revelation in the context of the doctrine of the Trinity. But undoubtedly, too, it is the Word that is spoken to men in revelation, Scripture and preaching. Hence we cannot speak or think of it at all without remembering at once the man who hears and knows it. The Word of God, Jesus Christ, as the being of the Church, sets us ineluctably before the realisation that it was and will be men who are intended and addressed and therefore characterised as recipients but as also themselves bearers of this Word. The Word of God thus sets us before the so-to-speak anthropological problem: How then can men be this? Before the "so-to-speak" anthropological problem, I said, and I indicated thereby that it can be called this only with some reserve. Or is this not so? Shall we say unreservedly that the question of the possibility of the knowledge of God's Word is a question of anthropology? Shall we ask what man generally and as such, in addition to all else he can do, can or cannot do in this regard? Is there a general truth about man which can be made generally perceptible and which includes within it man's ability to know the Word of God? We must put this question because an almost invincible development in the history of Protestant theology since the Reformation has led to an impressive affirmative answer to this question in the whole wing of the Church that we have called Modernist.

We have already mentioned incidentally the debates in Protestant orthodoxy on the question whether theology is to be regarded with Thomas Aquinas as an essentially theoretical
[192] science or with Duns Scotus as an essentially practical science. With increasing deliberateness and universality decision was made in favour of the latter, and this meant that the object of theology was no longer, as with Chemnitz (*Loci. theol ed.*, 1592, *De usu et util. loc. theol.*, p. 12), the nature and will of God, or, as with Walaeus, *res divinae, nempe Deus ipse ... et res omnes quae a Deo sunt*[EN3] (*Loci comm.*, 1640, 5), but rather, as already with J. Gerhard (*Loci theol.*, 1610, *Prooem.* 28), *homo quatenus ad aeternam beatitudinem est perducendus*[EN4], or, as with Wendelin (*Theol. christ. lib.* II, 1639, *Prol.* 1, 3), *vera religio, quae est ratio agnoscendi colendique Deum*[EN5], or, as with Burmann (*Syn. Theol.*, 1678, I, 2, 52), *vita hominis sive cultus ipsius erga Deum*[EN6], or, as with Mastricht (*Theol. theor. pract.*, 1698, I, 1, 26), *vita hominis formanda et dirigenda Deum versus*[EN7]. One can interpret this development *in meliorem partem*[EN8]. One of its most cautious proponents, F. Turrettini (*Instit. Theol. el.*, 1679, I, 5, 4), was well able to show that even so theology is still dealing with God, but *Deus quatenus revelatus est, Deus noster id est foederatus in Christo*[EN9]. Along Reformation lines there was a desire to shun proximity to *nuda speculatio de Deo*[EN10] (Quenstedt, *Theol. did. pol.*, 1685, I *cap.* 1, *sect.* 2, *qu.* 2, *font. sol.*, 7). There was already awareness that a "non-existential" theology is nothing: *theologia nisi ad*

[EN3] the divine things, namely, God Himself ... and all things which are of God
[EN4] man insofar as he is to be led to eternal blessedness
[EN5] true religion, which is the way in which God is acknowledged and venerated
[EN6] the life of man and his worship of God
[EN7] forming and directing human life toward God
[EN8] in the better sense
[EN9] God as revealed, our God, that is, the God who has covenanted with us in Christ
[EN10] mere speculation about God

praxin referatur ne theologia quidem est[EN11] (Burmann, *op. cit.*, I, 2, 51, cf. Cocceius, *S. theol.*, 1669, I, 8). It is true that H. Mulert (*Religion, Kirche, Theologie*, 1931, 28) and other modern authors claim that the orthodox regarded and pursued theology with rigid objectivism as *scientia de Deo et rebus divinis*[EN12], but this completely contradicts the tenor of the express declarations that are to be found in these theologians, even in the older ones who had not yet adopted the new fashion. From the very outset Protestant orthodoxy suffered from a surplus rather than a deficit in the regard it paid to the religious subject. Its aim at least—and this was the point of the turn to *scientia practica*[EN13]—was to understand the Word of God altogether as a word addressed to man. The only trouble was that there was another meaning to the development as well. It is patent that what was also sought and attained with this development was that the object of theology, as scientific consciousness after the Renaissance was increasingly demanding, was transferred from a Beyond genuinely confronting the place of man to the sphere of man himself. Though it did not have to be, this object could now be thought of as one that is embraced and conditioned by the general truths of man. An attempt could thus be made to view it, or the possibility of it, within the sphere of man's self-understanding. The contemporary reconstruction of a *theologia naturalis*[EN14] as the science of the *praeambula fidei*[EN15] in the ancient Thomistic sense, the slow but noticeable withdrawal of the doubts the Reformers had had regarding the value of this enterprise, shows that were was interest in this incorporation from other angles too. In the 18th century, at any rate, it cannot be denied that deductions were drawn in this direction. We now find the definition that can still be made to-day, namely, that theology is the science of religion, by which is meant "academic knowledge of the doctrines and truths that give us the instruction necessary for our felicity and contentment concerning our relations to God, the duties which arise out of these relations, and the hopes that we may build on these relations" (G. J. Planck, *Einleitung in die theol. Wissenschaft*, 1794, Vol. I, 29). A Herder and a Schleiermacher could do better than this in understanding religion in its depth and power and autonomy. But the "we" which strikingly dominates Planck's statement remains, or indeed becomes, the cornerstone of their view too. It is the same Schleiermacher who for the first time fundamentally relates this newly discovered independent reality of religion to a corresponding possibility that can be generally demonstrated anthropologically, and who for the first time fundamentally undertakes to interpret Christianity itself, in the form of a concrete historical analysis of human existence, within the framework of a general doctrine of man: 1. the [193]
encounter of man with God is now to be understood as a human religious experience that can be established historically and psychologically; 2. this experience is to be understood as the actualisation of a generally demonstrable religious capacity of man. For all the variety of types in individual interpretations, these are after Schleiermacher the two cardinal principles of the religious philosophy of the 19th and 20th centuries. The second of the two principles is naturally decisive. If we apply it to what we in our vocabulary call the doctrine of the Word of God it means that the real knowledge of the Word of God is the actualisation of a specific possibility of knowledge peculiar to man as such. If we accept this principle, then the answer to the question of possibility that now concerns us is to be sought in anthropology, and it is a secondary matter whether we follow the actual anthropology of Schleiermacher and his school or one more congenial to our age such as that of M. Heidegger. As it

---

EN11 theology cannot even be called theology unless it refers to practice
EN12 science of God and of divine things
EN13 practical science
EN14 natural theology
EN15 preamble to faith

is, we are spared the choice, for we are not in any position to accept the principle on the basis of which we would have to make such a choice.

The consideration that forbids us to acquiesce in it is this. In the first place it is true (and partially at least this was the point in at least the early stages of the development) that the Word of God must be understood as an event in and to the reality of man.

There can be no objection in principle to describing this event as "experience" and even as "religious experience." The quarrel is not with the term nor with the true and important thing the term might finally denote, namely, the supremely real and determinative entry of the Word of God into the reality of man. But the term is burdened—this is why we avoid it—with the underlying idea that man generally is capable of religious experience or that this capability has the critical significance of a norm.

And in the second place it is true that a possibility or capability on man's part must correspond logically and materially to this event.

Even the concept of the religious *a priori*, which played so big a part in religious philosophy around 1910, would not have to be rejected absolutely or intrinsically if it were not for the unfortunate fact that on the basis of a right or wrong understanding of Kant it is understood as a capability or property grounded in man as such and as the corresponding freedom of control.

The question is whether this event ranks with the other events that might enter man's reality in such a way that to be able to enter it actually requires on man's part a potentiality which is brought by man as such, which consists in a disposition native to him as man, in an organ, in a positive or even a negative property that can be reached and discovered by self-reflection, by anthropological analysis of his existence, in short, in what philosophy of the Kantian type calls a faculty. It might also be that this event did not so much presuppose the corresponding possibility on man's part as bring it with it and confer it on man by being event, so that it is man's possibility without ceasing (as such) to be wholly and utterly the possibility proper to the Word of God and to it alone. We might also be dealing with a possibility of knowledge which can be made
[194] intelligible as a possibility of man, but, in contrast to all others, only in terms of the object of knowledge or the reality of knowledge and not at all in terms of the subject of knowledge, i.e., man as such. In the light of the nature of God's Word, and especially of what we said in § 5, 2.3. about its purposiveness or pertinence, its being aimed at man, its character as an address to man, we must decide against the first view and in favour of the second. From this standpoint, the same that concerns us here, we had to understand the Word of God as the act of God's free love and not as if the addressed and hearing man were in any way essential to the concept of the Word of God. That man is the recipient of God's Word is, to the extent that it is true, a fact, and it cannot be deduced from anything we might previously know about God's nature. Even less, of course, can it be deduced from anything we previously knew about the nature of man. God's Word is no longer grace, and grace itself is no longer grace, if we

ascribe to man a predisposition towards this Word, a possibility of knowledge regarding it that is intrinsically and independently native to him. But the same results from what was said in the same passage about the content of the Word of God addressed to man. We then made the assertion that this content, whatever it might be *in concretissimo*[EN16] for this man or that man, will always be an authentic and definitive encounter with the Lord of man, a revelation which man cannot achieve himself, the revelation of something new which can only be told him. It will also be the limitation of his existence by the absolute "out there" of his Creator, a limitation on the basis of which he can understand himself only as created out of nothing and upheld over nothing. It will also be a radical renewal and therewith an obviously radical criticism of the whole of his present existence, a renewal and a criticism on the basis of which he can understand himself only as a sinner living by grace and therefore as a lost sinner closed up against God on his side. Finally it will be the presence of God as the One who comes, the Future One in the strict sense, the eternal Lord and Redeemer of man, a presence on the basis of which he can understand himself only as hastening towards this future of the Lord and expecting Him. To be sure, it is not these formulae which describe the real content of the Word of God, but the content of the Word which God Himself speaks and which He does so always as these formulae indicate, the real content of the real Word of God, that tells man also that there can be no question of any ability to hear or understand or know on his part, of any capability that he the creature, the sinner, the one who waits, has to bring to this Word, but that the possibility of knowledge corresponding to the real Word of God has come to him, that it represents an inconceivable *novum*[EN17] compared to all his ability and capability, and that it is to be understood as a pure fact, in exactly the same way as the real Word of God itself.

In 1 Cor. 2[6f.] we are told that the wisdom of God in Christ is a *σοφία ἐν μυστηρίῳ*[EN18] [195]
unknown to the rulers of this world, not seen by any eye, not heard by any ear, having entered into no man's heart, accessible only to the *πνεῦμα*[EN19] of God Himself and through the *πνεῦμα* of God Himself. It is not, then, accessible to the *ψυχικὸς ἄνθρωπος*[EN20] who as such does not have the *πνεῦμα* and who cannot know what is accessible only to the *πνεῦμα* and through the *πνεῦμα*: *οὐ δέχεται, οὐ δύναται γνῶναι*[EN21]. Man must receive (*λαμβάνειν*) not only the Word from Christ but also the *πνεῦμα* by which it is known, or he will not know it at all. *Ἐδίδαξεν ἡμᾶς ὁ κύριος, ὅτι θεὸν εἰδέναι οὐδεὶς δύναται, μὴ οὐχὶ θεοῦ διδάξαντος, τουτέστιν ἄνευ θεοῦ μὴ γινώσκεσθαι τὸν θεόν*[EN22] (Irenaeus, *C.o.h.* IV, 6, 4). "For what sort of a work is knowing? It meaneth neither fasting, watching, mortification, nor aught a man may do or suffer with the body, but it lieth right within in the

---

[EN16] in its utter concreteness
[EN17] new thing
[EN18] wisdom in a mystery
[EN19] Spirit
[EN20] natural man
[EN21] he does not receive, he is not able to understand
[EN22] The Lord has taught us that no one can know God, unless God is his teacher; that is, without God God is not known

deepest foundation of the heart. In a word knowing is no work but precedeth all works. For works follow after and from knowledge. Work is what we do, but knowledge is of what we receive and take. Thus by the one little word 'knowing' as by a mighty thunderclap is all doctrine smitten down which is founded on man's work, spiritual orders or divine service, as though thereby to be free from all sin, to reconcile God and to merit grace" (Luther, *Sermon on Jn.* 17[3], 1528, *W.A.* 28, 100, 21).

The Modernist view from which we must demarcate ourselves here goes back to the Renaissance and especially to the Renaissance philosopher Descartes with his proof of God from human self-certainty.

Among recent religious philosophers of this trend there have been some like G. Wobbermin (*System. Theologie*, Vol. 2, 1921, 455) and Heinrich Scholz (*Religionsphilosophie*, 2nd edn., 1922, 310) who have been open or incautious enough to appeal expressly to Descartes and to find fresh support in his train of thought.

"The I-experience establishes for man the surest certainty for reality that he can conceive of or that is possible for him at all. It is the presupposition ... of all validation of reality with reference to the external world" (Wobbermin, *op. cit.*). One might ask whether this Cartesianism is really as impregnable as it usually purports to be even on the philosophical plane. But that is not our present concern and we must beware of opposing to it a philosophy more suited to our theological interest or of so wearying of Descartes that we throw ourselves into the arms of, e.g., Aristotle or Thomas. Suspicious of the other side too, we shall simply make the point that at any rate in theology one cannot think along Cartesian lines.

In his essay "*Was hat die Rechtfertigungslehre dem modernen Menschen zu sagen?*" (1907 in *Ges. Aufsätze zur Kirchengeschichte*, Vol. 3, 1928, 559) Karl Holl once formulated as follows the fundamental principle that is "common to all men" and that constitutes "the plumb-line of their religion." "Nothing," he said, "is to be recognised as religiously valid but what can be found in the reality present to us and produced again out of our direct experience." This principle is in fact the principle of Cartesian thinking, which is quite impossible in theology. On the basis of this principle there is no knowledge of the Word of God. For we do not find the Word of God in the reality present to us. Rather—and this is something quite different—
[196] the Word of God finds us in the reality present to as. Again it cannot be produced again out of our direct experience. Whenever we know it, we are rather begotten by it according to Jas. 1[18].

The fact of God's Word does not receive its dignity and validity in any respect or even to the slightest degree from a presupposition that we bring to it. Its truth for us, like its truth in itself, is grounded absolutely in itself. The procedure in theology, then, is to establish self-certainty on the certainty of God, to measure it by the certainty of God, and thus to begin with the certainty of God without waiting for the validating of this beginning by self-certainty. When that beginning is made, but only when it is made, it is then, but only subsequently, incidentally and relatively validated by the necessary self-certainty. In other words, in the real knowledge of God's Word, in which alone that beginning is made, there also lies the event that it is possible, that that beginning can be made. Again, we do not base this rejection of the Cartesian way on a better philosophy. It is not our concern here whether there is such a philosophy. In relation to this object, the object of theology, we are content to say that one must affirm the possibility of its knowledge by men in this way and no other. Men can know the Word of God because and in so far as God wills that they know it, because and in so far as there is over against God's will only the impotence of disobedience, and because and in so far as there is a revelation of God's will in His Word in which the impotence of disobedience is set aside. We shall return to the problem indicated here in the third sub-section. For the moment we are simply stating that if one wants to call the problem of the knowability of the Word of God an anthropological problem, the reference must be to a Church (or theological) anthropology. The question is not how man in general and as such can know God's Word. This question is pointless, for *vis-à-vis* the Word of God there is no man in general and as such; the Word of God is what it is as it is concretely spoken to this or that specific man. The question is how these men to whom it is concretely spoken can know it. And our answer must be that they can do so when the ability is given to them by the Word itself. To this conclusion two elucidations must be appended.

1. We have made a positive assertion, pronouncing a definite Yes to the knowability of the Word of God. This must be pointed out already at this first stage in our deliberations because proponents of an answer to the question on the basis of general anthropology usually bring against all that has been said the objection that God's Word and man are finally held apart or even "rent asunder" thereby. In answer we argue that others ought not so stubbornly to hear only the No in what has been said. To be sure, what has been said denies a connexion between God and man, that is, a knowledge of God's Word by man, and thus a knowability of God's Word by him, in the sense that a capability of [197]
man in abstraction from the Word of God can serve as the condition of this connexion. This condition, of course, cannot be met. The very man who knows the Word of God also knows that he can bring no capability of his own to this knowledge, but has first to receive all capability. But is it too much to expect that even modern theologians will not set their hearts on this impossible condition? If one is alert, is it really possible to call the reference to the certainty of God that precedes all self-certainty an inadequate and unsatisfactory reference? Is not the reference to this way, the way from certainty of God to self-certainty, the only positive thing, and yet also the absolutely certain and decisive thing, that can be said on this question?

2. We have said something positive by the reference, of course, only to the extent that it was a reference, i.e., a reference to the event of the real knowledge of the Word of God. The power of this reference does not lie in itself; it lies in that to which it refers. That to which it refers, that event, the factual priority of the certainty of God over all self-certainty, the fact of the knowledge of God's Word that does not presuppose its possibility in man, but, coming to

man, brings the possibility with it—all this is something we can "presuppose" only as man can "presuppose" God. "Presupposition" in this case can only mean recollection of its promise and hope of its future, i.e., appeal to the biblical Word and expectation of its fulfilment. Our reference thus has just as much force as the promise is true and the future of the Lord is certain. Concretely it has just as much force as the text adduced (1 Cor. $2^{6f.}$) has truth and its content reality. In no respect, then, does the force of our reference lie in our hands. This applies not merely to the positive thing that we are trying to say but also and just as strongly to the associated negation. In other words, even the counter-thesis of theologians with Cartesian inclinations cannot be directly and strictly reduced *ad absurdum*[EN23] and overturned. The power with which their mouth must be stopped is not under our control, and they themselves do not dispose of the power to let their mouths be stopped. Even knowledge of the impossibility of knowledge of the Word of God outside its reality is possible only on the presupposition of this real knowledge. There is no philosophy that can render faith or theology even this negative service. The positive reference to the possibility of knowledge that the Word of God brings with it can be rejected and therewith also the negative reference to its unknowability apart from the possibility of knowledge it brings with it. But when we make the twofold affirmation its power is not under our own control even with reference to ourselves. Our affirmation as such might be powerless because it is destitute of real knowledge of God's Word, because it is merely verbal and mental
[198] instead of being real over and above that. If it is real, this does not lie in itself, not even in the seriousness and sincerity, nor the existential participation, with which we make it; it lies in the real thing that is affirmed therewith. In short the binding nature of what we affirm and deny depends wholly and utterly on our own relevance to the matter as speakers and hearers. But our own relevance to the matter depends wholly and utterly, not on us, but on the matter itself. And this is so precisely because the matter, God's Word, is no mere thing; it is the living, personal and free God. This elucidation must accompany us in all else that may have to be said on this question.

3. THE WORD OF GOD AND EXPERIENCE

What we have in view under this heading is the concrete application and execution of all that has been affirmed thus far. We have stated that knowledge of God's Word becomes possible for man in the event of the reality of God's Word. It "becomes possible for man"—this aspect of the thought is the one especially we must now interpret. We shall try to do it by means of the concept of experience.

H. M. Müller (*Glaube und Erfahrung bei Luther*, 1929), on the basis of certain passages in

[EN23] to absurdity

Luther, understands and considers experience in terms of the special experience of the trial of faith and the triumphant withstanding of the trial. Here we shall adopt a more general usage.

If knowledge of God's Word is possible, this must mean that an experience of God's Word is possible. We have defined knowledge as the confirmation of human acquaintance with an object whereby its truth becomes a determination of the existence of the man who has the knowledge. This determination of the existence of the man who has the knowledge we call experience. Man does not exist abstractly but concretely, i.e., in experiences, in determinations of his existence by objects, by things outside him and distinct from him. It is in past experience, i.e., as determined by the things that have thus far come to him from without in the way they have come, and then again in present experience, i.e., as he encounters specific external things in a specific way, that man is what he is, that he exists as man, and not otherwise. If knowledge of God's Word can become possible for men, this must mean that they can have experience of God's Word, that they can be what they are as determined by God's Word.

It should be stated explicitly that in this presentation we are adopting what might be rightly intended in the favourite 19th century formula of "religious consciousness." We cannot, of course, agree with 19th century thinkers when they say that "there is" or that "man has" a religious consciousness. But we might say that men can have a religious consciousness, or, in our own vocabulary. that the Word of God can become the ground and object of man's consciousness. Thus when Schleiermacher spoke of the Christian consciousness or of self-consciousness he had in view a "being affected" (to K. H. Sack, 9.4.1825, *Letters*, Vol. 4, 335) which is obviously very similar to our "being determined." If we prefer the concept of experience, it is because it expresses something more comprehensive. [199]

By the experience of God's Word which is possible for men on the presupposition of its reality, we understand the determination of their existence as men by God's Word.

If there is such a determination of human existence by God's Word, the primary point to be made is that this is not to be confused with a determination man can give his own existence. Naturally experience of the Word of God always takes place in an act of human self-determination. But it is not experience of the Word of God as this act. No determination man can give himself is as such determination by God's Word. Nor is there any place here for the view that this experience is a kind of co-operation between divine determining and human self-determining. Again, the undeniable fact that this experience takes place in an act of human self-determination does not mean that man in this self-determining accomplishes as it were a greater or lesser part of the whole and then leaves the rest to God's determining. Finally, we must also reject a view that is often commended as a solution—it was that of Augustine and is a central dogma in the school of Holl—namely, that we have here a simultaneity, interrelation and unity in tension between the divine and human determining: What is seen from the one side as grace is freedom when

seen from the other side and *vice versa.* All these theories are to be rejected because they are in contradiction to the self-knowledge of man in real experience of God's Word as we know it from the biblical promise. If man lets himself be told by the Word of God that he has a Lord, that he is the creature of this Lord, that he is a lost sinner blessed by Him, that he awaits eternal redemption and is thus a stranger in this sphere of time, this specific content of the Word experienced by him will flatly prohibit him from ascribing the possibility of this experience to himself either wholly or in part or from dialectically equating the divine possibility actualised in this experience with a possibility of his own. These theories—and not least the third—do not emanate from the only competent witness in this matter, namely, the man who stands in the event of real knowledge of the Word of God as this man is presented to us by Holy Scripture. They emanate from an onlooker who is interested in the event but only from outside, who regards the two determinations that are obviously present here, the one by God and the other by man himself, as the kind of determinations that might be rivals of one another, and who thus, as one would
[200] rightly do with other competing determinations, attempts to understand them in their co-existence, to effect a synthesis between them, his main interest obviously being in some way to maintain the self-determination of man in face of the determination of man by God. But the external onlooker with this interest fails to see—and as an external onlooker with this interest he is bound to do so—that the co-existence of God and man as it occurs in the experience of God's Word is not a co-existence on the same level, so that it is completely impossible to see it from a higher vantage point and to view it in its possibility. He also overlooks the fact that there can be no point in trying to maintain man's self-determination in some way, even dialectically, over against the determination of man by God. Precisely as self-determination, it is subject to determination by God. Our very self-determination needs this determination by God in order to be experience of His Word. In this relation of total subjection and need *vis-à-vis* determination by God it cannot possibly replace this, as Pelagius wished, or co-operate with it, as the Semi-Pelagians wished, or be secretly identical with it, as Augustine wished. Such solutions may be generally possible when the reference is to other competing determinations of man or of an object, but here, where it is a matter of the determination of man by God and by himself, they are impossible.

It would be a similar misunderstanding on a spectator's part, however, if he were to try to understand the situation of man in the experience of God's Word as an elimination of his self-determination or as a state of partial or total receptivity or passivity.

Because it almost of necessity gives rise to this idea, we prefer not to adopt Schleiermacher's concept of "dependence" in this connexion.

Even though there seems to be in this a very high appreciation of the idea of the omnipotence of God and His Word, it involves a misconception of the nature of the encounter between God and man. If God is seriously involved in experience of the Word of God, then man is just as seriously involved too. The very man who stands in real knowledge of the Word of God also knows himself as existing in the act of his life, as existing in his self-determination. We do not have to pronounce here whether this can and must really be said of man in general to the extent that one has to regard him as not just a natural being but as essentially and primarily a historical being.

More recent philosophy of various schools says this, and in so doing it is perhaps living more on borrowings from theology than is good for it as philosophy.

However that may be, the man who really knows God's Word, as this man comes before us in the biblical promise, can understand himself only as one who exists in his act, in his self-determination. The Word of God comes as a summons to him and the hearing it finds in him is the right hearing of obedi- [201]
ence or the wrong hearing of disobedience. Whether it is finally the one or the other is not, of course, in his hands. For that, for obedience or disobedience in his action, he cannot resolve and determine himself. As he decides, as he resolves and determines, he is rather in the secret judgment of the grace or disfavour of God, to whom alone his obedience or disobedience is manifest. And this is the overlapping determination by God which befalls his self-determination. Nevertheless, it does not alter the fact that his hearing is self-determination, act, decision. That the co-existence of God and man in man's experience of God's Word is not on the same plane, that it cannot be viewed in the same way as that of two other entities, that its possibility as co-existence cannot, then, be perceived, is something that has thus to be taken seriously on this side too. For the man who is concerned for God's omnipotence and wants to solve the problem on this side might also be an outside spectator trying to see and judge from a higher vantage point and for that reason having no understanding of the matter at all. At this point we can only repeat the two statements already formulated but with a shift of emphasis. Our very self-determination here is subject to determination by God. Our very self-determination needs determination by God in order to be experience of His Word. If human self-determination were not as it were the material which is subject and in need when we speak of the determination of human existence by the Word of God, then how could we speak of the determination of human existence or indeed of a determination by God's Word in any sense? If God's Word is not spoken to animals, plants and stones but to men, and if determination by God's Word is really a determination of human existence, in what, then, will it consist if not in the fact that the self-determination in which man is man finds its absolute superior in determination by God, that as self-determination, and without in the least being affected or even destroyed altogether as such, it receives a direction, is set under a judgment and has impressed upon it a character, in short, it is determined in the way that a self-determining being is by a word and that man is by the Word of God. The fact

that this happens to it, and what happens to it, is not the work of human self-determination. But conversely it is the work of human self-determination to which this happens, no matter what else may happen to it therewith.

When this is clear, the way is open for a more precise explanation of our statement that men can have experience of God's Word. This statement must now mean that men in their self-determination can be determined by God's Word: not just determined by any external factor that comes upon them, though naturally this can be true as well, but also determined by the Word of God. At this stage three points should be relatively easy to perceive.

[202] 1. To define the anthropological locus at which experience of the Word of God is possible, it is not necessary to emphasise one or another among the various possibilities of human self-determining, as though this and this alone were the chosen vessel of this experience. Will, conscience and feeling have been mentioned as such places, and whole theological systems have been built on the one preference or the other.

The reason why some prefer one anthropological locus and others another has always been that each has thought or hoped he could best justify a specific synthesis of the relations between divine and human determination, whether indeterministic, dialectical or deterministic, in terms of the one anthropological locus or the other. The unreality which is then, of course, inevitable on the presupposition of the necessity or possibility of such a synthesis has usually avenged itself in the form of a very one-sided view of religious experience and then of the Word of God which is supposedly experienced in this way. Now we have seen that the synthesis in question is neither necessary nor possible. We have thus no need to justify such a synthesis anthropologically. We have no need to stress the will in emphasis on human freedom, or conscience as the place where man becomes one with God's will, or feeling in order to make clear man's absolute dependence on God's omnipotence.

We may quietly regard the will and conscience and feeling and all other possible anthropological centres as possibilities of human self-determination and then understand them in their totality as determined by the Word of God which affects the whole man.

2. There is also no compulsion to invest certain anthropological centres with the fundamental distrust and suspicion that is often found in the history of theology. I have in mind especially the extraordinary polemic which it has been the fashion in recent years to wage against the so-called "intellect" of man, his powers of thought and understanding, as the locus of possible religious experience of the Word of God.

Two directly opposite reasons have been and are advanced for the special incompetence of the intellect in matters of religious experience. In the eyes of one group its activity in this area is a fatal sign that man, instead of actively determining his life himself, is on the point of sinking into the indolent passivity of mere reflection and contemplation. In the eyes of the other group the activity of the intellect is the peak of an overbold self-determination which, as they see it, ought to be broken and indeed completely smashed in experience of the Word of God. On the one side, then, the intellect lacks the real power, on the other the real humility, and on both the real depth which one hopes to encounter at other anthropological centres, e.g., conscience or feeling, as distinct from the intellect. What shall we say in answer? This surely, above all, that we, too, see no reason anthropologically to prefer the intellect especially. What man does when he uses this faculty, when he thinks and tries to understand, can in fact be indolence, hubris or both like any other human self-determination. But is not the same true of feeling, conscience, will, or anything else one might mention here? Are they not all self-determination, and no less so? Can they be less so seeing that the differences regarding the relation of spontaneity and receptivity which might call for consideration at this point drop seriously in importance *vis-à-vis* the comprehensive [203] determination of the whole of human existence by God's Word? Is it not an arbitrary pre-judgment that specifically in the act of thought man is man in a poorer sense than in his other self-actualisations? Is this pre-judgment really a judgment of the Christian faith, as is so often alleged? It is a well-known fact that only in retreat before modern agnosticism and not before has the Christian faith reached this extraordinary judgment. But this pre-judgment might imply a worse barricading of oneself against God's Word. We recall the fact established earlier that it is not just in the last resort, but primarily and predominantly, that God's Word is literally speech, i.e., an intellectual event. If this is so, then its being spoken to man must at least claim the intellect too, and experience of it must at least include also the intellect, and the claiming of the intellect. Does not the anti-intellectualism of modern theology involve on the one side a striving for sanctification which rests on self-delusion with reference to other anthropological possibilities and will necessarily end in disenchantment, and then on the other side a restriction of the possibility of experience of God's Word at the most decisive point, which might involve at once a complete denial of it? We can in no sense regard this as a respectable proceeding. We regard it as a form of cramp from which one must be healed to be able to see what is really to be seen here.

The Word of God that determines human existence is strong enough to deal also with man as he determines himself in thought. The same may naturally be said, and for the same reason, when attempts are made on the other side to discredit or exclude feeling or conscience as the locus of possible experience of the Word of God. If we have to reject it as more than a suspicious tyranny when Christian experience is interpreted expressly and preferentially as the experience of feeling or conscience, we obviously cannot assent to any exclusion of these anthropological centres.

In this sphere especially Evangelical theology is always threatened by the temptation to elevate the necessities of ephemeral polemics into denials in principle which cannot be carried through as such. We must resist this temptation in every direction.

3. Nor is there any need here to claim, discover, or assert any unusual or hidden anthropological centres as the basis of the possibility of human experience of God's Word. The existence of such unusual centres, which are more fully considered and investigated to-day than in earlier times, and the possibility that many more exist than are considered and investigated to-day, can indeed scarcely be doubted. Thus there are conscious and sub-conscious possibilities, and there would seem also to be semi-occult and occult possibilities of the human soul. There is also an intuitive grasp of objects apart from discursive thought and in all kinds of combinations with it. It may be that apart from the possibility of aesthetic feeling and attitude there is also that of a specifically religious variety.

One result of philosophical enlightenment as to the nature and limits of theoretical rea-
[204] son in particular was that from the time of Schleiermacher's discovery of the special "province" proper to religion in the mind of man theologians turned with a certain interested preference to these subsidiary areas of psychology. On our own presuppositions we shall have to say that we can really take no special interest in exhibiting such supposedly special places of possible religious experience. The possibilities which call for consideration in these subsidiary fields, both the generally recognised and the doubtful ones, are also in any case possibilities of human self-determination. So far as they can be claimed at all as human possibilities, they are rational possibilities in the broadest sense of the term. Their hiddenness and strangeness certainly do not qualify them as points of entry for the determination of man by God's Word. Here again, to the extent that we have specific human acts at all, our concern is still with acts of human self-determination, and it always will be no matter what discoveries may be made here nor what interpretations may be found. We do not say this in order to rule out these special places of human experience of the Word of God but to set them alongside the other, better known anthropological centres in the totality of human existence which is our concern here as the object of determination by God's Word.

Why should not the subconscious, or intuition, or whatever else might be mentioned here, have its place, too, among the possibilities of human existence in its determination by God's Word? But again, why should it have a special dignity alongside and among the other, better known possibilities? What depth psychology may have to say to us here along various lines may remind us of the breadth with which the concept of human existence will in any case have to be construed. All the same, from even the deepest depths of depth psychology we will not receive or expect information on this openness of human existence to the Word of God.

To summarise, human existence means human self-determination. If experience of God's Word involves the determination of human existence and hence also of human self-determination by the Word of God, then by self-determination we are to understand the exercise of all the faculties in whose exercise man is man without basic emphasis upon and also without basic repudiation of any specific human possibility. In this context all such emphases and repudiations are to be resisted already on the score of method, since they are the results or presuppositions of a general philosophical anthropology by whose constructions, however right or wrong they may be in their own sphere, we cannot allow ourselves to be influenced here. From different angles the determination of human existence by God's Word can be understood just as much as a determination of feeling, will, or intellect, and psychologically it may actually be more the one than the other in a given case. The decisive point materially, however, is that it is a determination of the whole self-determining man.

This settled, we push on a step further to the question in what the experience of God's Word, i.e., the determination of the whole self-determining man
[205] by God's Word, might then consist. To this question, which is so crucial for the whole problem of this section, an answer is given in the introductory thesis when it speaks of acknowledgment. I am aware of no word relatively so appro-

priate as this one to the nature of the Word of God whose determinative operation is our present concern. And in relation to what we know or think we know of man, this word is precise enough to say the specific thing that needs to be said about him here and yet also general enough to say this specific thing with the comprehensiveness with which it must be said here. To develop the concept of acknowledgment we shall borrow the nine points of orientation on the nature of the Word of God that we stated and explained in § 5.

1. The word acknowledgment entails first the concept of knowledge. This must be so because the Word of God is primarily and predominantly speech, communication from person to person and reason to reason, spirit, a rational event, the Word of truth, because it is addressed to the human *ratio*, by which one is not to understand the intellect alone, yet at any rate the intellect also and not last of all. If this is so, experience of God's Word must correspond thereto as far as possible. The word acknowledgment is at least an indication of this.

2. But this word also expresses the fact that experience of God's Word involves a relation of man as person to another person, naturally the person of God. We can also speak, of course, of the acknowledgment of facts, and we find this here too. But the kind of fact one acknowledges is not a fact of nature—one does not acknowledge a landslip or a rainbow or the like. The acknowledged fact is a fact created and presented by a person or persons. The determination of man's existence by the Word of God is created thus; it is determination by God's person. This is another reason why we call it acknowledgment.

3. Acknowledgment relates to a definite control (positive or negative) with respect to the one who acknowledges. It means not only subjection to a necessity, but adaptation to the meaningfulness of this necessity, approval of it, not just involvement in it but acceptance of it. Acknowledgment of God's Word relates to the purposiveness of God's Word, to its content as the Word of the Lord, the Word of man's Creator, Reconciler and Redeemer. It must consist in the fact that man approves this Word (even if in a very specific sense) and accepts its content (even if in a very specific sense) as truth valid for him. Acknowledgment of God's Word by man consists in avowal of and submission to the purposes of God declared in God's Word, in affirmation (naturally in a very specific way) of the "God with us" that the Word of God has to tell its hearers.

4. Acknowledgment of God's Word must also mean, of course, respect for the fact that takes place in God's Word. But this fact consists especially in its coming to us, in its contingent contemporaneity as revelation, Holy Scripture [206]
and Church proclamation. *Illic et tunc*[EN24] becomes *hic et nunc*[EN25]. Jesus Christ Himself lives in the message of His witnesses, lives in the proclamation of His

EN24 There and then
EN25 here and now

Church on the basis of this message, strides forward as the Lord of grace and judgment to meet the existence of the hearer of the Word. Experience of God's Word, then, must at least be also experience of His presence, and because this presence does not rest on man's act of recollection but on God's making Himself present in the life of man, it is acknowledgment of His presence.

5. In the word acknowledgment, as we have already said, there lies the relation to a control, a necessity. We have to remember that the Word of God has power, power as word has power, the power of God's truth, the power of His promise, claim, judgment and blessing which are its content, but power. Acknowledgment of the Word of God by man is naturally, then, approval of the Word of God by man, yet not approval on the basis of persuasion between equals, but the kind of approval that arises on the basis of obedience, of submission between those who are utterly unequal. To have experience of God's Word is to yield to its supremacy. Whether it comes to us as Law or Gospel, as command or promise, it comes at any rate in such a way as to bend man, and indeed his conscience and will no less than his intellect and feeling. It does not break him; it really bends him, brings him into conformity with itself.

6. Acknowledgment certainly means decision too. The coming of God's Word to man is the act of divine freedom and choice. It does not have to come to him. It comes according to God's good-pleasure, and it is again God's good-pleasure how it comes to him, whether for grace or judgment. In every case, then, experience of the Word of God is experience of the divine freedom and choice, and therefore it is itself decision, decision concerning man which is manifested as the characterising of man's decision as a decision for faith or unbelief, for obedience or disobedience. In the first instance, then, the conformity to God's Word to which we have just referred might mean either obedience or disobedience. Even in disobedience there is an acknowledgment of God's Word, though against man's will and to his perdition. Even in his disobedience man characterises himself as the man he is before God's Word. Even disobedience is in its own way a confirmation or approval of God's Word to the degree that it is disobedience against God's Word and to the degree that even in disobedience man's self-determination is a fulfilment of his determination by the Word of God. The same may naturally be said of the decision for obedience. Just because experience of God's Word is such decision, man can and must be summoned in the Church to ever new experience and therefore to decision.

[207] 7. There also lies in the concept of acknowledgment the fact that the act denoted thereby means halting before an enigma, acquiescence in a situation which is not open but which is unexplained from the standpoint of him who does the acknowledging. In § 5 we spoke of the secularity of the Word of God, i.e., of the fact that it comes to us in a form which also means its concealment. Experience of God's Word, then, must also consist in the fact that we receive it in this form and this concealment, in this twofold indirectness. Our very

acceptance of the Word, which will be especially important later, will participate in this twofold indirectness. It, too, will have a secular form, the form of all kinds of human acts, and this form will be its concealment, its ambivalence. Apart from this ambivalence, which is deeply rooted in the very nature of the matter, there is no experience of God's Word. It will always consist also in respect for, and acknowledgment of, the mystery of this Word.

8. Just because acknowledgment of the mystery of God in His Word is at issue, we must also stress the fact that the term acknowledgment denotes an act or movement on man's part, a movement which only as it is made is the acknowledgment required, so that it cannot be resolved into an attitude. What prevents the latter in experience of God's Word, and what makes this experience, where it is real, into a movement, is what we called in § 5 the one-sideness of the Word of God. We meant by this the fact that the total Word of God, whether veiled and unveiled, or unveiled and veiled, always encounters us, and that this is each time something specific for us, that it is one-sided for us, that now it encounters us in its veiling and now in its unveiling, that it is not manifest to us in the unity of the two, and yet that it always seeks to be heard by us as a complete Word of God. In view of this, acknowledgment of the Word of God necessarily means letting oneself be continually led, always making a step, always being in movement from the experience felt at one time or the thought grasped at one time to the opposite experience and thought, because hearing of God's Word always consists in also hearing the one in the other and the other in the one. In this movement which cannot be arrested by any synthesis a man acknowledges the mystery of the Word of God and he has Christian experience.

9. When acknowledgment takes place, there is a yielding of the man who acknowledges before the thing or person he acknowledges. He submits to the authority of the other. This is not in contradiction with the concept of self-determination but it does mean that the self-determination of man as such takes place at a specific point in a specific context. It has found its beginning and its basis in another higher determination. In the act of acknowledgment, the life of man, without ceasing to be the self-determining life of this man, has now its centre, its whence, the meaning of its attitude, and the criterion whether this attitude really has the corresponding meaning—it has all this [208] outside itself, in the thing or person acknowledged. So far as it has all this, it has it from the thing or person acknowledged. Thus acknowledgment as an attitude is in every respect the act of this man and yet from the standpoint of the meaning of the attitude it is not at all his act but a determination that has come upon him from the thing or person acknowledged by him and compelling his acknowledgment. First there is the thing or person acknowledged, and then in virtue of it, and in the last resort deriving wholly from it, there is acknowledgment. We are confronted here by what we called in § 5 the spirituality of the Word of God, i.e., the grounding not only of its being spoken but also of its being really heard by man in the Word itself, the appropriation of

God's Word as a gift of the Holy Spirit, and therefore as the Word's own act on man. Therewith we are also brought up against the frontier of what we can say about experience of God's Word as such. The final thing to be said is that while the attitude of acknowledgment *vis-à-vis* God's Word is really an attitude of man, an act of his self-determination, nevertheless it is the act of that self-determination of man whose meaning and basis, whose final seriousness and true content, whose truth and reality, cannot be ascribed to man himself but only to his determination by the Word of God. It is the act of pure acknowledgment, one might also say, the act in which acknowledgment consists in the fact that it merely seeks to be the answer to a "recognition"—at this frontier even the meaning of the word must change—which has come to man from beyond all his own acts or powers, of which he himself is not the subject, but in whose free truth and reality he must be acknowledged if he is to acknowledge its truth and reality.

It is as well to see and say at once that by taking place as an experience this experience ceases to be an experience. In the concluding sub-section, in order to close the circle of the problem of man's possibility of knowledge of the Word of God, or rather to indicate the point where it must finally be left open, we shall have to introduce and discuss at this juncture the concept of the faith which corresponds to the Holy Spirit of the Word of God. But before we do that it will be worth our while to look back for a moment and to state explicitly that experience of God's Word is possible, but that in respect of its meaning and basis, its final seriousness and true content, its truth and reality, it is not experience but more than experience.

We preface this negative and amplifying statement by a positive one. In what has been said thus far we have not denied but affirmed the possibility of human experience of God's Word. We have characterised it as genuine experience by emphasising as strongly as possible its character as human self-determination. We have not protested against the introduction of feeling or
[209] conscience or especially the intellect into experience of the Word of God. We have not combatted the concept of experience and we have even accepted "religious consciousness" without demur. We have described this experience, not in the form of a psychological study, but in the form of a conclusion from our earlier understanding of the nature of the Word of God, by mentioning a series of acts which with the partial exception of the frontier instance at the end can all be claimed as fully human acts possible to man. We shall not object if the nine or eight points in which we have developed acknowledgment are regarded and described in some fashion as an attempt to depict—formally as the situation here demands—the religious experience or consciousness of the Christian.

I must emphasise this because to my regret I am continually hearing it said that I am putting revelation and faith up in the clouds so far as the believer is concerned and teaching a *fides quae creditur*[EN26] "without regard for the *fides qua creditur*[EN27], the intimate personal conviction and experience of faith." "The intimate personal experience of faith is to be completely eliminated." The transmission of revelation is not thought of in such a way "that the nature of man is also to be taken into account in it" (cf. G. Wobbermin, *Richtlinien ev. Theol.*, 1929, 22, 104, 139, 141, etc.). Or again from E. Schaeder I continually hear the vague complaint (the last time in *Das Wort Gottes*, 1930, 37 f.) that I am in danger "of exaggerating in an untenable way the protest against the place and validity of the ego in faith and the theology of faith." In my work one is compelled as "believer and theologian" to do "the impossible, namely, to jump over one's own shadow." In me the necessary battle against idealism turns head over heels and even so pure distance between the Spirit of God and the human spirit or finite ego is not yet achieved (*op. cit.*, p. 41), etc. I do not doubt for a moment, and will return to this, that the difference between the view of Wobbermin and Schaeder (to mention these as spokesmen for many others) and the view presented here is as deep as it can possibly be within the Evangelical church, and I do not really have any thought of trying to commend myself to them by concessions. But it will clarify the issue in dispute if they and others will refrain from ascribing to me negations which I have never sponsored in this form, not even ten years ago. There cannot really be any dispute as to whether regard should be had to the "intimate personal experience of faith" or whether the nature of man should be "taken into account" or whether an exaggerated, i.e., an "absolute" protest should be made against the place and validity of the ego. What sense would there be here in even a relative negation and protest, let alone an exaggerated one? Nevertheless, I believe that the quiet affirmative that one can and must make at this point has still to be followed by different statements from those which Wobbermin and Schaeder would like to see and which would be as crucial for them in the whole dispute as my own further statements are for me.

We can concede everything that is in fact to be conceded here. We can thus state, as we have done in due form, that experience of God's Word involves an authentic experience possible for man. But we must then go on to ask whether experience of God's Word is possible in such a way that by it the store of human possibilities is enriched by a further one; whether man has a possibility, an organ, a capability that he did not have before; or, conversely, whether the [210]
possibility of experience of God's Word, being given to man in virtue of its actuality, is so given to him that it becomes a possibility which is certainly extraordinary, which may even perhaps be called miraculous, but which is still a possibility independently proper to him, the possibility of the religious man (of the pardoned man as one can and must also say), yet still of man. Does there take place in the reality of this experience a kind of divine emanation towards man, or, from man's standpoint, a divine *influxus*[EN28] whose outcome is the possibility in question? Can one deduce from the possibility of the experience of God's Word that there are men who have this possibility, perhaps in the same way as others have artistic possibilities as distinct from many of their fellow-men? Do these men exist in such a way that they can discover and recognise themselves as possessors of this possibility or be discovered and

EN26 the faith which one believes
EN27 the faith with which one believes
EN28 influx

recognised as such by others? Does experience of God's Word become real in such a way that its possibility may be advanced and presupposed as a predicate, as a specific characteristic of certain men, as the property of a human I or We which can be asserted directly, unequivocally and unreservedly in relation to this I or We?

This is obviously the deduction of, e.g., Schaeder from the general presupposition when he can speak of "a conjunction between the Word of God and the finite ego" (*op. cit.*, p. 41) which takes place and can be exhibited in faith, or of a "word-bound ego" (p. 45), or when "in the question of the Word of God" he wants to begin with the believing ego''—''what else can one do?''(p. 43), or when he claims knowledge of "a word-mediated synthesis between the Spirit of God and the finite spirit" (p. 46), an "inmost synthesis of word, history, human ego, Spirit of God and faith" (p. 50), a "relationship of the Word of God to the strict presence of him who receives it" (p. 49), or when on one occasion he can even describe the Word of God as "having arisen out of the synthesis of divine self-offering or revelation and the human relationship of faith effected by this revelation" (p. 105), or when he feels no difficulty in remarking incidentally: "We shall make no headway in promoting God's Word" until we have met such and such conditions (p. 103), or when finally his doctrine of the Word of God culminates in the reference to certain "men of sensibility" who represent the decisive operation of the Word of God or the Church of the Word (p. 170). It is a valuable service that should be mentioned here, since it spares us saying any more, that Robert Winckler has not only explicitly described this theory as "parallel in its main outlines" to that of his teacher Wobbermin but has also called it a "platform" on which to-day "all non-dialectical theology may find itself united" (*Th. Lit. Z.*, 1931, 550; cf. also Torsten Bohlin, *Th. Lit. Z.*, 1931, 570).

We must try to realise above all what it would mean if this theory were correct. It would obviously mean that we might now assert an aptitude of man for God's Word, a possibility of fulfilling man's determination by God's Word by means of human self-determination. I say "might" because this is not in the first instance asserted by the champions of this theory, i.e., not as a general
[211] possibility nor as one proper to man from the very outset. Indeed, it can even be emphatically denied by them as a possibility in this sense. On the basis of this theory it can even be said very zealously that the possibility of this experience is given to man by God and by God alone.

What was expressly stated in the first edition of this book (p. 92f.) must be repeated here. We do injustice to Schleiermacher (and his followers right up to our own day) if we foist upon them the intention which was, of course, that of Feuerbach, namely, that of making the human subject the creator of his determination by God, as though their theology were direct Cartesianism. I do not think I missed the significance of Schaeder's catchword "theocentric theology" in the polemic which I then conducted against him. Schaeder now sets store on the fact that he can understand as a "word-bound ego" the ego which on his view is to be questioned about the Word of God in theology. Now at that time I quoted sentences like the following from his earlier book: "The factors with which we deal in knowledge are all factors of consciousness or they are not there for us to deal with. The God with whom theology has to do is the God of our consciousness and no other. Or He is the divine spirit-content of our consciousness. .... The present finite spirit or personal consciousness is investigated by theology respecting its possession of God or the divine Spirit and the conditions thereof. It is not easy to see how it could be otherwise. This I term the theocentric in theology. Naturally theology in selecting this term starts with man or the spiritual consciousness of man. What sensible man would not do this? But in consciousness or on the basis of consciousness it seeks to grasp by the means of knowledge available the divine reality of the Spirit, the pneumatic element, the reality of God" (*Das Geistproblem der Theologie*, 1924, 2, 4). But already at that time I also cited and considered Schaeder's further statement :"We reach God only in the way He reaches us, i.e., only on the basis of His revelation to us, which at least ultimately and conclusively is achieved in our consciousness if it is to count as revelation" (*op. cit.*, p. 63). I also think I understood Schaeder then exactly as he has now interpreted himself (*Das Wort Gottes*, 1930, 43 f.), i.e., I presented as his meaning just what he has now added by way of interpretation. And it should be expressly emphasised that in Wobbermin, too, one can find statements like the following:"The way in question leads from God to man, not *vice versa* from man to God. Man, who is always entangled in sin and guilt, does not enter the way to God on his own. For sin and guilt lead him away from God. Only God can make a connexion between God and man, and bridge the chasm which is torn open, and continually torn open afresh, by the sin of man" (*Richtlinien ev. Theol.*, 1929, 102). Thus on the points that man is not apt for God's Word *a priori* and in general, that in experience of God's Word he does not act at all creatively, that the possibility of this experience is not to be regarded as one originally pertaining to him but rather as one accruing to him, there can be no quarrel with the representatives of this theory.

But what at first seems to hold good and is maintained on the basis of this theory, the action, creation or gift of God in the experience of His Word, suddenly ceases to apply at a specific point. And what at first seems not to hold good and is denied on the basis of this theory, the aptitude of man for this experience, suddenly comes into play at a specific point. The start is apparently not Cartesian but the subsequent course is plainly so. The reality of this experience, i.e., man's determination by the Word of God, is thought of in [212]
such a way that in it God hands something over to man in the sense that it really passes out of God's hand into the hands of man, or, from man's standpoint, in such a way that man receives something from God in the sense that it is really put in his hands. A conjunction or synthesis has taken place. Man's consciousness now has a divine content of spirit in the light of which it can be contemplated and investigated. The statement *homo capax verbi Dei*[EN29] suddenly comes to life. There arises in the reality of this experience as something that is present and can be demonstrated and presupposed a new man, new not only in the sense that he is man addressed by the Word of God, new, then, not only in Christ—who could or would oppose that?—but new in himself, changed in the immanent constitution of his humanity. Even if on the basis of his being addressed by the Word, this man now acquires autonomy and independent interest as a participant in the reality of the Word, so much so that if the introduction of the concept of mysticism is not quite indispensable it is at least obvious and desirable.

Cf. Schaceder, *Das Geistproblem*, p. 118 f. and more cautiously *Das Wort Gottes*, p. 54. I do not know whether to regard it as uncertainty in terminology or as material wavering when in his final statements Schaeder describes "faith-mysticism" primarily as the "active proximity of

EN29 the human being is able to receive the word of God

God," as the claiming, adoption and justification of man (*Das Wort Gottes,* 33 f., cf. also p. 47), but then goes further and says that it is not only that but also "a characteristic inner transformation of the ego or enrichment of its content" (*op. cit.*, p. 41). The decisive step is not the introduction of the concept of mysticism but the definition of it in this way, the assertion of the "conjunction" or "synthesis."

The man thus distinguished is not, then, man in general, nor does any possibility presupposed as such in man correspond to the content of divine Spirit. This man is the particular man usually called the religious man or the believing Christian man. And his possibility of being a bearer of the content of divine Spirit is the possibility he has received in the reality of experience of the Word of God. Nevertheless—and this is the point—it is a possibility which is proper to him, which has become proper to him, as this man, the religious man. In a depth of his being which is hidden, yet not completely hidden but penetrable, his existence or self-determination is identical with the fulfilment of his determination by God's Word. He does not stand only on the Word of God. While constantly appealing to the Word of God, he also stands on himself, on the conjunction or synthesis which is actual in him and therefore possible for him, on the *esse capax verbi Dei*[EN30] imparted to him.

His "own personal experience of faith" now becomes, in the words of Wobbermin, the "opposite pole" to the Word and hence a "methodical aid" to knowledge of the Word, even though this be understood as a subordinate entity (*Richtlinien,* 140 f.).

[213] And the reality of the experience of God's Word no longer rests on itself; it has become an ellipse instead of a circle, and one of the poles, the one nearer us and opposite God, is the man who has the experience.

Is it not inevitable that the man who is thus characterised as the opposite subjective pole will find that he is nearer himself than the Word of God is, that the new epistemological order of man to God will come into force afresh, and that even with the double safeguard that the reference is to pardoned man and that the material order is the reverse (cf. Wobbermin, *Wort Gottes und ev. Glaube,* 1931, 9 and Robert Winckler, *Theol. Lit. Z.*, 1931, 550–51) it will come into full force for the first time? When a theology starts with the believing ego in the question of God's Word (Schaeder, *Das Wort Gottes,* 43), can it avoid making the believing ego, the known Christian believer, the criterion and standard of its statements about God's Word? And can it be denied that the Cartesianism which has apparently been rejected is thereby brought back into theology as, so to say, an indirect Cartesianism, the Cartesianism of the believing Christian? In this event has not the concept "theocentric theology" become a *lucus a non lucendo*[EN31]?

Thus in real experience of the Word of God man becomes an independent actualisation of this experience with his own independent interest. He thereby makes the experience possible. There are religious men into whose existence and nature the Word of God has entered and is present and whose existence

[EN30] to be able to receive

[EN31] "lucus" which is the word for forest because it is dark in there ("non luceat")

and nature are therefore bound to become the depository and the first and decisive criterion and standard of knowledge of the Word of God. This thesis we must oppose.

Let it not be thought that this thesis and our opposition to it are just a theological quibble that might well be left unsettled. Behind Professors Wobbermin and Schaeder and their view of the independent being and possession of religious man with its independent interest there stands the *Ecclesiam habemus*[EN32] of General Superintendents Dibelius and Schian, the "common sense" of practically the whole of our positive and liberal ministry, and the prevailing tendency in the pietistic community-movement, which at this point is intimately bound up with the prevailing tendency in the Church at large. Tell them what Wobbermin and Schaeder are also trying to tell them, that the material order with reference to experience of God's Word must run from God to man and not *vice versa*, and they will all applaud and agree with you to-day. Tell them further that for man generally, for man without faith or before faith, the epistemological order must also be from God to man, that without preceding revelation there can be no faith, and they will concede your point, not yet being affected themselves. But tell them that this epistemological order applies also and particularly to the religious man, that he also and particularly has no possibility, not even a received possibility, but can only receive the possibility of experience of God's Word, can use it only as it is conferred in the actuality of reception, tell them that this possibility is and remains God's possibility and does not pass out of His hands into any other hands, tell them this and at once bitter and irreconcilable controversy breaks out. When we tell them this, when we oppose to that thesis our counterthesis, which is separated from it only by a blade's breadth and yet by a chasm's depth, then an impressive majority among both the leaders and the led in the modern Evangelical Church is passionately against us. Now the feeling on the other [214] side that everything is at stake here for faith and love and hope, for thought and life, for the world and the Church—this feeling is in every respect ours too, and anyone who sees the issue will have this feeling, no matter what position he may adopt. Let everyone make his choice and let none continue to look around for new and tiresome attempts at mediation!

We must now develop the reason for our rejection of this indirect Christian Cartesianism and also our own thesis regarding the possibility of experience of God's Word.

To do this we must first summarise again the positive content of our train of thought thus far. We have stated that if there is any Church and Church proclamation in a serious sense, this implies that knowledge of the Word of God is possible for some men. The fact that this knowledge is possible for them necessarily means that experience of God's Word is possible for them, i.e., that it is possible that certain men may be determined by the Word of God in their existence, i.e., in the totality of their self-determination. It is possible, as we have said more precisely in the light of God's Word, that the relation of these men to the Word of God may be the relation of acknowledgment. In the possibility of acknowledgment of the Word of God there thus consists the possibility of experience and therefore of knowledge of the Word of God. At this point Cartesianism now encounters us a second time in the specific form of indirect Christian Cartesianism. This interprets the possibility as one which in the act

EN32 We have the Church

of real acknowledgment (or experience or knowledge) of the Word of God, and in the form of an emanation from the Word of God spoken to man or an *influxus*[EN33] into the man addressed by the Word of God, becomes man's own, a predicate of his existence, a content of his consciousness, his possession. We must now make a demarcation against this interpretation of the possibility in question.

To this end we return again to the beginning. We are dealing with the possibility of knowledge of God's Word. We are thus dealing with the possibility of confirmation of the acquaintance man has with God's Word. We are dealing with the fact that for men acquainted with God's Word through revelation, Scripture and proclamation, God's Word can and must become true in such a way that its truth becomes their own and they become responsible witnesses to its truth. We are dealing with the fact that the Church and Church proclamation can be there in truth among men and through men. As stated already at the beginning of the section, no small thing depends on this possibility. On our understanding of this possibility depends the way in which we understand the Church and Church proclamation, and as regards dogmatics the way in which we understand its particular ministry in the Church, the testing, criticising and correcting of Church proclamation. For the Word of God is the criter-
[215] ion of the Church, Church proclamation and dogmatics. When we ask where the possibility of knowledge of God's Word is to be sought, we are asking where the criterion is to be sought with which dogmatics works. It makes a great difference whether in answer to this question we say with indirect Christian Cartesianism that it is given by God to the religious man, the Christian believer, that it is handed over to him by God, that we are thus to seek it in him, in his own personal experience of faith as such, in his "word-bound ego," among the contents of his consciousness—whether we have to say all this or whether we are perhaps not to say it at all. Dogmatics will be very different, Church proclamation will be very different and finally the whole Church will be decisively different according to whether this must be said or not. The whole question of the relation of the Church to the truth will be put very differently according to whether the answer here is Yes or No, and so too will the relation of the truth to the Church. The presence of truth in the Church or its absence from it might depend on whether the Church goes the one way or the other at this point. Jesus Christ can and will confess in some way—and that a salutary and victorious way—even a Church with a bad dogmatics and a bad proclamation due to a wrong decision at this point. This can and should be said by way of comfort. But we neither can nor should be content with that. We must open our eyes as widely as possible at this cross-roads and only with the best possible conscience should we decide for the right hand or the left. We must be as sure of ourselves as men can possibly be when we seek the possibility of knowledge of God's Word either the one way or the other. And

---

[EN33] influx

the question must now be: Can we be sure of ourselves if we seek this possibility in the religious man, the believing Christian? Are we certain that in what we can find, affirm, consider and analyse in him as the possibility of such a man we can really find and affirm the possibility of knowledge of the Word of God? Or, from the opposite angle, can we be sure that we can really find among the possibilities of such a man, and affirm in one of the possibilities of such a man, the possibility of knowledge that corresponds to real knowledge of the Word of God, this possibility on the understanding of which so much later depends? Can we say with final human certainty that this is so? Can we put our hand in the fire for it? (We can only *ask* in relation to this decision, but at all events we *must* ask; we must ask whether we can be responsible with ultimate human seriousness for ascribing the possibility of knowledge of the Word of God to the religious man as such.) And it is to the question as put in this way that our answer must be No. We could give an affirmative answer only with penultimate seriousness, only with a wavering conscience, only with semi-certainty.

We might well be responsible for saying Yes here if it were not a matter of the possibility of knowledge of the Word of God but only, e.g., the possibility of [216]
understanding Plato's wisdom and culture. Where else should we seek and find and study this if not in the representatives of this wisdom and culture, in the men gripped by its pathos and ethos? We might well take the responsibility of saying Yes at this point if it were not a question of the criterion of dogmatics but the principle of a philosophy or world-view, if it were not a question of the proclamation of the Church but of the message of a union of *illuminati*[EN34] and men of profound insight, if it were not a question of the Church but of a society of stirred partisans seeking to stir others. If we were dealing with the possibility of human knowledge of things in man's sphere, it would in fact be natural and necessary to seek this possibility, whatever its objective content, in the appropriate experts, i.e., in ourselves if we are among them, or in others, or at all events in those involved. We might entertain with ultimate human certainty the expectation of really finding it there and getting orientation and instruction there.

But in the case of the possibility of knowledge of the Word of God the situation is quite different. To be sure, it, too, has its special bearers, its experts, its representatives. There are indeed men who have this possibility. We ourselves are perhaps among those who have it, namely, as the reflection or echo of its reality, in the act of the Word spoken to us, in the event of experiencing it. But if we regard ourselves or others among such men, and then affirm in ourselves or in them this possibility that has as it were been infused by God, do we not come up at once against an insuperable difficulty which proves to be the end of all, yes, *all* certainty in any such assertion? When we try to find the content of divine Spirit in the (pardoned) consciousness of man, are we not like the man who wanted to scoop out in a sieve the reflection of the beautiful silvery

[EN34] enlightened folk

moon from a pond? What can or shall we find there to investigate? As the substance of human experience of God's Word, obviously that which we have designated and described as the act of acknowledgment of God's Word: a human process of a very characteristic and differentiated and at the same time comprehensive kind. Because this process is indeed present and may be lived, asserted and described, we speak of a possibility of human experience of the Word of God. In establishing this process in ourselves or others, we take this possibility into account. But does this mean that we really find this possibility in the process, that we reckon with the possibility because we have found it in this process? Is it not the case that we do not see or grasp the possibility at all in this process as such, that what we do see and grasp is never more than the process itself, which might as such be something very different from that possibility? Is it a fact that the acknowledgment that takes place in us or others must really be acknowledgment of the Word of God, that it can refer only to this, the
[217] counterpart of the divine Word, that it is a faithful mirror of this counterpart, that we may deduce this counterpart from the human acknowledgment, that we may regard man as confronted with this counterpart? Who tells us that? Who guarantees it? Who, when we have in view the ascertainable human possibility as such, can vouch for it that this is the possibility corresponding to the reality of the Word of God and not a completely different possibility? For all the nine elements we assembled under the concept of acknowledgment (with the possible exception of the last, to which we ventured to apply the concept of experience only in part), cannot striking parallels be adduced among possibilities of a very different kind? Can this acknowlegment of God's Word be differentiated even from the phenomenon of what are called "other religions" with any clear distinctiveness or individuality? To the degree that it has its reality in this human acknowledgment, does not Christianity undeniably belong to the sphere of general religious history in which there are no doubts hills and valleys but no heaven? And does not the whole sphere of religious history itself lie in the comprehensive sphere of the general history of culture? Is there even a single so-called religious phenomenon which cannot be more or less completely interpreted as the prototype or residuum of a thoroughly this-worldly attempt at civilisation, as a phenomenon of work in the broadest sense of the term? And is culture anything but the life-act of man understood from the standpoint of work? If we cling to what we can affirm and investigate as the human acknowledgment of God's Word, to what can be experienced in Christian experience, where shall we find there the criterion by which to distinguish this experience from others, the authentic from the inauthentic? What is there here to stop us interpreting everything in terms of the religious, the cultural, the human generally, or finally indeed the biological? With what certainty can one know and maintain that in what is seen to take place as an act of acknowledgment in the religious man there is really present the acknowledgment of the Word of God spoken to him and therefore the possibility of his experience or knowledge of it? No, the certainty that dogmatics, Church proclamation

and the Church itself need in relation to the possibility of knowledge of God's Word is not to be attained here. All that can be attained consists only of vague assertions in support of which one can hardly avoid having recourse to direct philosophical Cartesianism.

Schaeder's dictum is simply not true, that "every subjective explanation of these subjective phenomena of consciousness breaks down" (*Das Geistproblem d. Theol.*, 1924, 65). And when Wobbermin insists that "the ultimate supreme reality" which is the opposite pole of the "basic act of religion" shows itself to be secure against the suspicion of subjective illusion by the fact that this basic act, as I-related, enjoys "the primal reality of the whole certainty and validity of reality," namely, the I-consciousness (*Syst. Theol.*, Vol. 2, 1921, 456), this simply shows that even as a follower of indirect Cartesianism one is forced at the crucial point to [218] take refuge in the original and direct form and to swear by the certainty of the self-certainty of man in general. In fact what happens to us when we point to what the Word of God itself does to and in and through us is exactly what happened to Aaron when he caused his rod to turn into a serpent before Pharaoh and his court: "Then Pharaoh also called the wise men and the sorcerers: now the magicians of Egypt, they also did in like manner with their enchantments. For they cast down every man his rod, and they became serpents" (Ex. 7^10f.^). The only thing is that we unfortunately cannot command the sequel: "But Aaron's rod swallowed up their rods."

It might be objected, of course, that in all this we have been looking only, so to speak, at the outward aspect of the act that we may experience, that we have been viewing it only, so to speak, as a phenomenon. It would have to be granted that it cannot be recognised as this specific act, and that certainty as to its authenticity cannot be reached, when it is viewed thus. But things are quite different, it might be argued, when we ask what the man engaged in the act knows about himself, whether for this man—and therefore universally in so far as this man is a normative witness to the matter in question—the act is not distinctively, unequivocally, visibly and perceptibly this act and not another, whether the possibility of experience or knowledge of God's Word that is sought is not, then, visibly and perceptibly distinct from all other acts and possibilities. Our reply is that in fact the apparently unavoidable relativising of the act might find its own limit in the limit of its external aspect, of its purely theoretical consideration, and that beyond this (on the basis of its inner aspect and hence in analysis of its existential character) new territory might open up, and there might also result a certain interpretation of the act with reference to its relation to the Word of God. How could we refuse, then, to entertain the proposal that the question be put in this broader or deeper form? One thing, however, we must stipulate. The man engaged in this act, who is to be a witness here and whose self-understanding must decide, must be the man we know from the promise. Only this man can tell us about the possibility that corresponds to real experience of the Word of God. My self-understanding can be significant here only to the degree that I understand myself as confronted with the promise, i.e., with the Word of God as it encounters me in revelation, Scripture and proclamation, only to the degree that I see myself in the specific light that falls upon my existence from this. Analysis of my self-understanding

here can only mean appealing to what the promise tells every man about himself, and to what only the promise can tell him decisively and effectively about himself. Asseverations about a personal situation, if this is what existential talk means, can be of no importance here. If on these conditions we accept the demand that the inner aspect of the apprehensible act of acknowledgment
[219] and therefore of Christian experience be given its say, then we are simply saying that from this angle it is not the human act as such, not what can be and is experienced as such, not what is really put in our hands as such, not what can be achieved and established by man as such, that absolutely distinguishes, characterises and qualifies this specific act among and alongside man's other possibilities as the act in which the determination of man by the Word of God takes place. To be sure, the man who is really determined by God's Word will perform this act. There is no real knowledge of the Word without performance of this act. As man knows God's Word, all that we have said about this act can be and is experienced. It becomes real and can be established psychologically. There takes place an understanding, a personal involvement, an acceptance, an assent, an approval, a making present of remote times, an obedience, a decision, a halting before the mystery, a stimulation by the inner life, a basing of man's whole life on this mystery that is beyond himself. All this takes place and has to do so.

That man's encounter with God according to the Old and New Testaments is the very opposite of a transcendental drama which man confronts almost as a bored spectator, that the biblical concepts of renewal and sanctification, of faith, knowledge and obedience, of repentance, love, humility, gratitude, etc., invariably point also to a very concrete event and act that can be experienced and established psychologically, is something that admittedly no less a person than Luther repeatedly emphasised. We may simply recall in this connexion some of the most general passages in which the accent falls especially on the fact that this event can be experienced: "The same peace hovers over all sense, reason and understanding. Hence thou must not think of it as though none could feel or experience it; for if we are to have peace with God, then we must first feel it in heart and conscience, how else could our heart and mind be kept by it? ... (*Adventspostille*, Phil. $4^{4f.}$, 1522, *W.A.* 10^{12}, 186, 15). "For if a man enter into the illusion he has faith and yet never experiences it, he will rot and dry up, and nought is found when it comes to the point it should be found" (*Sermon on Jn.* $4^{10f.}$, 1532, *W.A.* 36, 468, 29). "If then ... ye have grasped the resurrection of Christ with faith and have received power and comfort of the same, and are therefore risen together with Him, that must prove itself in you such that it is felt and traced in you as it hath begun to work in you, that it is not alone word but truth and life. For to those that feel it not thus, Christ hath not yet arisen ... (*Cruc. Sommerpostille, Sermon on Col.* 3^{1-7}, *W.A.* 21, 266, 20). " ... take to thyself the Word of God, go and listen to man's preaching, or read or write or even sing it, so that thy sole concern and act is with it, then wilt thou feel somewhat, that will not fail" (*Sermon on Lk.* $24^{13ff.}$, 1523, *W.A.* 12, 500, 10). " ... the call of the spirit in the heart must thou feel, for it is always also thy heart's call, how shouldst thou not then feel it? ... If thou feelest not the call, take thought and cease not to pray till God hear thee; for thou art Cain and it standeth not well with thee ..." (*Kirchenpostille*, 1522, *Sermon on Gal.* $4^{1f.}$, *W.A.* 10^{11}, 372, 10; 373, 2). Cf. also Calvin: *Consequitur fidem a pio affectu nullo modo est distrahendam.* [EN35]

[EN35] It follows that faith must not in any respect be separated from pious devotion

(*Instit*, III, 2, 9). *Id autem* (assurance of faith) *fieri nequit, quin eius* (God's goodness) *suavitatem vere sentiamus et experiamur in nobis ipsis*[EN36] (*ib.*, III, 2, 15).

But the fact that all this happens and must happen does not mean in the least that the possibility of experience of God's Word is to be seen and found in [220] this event, that in it human self-determination becomes the opposite pole of the divine determination, that man becomes a "word-bound ego" in contemplation of which we must orientate ourselves in the question of the Word of God. The very man who is really engaged in this act will never even partially, not even in the tiniest part, see in this act as such something that makes possible what is the meaning, basis and end, the truth and reality of this act. No matter how authentic and good and strong he feels, he will not "feel" himself to be an "opposite pole," he will not think that as a "word-bound ego" he can leave his own sphere, he will not expect new experience, not even partially, in the form of self-experience. He will indeed be called by God in his whole existence; "with all his heart and soul and mind and strength" he will be involved. But not for a moment or in any respect will he think that his being involved is even approximately an adequate counterpart to the promise and claim confronting him. Not for a moment or in any respect will he rely upon the fact that he is involved, or orientate himself by it, or take from it the standard for understanding the reality in which he stands: he will not want to reflect on it but will simply be in it. Not for a moment or in any respect will he want to come back to his involvement or cling to it or build upon it. The judgment of the divine Word is passed on his involvement even as it takes place. What acknowledgment of God's Word in our experience, what understanding, involvement, assent, obedience, etc., can even remotely deserve to be called real acknowledgment of God's Word? What acknowledgment of God's Word in our experience is not unmasked and convicted by the Word of God even as it takes place, convicted not of its imperfection and inadequacy but of its total corruption and futility?—for as surely as all else we do it is the work of the human heart whose inventions and endeavours are bad from youth up and can be helped only by forgiveness. In what acknowledgment of God's Word in our experience, then, can there be anything like a sure and necessary correspondence to the Word of God? If there really is, then it is in virtue of the acknowledgment which man cannot achieve and therefore cannot assert, but which comes by grace upon his work that is corrupt and dead through sin, for Christ's sake and not for the sake of his inner disposition. How else can it be even in the religious man, the believing Christian? He it is specifically who knows, who alone knows, that this is how it is and not otherwise. The saying *finitum non capax infiniti*[EN37] cannot really prove what has to be proved at this point. If the real experience of the man addressed by God's Word is against this saying, then the

[EN36] And this (assurance of faith) cannot be present, unless we truly feel its sweetness (the sweetness of God's goodness) and experience it within ourselves

[EN37] the finite cannot contain the infinite

saying must go, as every philosophical statement in theology that is in contradiction with this experience must go. As a philosophical saying it does not interest us in the slightest. We do not say *finitum*[EN38] but *homo peccator non*
[221] *capax*[EN39], and we do not continue *infiniti*[EN40] but *verbi Domini*[EN41]. The real experience of the man addressed by God's Word is the very thing that decides and proves that what makes it possible lies beyond itself.

We think of Peter's ἔξελθε ἀπ' ἐμοῦ ὅτι ἀνὴρ ἁμαρτωλός εἰμι[EN42] (Lk. 5^{8}) and of the saying of the father of the epileptic boy: πιστεύω· βοήθει μου τῇ ἀπιστίᾳ?[EN43] (Mk. 9^{24}). The same Luther who rates experience so highly can also say along this line: "Faith is such that it feeleth not but droppeth reason, shutteth the eyes and simply surrendereth to the Word, and followeth the same through death and life. But feeling goeth not beyond what can be grasped by reason and the senses, as what is heard, seen and felt, or known by the outward senses. Therefore feeling is counter to faith, faith to feeling .... Whoso then pursueth feeling, he is destroyed, but whoso counter to feeling dependeth heartily upon the Word, he will be brought through" (*Sommerpostille*, 1526, *Sermon on Mk.* $16^{1f.}$, *W.A.* 10^{12} 222, 21 and 223, 34). "But an I believe God and be born anew, I close my eyes and grope not and let the soul's being wholly perish and exclaim. Ah, God, in thy hand standeth my soul. Thou hast preserved it in my life, and I have never known where Thou hast set it, therefore will I likewise not know what Thou wilt do with it now and henceforth, of this alone am I sure, it standeth in Thy hand, Thou wilt surely help it" (*Sommerpostille*, 1526, *Sermon on Jn.* 3^{1-15}, *W.A.* 10^{12}, 301, 20). "The Word I speak thou hearest well, but thou knowest neither its beginning nor its end. Just as thou knowest not where the wind starteth or where it ceaseth, so also thou knowest not whence the Word cometh and whither it goeth. The bodily voice and the outward sound thou hearest well, but the power of the Word thou seest not, what it doeth, how the Spirit worketh with and by the Word. Therefore the Word must be believed against all sight and feeling of the understanding. If we would discuss much how it befalleth, 'tis all up" (*Sermon on Jn.* 3^{1-15}, 1532, *E.A.* 4, 177). "And so not a Christian do I see. Nor can I myself say. This hour or in that place shall I become a Christian. In short 'tis not within sight or time or place, 'tis beyond grasp or feeling, it dependeth not on apparel or on this or that we see or feel, 'tis literally nought. Well, what concern of mine, if 'tis nought? Yea, 'tis nought if thou quiz thy five senses thereon or take counsel with thy reason and wisdom. But thou must set aside sense and reason and consider 'tis somewhat other that maketh a Christian, whereof thou hearest no more than the breath and rustle. An thou hearest the voice, follow it and have faith in it, so shalt thou be born anew" (*Expos. of Jn* 3, 1538–40, *W.A.* 47, 29, 22). This, too, is the place to recall a thought that Calvin was fond of expressing, namely, that the weakness and folly of all philosophical talk about the "supreme good" is that in it man is riveted to himself: *quum necesse sit extra nos exire*[EN44]. The "supreme good" is *coniunctio cum Deo*[EN45]. But this demands a *conformatio*[EN46] of man with God. But this can take place only in a negation of man, in a full *quiescere ab operibus nostris*[EN47]. And so: *hinc semper faciendum est*

[EN38] the finite
[EN39] the human sinner cannot contain
[EN40] the infinite
[EN41] the word of the Lord
[EN42] Depart from me; for I am a sinful man
[EN43] I believe; help my unbelief
[EN44] although it is necessary to go outside of ourselves
[EN45] a conjoining with God
[EN46] conformity
[EN47] leaving off from our own works

exordium, quum de regula pie sancteque vivendi agitur, ut homo sibi quodammodo mortuus Deum patiatur vivere; ferietur ab operibus propriis, ut locum Deo agenti concedat. Fateri enim necesse est, tunc recte demum constitutam esse vitam quum Deo subiecta est. Atqui propter ingenitam pravitatem hoc nunquam fit, donec a propriis operibus supersedemus. Talis inquam repugnantia est inter Dei gubernationem et nostros affectus, ut in nobis agere, nisi otiosis, nequeat[EN48] (*Comm. on Heb.* 4^{10}, *C.R.* 55, 48).

The "perishing of the being of the soul" or the "'tis literally nought" of Luther and Calvin's *locum concedere Deo agenti*[EN49], the passivity and even death [222] of man in face of the divine act, undoubtedly mean that a mystical vocabulary has already appeared. We should not object to it, for this vocabulary can hardly be avoided at this point. If experience of God's Word is such that it can have its basis and certainty only outside itself, then understanding of it as true and actual experience is in fact understanding of its own radical end and of the fact that there is here a real perishing and dying of man. This is the new land which opens up when one does not just consider Christian experience as a phenomenon but lets it speak for itself. If we want to call the thought of the far side of all experience that comes to light here a mystical one, it is not worth while contesting the word so long as it is clear—and this is not often clear in what is called mystical thinking—that this far side cannot be as it were a hinterland of the sphere of human acts, experiences and possessions, a hinterland which we have still to tread and occupy, a human act, or the content of a human act, which can now be established by new methods. The far side in which real experience seeks and finds its true basis, in relation to which it knows it is true and actual experience, in acknowledgment of which alone it is ready to consist, to consist without claim to a content or seriousness of its own, so to consist that it is ready to consist as acknowledgment from and to this alone—this far side is to be understood as a genuine and immutable far side which cannot be changed into this side, as the side of God the Lord, the Creator, the Reconciler and the Redeemer. Human self-determination as it takes places also and precisely in acknowledgment of God's Word, i.e., human experience of God's Word, will never be able to see, perceive or understand itself, if it is real, as determined by the Word of God. It will be this without seeing or understanding itself in this being. It will just be true from God that human existence is engaged here in acknowledgment of the Word of God. For it will be true that God has spoken and man has heard. A new, regenerate man will arise in the act of this acknowledgment as the man whom God has addressed and who

[EN48] when we are speaking of the rule to live in a pious and holy manner, it is always necessary to begin from the principle that a man, in some sense dead to himself, must allow God to live; that he must refrain from his own works in order to leave a place for God to act. Moreover, it is necessary to acknowledge that a life is not rightly established until it is subjected to God. And on account of our inborn depravity, this never happens, until we desist from our own works. So strong, I say, is the opposition between God's governance and our own sensibilities, that God cannot act in us, unless we are idle

[EN49] leaving a place for God to act

hears God, unknown, of course, to himself and others, in a newness that cannot be ascertained, for what can be ascertained in him will always be the old, not possessing himself, for to the extent that he possesses himself he certainly does not possess this regenerate man. But it will be true that he is kept in the peace of God which passes all understanding. It will be true in absolute independence of all the criteria of truth that the secular or even the religious man has first to provide and apply critically before he very kindly resolves to let what is true be true. All this will be true in itself just as the Word of God is true in itself. Its truth will be nothing other (no opposite pole! no subjective counterpart!) than the truth of God's Word itself. The possibility of knowledge of God's Word lies in God's Word and nowhere else. In the absolute sense its
[223] reality can only take place, and it can do so only as a miracle before the eyes of every man, secular and religious, Greek and Jew.

"It is only an appearance that the rainbow stands on the earth, in reality it arches over the earth; true, it stoops down to the earth, yet it does not stand on our earth, but is only perceived from it. So it is with divine truth; this needs no human support, as the rainbow does not need the earth. True, it shines on man and he receives it; yet it is not dependent on man. It withdraws and man remains in darkness; it returns and man walks in light. But man is not its assistant; he cannot produce the light; similarly he cannot store it" (Eduard Böhl, *Dogmatik*, 1886, p. XXV). "Therefore when I die—but I die no more—and someone finds my skull, let this skull preach to him and say: I have no eyes, yet I behold Him; I have no brain nor understanding, yet I comprehend Him; I have no lips, yet I kiss Him; I have no tongue, yet I praise Him with all who call upon His name. I am a hard skull, yet I am quite softened and melted in His love; I lie outside here in the churchyard, yet I am within in Paradise. All suffering is forgotten. This His great love has done for us, since for us He bore His cross and went forth to Golgotha" (H. F. Kohlbrügge, *Passionspredigten*,[3] 1913, 173 f.). This is the voice of true Christian experience.

This miracle is faith, and in the fourth sub-section we shall say what needs to be said about this in the present connexion.

Let us make here the final statement in the present train of thought. We have put to Christian Cartesianism the question whether we can be responsible for the thesis of the immanence of the possibility of experience of God's Word in the consciousness with the final human seriousness commensurate with its significance for dogmatics, Church proclamation and the Church generally, whether we can put our hand in the fire for it, whether, one might also ask, we can pledge ourselves to champion and defend it as *articulus stantis et cadentis ecclesiae*[EN50]. We have seen that the act of acknowledging the Word of God, so far as its immanence in the consciousness can be established from outside, historico-psychologically, by observation of ourselves or others, cannot even be characterised unequivocally as this act, let alone known in its relation to the Word of God. All that can be established are human possibilities in immovable proximity and indissoluble similarity to other human possibilities. We have also seen that even the transition to "existential" thinking does not

[EN50] an article by which the church stands or falls

help us here but proves definitively that nothing is to be gained along these lines. For if this thinking is the self-understanding of the man who has learned about himself from God's Word, then this inward aspect of Christian experience will itself bear witness that real acknowledgment of the Word of God does not rest at all on a possibility imparted to man and thus integral to him or immanent in him, but that it rests in God's Word itself, which man and his possibilities can in no sense precede but only follow. And now we for our part must advance the following positive conclusion. This possibility, in distinction from others that slip through our fingers, the possibility of human experience of the Word of God understood as the possibility of this Word itself, is one that [224]
we can and must affirm with certainty, with final human seriousness. It can and must be championed and defended as *articulus stantis et cadentis ecclesiae.* We can and must actually put our hand in the fire for its character as a unique possibility. When we refer to this possibility in dogmatics, in Church proclamation and in the Church generally, we are in all circumstances building on the rock and not on the sand.

H. M. Müller ("*Credo ut intelligam,*" *Theol. Bl.*, 1928, 167 f.) has brought against me the charge that in my dogmatics I merely confront the one "unheard of assurance" of Neo-Protestantism with another. Of course! is my only possible reply. The "assurance" of the Neo-Protestant thesis is not "unheard of" because it is assurance, but because it is not and cannot be what it purports to be. The assurance with which dogmatics, Church proclamation and the Church may refer to the possibility of human knowledge of God's Word cannot be great enough, and it is my opinion—and naturally not mine alone—that in relation to the unique and distinctive possibility at issue here, in relation to the self-certainty of the divine Word, it must even be an "unheard of" assurance.

It will be continually asked, of course, whether we know this possibility. Now it stands or falls with the real utterance of God's Word to us, which we cannot anticipate as such, which we can only have before us and expect as the event of God's grace. In this event the possibility of knowledge of God's Word comes into view for us, not otherwise and not before. But this means that it comes into view as it is actualised, as we have knowledge of God's Word, as our self-determination is determined by God. We know it when we can only affirm it because we ourselves are its actualisation in our entire existence. It may be asked whether we know it because this event, as it comes into view for us, stands in the freedom of God. Grace would not be grace if God could not give and also refuse us this reality and with it this possibility too. The knowability of the Word of God stands or falls, then, with the act of its real knowledge, which is not under our control. On this actualisation, then, there also depends whether we can know and affirm it. On it there also depends the assurance of this affirmation. It can only be the assurance of faith, the assurance of the man whom God in His free grace has not passed by but whom He has called to faith by His Word, and who, called by His Word, stands in faith. In faith man has and knows and affirms only this possibility of knowledge of God's Word, the possibility which lies in the Word of God itself, has come to him in the Word, and is

present to him in the Word. Hence the assurance of his affirmation of this possibility can only be that of the Word of God itself. This means, however, that it cannot be self-assurance. He is not sure of himself but of the Word of God, and he is not sure of the Word of God in and of himself but in and of the Word.
[225] His assurance is his own assurance, but it has its seat outside him in the Word of God, and it is his assurance in this way, as the Word of God is present to him.

Quare facile senties, si advertas, hunc affectum ex tuis viribus in te non esse: impetrandus ergo per humilem et in seipso desperatum spiritum. Fabulae ergo sunt opinatorum Scholasticorum, hominem esse incertum, in statu salutis sit nec ne. Cave tu, ne aliquando sis incertus, sed certus, quod in te ipso perditus: laborandum autem. ut certus et solidus sis in fide Christi pro peccatis tuis traditi[EN51] (Luther, *Comm. on Gal.* 1⁴, *W.A.* 2, 458, 26).

When the Word of God is present to us, this means that we are turned away from ourselves and towards the Word of God, that we are orientated to it. To stand in faith means to be called to new faith. The presence of the Word and standing in faith mean, then, having the Word and faith before one and expecting them, being directed anew to the free actualisation of the grace experienced, clinging anew to the promise, looking anew for the event in which the possibility of knowledge of God's Word comes into view for us.

ἐλάβομεν καὶ χάριν ἀντὶ χάριτος[EN52] (Jn. 1¹⁶). The righteousness of God is revealed ἐκ πίστεως εἰς πίστιν[EN53] (Rom. 1¹⁷). This can and must also mean παρ᾽ ἐλπίδα ἐπ᾽ ἐλπίδι ἐπίστευσεν[EN54] (Rom. 4¹⁸).

If a man, the Church, Church proclamation and dogmatics think they can handle the Word and faith like capital at their disposal, they simply prove thereby that they have neither the Word nor faith. When we have them, we do not regard them as a possession but strain after them, hungering and thirsting, and for that reason blessed. The same is true of the possibility of knowledge of God's Word. When we know it, we expect to know it. The assurance of its affirmation is thus the assurance of its expectation—the expectation which rests on its previous presence, on the apprehended promise, or, as we can already say here, on received and believed baptism—but still the expectation. When we maintain the possibility of knowledge of God's Word, this means that we relate ourselves to the event of its actualisation. And this means again that we do not maintain it but confess it, as we must confess faith when we believe and as we can only confess the event of the grace of God. This event, grace,

---

[EN51] Therefore you will easily feel, if you pay attention, that you cannot achieve this state of mind by your own strength: you will need to obtain it through a spirit that is humble and in itself without hope. Nonsense is the Schoolmen's claim that a person can never be certain whether or not he is in a state of salvation. But you beware of being in any way uncertain. Be certain that you are lost in yourself: but strive to be sure and certain in faith in the Christ who was handed over for your sins

[EN52] we have also received grace upon grace

[EN53] from faith to faith

[EN54] in hope he believed against hope

and in and with grace faith, must come first. Confessing, relating ourselves to the grace already proclaimed and received, we then affirm the possibility of knowledge of God's Word that is given to man. Affirming this possibility, then, we are asked in all earnestness how we get to that point, whether we are not thereby presuming something one cannot presume, whether we are not perhaps trying to build a tower without counting the cost, whether we are not thinking and alleging we can be something that we must first have received in order to be it in truth. The Church, Church proclamation and dogmatics have to realise that when they explicitly or implicitly affirm the possibility of know- [226]
ledge of God's Word they stand in the crisis of this question, the question: Where do they come from? Do they really come from the Word and faith and believed baptism? And even if they do come from there, their affirming of this possibility can only be a self-relating to the new and future event of the actualisation of this possibility which is always included and taken up in its actualisation. It is from this that it seeks to make itself known and to give itself to us, and that when made known and given it wants to be sought and found afresh. The assurance of its affirmation is really the assurance of its expectation. The assurance of grace, of faith, of believed baptism, is the assurance of the faith that constantly looks ahead in new hope. It cannot be but that the assurance of this expectation is an assurance in the deepest jeopardy. In this expectation man must let go and surrender all the assurance he himself brings. He is thrown back completely on free grace, which might well be replaced by merited condemnation. Apart from its actualisation in God's Word it would then be all up with the possibility of knowing it, and what would then become of our cocksure affirmation of this possibility? Thus the assurance of this expectation is as it were a trembling assurance. Its power lies in submission to grace or non-grace. Seen alone it has no foundation, no hold on God, and it is empty compared with other human assurances which do not have their seat so strictly outside man. It is more human, i.e., more unsure, than all other human assurances just because it is the assurance of expectation, of this expectation. And yet it is an "unheard of assurance"? It is an assurance which one may quietly and confidently compare with the assurance that has its basis in the human self-consciousness, the assurance of the directly or indirectly Cartesian thesis about the knowability of the Word of God, and find it superior in every respect? Yes indeed, for again it cannot be but that just because it is so profoundly jeopardised, just because it relates itself to the confirmation that we cannot achieve but can only hope for, just because it is included in the divine actualisation, and is thus withdrawn from our grasp, and is thus to be sought there alone and expected thence alone, for this reason and in this way it is an assurance with a metal that makes it superior to every other assurance: because and so far as it is confession of God's free grace, because and so far as it is surrender to grace and non-grace, i.e., an appeal to God Himself. But again it is all this only to the extent that it is assurance of grace already received, the grace of faith, the grace of baptism. If it is this assurance—the question is

whether our assurance is this assurance and this depends on God—but if it is this assurance, then our affirmation of the knowability of God's Word is the knocking to which it shall be opened. It is then in the circle of promise and
[227] faith in which is no Yes and No but only Yes. Praying that it might be this boundless affirmation, it is even in its total humanity an affirmation of "unheard of" assurance.

"(Man) must not doubt or waver as to whether he is one of those to whom such grace and mercy are given, who have surely received them by baptism or sacrament. When he believeth this, then he must freely say of himself that he is holy, pious, righteous and God's child, certain of blessedness, and must not doubt therein at all, not because of himself or his merit or work, but of the pure mercy of God poured out upon him in Christ. The same he seeth to be as great as it is, so that he doubteth not that it maketh him holy and God's child. And when he doubteth it, he doeth his baptism and sacrament the highest dishonour and giveth the lie to God's Word and grace in the sacrament. For there should be no fear or doubt that he is pious and God's child by grace, but only fear and care how he may remain steadfast to the end, in which alone all fear and care stand; for there all bliss is assured. But it is uncertain and a matter of concern whether he stand fast and maintain it, there one must walk in fear; for such faith boasteth not of work or self but only of God, and His grace cannot and may not leave him so long as the boasting lasts. But how long it will last he wots not; whether some temptation may drive him that the boasting ceaseth, and so grace ceaseth also. So Solomon means in Eccles. 9: "The righteous and their works are in the hands of God"; yet is it all set in future uncertainty, so that man knoweth not whether he is worthy of grace or the reverse. He saith not that it is uncertain in the present but in the future, hence that man knoweth not whether he will withstand the assaults of temptation" (Luther, *Kirchenpostille*, 1522, *Sermon on Gal.* $1^{4f.}$, *W.A.* 10^{11}, 331, 17).

Because it is surrounded by this ultimate uncertainty, by the freedom of God, the assurance of our affirmation of the knowability of the Word of God cannot be great enough. Good care is taken that it will be limited enough in its appearance, and we really need not fear the absolutising so fearfully portrayed at this point by those who have no understanding.

4. THE WORD OF GOD AND FAITH

At the beginning of this section we said that we could investigate only the knowability and not the knowledge of God's Word, because the knowledge of God's Word is no other than the reality of the grace of God coming to man, whose How as a reality is as hidden from us as God Himself is, so that we can only relate ourselves to it with our questions and answers. God has revealed it and will always reveal it, and man may proclaim it. We cannot ask how that happens but only, assuming that it does, how it can happen, how we are to understand it that men become the subject or object of this event. Now this very question has led us back again, and for the first time in full truth, to the event itself. We have found that the possibility of the knowledge of God is

absolutely grounded, implied and included in the event of its actualisation, [228]
and our Yes to this possibility is one long reference to this event. We cannot produce this event and so we cannot give a basis for our reference; we could do so only by producing the event to which it points and letting it speak for itself. Hence we can only ask—and we certainly must ask—what the reference means in this context, how far, in what sense, with what special necessity we refer to that event as the place where the question of the knowability of the Word of God is decided. To the question so put the answer is that we refer to this event as the event of faith. Faith—we could no longer avoid the term at the end of our deliberations on experience in the third sub-section—is the making possible of knowledge of God's Word that takes place in actual knowledge of it. The event concerned can and must be understood under many other concepts. Following the general tradition of the Church and theology, we choose this particular term here because it does in fact denote both precisely and yet also comprehensively the element in this event which constitutes it the making possible of knowledge of the Word of God. If one asks about the reality of the knowledge of God, which is so inconceivable in its How, which can be revealed only by God, which can be proclaimed by man only in the service of God and in virtue of His presence; if one asks what this reality is in so far as the knowability of God is included within it, the only possible answer which is both accurate and exhaustive is that this reality is faith.

We best make this clear to ourselves if we think of the use of the term *πίσῖις*[EN55] in the New Testament. *πίσῖις* may signify, as one sees from Rom. 3^{3} and especially from the use of the adjective *πίσῖις*, the faithfulness of God, the reliability and trustworthiness of God and His Word, and therefore that attribute of God and His Word in virtue of which man attains to a knowledge of God from God, because God is *πιστός*. But already in Paul (Rom. 12^{6}; Gal. 1^{23}; $3^{22f.}$; 1 Tim. 4^{1}, ^{6}), and then in Jude (v. 3, 6), *πιστός* also means the doctrine of faith, the Gospel revealed to man, and therefore the way on which knowledge of God is made possible from God by His making Himself known. Again and especially—think of the so-called *genetivus mysticus πίσῖις Ιησοῦ Χρισροῦ*[EN56] and of the many Pauline and Johannine passages to the same effect—*πίσῖις* denotes the state created by God's revelation in Christ, the being of Christians, their being *ἐν Χρισῷ*[EN57], by which they are put in a position to achieve for their part the knowledge of God or of Christ as the Kyrios, the reality of man in which this achievement is an event. In the *πίσῖις Ιησοῦ Χρισροῦ*[EN58] we see the divine decision made about man. Only then and on this basis does the word slip down, as it were, into the sphere of human actions; now—and this includes most of the Synoptic references and a number from the Epistles too—*πίσῖις* is fairly frequently and clearly described as trust, as the attitude in men in which they honour and revere the worth of God, His readiness to help, His might, His truth as it encounters them in Christ, by their acknowledgement as such, by their submission thereto; the possibility of knowing His Word which is offered by God in Christ is now actualised in them. *Πιστεύειν*[EN59] is now the decision made by man's own attitude.

[EN55] (*pistis*) faith
[EN56] mystical genitive in the phrase 'the faith of Jesus Christ'
[EN57] in Christ
[EN58] faith of Jesus Christ
[EN59] To believe

Πίστις, as is known, can then be used in the further and more concrete sense of a Christian
[229] *charisma* or virtue beside which there are others, and beside these others it has no particular prominence and may even (1 Cor. 13^{13}) be of less account. Finally *πίστις, πιστεύειν, πιστός*[EN60] can simply denote what one might call the Christian religion or adherence to it. In this respect it is a term for the historical phenomenon which can be seen very directly in the form of a specific community, a specific cultus, a specific confession and a specific manner of life, and the relativity and ambivalence of which can also be stressed in the very sharp way familiar to us from the Epistle of James. At this point we seem to be far removed from the very objective *πίστις θεοῦ*[EN61] of Rom. 3^{13} and also from the very cryptic, important and effective *πίστις Ἰησοῦ Χριστοῦ*[EN62]. In reality, however, all these meanings of the term stand under a common denominator. Invariably, no matter how objective or subjective, how central or peripheral, how simple or manifold the use of the term may be, from the mystery of God to what could be seen directly on the streets of Corinth and Rome, *πίστις* is the real event which rests on the will and Word of God and relates to the will and Word of God, in which is also included at all events the fact that the proclamation of Christ confirms itself to men, in which men, touched by its truth, themselves become its bearers, and in which the knowledge of God becomes real. *Πίστις* says more than *γνῶσις*[EN63], but in all circumstances it says *γνῶσις* too. Augustine rightly says: *Si tollatur assensio. fides tollitur; quia sine assensione nihil creditur*[EN64] (*Enchir.*, 20). And Thomas Aquinas has the correct definition: *fides cognitio quaedam est, in quantum intellectus determinatur per fidem ad aliquod cognoscibile*[EN65] (*S. theol.* I, *qu.* 12, *art.* 13). At the crucial point the same may be said of Bonaventura: *Fides non est aliud nisi habitus, quo intellectus noster voluntarie captivatur in obsequium Christi*[EN66] (*Sent.* III, *d.* 23, *a.* 1, *qu.* 1, quoted acc. to R. Seeberg, *Dogmengeschichte*, Vol. 3, 2–3. edn., 1913, 336). Along the same lines cf. Luther too: *fidem nihil aliud esse quam veritatem cordis hoc est rectam cogitationem cordis de Deo*[EN67] (*Comm. on Gal.* 3^{7}, 1535, *W.A.* 40^{1}, 376, 23). *Apprehenditur Christus ... ratione seu intellectu informato fide et illa apprehensio Christi per fidem proprie est speculativa vita*[EN68] (*ib. on Gal.* 3^{13}, *W.A.* 40^{1}, 447, 15). *Fides est in intellectu .... Fides dictat et dirigit intellectum .... Est igitur fides doctrina seu notitia .... Fides habet obiectum veritatem .... Primum omnium pius habere debet rectam opinionem et intellectum fide informatum .... Fides igitur est Dialectica, quae concipit ideam omnium credendorum*[EN69] (*ib., on Gal.* 5^{5}, *W.A.* 40^{11}, 26, 11 f. and 28, 9 f.). And Calvin: *Non in ignoratione, sed in cognitione sita est fides*[EN70] (*Instit.*, III, 2, 2). *Fateor ... generale fidei obiectum ... esse Dei veritatem*[EN71] (*ib.*, III, 2, 30). But the content of the

---

[EN60] faith, to believe, faithful

[EN61] faith (= faithfulness) of God

[EN62] faith of Jesus Christ

[EN63] gnosis

[EN64] If assent is taken away, so is faith; because without assent there is no belief

[EN65] faith is a kind of knowledge, inasmuch as the intellect is determined by faith toward something knowable

[EN66] Faith is nothing else than the disposition by which our intellect is willingly made captive to obedience to Christ

[EN67] faith is nothing else than the truth of the heart, that is, the heart's thinking rightly of God

[EN68] Christ is apprehended ... by the reason or intellect that has been formed by faith, and that apprehension of Christ through faith is what is properly termed the speculative life

[EN69] Faith is in the intellect .... Faith orders and directs the intellect .... Therefore faith is a teaching or understanding .... Faith has truth as its object .... First of all the pious person must have right opinion and an intellect informed by faith .... Therefore faith is that kind of Dialectic, which produces the conception of all things that ought to be believed

[EN70] Faith rests on knowledge, not ignorance

[EN71] I admit ... that the common object of faith ... is God's truth

term γνῶσις[EN72] is so included in the term πίστις[EN73] that it is patent how God Himself or Christ is at once the object, meaning, empowering and measure of the real knowledge of God and yet this does not cease to be a wholly concrete act performed by men and experienced by men.

Thus it is in faith, as the possibility given in faith, that we have to understand the knowability of the Word of God. In the event of faith it is as it were born, it comes into view, and it is to be sought and found.

Of the event of faith according to the understanding of the New Testament peculiar to the Evangelical Church, three things at least must be said as important in the present context, and these will yield three different definitions of the concept of the knowability of the Word of God.

1. In faith as real experience the acknowledgment of God's Word which we have understood to be the concrete form of its experience by man is as it were put into effect by the Word of God known. In however perfect or imperfect a [230] form, human action understood as acknowledgment comes into play. In faith it is true, accepted and acknowledged acknowledgment, not because man himself has the power or he himself has been able to achieve this proper acknowledgment, but because what he can do and does is acknowledged by the acknowledged Word of God, not as self-determination but as the self-determination determined by God's Word. We insist that faith is experience, a concretely ascertainable temporal act of a specific man, the act of acknowledgment. But experience is not self-evidently real experience, experience of God's Word. Of no experience as such, however perfect its form, can this be said. Not, then, as experience is faith faith, i.e., real experience, even though it is certainly experience. Or, the act of acknowledgment is not as such acknowledgment of the Word of God. Nor is it this in virtue of any perfection with which it is performed. It is the Word, Christ, to whom faith refers because He presents Himself to it as its object, that makes faith faith, real experience. Let it be clearly understood: because He presents Himself to it as its object. For faith is not faith by the mere fact that it has or is a reference—it might well be in reality a pointless reference to an imagined object. It is faith by the fact that the Word of God is given to us as the object of this reference, as the object of acknowledgment, and therefore as the basis of real faith.

As regards the epistemological problem a particularly instructive document for the constitutive significance for faith of the object of faith is the first chapter of the *Proslogion* of Anselm of Canterbury. In the closest material relation to the famous proof for the existence of God immediately following, there is brought up here in the form of a prayer the problem whether God is present at all to the thinker who sets out to understand and explain the existence and nature of God. He needs Him to be the man who can see and understand Him aright, but beyond that to have Him at all as the discoverable object of his search. *Quando illuminabis oculos nostros et ostendes nobis faciem tuam? … Nec quaerere te possum, nisi te doceas, nec*

[EN72] gnosis
[EN73] faith (pistis)

invenire, nisi te ostendas[EN74]. And Anselm does not find himself at all in this presence which is so necessary to him in the twofold sense. God's face is hidden from him as if he himself were blind. The twofold encounter he needs on God's part does not take place. He does not have in mind here the philosophical incomprehensibility of God but specifically the mystery of God which can be regarded only as a punishment on sinful man. As a son of Adam he knows his exact situation in this respect. But he is not as it were rhetorically putting himself in the place of the heathen in speaking thus. No: *Tu me fecisti et refecisti et omnia mea bona tu mihi contulisti et nondum novi te*[EN75]. It is altogether as a Christian, then, that he thinks he must say what he says. Again, it cannot be merely that this Christian is experiencing an accidental and passing relapse from faith to unbelief, for in the same breath he describes his concern as follows: *Desidero aliquatenus intelligere veritatem tuam, quam credit et amat cor meum*[EN76]. Apart from this there is really no special need to recall that the whole thing occurs in the sphere of the Catholic Church and against the background of its unshakably acknowledged creed. "The archbishop (? not till thirty years later!) is not a bad Catholic" (H. M. Müller, *Theol. Bl.*,
[231] 1928, 169 f.). All this, and all that was said before, undoubtedly means that the unrest with which Anselm seeks the presence of God is not an absolute unrest. It is not the direct opposite of the peace of God. It is the relative unrest of man which has as such its definite place and play, and which has somewhere and somehow in the Church the counterpart of a rest that may be his own or may not be his rest at all, but that is at least superior to his unrest. Would not the desire for unrest which the prospect of this superior rest excludes, would not the assertion of an absolute unrest, be the most foolish of all the foolish self-apotheoses of man? Can and should a destruction of man's possibility of knowing God such as seems to be assumed at least in this chapter of Anselm really be carried through with full consistency? Can one persist in standing in crisis either in the Roman Catholic or the Evangelical Church, as H. M. Müller seems to demand of Anselm and theologians generally? As though man could in fact stand in an absolute crisis on this side of the end of all things! If there is true and honest human seeking in the Church, will it not show itself to be one on which, for all its perhaps hopeless despair, there does not still lie the reflection of having found, and there does not already lie the reflection of finding again? But be that as it may, it is humanly not good, it has no basis in the text or in other texts of Anselm, and there is something extraordinarily foolish and unspiritual about it, when H. M. Müller dismisses this chapter of Anselm out of hand, assigning no importance to the question it raises, because it is raised only within the "system," and therefore it has its answer secretly within it. In so doing he suppresses at once the fact that the question in the chapter is at least an open one as a question, and that it is solved neither by appealing to the creed of the Church or the *credere*[EN77] of the Christian thinker, nor dialectically, nor by pointing to an answer to prayer already received. Why in the world should it not have been as bitterly serious for Anselm as only an open question can be serious for a man, even and especially if he knows that with his question he is in the sphere of the Church and therefore of the answer that he has still to find but that is already given and will certainly come? And above all H. M. Müller fails to see that if in Anselm this question does in fact stand in the reflection of the solution that has been achieved already and also comes afresh, and yet it is still a radically open question, then the reference to Anselm's Catholicism cannot really be enforced as the only possible interpretation. One might also say that it is far from being proved that the reference to Anselm's Catholicism necessarily

---

[EN74] When will You lighten our eyes and show us Your face? ... For I cannot seek You, unless you teach me how; nor find You, unless You show Yourself

[EN75] You made me and remade me, and you showered me with all your good things, but still I did not know you

[EN76] I desire some understanding of that truth of Yours which my heart believes and loves

[EN77] belief

implies an interpretation *in malam partem*[EN78]. Why should not the remarkable coincidence of ultimate disquiet and ultimate peace that characterises this chapter in Anselm be viewed from the standpoint that Anselm prays as he asks and asks as he prays. Is it not more pertinent and respectful to keep to this fact? Can one ignore this, or discredit it as bad Catholicism, because of a completely unprovable suspicion that there might be a "system" here? Only if one assumes this—and the inhumanity and at the same time the unspirituality of H. M. Müller's exposition of the matter is that he does assume this—only then can one treat as lightly as he does the unrest of Anselm, which is not absolute but limited, of course, against the background of the doctrine of absolute unrest. If we take seriously the fact that Anselm prayed in this unrest and that he suffered this unrest in prayer, one will evaluate the chapter as in its own way a distinctive illustration of the truth that authentic, utterly certain and hidden faith is always in transition from expectation to fresh expectation. All faith's unrest is, in fact, set aside in prayer, but its prayer is its profound unrest. And both as prayer and also as unrest it is expectation, expectation of its object. It lives by its object, at rest or in unrest, having found, seeking, finding again and seeking anew. But this object is the free God who is hidden from man because he is a sinner, who has, of course, put man in the new state of faith in which He can be known by him, but who in this very state—it is indeed that of faith—wills [232]
to be sought and found anew and then anew again. For faith, He is and remains enclosed in objectivity, in the externality of the Word of God, in Jesus Christ. He must teach man to seek Him and He must show Himself to him in order that he may find Him. But it is by this external object that Christian faith lives.

Non ex visione credentis, sed a visione eius cui creditur results the *determinatio intellectus ad aliquod cognoscibile*[EN79] (Thomas Aquinas, *S. Theol.* I, *qu.* 12, *art.* 13, *ad.* 3). *Non enim fides assentit alicui nisi quia est a Deo revelatum*[EN80] (*ib.*, II², *qu.* 1, *art.* 1). *Tolle verbum et nulla jam restabit fides*[EN81] (Calvin, *Instit.* III, 2, 6). *Quoties nos de fide loquimur, intelligi volumus obiectum scilicet misericordiam promissam. Fides non ideo iustificat, quia ipsa sit opus per sese dignum* (not because ... in itself 'tis our work or ours),[EN82] *sed tantum quia accipit misericordiam promissam*[EN82] (Melanchthon, *Apology, art.* 4, *De justif.* 55 f., cf. 86). *Non enim in sensum sed in promissionem recumbit fides*[EN83] (C. Olevianus, *De subst. foed.*, 1585, 304, *cit.ap.* Heppe, *Dogmatik d. ev. ref. Kirche,* 1861, 388). *Non propter fidem quatenus est virtus vel opus nostrum justificamur*[EN84] (M. Chemnitz, *Loci theol.*, 1591, Vol. II, 255) ... *sed propter objectum quod fides apprehendit Christum*[EN85] (*ib.*, 252). *De fide non est statuendum ex sensu consolationis et gaudii spiritualis: quia quintus ille gradus sequitur fidem, non est de essentia fidei et Deus sensum illum pacis credentibus saepe subtrahit*[EN86] (*ib.*, 252). *Ancoram fidei nostrae iactam esse in ipsum coelum et*

EN78 in a bad sense

EN79 Not from the vision of the believer but from the vision of the one whom we believe results the determination of the intellect toward something knowable

EN80 For faith does not assent to anything unless it is revealed by God

EN81 Take away the Word and no faith will remain

EN82 Whenever we speak of faith, we wish to be understood that faith has an object, namely (God's) promised mercy. For faith does not justify because it is a work that is worthy in itself (not because ... in itself 'tis our work or ours) but only because its accepts (God's) promised mercy

EN83 For faith does not rest on feeling, but on the promise

EN84 We are not justified by faith insofar as it is a power or work of our own

EN85 ... but on account of Christ as the object which faith apprehends

EN86 Statements on faith must not be based on feelings of consolation or spiritual joy: because those special gifts follow faith, but are not of the essence of faith, and God often takes that feeling of peace from believers

quidem ubi Christus pro nobis sacerdos[EN87] (*ib.*, 257). Then with delightful precision High Orthodoxy explains that *fides*[EN88] is *justificans*[EN89] not as a *qualitas inhaerens*[EN90] nor as an *actio*[EN91] of man but *ut est in praedicamento relationis*[EN92], as a relation (σχέσις) to its object; and again not *per relationem* (through relating to itself) but *in relatione: quatenus sibi applicat et appropriat meritum Christi, cui unico dignitas illa competit*[EN93]. Finally it may be said that the act of justifying faith (*fides quae justificat*), while it is, of course, correctly described by such terms as *notitia, assensus, fiducia*[EN94], is to be understood as justifying (as *fides qua justificat*) only to the extent that beyond what makes it an act it is a *nuda apprehensio seu fiducialis acceptatio bonorum foederalium et beneficiorum Messiae passiva, admissiva motuum Spiritus, requietoria in sanguine et meritis Christi*[EN95] (Quenstedt, *Theol. did.-pol.*, 1685, III, *cap.* 8, *sect.* 2, *qu.* 6, *ekth.* 8–10).

In this context we must speak especially of Luther. There are two sayings of Luther, one of which is adduced time and again in the modern theological debate by Wobbermin, who obviously never grows tired of it (cf. *Richtl. ev. Theol.*, 1929, 124 f.; *Wort Gottes und ev. Glaube*, 1931, p. 5), after having played, with its whole context, a very similar role the previous century in A. Ritschl (*Rechtf. u. Vers.*, 4th edn., Vol. I, 218 f.; Vol. 3, 201 f.); it is to the effect that "faith and God belong together" and it stands at the beginning of the exposition of the First Commandment in the *Larger Catechism*. The other is in the Lectures on Romans and, as every reader of Wobbermin knows, it runs: *fides et promissio sunt relativa*[EN96] (Wobbermin persistently writes *correlativa*[EN97] for this, cf. *Richtl.*, 109, 125 and *Wort Gottes*, p. 5). The first saying occurs in the following passage: "What does it mean to have a God, or what is God? Answer: A God is that by which one is to be supplied with all good and with which one should take refuge in all afflictions. Thus, to have a God is nought other than to trust and believe in Him from the heart, as I have often said, which thing alone, the trust and faith of the heart, maketh both God and false god. If the faith and trust is right, so also is thy God right, and again where the trust is false and wrong, there also the right God is not. For the two belong together, faith and God. Whereupon then (I say) thou hangest and confidest thy heart, that is really thy God" (*Deutscher Catechismus*, 1529, *W.A.* 30^1, 132, 34). And the other: *fides et promissio sunt relativa; idem cessante promissione cessat et fides et abolita promissione aufertur et fides*
[233] *et econtra*[EN98] (*Gloss on Rom.* 4^{14}, *Fi.* 40, 24). For the sake of completeness we will add two further sayings of Luther that tend in the same direction. The first is parallel to the passage from the *Larger Catechism*: "As thou turnest and wheelest, so God, too, turneth and wheeleth. Thinkest thou that He is wroth with thee, so He is wroth. Thinkest thou that He is unmerciful to thee, and wishful to thrust thee into hell, then so He is. As thou believest of God, so thou hast Him" (*Sermon on Jn.* $4^{47f.}$, 1534, *E.A.* 5, 224). "Therefore, as we believe, so it

---

[EN87] The anchor of our faith is cast into heaven itself, the place where Christ is priest on our behalf

[EN88] faith

[EN89] justifying

[EN90] inherent quality

[EN91] action

[EN92] as it is in a predication of relationship

[EN93] in relation: to the extent that it applies to itself and appropriates the merit of Christ, the only one to whom such merit belongs

[EN94] understanding, assent, trust

[EN95] bare apprehension or passive, trusting acceptance of the good covenants and benefits of the Messiah, open to the Spirit's influence and resting on Christ's blood and merits

[EN96] faith and the promise are interrelated

[EN97] correlated

[EN98] faith and the promise are interrelated: so when the promise ceases, so does faith; and when the promise is taken away both faith and its opposite are banished

befalleth us. If we hold Him for our God, He will certainly not be our devil. But if we hold Him not for our God, He is certainly likewise not our God, but must be a consuming fire" (*ib.*, 5, 229). The other is a parallel to the gloss on Romans: "So ought Word and faith to stand splendidly together. For the one cannot exist without the other. Whoso hath faith and not the Word believeth like Turks and Jews. They have the faith that God is gracious and merciful. But the promise is lacking, for God will not be gracious apart from Christ. Thus, whoso hath the Word but not faith, there the Word accomplisheth naught. Thus Word and faith are given together in wedlock, and naught can cause them to part from one another" (*Hauspost.*, 1544, *Sermon on Mt.* $9^{1f.}$, *W.A.* 52, 498, 22). Wobbermin wants to show from these sayings that the relation between the Word of God and faith according to Luther is to be regarded as a relation of "connexion" or "correlation," as a "circular" relation, a relation of "reciprocity" or "two-poled relation" (*Richtl.*, p. 125, 140 f.; *Wort Gottes*, 5 f., 14, 27, etc.). I do not wish to contest these descriptions, though they are too ambiguous for me to adopt. I would only say regarding Luther that he is simply stating that in a man's faith or erroneous faith or unbelief the decision is made what kind of a God he has, so that man always has the God he believes in. But this is not at all the same thing as saying that faith is as it were the human counterpart of the Word of God, that the relation between the Word of God and faith is the symmetrical one of two partners, one superior and the other subordinate but still two partners, and that this relation is just as basically grounded in faith as it is in the Word of God. To be sure, it is only in faith that one has the true God, and this God, as the God believed in, is that on which man sets his heart's trust. But it is not at all true that the fact that He is believed in, that the heart's trust, man's "interest" in Him as A. Ritschl puts it, makes Him the true God. As the object of faith or trust he might equally well be a false god. What makes Him the true God is that one believes in Him in true faith. And the fact that the faith in which the true God is believed in is true faith is not due in any way or in any sense to itself but to the fact that the true God has revealed Himself to it, i.e., it is due to the Word of God. In this concept the circular movement of reflection necessarily ends, and it does so in Luther, for he is denoting the point where the true and irreversible circular movement of Word and faith takes its beginning, which is not conditioned by an opposite pole. Wobbermin thinks the saying that "faith and God belong together" might be rendered by the different one that "faith and the Word of God belong together" (*Wort Gottes*, 5). This might be conceivable if we had only this saying to deal with. But in view of the content of the rest of the passage from the *Catechism* this translation is quite untenable. Obviously Luther neither intended to say nor could he say that the trust and faith of the heart constitute the Word of God, that when man's faith and trust are right God's Word is right. All that he says in the *Catechism* is that always and in every sense of the term "God" is for man that whereon he sets his supreme trust. There is thus no point in building one's understanding of Luther or one's whole theology on this popular preamble. Neither in the *Larger Catechism* nor elsewhere did Luther teach the God defined thus but only the true God of true faith, and in the question of this God he never referred to faith as such or its immanent correctness nor did he ever raise it to the rank of a counterpole or partner of God's Word. What we read is that [234]
"to believe aught without God's Word is no faith but a false delusion, for naught will ever come of it, just as if thou shouldst believe thou wouldst yet become the Roman Emperor ..." (*Hauspost.*, 1544, *Sermon on Jn.* $4^{47f.}$, *W.A.* 52, 518, 22). "Whoso then hath not nor knoweth God's Word can have no such confidence and must get this good comfort" (*Ib.*, *Sermon on Lk.* $5^{1f.}$, *W.A.* 52, 396, 7). "It is this, then, that I have said, that God will not suffer it that we rely on aught else or with the heart depend on what is not Christ in His Word, be it as holy or spiritual as it like. Faith hath no other ground on which it can stand" (*E.A.* 11, 26). "In faith all things must be put out of sight save the Word of God. Whoso alloweth aught else to come

into view but the Word itself is already lost. Faith dependeth on the pure Word alone, turneth not its eyes therefrom, regardeth naught else, neither its work nor merit. If the heart standeth not simply thus, it is already lost" (*Sermon on Jn.* $4^{4f.}$, 1522, *W.A.* 10^{III}, 423, 17). "This is the nature and property of faith, that it may suffer naught beside it by which man steers or turns save the simple Word of God or divine promise ... faith letteth go all creatures, all visible things in the world, even itself, and dependeth on God's Word. Thus it must be, dear friend, faith relieth on naught, gropeth not after aught, what it is sure of that will it cling to" (*Festpost.*, 1527, *Sermon on Lk.* $1^{26f.}$, *W.A.* 17^{II}, 400, 14, 32). In faith there takes place a *speculatio qua Christus apprehenditur, a speculatio theologica fidelis et divina inspectio serpentis suspensi in palo hoc est Christi pendentis in cruce pro meis tuis et totius mundi peccatis*[EN99] (*Comm. on Gal.*3^{13}, *W.A.* 40^{I}, 447, 18). It should also be noted that in the Romans gloss and the sermon on the marriage between the Word and faith the emphasis of Luther's expositions lies throughout on the thought that without the Word there can be no faith. The dialectical supplement that without faith one cannot have the Word is simply added in both passages but not developed. In sum, when Luther speaks of the Word and faith he is saying, of course, that where there is no faith the Word cannot be, or cannot be fruitful, but he is saying primarily, and this is the point, that where faith is, it does not have its ground and its truth and its measure in itself as a human act or experience, but even though it is a human act and experience it has these things in its object, in Christ, or God's Word. In my view terms like circular or reciprocal or correlative relation are very imprecise descriptions of what Luther meant to say and did say in this matter. In fact, what we learn from Luther about the Reformation insight into this matter is exactly the same as what we learn from Melanchthon.

In the light of this it should now be quite plain that the interpretation of faith as *fiducia*, trust, or confidence in the older Reformers and the whole of the older Protestant theology (*Est itaque fides non aliud, nisi fiducia misericordiae promissae* ... [EN100], Melanchthon, *Loci*, 1521, *De justif. et fide* IV; cf. *Conf. Helv. post.*, 16; *Heidelb. Cat. qu.* 21) has nothing whatever to do with a shifting of the reality of faith from its object to the believing subject. The stressing of *fiducia* is designed to differentiate real faith from a mere *opinio historica*[EN101], from a neutral recollective knowledge and affirmation of biblical or ecclesiastical statements such as is possible apart from the reality of faith. The possibility of excluding the element of *notitia* or *assensus*[EN102], i.e., the element of knowledge from faith, of making faith a trust either devoid of intellectual form or indifferent to it, of viewing it as any kind of trust in any kind of object, of throwing doubt on the object of faith and transferring the reality of faith to the believing subject, was one of which we can say with complete certainty (in spite of what K. Aner seems to assume in *RGG*², Art. "*Glaube, IV, dogmengeschichtlich*") that even in the early days of the Reformation none of the responsible leaders ever considered it seriously even for a single
[235] moment. For Older Protestantism faith is *fiducia*, and hence more than *notitia* and *assensus* in relation to the content of God's Word, to the degree that in faith man accepts the merciful Immanuel spoken by God's Word, i.e., applies to himself the mercy of which the Word speaks, takes comfort in it on the basis of the Word, relies upon it in the light of the Word, to the degree that the believer is a man who is comforted by the Word of God. To be sure, faith becomes faith only when it is *fiducia*. *Notitia* and *assensus* alone would not be faith, but only

---

[EN99] a speculation by which Christ is apprehended, faithful theological speculation and a divine gazing at the serpent suspended on the pole, that is, Christ hanging on the cross for my sins, your sins, and the sins of the whole world

[EN100] And so faith is nothing else than trust in [God's] promised mercy ...

[EN101] historical opinion

[EN102] understanding or assent

the *opinio historica* that the ungodly can have too. Nevertheless, how can faith be *fiducia* without also being, even as *fiducia, notitia* and *assensus, fiducia promissionis*[EN103], trust in the mercy of God which encounters us as *misericordia promissa*[EN104], i.e., in the objectivity of the Word, which has form and even a form of words, and therefore has also a form of knowledge, of acceptance of its truth, in the faith which receives it? A few lines before his well-known definition of *fides* as *fiducia* Melanchthon himself has the definition: *Quid igitur fides? Constanter assentiri omni verbo Dei*[EN105]. He would certainly not have said with Wobbermin (who in *Wort Gottes,* 10 f.; *Richtlinien,* p. 131 can even speak of a "radical rejection of *fides historica*"[EN106]) that this *assentiri*[EN107] is subordinate to *fiducia,* because for him there can be no question of a true and serious and theologically important subordination of *assensus* to *fiducia* in real faith, only of both to their object. Hence Melanchthon, as we have seen, said of faith understood as *fiducia* that it can be regarded as true justifying faith, not as *opus per sese dignum*[EN108], but only with reference to its *obiectum.* With reference to its object, however, faith is necessarily and in no way secondarily *notitia* and *assensus* too (Melanchthon seems not to distinguish the two in the *Loci* of 1559, *C.R.* 21, 242 f.); it is knowledge, accepting as true the Word of the divine person in which it reposes its trust. The word *fiducia* itself shows clearly that this is so, and that it has to be so. With its psychological sense it also has a legal sense, and it is linguistically legitimate at least to refer to the latter for an understanding of the former. Legally *fiducia* means leaving a property in trust, or the contract arranging this transfer (e.g., a fictitious sale), or even the security given as a mortgage in such a case. *Fiducia* then, in a legal transaction by which a man provisionally and temporarily puts something of his own in the hands of another, is that which he retains in his own hand as a pledge establishing his legal claim both before and after the transaction. It may be simply belief in the integrity of the other person, or a contract guaranteeing his integrity, or a deposit guaranteeing the contract. *Fiducia* relates, therefore, to the reliability or *bona fides*[EN109] of the other with whom what is mine, without ceasing to be mine, is now lodged. To have *fiducia* is thus to have reason to rely on his reliability. Without the reference to this object, to the *bona fides* of the other, there is no *fiducia.* I have it as I stand in this relation to him and in order to be able to stand in this relation to him, not otherwise. This is the *tertium comparationis*[EN110] between the legal and the psychological and then the theological concept of *fiducia.* It should be noted that already in the New Testament it can be said incidentally of God: *πίστιν παρασχὼν πᾶσιν ἀναστήσας αὐτὸν ἐκ νεκρῶν*[EN111], i.e., in the resurrection of Jesus He gave a surety to all, and this surety is simply what they can now have in the form of faith (Ac. 17^{31}). No less than *notitia* and *assensus, fiducia* denotes the objective reference of faith. But *fiducia,* the reliance on God's reliability that takes place in faith, denotes this objective reference in a specific way, and in virtue of the material content of faith expressed in the term *fiducia* the terms *notitia* and *assensus* with their reference to the divine opposite as such are needed to mark off its formal content. *Ultimus actus fidei nempe fiducia anima fidei justificantis est, sive perfectio eius formalis qua stante impossibile est hominem perire. Interim tamen praesupponit*

[EN103] Assent, trust in the promise
[EN104] promised mercy
[EN105] What then is faith? To give constant assent to every word of God
[EN106] a merely conventional faith
[EN107] act of assent
[EN108] a work that is worthy in itself
[EN109] good faith
[EN110] basis of comparison
[EN111] he has given assurance to all by raising him from the dead

obiecti justifici cognitionem explicitam et assensum generalem ... et specialem[EN112] (Quenstedt, *Theol. did.-pol.*, 1685, III, *cap.* 8, *sect.* 2, *qu.* 6, *ekth.* 7).

[236] A word in closing might be said about two terms which have recently enjoyed a considerable vogue again (especially in Wobbermin), namely, *fides quae creditur*[EN113] and *fides qua creditur*[EN114]. This distinction originates with Augustine: *Aliud sunt ea, quae creduntur, aliud fides qua creduntur. Illa quippe in rebus sunt ... haec autem in animo credentis est* (*De trin.*, XIII, 2, 5).[EN115] Anselm of Canterbury then divides the element of *fides qua* by distinguishing between *credere id*[EN116] and *credere in id, quod credi debet*[EN117] (*Monol.*, 76–78). This *in id* also derives from Augustine (e.g., *Tract. in Ioann.*, 29, 6). Peter Lombard first adduces the first reference from Augustine and then (is this original?) even uses a threefold formula for the *fides qua creditur*[EN118] in relation to the second: *aliud est enim credere in Deum, aliud credere Deo, aliud credere Deum*[EN119] (*Sent.*, III, 23 C. and D.; cf. the marginal note of Luther on this, *W.A.* 9, 90, 15). J. Gerhard then found the first Augustine passage in Peter Lombard and in relation to it he was probably the first to use the terms so familiar to us to-day, *fides quae creditur*[EN120] and *fides qua creditur*[EN121], the first denoting the object of the second, the *materia circa quam*[EN122], the second the πεποίθησις et πληροφορία *in animo credentis*[EN123] (*Loci theol.*, 1610; *Loc.* 16, 66). But Gerhard also found in Lombard the threefold formula for the *fides qua creditur*, and, believing it to be Augustinian, he regarded it as a confirmation of his own formula *fiducia, assensus, notitia*[EN124] (*ib.*, 67). The *fides quae* and *qua* and the three terms in explanation of *fides qua* then became more or less the common stock in trade of Protestant Scholasticism. In J. Wollebius (*Chr. Theol. Compend.*, 1626, I. 26, 1 and 7) the two had already been adopted by Reformed dogmatics, though, e.g., M. Chemnitz on the Lutheran side and W. Bucan on the Reformed side do not yet seem to have taken them for granted as familiar formulae. Obviously the distinction between *fides quae* and *qua* can only have the significance of denoting the dialectic of the object-subject content of the term faith as it has met us already in the New Testament use of πίστις, the problem of faith and the object of faith as such. To the discussion of this problem the distinction itself makes no contribution, for, as the labours of Anselm and Lombard show, everything depends on defining what is meant by *fides qua*. We ourselves have been examining the decisive term *fiducia* and we have made the point necessary in the present context, namely, that *fiducia* itself—and with it *fides qua* generally, which is not for this reason mere *fiducia*—refers beyond itself to the object in relation to which it is *fiducia*. The realist Augustine, who seems to have

---

[EN112] The final act of faith, namely, trust, is the soul of justifying faith, or its formal perfection, so that, if this is present, it is impossible for a person to perish. Nevertheless, it presupposes an explicit knowledge of and a general and specific assent to the object that is the cause of justification

[EN113] the faith which one believes

[EN114] the faith with which one believes

[EN115] That which is believed is one thing, the faith with which it is believed is another ... The first is in external things, the second in the mind of the one who believes

[EN116] to believe that something is the case

[EN117] to believe in something, which must be believed

[EN118] the faith with which one believes

[EN119] for it is one thing to believe in God, another to believe God, and still another to believe that there is a God

[EN120] the faith which one believes

[EN121] the faith with which one believes

[EN122] matter about which

[EN123] confidence and certainty in the mind of the believer

[EN124] trust, assent, understanding

been the first to speak of this *quae* and *qua*[EN125], certainly did not understand his *fides qua* any differently.

If this is how it stands with faith, then one may say of the knowability of the Word of God given in the event of faith that it is not a possibility which man for his part brings to real knowledge, nor is it a possibility which in real knowledge accrues to man from some source as an enrichment of his existence. But as faith has its absolute and unconditional beginning in God's Word independently of the inborn or acquired characteristics and possibilities of man, and as it, as faith, never in any respect lives from or by anything other than the Word, so it is in every respect with the knowability of the Word of God into which we are now enquiring. We cannot establish it if, as it were, we turn our backs on God's Word and contemplate ourselves, finding in ourselves an openness, a positive or at least a negative point of contact for God's Word. We can establish it only as we stand fast in faith and its knowledge, i.e., as we turn away from ourselves and turn our eyes or rather our ears to the Word of God. As we hear [237] it, we have the possibility of hearing it. Hence we do not affirm our own possibility but its reality, which we cannot do except as we stand fast. In its reality we also have our own possibility, not to contemplate it, but only to use it. Contemplating it, we no longer hear, and we thus lose the reality and with it our own possibility that we want to contemplate. As the possibility which comes to us in the Word's reality it is our possibility, just as faith is our possibility as that which comes to us. It is really ours, the possibility of the entire creaturely and sinful man; yet not in such a way that contemplating this man one can discover it or read it off somewhere in him or on him; only in such a way that this creaturely, sinful man waits for the Word that comes to him and therewith for his faith, so that he believes already, he who, contemplating himself, will continually have to say that he cannot believe.

P. Althaus has a very fine and pertinent saying about this: "I do not know whether I believe, but I know in whom I believe" (*Grundriss d. Dogm.*, 1929, 19; cf. *Communio sanctorum*, 1929, 92 f.).

This is exactly how it is with the knowability of God's Word in faith. It is not an extraordinary art. Or should one rather say conversely that is it a highly extraordinary art? Its practice does not presuppose any special endowment whether natural or supernatural. The believer is the same ungifted and idle or gifted and busy man he was as an unbeliever and may become again. He believes as the man he is, with the inventory corresponding to his condition. There is no question of an exalting or abasing of his existence; what is at issue is the grace or judgment of God on his existence. Therefore there is nothing extraordinary here in so far as it is a matter of man and his knowledge as he is. It is all highly extraordinary, of course, in so far as the Word of God becomes the truth here to this man and his knowledge. But whether extraordinary or

---

[EN125] which and by which

not it is at least a possibility given to us, a possibility given for use, not for putting in an inventory or catalogue, not for storing on ice or placing in a museum.

Even in its details the story of the "manna" in Ex. 16 is an illustration of what has to be said about faith in this connexion.

The possibility, then, is not one we can exhibit but only one to which we can point, like faith, or the Word of God itself, or the child born of the Virgin Mary in the manger at Bethlehem. The force and seriousness of this pointer must be the force and seriousness of God if we are really to point. Thus the first thing that must be said about the knowability of the Word of God as the possibility given to us in faith is that it arises and consists absolutely in the object of real knowledge.

[238] 2. If what happens in faith is that acknowledgment of God's Word, as it can become a human act and experience, is, as it were, brought into force not by itself but by the Word of God acknowledged, so that it is real acknowledgment, we must now make the positive statement that in faith men have real experience of the Word of God, and no *finitum non capax infiniti*[EN126], no *peccator non capax verbi divini*[EN127], can now prevent us from taking this statement seriously with all that it involves. The statement refers, not to our human capacity, but to men on the assumption of their complete incapacity. The principle of the incapacity of the *finitum* or the *homo peccator*[EN128] must be accepted. And what we say about the man who can have real experience of God's Word does not invalidate it. But it transcends and brackets it. Faith is not one of the various capacities of man, whether native or acquired. Capacity for the Word of God is not among these. The possibility of faith as it is given to man in the reality of faith can be understood only as one that is loaned to man by God, and loaned exclusively for use. The moment we regard it as a possibility which is in some sense man's own, the opposite statement regarding man's incapacity comes back into force. We do not understand it as a possibility which is in any sense man's own. But for this reason there can also be no objection from the standpoint of man's possibilities when we say that in faith there takes place a conformity of man to God. We do not say a deification but a conformity to God, i.e., an adapting of man to the Word of God. In faith, as he really receives God's Word, man becomes apt to receive it. If one were to deny this one could no longer describe and understand faith as the act and experience of man nor man as the subject of faith. But if we ascribe to man this aptness which is not his own but is loaned to him by God, which is not to be contemplated but simply used in faith, an aptness to receive the Word of God, then we cannot shrink from speaking of a conformity to God proper to him in faith. There can be no receiving of God's Word unless there is something common to the

---

EN126 the finite cannot contain the infinite
EN127 a sinner cannot receive the divine Word
EN128 sinful human being

speaking God and hearing man in this event, a similarity for all the dissimilarity implied by the distinction between God and man, a point of contact between God and man, if we may now adopt this term too.

This point of contact is what theological anthropology on the basis of Gen. 1^{27} calls the "image of God" in man. In this connexion we cannot possibly agree with E. Brunner (*Gott und Mensch*, 1930, 55 f.) when he takes this to refer to the humanity and personality which even sinful man retains from creation, for the humanity and personality of sinful man cannot possibly signify conformity to God, a point of contact for the Word of God. In this sense, as a possibility which is proper to man *qua* creature, the image of God is not just, as it is said, destroyed apart from a few relics; it is totally annihilated. What remains of the image of God even in sinful man is *recta natura*[EN129], to which as such a *rectitudo*[EN130] cannot be ascribed even *potentialiter*[EN131]. No matter how it may be with his humanity and personality, man has completely lost the capacity for God. Hence we fail to see how there comes into view here [239] any common basis of discussion for philosophical and theological anthropology, any occasion for the common exhibition of at least the possibility of enquiring about God. The image of God in man of which we must speak here and which forms the real point of contact for God's Word is the *rectitudo* which through Christ is raised up from real death and thus restored or created anew, and which is real as man's possibility for the Word of God. The reconciliation of man with God in Christ also includes, or already begins with, the restitution of the lost point of contact. Hence this point of contact is not real outside faith; it is real only in faith. In faith man is created by the Word of God for the Word of God, existing in the Word of God and not in himself, not in virtue of his humanity and personality, not even on the basis of creation, for that which by creation was possible for man in relation to God has been lost by the fall. Hence one can only speak theologically and not both theologically and also philosophically of this point of contact, as of all else that is real in faith, i.e., through the grace of reconciliation.

"Conformity to God" was what we called the possibility of receiving God's Word. The concept of the *imago Dei*[EN132] is to the same effect. But we have to realise that at this point we are only a hair's breadth from the Roman Catholic doctrine of the *analogia entis*[EN133]. Even and precisely in this close proximity, however, our teaching must be very different. We do not construe the analogy, similarity, or conformity to God that is actually to be maintained here as an *analogia entis*, i.e., as an analogy that can be surveyed and perceived, as an analogy that can be understood in a synthesis from an onlooker's standpoint. Not a being which the creature has in common with the Creator for all their dissimilarity, but an act that is inaccessible to any mere theory, i.e., human decision, is in faith similar to the decision of God's grace for all its dissimilarity. Of more than an analogy or similarity we should not speak. And it must be emphasised, as the Roman Catholic doctrine of the *analogia entis* also emphasises for that matter, that this is a similarity in great dissimilarity. This helps us to understand why the previously mentioned theory of Augustine (and of the Holl school) about the secret identity of the divine and human decision is inadmissible. If secret identity existed here, one would not have to speak of similarity in dissimilarity but of equality in inequality, but then we would not be dealing with mere conformity to God but with a deification of man. Nevertheless, we cannot be dealing with less than conformity to God. In rejecting the Thomist *analogia entis* we affirm the other idea of Thomas in which, for that matter, one might discern the content

EN129 the good nature
EN130 goodness
EN131 potentially
EN132 image of God
EN133 analogy of being

of truth in even the so-called *analogia entis: quum igitur christiana fides hominem de Deo ... instruit ... fit in homine quaedam divinae sapientiae similitudo*[EN134] (Thomas Aquinas, *S. c. gent.*, II, 2). Luther speaks similarly of the act of justification; it happens in such a way that God *nos tales facit, quale est verbum suum, hoc est justum, verum, sapiens, etc. Et ita nos in verbum suum, non autem verbum suum in nos mutat. Facit autem tales tunc, quando nos verbum suum tale credimus esse scilicet justum verum. Tunc enim iam similis forma est in verbo et in credente, id est veritas et justitia*[EN135] (*Schol. on Rom.* 3^{4}, *Fi.* II, p. 65, 16). And elsewhere: *Necesse est sapientiam carnis mutari et suam formam relinquere ac formam verbi suscipere. Quod fit, dum per fidem se ipsam captivat et destruit, conformat se verbo, credens verbum esse verum, se vero falsam*[EN136] (*ib., on* Rom. 6^{14}, *Fi.* II, 160, 3). And again: *per fidem fit homo similis verbo Dei*[EN137] (*Schol. on Heb.* 3^{13}, *Fi.* II, 44, 4). And again in another passage: "As is the Word, so becometh also the soul by it, like as iron becometh glowing red like fire from union with fire" (*Freedom of a Christian Man*, 1520, *W.A.* 7, 24, 33). With reference to the righteousness that man receives in faith, Luther could well say: *fides ita exaltat cor hominis el transfert de se ipso in Deum, ut unus spiritus fiat ex corde et*
[240] *Deo*[EN138] (*Schol. on Heb.* 7^{1}, *Fi.* II, 74, 9). With reference to the constancy and certainty of faith he could even say: *fide homo fit Deus*[EN139] (*Comm. on Gal.* 2^{7}, 1535, *W.A.* 40^{1}, 182, 15). With reference to the power of real faith: *Qualia diligimus, tales efficimur. Deum diligis, Deus es*[EN140] (*Schol. on Rom.* 3^{12}, *Fi.* II, 78, 12). "God help us, what a boundless, rich and mighty thing is faith! for it maketh man in all things a god, to whom naught is impossible ..." (*Kirchenpost.*, 1522, *Sermon on Lk.* 2^{21}, *W.A.* 40^{1}, 518, 5). And with reference to the fact that in faith and only in faith does man honour God as God, he says even more boldly: *Ea* (*sc. fides*) *consummat divinitatem et, ut ita dicam, creatrix est divinatitis, non in substantia Dei, sed in nobis. Nam sine fide ... nihil maiestatis et divinitatis habet Deus*[EN141] (*Comm. on Gal.* 3^{6}, *W.A.* 40^{1}, 360, 21). In the same sense Augustine had already been able to say that in man's *justificatio*[EN142] in so far as it makes us God's children, a *deificatio*[EN143] takes place, though he does not neglect to add the comment: *sed hoc gratiae est adoptantis non naturae generantis*[EN144] (*Enarr. in* Ps. 49^{2}). Neither in Augustine nor in Luther is there anything about a deification in faith in the sense of a changing of man's nature into the divine nature. What makes the expressions possible is the *apprehensio Christi*[EN145] or *habitatio Christi in nobis*[EN146] or *unio hominis cum Christo*[EN147] that takes place in real faith according to the teaching of Gal. 2^{20}. In emphasis-

---

[EN134] when the Christian faith instructs a person about God ... there is created in the person a certain likeness to the divine wisdom

[EN135] makes us like His Word, that is, righteous, true, wise, etc. And thus He changes us into His Word, but does not change His Word into us. He makes us such when we believe His Word to be such, namely, righteous and true. For then a similar form is in the Word and in the believer, i.e., truth and justice

[EN136] It is necessary for the wisdom of the flesh to be changed by giving up its form and taking up the form of the Word. This happens when it through faith takes itself captive and destroys itself, conforming itself to the Word, believing the Word to be true and itself false

[EN137] through faith a person is made like God's Word

[EN138] in this way faith exalts the human heart and transfers it from itself into God, so that there is one spirit uniting the heart and God

[EN139] by faith a person becomes God

[EN140] What we love, this we are being made. You love God, you are God

[EN141] This (namely, faith) perfects divinity and, if I may say so, is divinity's creator, not in God's own substance, but in us. For without faith ... God has nothing of majesty and divinity

[EN142] justification

[EN143] deification

[EN144] but this is the effect of grace adopting, not of nature generating.

[EN145] apprehending of Christ

[EN146] Christ's dwelling in us

[EN147] union of the person with Christ

ing this more than mystical and more than speculative principle that faith means union with what is believed, i.e., with Jesus Christ, Calvin did not lag in the least behind Luther nor either of them behind an Augustine, Anselm, or Bernard of Clairvaux. Without this principle it is impossible to understand the Reformation doctrine of justification and faith. How it was distinguished from the idea of an essential deification of man in the Reformation period may be seen especially from Calvin's controversy with A. Osiander (*Instit.* III, 11, 5 f.); there can be no question of a *mixtura Christi cum fidelibus*[EN148]. It is *in media tenebrarum*[EN149] (Luther on Gal. 2[16], *W.A.* 40[1], 229, 18), in full concealment, that there takes place this *unio*[EN150], this self-presentation of Christ or the Word of God or God Himself in the believer, this *inhabitatio totius sacrosanctae trinitatis*[EN151] as was said later. In this relation man remains man with his possibilities and limitations, and Christ Himself and alone, or the Word, remains the object of faith and it is not an inpoured love or the like that is the *forma fidei*[EN152] (Luther, *ib.*, 229, 28), i.e., that which distinguishes the believer from the unbeliever, that which makes his experience and act real faith and therefore a possibility that is given to him for use. But at any rate there is this distinction. Its complete concealment corresponds only to its complete reality as divine grace, a reality about which so much can be said without exaggeration.

In faith man is in conformity to God, i.e., capable of receiving God's Word, capable of so corresponding in his own decision to the decision God has made about him in the Word that the Word of God is now the Word heard by him and he himself is now the man addressed by this Word. One is not to seek this capability among the stock of his own possibilities. The statement about the indwelling of Christ that takes place in faith must not be turned into an anthropological statement. There must be no subtraction from the lostness of natural and sinful man, as whom the believer will for the first time really see himself. But this natural and sinful man that he is, and that in faith he must see himself to be, is dead in faith, in Christ, according to Rom. 6[3f.], and I am alive in faith, a miracle to myself, another man, and as such capable of things of which I can only know myself to be absolutely incapable as a natural sinful man.

Part of this capability is that the Word of God is knowable to man in faith, [241]
that it can be spoken to him, and that he can hear it, that he can receive it as a word, and indeed as God's Word.

It can come about in faith that man has a *ὑπόστασις ἐλπιζομένων*[EN153], i.e., a confidence corresponding and open to the nature of the thing hoped for, an *ἔλεγχος οὐ βλεπομένων*[EN154], i.e., a proof of that which is invisible and inaccessible to him (Heb. 11[1]). To the man who is righteous before God in faith it may be said: *ἐγγύς σου τὸ ῥῆμα ἐστιν, ἐν τῷ στόματί σου καὶ ἐν τῇ καρδίᾳ σου*[EN155] (Rom. 10[8]). What Irenaeus once demands is

EN148 blending of Christ with the faithful
EN149 in the midst of the darkness
EN150 union
EN151 indwelling of the entire most holy Trinity
EN152 form of faith
EN153 assurance of things hoped for
EN154 conviction of things not seen
EN155 The word is near you, on your lips and in your heart

now possible: ἵνα ἀεὶ μὲν ὁ θεὸς διδάσκῃ, ἄνθρωπος δὲ διὰ παντὸς μανθάνῃ παρὰ θεοῦ[EN156] (*C. o. h.*, II, 28, 3). This ability with reference to God's Word is the conformity of the believer to God and in particular it is the knowability of the Word of God which is the object of our present enquiry.

To the image of God in man which was lost in Adam but restored in Christ there also belongs the fact that man can hear God's Word. Only as the Word of God is really spoken in spite of his sin and to his sin, only in the grace with which God replies to sin, can this possibility revive. But in grace it does revive: not, then, as a natural capacity in man—it is grace after all that comes to sinners, to incapable men—but as a capacity of the incapable, as a miracle that cannot be interpreted anthropologically, nevertheless as a real capacity which is already actualised in faith, regarding whose existence there is no further room for discussion, whose existence can only be stated, since in becoming an event it already showed itself to be a possibility even before any question about it could arise.

What no eye has seen, nor ear heard, what has not entered into the heart of man, God has already prepared for those who love him (1 Cor. 2[9]). There are men—God has vouchsafed that there should be such—who know God's gracious acts (2[12]), who search out the "deep things of God" (2[10]), who can discern what is spiritual spiritually (2[13]), men to whom one can speak about their acquaintance with the Word of God: δέξασθε τὸν ἔμφυτον λόγον[EN157] (Jas. 1[21]), who can "stand" in faith (1 Cor. 16[13]).

As God's Word is spoken to man, it is in him and he is in the Word. The only proof of this mutual indwelling of the Word and man is a reference to the fact that as the Word of God is spoken to some other man it can be in him too, and he in it. The proof of faith consists in the proclamation of faith. The proof of the knowability of the Word consists in confessing it. In faith and confession the Word of God becomes a human thought and a human word, certainly in infinite dissimilarity and inadequacy, yet not in total alienation from its real prototype, but a true copy for all its human and sinful perversion, an unveiling of it even as its veiling. This does not imply an immanent transformation of human thought or human speech. It does not imply even a modest removal of the offence with which the Word is flesh here. Nor does it imply any diminution of the miracle of the mutual indwelling, any supernatural physics trying
[242] to make the incomprehensible comprehensible. Again, what must be said here cannot be meant as analysis of a present reality, for as such it evades our grasp and knowledge. In the strict sense it is meant only as recollection of the promise and as expectation of its future fulfilment. But in this sense the mutual indwelling and indeed the union of the divine and human logos in faith cannot be ignored or denied. This mutual indwelling or union is the knowability of the Word of God, the possibility of Church proclamation whether from the preacher's standpoint or the hearer's, and therefore the possibility of dogmat-

---

[EN156] that God should always teach and human beings continually learn from God
[EN157] receive the engrafted word

ics too. As the Church provides the ministry of proclamation and as we pursue dogmatics, we confess that we believe this possibility. For all the menacing proximity of the *analogia entis*[EN158], mysticism and identity philosophy, and in spite of all the so-called dangers, we have every reason to speak out clearly on this point.

Uniatur tecum cogitatio mea, una et singularis sit tecum intentio mea ubi tecum a te misericorditer suscepta beata iam regnat substantia nostra[EN159] (Anselm, *Medit.*, 1, 6). So, too, Luther: *In ipsa fide Christus adest. Fides ergo est cognitio quaedam vel tenebra, quae nihil videt et tamen in istis tenebris Christus fide apprehensus sedet sicut Deus in Sinai et in templo sedebat in medio tenebrarum*[EN160] (*Comm. on Gal.* 2^{16}, *W.A.* 40^{1}, 229, 15). "The statement of revelation that God speaks is identical with the statement that man hears" (E. Thurneysen, *Das Wort Gottes und die Kirche*, 1927, 222; Wobbermin's indignation at this sentence in *Wort Gottes u. ev. Glaube*, 1931, 27 is not very penetrating either actively or passively).

With our statement about man's conformity to God in faith and therefore in his possibility of knowing God's Word we are saying—and this is our second definition of the knowability of the Word of God—that when and where the Word of God is really known by men the manner of this knowing corresponds to that of the Word of God itself. If as our first definition of the knowability of the Word of God we construed it as a human possibility that becomes a possibility in face of the object that encounters man, in face of the Word of God itself, as a reflection of its own self-grounded possibility, we must now say that it becomes a possibility in the same way as the Word of God itself and in itself is possible. We have thus described what acknowledgment of God's Word by man is, not in the form of an analysis of man's consciousness of faith, but in the form of a postulate directed to man's consciousness of faith by the nature of the Word of God. We have to think of man in the event of real faith as, so to speak, opened up from above. From above, not from below! What can be seen and grasped and analysed from below, as human experience and act, as the consciousness of faith, is not the fulfilment of this postulate. It is in itself a vacuum which might be filled in quite another way than by the Word of God. The true believer is the very man who will not hesitate to acknowledge that his consciousness of faith as such is human darkness. Hence we cannot omit to [243] investigate the consciousness of our known ego with reference to the content of God's Word. The opening up from above that takes place in the event of real faith remains just as hidden for us as the event itself or God Himself. But we must also say that it is as manifest to us as this event is manifest or God is manifest, i.e., in recollection of the promise and hope of its fulfilment. As we can and should believe the Word of God itself, as we are summoned to believe

EN158 analogy of being

EN159 Let my thought be united with You, let my purpose be one and single with You where our blessed substance, mercifully received and sustained by You, already reigns with You

EN160 In faith itself Christ is truly present. Therefore faith is a kind of knowledge or darkness which sees nothing, and yet Christ, apprehended by faith, sits enthroned in this darkness, in the same way that God sat enthroned on Sinai and in the temple in the midst of darkness

it, so we must believe our faith in the Word, our possibility of knowing it or its knowability for us, the presence of the *forma Dei*[EN161] in the midst of human darkness, Christ's presence in the *tenebrae*[EN162] of our heart. If the event of faith is the event of the presence of the believed Word in man, the union of man with it, then this must mean that the darkness of man—we can never see or understand it as anything else—can be light. Thus the possibility of man, inadequate in itself, can become the adequate divine possibility. In its fulfilment it is the adequate divine possibility. In affirming the knowability of God's Word as it is promised to us and as it takes place in the event of faith, we affirm the divine possibility. To the extent that we can affirm it only in its concealment, in the husk of the human possibility that meets us as darkness, we will not deny the dissimilarity between the divine possibility in itself and what it becomes in our hands. We can see the stick dipped in water only as a broken stick. But though we cannot see it, it is invisibly and yet in truth a completely unbroken stick. For all the dissimilarity, the possibility of grasping the promise in faith is not without similarity to the divine possibility of its actualisation: not in itself, not as a human possibility, but, according to our first definition, in terms of its object, as the possibility of grasping the promise. In virtue of this similarity our possibility of knowing God's Word is the possibility of a clear and certain knowledge, not equal but at least similar to the clarity and certainty with which God knows Himself in His Word. In virtue of this similarity the confession of faith, corresponding to the knowledge of God's Word, acquires the definiteness which distinguishes it basically from all human convictions, however profound or serious; it acquires the final human seriousness which belongs only to confession, to the confession of faith. In virtue of this similarity the Church, Church proclamation and dogmatics are possible. The clarity and certainty of knowledge, the confession of faith and the Church rest on the fact that whenever and wherever the Word of God is really known it is known after the manner of the Word of God itself, in this similarity to what is believed and known.

Our reply to the Roman Catholic doctrine of the *analogia entis*[EN163] is not, then, a denial of the concept of analogy. We say rather that the analogy in question is not an *analogia entis* but according to Rom. 12[6] the ἀναλογία τῆς πίστεως[EN164], the likeness of the known in the
[244] knowing, of the object in thought, of the Word of God in the word that is thought and spoken by man, as this differentiates true Christian prophecy in faith from all false prophecy. This *analogia fidei*[EN165] is also the point of the remarkable passages in Paul in which man's knowledge of God is inverted into man's being known by God. Paul calls Christians γνόντες θεόν[EN166] only to amend it once at: μᾶλλον δὲ γνωσθέντες ὑπὸ θεοῦ[EN167]. It is obviously

[EN161] form of God
[EN162] darkness
[EN163] analogy of being
[EN164] analogy of faith
[EN165] analogy of faith
[EN166] people knowing God
[EN167] rather known by God

this γνωσθῆναι[EN168] that distinguishes their γιγνώσκειν[EN169] as Christians from their previous non-knowing of God as pagans (Gal. $4^{8f.}$). If here in the Christian community a man thinks he has known something, he has not known what must be known. One can never look back on the human, even the Christian act of knowledge as such as on a successful work corresponding to its object. The man who loves God οὗτος ἔγνωσται ὑπ' αὐτοῦ[EN170]. Again it is the divine act of knowledge which takes place on man rather than through man that distinguishes those whose knowledge is grounded in love of God and therefore in true fellowship with Him, in the presence of God (1 Cor. $8^{2f.}$). But even in the Christian this being known, the divine possibility, remains distinct from the human possibility of knowing; this cannot exhaust it; there is only similarity, analogy. To see God "face to face" without dissimilarity must await the eternal consummation even in the case of Christians: τότε δὲ ἐπιγνώσομαι καθὼς καὶ[EN171] (i.e., not just correspondingly, similarly, analogously, but exactly as) ἐπεγνώσθην (1 Cor. 13^{12}). We find the same reversal in the words of Augustine: *Qui autem per Spiritum tuum vident ea* (*sc. opera Dei*) *tu vides in eis. Ergo cum vident quia bona sunt, tu vides quia bona sunt: et quaecumque propter te placent, tu in eis places et quae per Spiritum tuum placent nobis, tibi placent in nobis*[EN172] (*Conf.* XIII, 31, 46). One must also be sufficiently impartial not to overlook that which for all the dubious elements can still be taken *in bonam partem*[EN173] in the words of the Hegelian P. Marheineke: "In the human spirit God is not manifest through this but through Himself, and hence manifest also to the human spirit. This, as reason, is annulled in Him. The hardest thing that science requires of every devotee is that pure substance show itself as subject, that he with his spirit should subject himself to the divine spirit and be patient under it. His true knowledge of the absolute is itself absolute" (*Grundlehren d. ch. Dogm. als Wissenschaft,* 1827, § 115). Precisely when we describe both the conformity of man to God that takes place in faith and also the point of contact for the Word of God posited in this conformity, not as an inborn or acquired property of man but only as the work of the actual grace of God, our only final word at this point can be that God acts on man in His Word. Because man's work in faith is that on which God's work is done, man can know the Word of God. He knows as he is known by God.

3. The last turn in our discussion of the concept of the *analogia fidei* has brought us already to the third and final thing which must be said in this connexion about faith and the knowability of the Word of God for man. If it is true that man really believes 1. that the object of faith is present to him and 2. that he himself is assimilated to the object, then we are led in conclusion to the third point that man exists as a believer wholly and utterly by this object. In believing he can think of himself as grounded, not in self but only in this object, as existing indeed only by this object. He has not created his own faith; the Word has created it. He has not come to faith; faith has come to him through the Word. He has not adopted faith; faith has been granted to him through the Word. As a believer he cannot see himself as the acting subject of

---

EN168 being known

EN169 knowing

EN170 is known by Him

EN171 then I shall know fully, even as I am fully known

EN172 And those who see them (namely, the works of God) through Your Spirit, You see in them. And when they see that they are good, you see that they are good: and whatever is pleasing because of You, You are pleased in them; and whatever pleases us through Your Spirit is pleasing to You in us

EN173 in a good sense

[245] the work done here. It is his experience and act. He is not at all a block or stone in faith but self-determining man. He does not sink into passive, apathetic contemplation in faith, and even if he did he would still do so as self-determining man. Whatever his state of soul, at least in thinking, willing and feeling he is himself and lives his own life. Nevertheless, the point is that in faith he must regard this in no sense diminished self-determination, himself in his own activity, in the living of his own life, as determined by the Word of God. In his freedom, in the full use of his freedom as a man, he must see himself as another man that he had no power to become, that he still has no power to become, that he is not free to become or to be (though he is free as he becomes and is), in short, that he can be only by being this man. Man acts as he believes, but the fact that he believes as he acts is God's act. Man is the subject of faith. Man believes, not God. But the fact that man is this subject in faith is bracketed as a predicate of the subject God, bracketed in the way that the Creator encloses the creature and the merciful God sinful man, i.e., in such a way that man remains subject, and yet man's I as such derives only from the Thou of the subject God.

The older theology was describing this when it called faith a gift of God, of the Holy Spirit. This could be meant and said with varying degrees of strictness. We must take it in a more incisive sense than it is stated and understood, e.g., in Augustine. Augustine, of course, taught very explicitly and impressively against the Pelagians that faith is grace. But his *Ut credamus Deus dedit*[EN174] remained equivocal, for there was always the other saying: *fides in potestate est*[EN175], in which *potestas*[EN176] meant the *facultas faciendi*[EN177] (*De Spir. et lit.* 31, 55), and the relation of the two is described thus: *Quid habeat et quid accipiat, Dei est; accipere et habere utique accipientis est*[EN178] (*ib.*, 34, 60). In one of his last writings against the Semi-Pelagians he certainly tried to correct this: *Habere fidem gratiae est fidelium*[EN179], but over against this there is still the other saying: *Posse habere fidem naturae est hominum*[EN180]; there is a general human *natura in qua nobis data est possibilitas habendi fidem*[EN181] (*De praedest.* 5, 10). Since it is hard to find any basis in man even for this *possibilitas habendi*[EN182], let alone a *habere*[EN183], it is better to say with Luther: *fidem esse ... simpliciter donum Dei, qui ut creat ita conservat fidem in nobis*[EN184] (*Comm. on Gal.* 1[12], 1535, *W.A.* 40[1], 130, 13). "Here we must not regard reason or its work when we speak of faith and God's work. Here God worketh alone and reason is dead, blind, and compared to this work an unreasoning block, on which Scripture insists when it says, 'God is marvellous in his saints,' also Is. 55: 'As heaven is high above the earth, so are my ways high above your ways'" (*Fastenpost.*, 1525, *Sermon on Mt.* 8[1f.], *W.A.* 17[11], 85, 10). "But they who gladly hear God's Word and to whom Christ hath said as here to

[EN174] That we believe is a gift of God
[EN175] Faith then is in our power
[EN176] power
[EN177] a capacity to make it happen
[EN178] What he has and what he receives are of God; the acts of having and receiving are both the receiver's
[EN179] To have faith is a grace given to the faithful
[EN180] The capacity to have faith is part of human nature
[EN181] nature through which the possibility of having faith has been given to us
[EN182] possibility of having
[EN183] having
[EN184] faith is ... simply a gift of God, who equally creates and preserves faith in us

the deaf, 'Ephthatha, ear, thou shalt stand open,' 'tis these are rightly holpen against the devil, for God hath given us no other stairs nor shown us any other way whereon we may go up to heaven save His dear Word, the holy gospel. Whoso gladly heareth the same, marketh it with diligence, and hath desire and love thereto, he receiveth help. This is a miraculous work which is still done daily in Christendom, that our ears which the devil hath stopped by sin are opened again by the Word, that we hear God's Word" (*Hauspost.*, 1544, *Sermon on Lk.* 18[9f.], *W.A.* 52, 452, 14). "Like then as God giveth the Word, 'tis His and not our Word, so too giveth He faith in the Word. For both are God's work, Word and faith" (*Hauspost.*, 1544, [246]
Sermon on Mt. 9[1f.], *W.A.* 52, 501, 19). "But that thou hearest and apprehendest such, is likewise not of thine own power, but of God's grace, who maketh the gospel fruitful in thee, that thou believest it ..." (*Adventpost.*, 1522, *Sermon on Mt.* 21[1f.], *W.A.* 10[12], 30, 5). "Where Christ sat not on the right hand of God nor daily poured forth of His Spirit, Christian faith could not exist. For 'tis counter to all human reason and the devil is hostile to it. Therefore, where the outpouring of the Holy Ghost kept not continual guard, the devil would not let a single man abide by the preaching of Pentecost and by faith in Christ" (*Sermon on Acts* 2[14f.], 1534, *E.A.* 4, 105). It should be noted that Luther here is not dealing with a mere assent to truth but with the living and direct relation to Christ that takes place in faith, with the faith that lives in works. It is this that he traces back to and nails to the fact that it is not a human work (as mere assent to truth might be) but the gift of God. "There be some that hear and read the gospel and what is said anent faith and they fall swiftly thereon and give the name of faith to what they think. But they think no further than that faith is a thing that standeth in their power to have or not to have, like any other natural human work; therefore, when in their heart they effect a thought that saith, Verily the doctrine is right and I believe it is so, at once they think faith is there. When they then see and feel in themselves and in others that there is no change .... Lo, they then fall away and cry and say, Ah, faith doeth it not alone. Why? Ah, for this reason that there are so many of them that believe and do nothing more than before, they likewise find themselves no otherwise minded than before. These are they whom Jude in his Epistle (v. 8) calleth dreamers who deceive themselves with their own dream. For what other is this thought of theirs that they call faith than just a dream and a mere ghost of faith which they themselves of their own power, without God's grace, have made in their hearts? who become thereafter worse than they were before .... But the right faith whereof we speak letteth not itself be made with our thoughts but 'tis a pure work of God in us without any aid of ours .... Therefore, 'tis likewise a mighty, active, restless, busy thing, which alike reneweth a man, beareth him elsewhere, and leadeth him altogether into a new way and nature, such wise that 'tis impossible that the same should not do good works without intermission" (*Sermon on* Lk. 16[1f.], *E.A.* 13, 235, cf. *Hauspost.*, 1544, *Sermon on Jn.* 16[5f.], *W.A.* 52, 292, 31).

The application to the problem of knowledge is self-evident.

We may now rejoin Augustine: *Non parva ex parte intelligit et scit Dominum, qui intelligit et scit etiam hoc a Domino sibi dari, ut intelligat et sciat Dominum*[EN185] (*Conf.* XVII, 4, 8). And Anselm: *Intellectus ex auditu gratia est*[EN186] (*De concordia, Qu.*, III, 6).

The Word of God becomes knowable by making itself known. The application of what has been said to the problem of knowledge consists in stopping

EN185 The one who understands and knows that even what he understands and knows of the Lord has been given to him by the Lord does not understand and know the Lord in a small way

EN186 The understanding that comes through hearing is grace

at this statement and not going a single step beyond it. The possibility of knowing the Word of God is God's miracle on us just as much as is the Word itself or its being spoken. Here again we are not arguing for a passivity in man which sets aside or even limits his freedom. Here again our concern is to realise that the mutual indwelling or union of the divine and human possibility, of man's knowing and his being known by God, is an event in the freedom of man, and
[247] yet that it cannot in any sense be regarded as its product, as the result of an intuition, of a conceivable or attainable deepening or enhancing of the life of the human soul. This may take place—and why should it not?—but it does not have to take place. And in any case it is not the thing that brings about that union and therefore the knowability of the Word of God. Even the idea of a *sacrificium intellectus*[EN187] is only a last desperate attempt to make the knowledge of God a work of man, to have a human possibility correspond to what is God's work alone. If we have understood that the knowability of God's Word is really an inalienable affirmation of faith, but that precisely as such it denotes the miracle of faith, the miracle that we can only recollect and hope for, then as a final necessity we must also understand that man must be set side and God Himself presented as the original subject, as the primary power, as the creator of the possibility of knowledge of God's Word. Christ does not remain outside. And it is true enough that man must open the door (Rev. 3^{20}). But the fact that this takes place is *quoad actum*[EN188] and *quoad potentiam*[EN189] the work of the Christ who stands outside. Hence it is also unconditionally true that the risen Christ passes through closed doors (Jn. $20^{19f.}$).

[EN187] sacrifice of the intellect
[EN188] with respect to the act itself
[EN189] with respect to its possibility

§ 7 [248]

THE WORD OF GOD, DOGMA AND DOGMATICS

Dogmatics is the critical question about dogma, i.e., about the Word of God in Church proclamation, or, concretely, about the agreement of the Church proclamation done and to be done by man with the revelation attested in Holy Scripture. Prolegomena to dogmatics as an understanding of its epistemological path must therefore consist in an exposition of the three forms of the Word of God as revealed, written, and preached.

1. THE PROBLEM OF DOGMATICS

In the three preceding sections we have described the criterion of dogmatics, its three forms, its nature and its knowability. What we had in view when in § 3 we called the Word of God the standard by which dogmatics must measure Church proclamation should now have become provisionally comprehensible in all its incomprehensibility. Provisionally, we shall have to say, for all that we have said thus far implies only a turning around and placing ourselves in the direction in which we must look to see the point from which the Church realises that its proclamation is perceived and judged and from which, therefore, it must make every effort to think about itself so that, fully aware of its responsibility, it may submit to the necessary self-examination in respect of its proclamation. In all that has been said thus far we have as it were only sketched the sphere of this criterion, trying to visualise its distinctiveness as compared with other objects of human and even Christian reflection and its difference from other intrinsically possible criteria. Although with constant regard to the concrete content of this criterion, we have put only the formal question and received the corresponding formal answers. More can and must be said about the Word of God than has been said thus far, though always in recollection of the promise made to the Church and in expectation of its fulfilment. The recollection to which the Church knows it is summoned relates to a wholly concrete content of the Word of God, and so, too, does the expectation inseparable from the recollection. This concrete content of the criterion of dogmatics has not yet been put in the centre of our attention or discussed independently. But this must be done. Only when we have understood it in the unity of form and content, only when it is clear that the form that has concerned us thus far is the form of a very concrete content, have we understood [249]
the Word of God in such a way that its application as the criterion of Church proclamation has meaning and authority. As yet, therefore, our doctrine of the

Word of God is far from complete. Its most characteristic statements have still to be made. In one sense we cannot go further or expect to hear more. We have said that what is meant by the Word of God must have become comprehensible now in all its incomprehensibility. First, we accept and shall continue to accept the incomprehensibility of the fact that the Word of God is spoken to man. No consideration yet to be adduced, not even that which must and will be directed to its specific content, will ever help us to see how this reality comes to be. We have investigated its constitution and will investigate it further. We have been able to ask *a posteriori* concerning its possibilities, namely, those grounded in itself. How it came about and comes about as thus constituted, what is the possibility of its possibilities, must and will always remain incomprehensible to us. Secondly we accept and continue to accept the incomprehensibility of the nature of the Word of God in itself. For one thing, as what it is it is only the content of the specific event of its being spoken to this man or that. Then again, as what this man or that receives and accepts and can give an account of as God's Word in the event of faith, it is no longer what the Word of God that is spoken to him is in itself, but only his recollection of what is said to him and his expectation of what will be said to him afresh. Dogmatics cannot get round this twofold barrier even by turning its attention to the concrete content of the Word of God. With the whole Church it can know its concrete content only in recollection and expectation and therefore neither in its That nor (in the narrower sense) in its concrete What, neither with a proof lying outside itself nor as the *verbum concretissimum*[EN1] that comes to specific men but is veiled from each man even as it is revealed to him. One should not expect anything superhuman from dogmatics; its office cannot be to tear down the barriers of faith that are set for the Church. Part of its task is rather to make these barriers known as such, to say what can be said and therewith to warn against violations or illusions regarding things one cannot say. In this sense it should now be comprehensible what is meant by the two terms "God's Word": provisionally comprehensible and comprehensible in all its incomprehensibility. To say "provisionally" is to indicate the possibility of further insights. To say "in all its incomprehensibility" is to imply that we shall still be moving within fixed limits even in all these further insights.

But before we can enter upon this further path, we must turn once again, instructed to some extent about the one thing needful, to the task of dogmatics as such. In § 1 we generally defined this as the Christian Church's task of
[250] self-examination regarding the content of its specific talk about God. Then in § 3 we said rather more precisely that it is a matter of investigating the "responsibility" of this talk, namely, of Church proclamation measured by the Word of God that it is seeking to proclaim. The primary result was a need to ask and say what is meant by this standard by which Church proclamation is to be measured and by means of which that self-examination is to be performed. Now

---

[EN1] utterly concrete word

that this has been done we move on to a third and even more precise definition of the dogmatic task. It should be noted that even this cannot be the last one. That can be reached only when we have examined the criterion according to its concrete content, or rather in the last stage of this examination itself. But in order to determine in which direction we must move we must now for a moment turn our attention afresh to the task as such for whose sake the question of the criterion has been put and is still to be put.

The task of dogmatics is the examination of Church proclamation in respect of its agreement with the Word of God, its congruity with what it is trying to proclaim. In the human form of the proclamation offered by the Church, the Word of God should, of course, be present too. This is the claim with which the Church advances its proclamation and also the expectation by which it is surrounded. Dogmatic work begins by taking this claim and expectation with full seriousness, by taking the Church at its word, so to speak, in respect of this claim and this expectation. In dogmatics the Church accepts what it is undertaking in its proclamation. It tests this undertaking by confronting it critically, by suspending the claim and expectation for a moment to the degree that it dissociates proclamation and the Word of God in thought, not in order to measure the Word of God by its proclamation, but in order to measure its proclamation by the Word of God. The Church does not cease to believe that God will confess it and its work, that He will put His Word in its proclamation and thus make its proclamation real proclamation. But the fact that it believes this means that it grasps God's promise. "It believes" does not mean "it thinks it possesses," but "it hopes it will be given." The reflection of faith, then, consists in the fact that the Church holds apart God's Word and its own and questions the latter in the light of the former. Faith knows that it is asked whether as a human work it is also obedience. To faith the judgment of God to which all human work is subject as such is no idle thought. It is a summons to judge itself regarding this work. The corresponding critical concern for Church proclamation is the task of dogmatics. But can it do justice to this task? How and where may it see the Word of God as an entity distinct from Church proclamation so as to compare the latter with it and measure it by it? Is there any possibility of this at all? If there were no such possibility, we should be faced by a remarkable dilemma.

We might still scrutinise Church proclamation in many different ways. We [251]
might ask whether it is really commensurate with the Word of God that it purports to proclaim and indeed to be. Disturbed by its human imperfection, we might examine it in terms of this congruity and improve it accordingly. We might test it philosophically in terms of its epistemological, logical, cosmological and psychological content, or test its form historically, ethicopedagogically, or politically. We might adjust it to the prevailing modern philosophy, or the most pressing practical needs and tasks, or the most eloquent forms of expression. There are many such criteria which one might advance in place of the absent criterion of the Word of God. It might be that

Church proclamation would correspond to God's Word to the degree that it stands the test of one or other of these criteria or all of them together. Theology would then consist in administering these criteria and their relevance with the utmost possible strictness of application, always on the assumption that in this way justice is done to the inconceivable true criterion of theology, the Word of God.

The theology of Modernist Protestantism might be understood in this way and against this background. It too, gripped and impelled in its own way by concern for the Church, was trying to do justice to the task handed down by the Reformation and the older Church. It, too, was trying to promote concern for correct Church proclamation in accordance with the Word of God. It, too, desired and therefore had its dogmatics. But it had lost the proper criterion above and over against Church proclamation as the Reformation especially had put this in its hands. It still knew it, but it no longer regarded it as a criterion in its distinction from and superiority to the present action of the Church. It still took it into account, but it no longer understood its dignity, its character as a final court of appeal. It forgot to look to this and to this alone in the question as to the Word of God by which Church proclamation must be measured. In this question it constantly looked elsewhere. The empty place of the criterion of Reformation theology had to be occupied, and was occupied, in some other way. Even though one regards as heretical this newer theology which attained to leadership with Pietism and the Enlightenment, we must admit that it wanted to continue the critical function of theology. It still wanted to be the conscience of the proclaiming Church. It also saw that conscience must have a criterion. And if it no longer understood the criterion of Reformation theology as such, and therefore seized on other criteria, it did so with the idea of finding in these other criteria a full and equal replacement or substitute for what had been lost. It was out of good intentions rather than bad intentions that it became as philosophical, as moral, as secular, in short, as culturally Protestant as it became and continued to become in ever new forms throughout the 18th and 19th centuries and on into our own. The golden calf (Ex. 32), too, was not meant to represent a strange god but the God who had led Israel out of Egypt. Israel, too, acted out of piety in this matter, and Aaron met its wishes with the best of intentions. This is how we might regard the theology of Modernist Protestantism. It could see no further possibility of viewing the Word of God as an entity distinct from Church proclamation. But it could clearly see other entities distinct from Church proclamation and at least very normative. Their epitome was modern cultural
[252] awareness. It therefore set up this cultural awareness as a surrogate in the place of the Word of God which had now lost all concreteness for it and had volatilised into a mere idea. And it now judged according to this surrogate.

If we cannot make the distinction, if the Word of God is not for us a concrete entity distinct from Church proclamation, then we might be tempted to take this course—and it is not the only one available at this point. But if we do, we should be aware of the serious problems that arise on this path, and the question is whether they are surmountable.

1. How do we know what we obviously think we know on this path, namely, that the process of losing the Word of God as a concrete theological criterion, and therefore of losing a specifically theological relevance, is a good and necessary process whose results one can and should simply accept?

2. How do we know whether the criteria newly selected to replace that which

is lost are really commensurate with this undertaking, with Church proclamation, whether in applying them we are not causing confusion where there should be order and destroying where we ought to build?

3. How do we know whether here, where perhaps only an absolutely given criterion ought to come into consideration, we are not decisively in error in the very fact that, however good our intentions, we even look around for criteria, choose them, and set them up as such?

4. How do we know, finally, whether any other criterion can replace the Word of God that we can no longer grasp, whether we are not rather to accept the impossibility of seeing the Word of God concretely, whether it would not be better to renounce all critical concern for Church proclamation, i.e., all theology?

Naturally these questions will really harry and possibly force off that path only those who have not completely lost sight of the Word of God as a concrete independent criterion, so that for them the possibility of a comparison between this criterion and the others has not been totally cut off.

This stage has not been reached even in the age of theological Modernism. The very different approach of the first centuries of the Reformation churches has not ceased to have an unsettling effect. Its influence, of course, was often reduced to a minimum. If anything served to restrict it and hence to harden the Modernist position, it was the resistance which the official ecclesiastical authorities offered to theological Liberalism from the days of Wöllner's edict on religion, through the disastrous period of Frederick William IV and up to the time before the First World War. For this opposition was not based on better theology or on real perception of what Modernism could no longer see. In the main it rested on blind conservative instincts. Again, the opposition did not follow the only way that is possible in the Church, that of spiritual conquest. Instead, it took the form of political repression of what was then the new theology. The human brilliance which has enveloped theological Liberalism right up to the final phase characterised by such names as Harnack and [253]
Troeltsch, and the religious passion with which it could be presented at the same period in the theology of W. Herrmann, were the brilliance and passion of a martyrdom by which the Church authorities, powerless to oppose to it a superior word, continually vindicated it in its own eyes and in the eyes of the world. What an ecclesiastical orthodoxy that was so unsure of its cause as that of the 18th, 19th and 20th centuries could and did accomplish when faced by the great Modernist *Quid pro quo*[EN2] was far from being a salutary unsettling of this new Protestantism by Reformation insights. And if to the very last Liberal theology was opposed by a "positive" theology of imposing power which did formally maintain the Reformation thesis with respect to the criterion of dogmatics, this ought to have steered clear of any alliance with the unspiritually conservative Church authorities; it ought to have declined their political support; it ought to have shown itself much more unequivocally to be what it meant to be, namely, a theology of revelation. But did the modern positive block in which the remnants of the former Erlangen and Leipzig schools regrouped in the first decade of the present century really have so much to reproach its Liberal opponents with as it made out? In the last resort, where was the theological orthodoxy about which Liberal journals had so much to say? How it had joined in the chase after new criteria! How it had dabbled in apologetics! How many of its members could waken up one morning with no particular

[EN2] tit for tat

transformation to find themselves tolerably authentic religious philosophers, religious historians or religious psychologists! How in the field of exegesis in particular it even increased the confusion of approaches by a historicism which was not better because it was a traditionally inclined and supernatural historicism, which certainly had not the slightest influence on the opposition and which could not prevent the increasing and final obliteration of the frontiers between "positive" and "liberal" Old and New Testament scholars, always to the disadvantage of the so-called "positives"! And how finally, when the great moment came (in 1914) in which a theology of revelation had to differentiate itself at least in some measure from a theology of culture within the relativity of all things human, it went along with it hand-in-hand in both ethos and ethics! I make these points, which are not really my concern here, only because the complaint is continually made to-day (especially in the writings of E. Schaeder, though cf. also P. Althaus, "*Die Theologie*" in C. Schweitzer, *Das. relig. Deutschland der Gegenwart*, Vol. 2, 1930, 140) that it has now been largely forgotten that there has been a constant theological protest against cultural Protestantism for a long time. Certainly there was this protest. Indeed, it was there in Liberal theology itself. It had to be if theology was not going to sell out completely and retire. Liberal theology was not really as bad as it often made itself out to be. Under the pressure of the problem there were some note-worthy counter-movements even in its own ranks. To-day Wobbermin, e.g., in the Preface to *Richtlinien*, 1930, or *Wort Gottes*, 1931, 4, n. 2, is no less zealous than E. Schaeder in announcing that he was long ago "in the sharpest conflict not only against all psychologism but also against all historicism" (*op. cit.*, p. 6). But what point or value is there in contesting or maintaining priorities here? If and to the degree that "it" was really said long ago by Positives and by Liberals themselves, it had then the effect and significance that it could have in the form in which it was said. The one thing that is certain is that the real power to unsettle did not come from the Church authorities or the theology of the period but from the simple fact that the Church lived on and its proclamation continued, that whether led or led astray, whether promoted or devastated by Modernist theology, it nevertheless continued through the 18th and 19th centuries and on into the 20th century. The Church lived on because the
[254] Bible was preserved for it, a Bible much relativised by history and psychology, a Bible misinterpreted by religious philosophy, a Bible whose right and claim to constitute the textual basis of Church proclamation were disputed, a Bible which was affirmed in fact rather than theoretically and in large measure even against theological theory, a Bible to which only relative commitment was felt, nevertheless the Bible, and with the Bible the problem, and with the problem a sense of dissatisfaction with the Neo-Protestant solution. It is in this way, by ongoing proclamation bound somehow—very much "somehow"—to the Bible, by the ongoing life of the Church in this its decisive function, that a challenge has always been maintained to the Modernist answer in this matter.

When in face of the possibility of replacing the Word of God by other criteria in dogmatics, we raise those four questions, when we say that there is no way of knowing what is thought to be known at all those points, when we thus state that that whole possibility of solution is unsound, we are appealing to the simple fact that Church proclamation, whether this be understood or not understood, whether it is inwardly reasoned out or merely a matter of tradition, is in fact confronted with the Bible. So long as this confrontation is not set aside, no one can truly say that the problem does not exist for him, that the possibility that the Word of God is the true and concretely independent criterion of Church proclamation has been completely banished from his field of vision.

1. *The Problem of Dogmatics*

From the book by Wilhelm Pauck, *Karl Barth, Prophet of a New Christianity?*, 1931, 99, I take the following observation. "It is important to remember ... that the difference between modern preaching in America and Protestant Europe is fundamental. The American sermon is seldom Biblical and expository. Its reference to the Scripture is in the majority of cases casual or superficial. It deals generally with 'religious' topics. The European Protestant, however, follows the old tradition of preaching the 'Word' whether he is affiliated with liberal or orthodox theology." If this is generally true as concerns America, then even the actual confrontation with the Bible which is presupposed here is no longer, or scarcely any longer, an event there. And if not, then naturally the problem based on this confrontation does not arise. In that case I may expect from the descendants of the Pilgrim Fathers neither interest nor understanding for what follows, nor indeed for the whole of this Dogmatics. But perhaps even in America there is at least a dim recollection that the preaching of the Church might stand in some sort of special connexion with the Bible. And even there it will surely happen some day that "religious" topics will become so stupid and stale that the dim recollection might become once again a clear recollection.

From the situation of the parson in the pulpit, who not only has to say something somehow, but has to say it in face of the open Bible and supposedly in accordance with the Bible and in exposition of the Bible, from this situation even the man outside the Church, the abjurer of faith, can at least gather this, that here there is at the very lowest the possibility of a protest against the introduction of other criteria of Church proclamation, or as we might also put it, of the assertion of the Bible as the criterion, as the concrete form of the Word of God. Or it might be that the Bible has already spoken or will speak to us again as the Word of God and that we have to think and judge in this matter, not as [255] outsiders, but as those who stand on the Church's own ground. Considered as a human place of human willing and doing, the Church rests, not on the presupposition, but very definitely on the recollection and the expectation that God in fact has spoken and will speak the Word to us in the Bible. Can one stand in this recollection and expectation, and to that extent in the Church, without having to raise those four questions? And can the questions be answered except as follows?

1. If it is true that we no longer know concretely whether and how far the Word of God is the standard by which Church proclamation is to be measured, if the Word of God has really dissolved from a concrete counterpart into a mere idea, then we do not have to accept this as a historical fate in intellectual history, but it is a sign of the wrath of God, a trial of faith, a falling into the consequences of disobedience in which one cannot be a mere spectator of oneself, with which one cannot come to terms in the Church, but, realising that it is a matter of divine chastisement, one can only reply by crying to the hidden God that He will give again the standard that has been lost. This is in keeping with the recollection and expectation of faith. At any time faith can fall into unbelief and then theological relevance is indeed lost and the temptation arises to make a golden calf representing the God of Israel, the temptation as it were to settle down comfortably in unbelief and to fend for oneself.

Faith overcomes this temptation. Faith does not make a virtue of the necessity. Even and precisely in the depths of unbelief faith hears the new summons to faith. In the trial regarding God's Word which did not indeed come only with the 18th century, faith may thus lose theological relevance, but it can lose it only to find it again.

2. In fact Church proclamation is not an undertaking which can come under other criteria than God's Word in respect of its content. What is undertaken in it is exempt from the claim to be judged by any philosophy or ethics or politics, if not in respect of its human motives and forms, at least in respect of its believed intention. The introduction of other criteria here can only mean that the undertaking itself has become a different one, that it ceases to be the Church's undertaking laid upon it by commission and accompanied by the divine promise. For the introduction of another criterion means renunciation of the believed intention of this undertaking. To the extent that another standard is really applied here and not the Word of God itself, only confusion and destruction can actually result, no matter how true or weighty the other standard may be in and for itself. For the decisive word about its proclamation the Church cannot listen to any other voice than the voice of its Lord. If it does [256] not hear this, the darkness of an utter lack of counsel or leadership would be ever so much better than the light of strange lights however bright.

3. It is indeed a decisive mistake to think that other criteria can be sought and chosen and set up in matters of Church proclamation. The criterion to which the Church knows it is subject is not one it has chosen and adopted; it has been given to it. It is in force before and as proclamation is undertaken; proclamation is undertaken on the basis of the fact that it is already in force. It may be regarded or not regarded, acknowledged or not acknowledged, but when it is regarded and acknowledged it can be regarded and acknowledged only in an act of obedience, only in a finding preceded by no human seeking. The choice of other criteria in place of God's Word betrays itself already as an act involving abandonment of the Church's ground, of its recollection and expectation and to that extent of its faith, by the very fact that it is a choice, an act of human perplexity and prudence, instead of an act of acknowledgment of God's prevenient goodness.

4. But if it is finally objected that there is not any real surrender of the one criterion of the Word of God, that the other criteria are merely brought in to represent this one (in view of its incomprehensibility), that theology is not giving up its task but simply assuming as it were an incognito by putting other standards alongside the one standard that is not thereby denied or replaced but merely given surrogates or a surrogate (always in view of its in comprehensibility), the answer is that these other criteria are to be rejected as irrelevant and injurious because they cannot serve vicariously as surrogates, because all vicariate is fundamentally impossible here. Philosophy, ethics, politics and anything else that might be suggested here may all have their own dignity and justification in their own spheres but they are the philosophy, ethics and polit-

ics of sinful and lost man whose word, however profound and true it may be, cannot be recognised as judge over the Word which is addressed in the name of God to these sinful and lost men, as judge, therefore, over Church proclamation. In seeking to judge himself here, man would not be judged. Trying to serve proclamation on this basis, dogmatics would not serve it with true and serious criticism and correction. Theology itself would be only one of the many forms of dialogue that man has with himself about himself when what it ought to do is to serve the discourse that God directs to man. The true problem of Church proclamation, the problem of the question how sinful man can be a messenger of the divine Word, would be ignored, for even the best-founded and most considered human judgment cannot help with this problem. If theology had no answer to this true problem of the Church, it might in fact be just as well abandoned.

The other possibility in the dilemma in which we would be placed if we did [257]
not know any concrete form of the Word of God as the supreme criterion of Church proclamation would consist in our having to start with the fact that the Church with its proclamation is indeed left to itself and cast back on its own resources. But, it might then be asked, would this really mean that it is without God's Word and therefore in no position to control, criticise and correct itself by God's Word? May not and must not the juxtaposition of God's Word and Church proclamation be viewed as a relative one? Have we not said ourselves that the reflection in which the Church makes this distinction is the reflection of faith, which, even as it makes the distinction, lays hold of the divine promise, Lo, I am with you alway! and precisely in so doing abrogates the distinction again? Might not the distinction amount to no more than a distinction within the reality of the Church itself, the distinction between the human and divine elements of its reality, which are both still to be regarded as elements of its reality? Is the Word of God not given to it as the Church of Jesus Christ? Is not, then, the absent concrete authority established and alive within itself? Is not precisely this the glory of the Church, the presence of its Lord within it, that on the one hand it can and should proclaim the Word of God and on the other hand it can and should itself regulate, criticise and correct its action in this respect by means of the same Word of God?

In this possibility we are primarily confronted again by the Roman Catholic view of the relation of the Bible to the teaching office, which we discussed already at an earlier stage. According to this view the Church has, of course, a lord and judge over its acts. It has, of course, the Word of God over it. But it has this over it as it has it in it, indistinguishable from itself. Though it puts tradition alongside the Bible, the Roman Catholic Church, too, has and reads and honours the Bible. But this is not the Bible in itself, the emancipated Bible, the Bible which confronts the Church as an authority. The fact that the Bible in its own concreteness is the Word of God, and that as such it is the supreme criterion of Church teaching, is not acknowledged here. What we have here is the Bible as it is authoritatively interpreted by the Church itself or by its teaching office, which is the living voice of Christ. What we have here is the Bible which belongs to the Church, which is understood aright and expounded aright and applied aright by its teaching office. This Bible is the Word of God by

which all proclamation is to be measured. The *regula proxima fidei*[EN3], the nearest immediate plumbline of Catholic faith, is not, then, the verdict of the Bible but the verdict of the teaching office on the Bible. (Cf. Diekamp, *Kath. Dogm.*, Vol. 1, 1930, 63 f.) Even and especially in relation to the Bible the Church keeps in its own hand both proclamation and also the norm of its necessary criticism, i.e., the Bible correctly understood and applied, which is in fact the norm employed in this criticism. There is in fact only a relative difference between the two, and their synthesis can cause no surprise to the Church which in its head is both *norma normata*[EN4] and *norma normans*[EN5], both *ecclesia audiens*[EN6] and *ecclesia docens*[EN7], for at least in its head, i.e., its teaching office, it has oversight of both and full authority and power to effect the synthesis and therefore to pursue dogmatic criticism according its own free judgment. But in this possibility we are not merely confronted by the Roman Catholic view of the
[258] teaching office. For according to the teaching of Protestant Modernism as well we ultimately find the Church dependent on itself and left to its own devices. Here again this does not have to mean that the Church is necessarily without the Word of God and consequently without the criterion of its proclamation. Here again the Bible has not just been pushed aside in favour of philosophical, historical, political and other criteria. Here again the connexion of proclamation with the Bible and therefore a certain critical participation of the Bible in dogmatics remain. There even remain as a rule—and this largely serves to obscure the issue—strong traditional theoretical statements about the normativity and even the sole normativity of the Bible. "I am quite serious in bringing to full and unrestricted validity the principle of Luther that the Word of God alone has to set up articles of faith ... that Holy Scripture alone must be accepted exclusively and unconditionally as the source of dogmatic work, all so-called subsidiary sources being sharply rejected." So Wobbermin! (*Chr. u. Wiss.*, 1932, 179). But here again the Church does not have the Bible over it as a concrete and supreme criterion. Here again it has the Bible over it only as it has it in it. To be sure, there is no infallible teaching office authoritatively representing the Bible's being in the Church and constituting with its interpretation of the Bible the *regula proxima fidei*[EN8]. But the fact that the Church in its unity as *norma normata* and *norma normans* does have this specific representative in Roman Catholicism is not the essential point of this position even there. The essential point is rather the presupposed relativity of the difference between the Church and the Bible, or the insight into this relativity which is ascribed to the Church, its ascribed competence to determine for itself how far it will let itself be judged by the Bible, and therefore to be finally the judge in its own cause. Protestant Modernism does this without a teaching office. That this is so is perhaps seen most plainly in that one of its many schools in which, apart from Schleiermacher, its essence has in general been most clearly and consistently developed, namely, in theologians philosophically orientated to Hegel. When P. K. Marheineke ascribes quite unreservedly to the Christian community the "holy spirit of Jesus Christ" who "not only has knowledge in himself but is knowledge" (*Grundlehren der christl. Dogmatik*, 1827, § 15), when he can thus say of the Christian religion that "in it God is known humanly as He knows Himself. It is truth in and for itself" (§ 69), when in this Christian "spirit" he finds not only reason but also Church tradition and the Bible "abrogated in their aseity" (§ 113), and when he then expressly makes this "spirit" the normative expositor not only of tradition but also of the Bible (§ 112 and 588), the expositor who, being himself the spirit of the Bible, takes his own standpoint in this, and therefore in dogmatics as in Church

[EN3] the most immediate rule of faith
[EN4] standardized norm
[EN5] standardizing norm
[EN6] listening church
[EN7] teaching church
[EN8] most immediate rule of faith

tradition simply repeats what he already has and indeed himself is (§ 116), what does all this mean but that the Bible is retained as a stage which the self-movement of the Christian spirit must pass through but which has completely lost as such the character of a court that is independent of this self-movement and that really judges it? What does all this mean but that the difference between the divine and the human word is already perceived and overcome in its relativity by the Christian thinker even as it discloses itself to him? Does it make any basic difference if this Christian thinker is not the pope and does not have a pope over him to decide authoritatively the extent of this perceiving and overcoming? Is not the nature of the basic view more clearly exposed, perhaps, if every man is called upon to be his own pope in virtue of the spirit that is alive within him as a member of the Christian community? And when A. E. Biedermann sets dogmatics the task of logically developing our experiential knowledge of the Christian act of faith and thus gaining autonomously an understanding of its nature, of the Christian principle (*Christl. Dogm.*, 1869, § 92), when he thinks he sees this Christian principle in the "religious personality of Jesus," i.e., in the reciprocal relation [259]
between God and man which is in Jesus the fact of His religious self-consciousness" (§ 99), when be thus calls the Bible the place where "in the first instance" (alongside it, as in Marheineke, Church tradition, i.e., the historical development, calls for consideration on the same level) the Christian principle is to be communicated by historical science in the "original form of the Christian faith" (§ 140), what does all this mean but that the relation of dogmatics to the Bible is understood as a dialectical circle whose course is determined by the dogmatician himself? He develops his experiential knowledge of the act of faith in just the same way as he controls (as historian) the Christian principle in so far as this meets him in the original biblical form of the Christian faith and in the development of the Church. There can be no confrontation by a *ἕτερος νόμος*[EN9] on this theory in spite of its acceptance of a historical point of reference. The Church of the present, which always has the Word of God already within itself, is left in splendid isolation. And it is only a secondary question of no great significance whether this isolation is the more impressively symbolised by the Roman Catholic establishment of an authoritative teaching office or by the obvious lack of any such teaching office in Protestant Modernism. The Roman pope infallibly interpreting the Bible and the Neo-Protestant professor of theology who bears the Christian principle or the Christian spirit no less surely in himself than he rediscovers it in the Bible are figures which perhaps stand out equally effectively against the same background.

With regard to this second possibility, too, there is no direct proof of its impossibility. If we were to presume to attempt such a proof we should as it were confound ourselves; we should ourselves prove *ipso facto*[EN10], not its impossibility, but in the closest accord with the adversary whom we are supposed to refute, its possibility. To prove that the juxtaposition of the Word of God and Church tradition is not just a relative one as maintained, that it is not a distinction within the Church of the present itself, that the Word of God in the Bible encounters and continually confronts Church proclamation as a judicial authority, that the Bible as this supreme authority which addresses the Church is not at all the Bible that is already dogmatically and historically interpreted by the pope or the professor but the Bible that is not yet interpreted, the free Bible, the Bible that remains free in face of all interpretation—to

EN 9 different law
EN10 by that very fact

prove that we should obviously have to put ourselves in a place above proclamation and the Bible, we should have to share the opinion that it is for us to make this relation clear, to order it one way or the other, and that we can establish the supremacy of the Word of God in this relation. But then the Bible whose supremacy we could establish would obviously not be the free Bible which constitutes an effective court. It would obviously have become a Bible interpreted already in a particular way, a Bible made over to us and thus put as an instrument in our hands. To that degree, even though we could perhaps prove its supremacy, it would still be only an element in the Church of the present which we ourselves constitute. We shall thus be on our guard against attempting this kind of proof. It could only prove the opposite of what it is
[260] supposed to prove. At this point we can only point to a fact, and in view of this fact, with no more proof than before, lodge an objection. The fact is again the significance that the Bible actually has in the Church irrespective of all theories about its significance.

It has this even in the Roman Church in spite of the fatal doctrine of the teaching office, and it has it also in Protestant Modernism in spite of the equally fatal doctrine of the spirit of the Christian community or the Christian principle.

It has never wholly lost the significance of a relative court over against the consciousness and proclamation of the present-day Church, the significance, so to speak, of a second voice which the Church has always wished to hear alongside its own voice and in harmony with it. Some care and concern for this harmony, for establishing and maintaining it, has never completely vanished. But this means that in spite of the theory, or in a fulfilment of the theory that was better than the theory itself, the possibility always remained, not that the Church would rule the Bible but that the Bible would rule the Church, that the controlling relation which is theoretically ordered so completely in favour of the Church or of man in the Church, that the relation of "over" and "in" the Church, could be completely reversed in practice. There remained at least the possibility of resistance by the free Bible which perhaps cannot be wholly taken captive by any interpretation. Even the Bible which seemed to be assimilated to the Church was never so completely assimilated that there was utter failure to call to awareness from time to time at least the relative distance between it and ourselves, that a complete denial of even the formal—and perhaps in fact the purely formal—distance as such was hazarded. The Bible found a voice and finds a voice *in* the Church. Hence the possibility is not ruled out that it may also find a voice *over against* the Church. Certainly this fact and the implied possibility are only a sign. The sign may be overlooked. The story of the Bible in the Church may be viewed and interpreted in such a way that the pope and the professor have always done as they wanted with the Bible. But we do not have to view and interpret it thus. Even if we do view and interpret it thus, we have to concede that it might be viewed and interpreted otherwise—not perhaps that it can be, but at any rate that it might be. The sign as such,

whether understood or not understood or however understood, cannot be refuted. Of course the sign as such is not an answer to the question whether the Bible is God's Word over the Church and to the Church. This question is the question of faith. How can it be answered by the existence of a sign? One cannot even say more generally that the question of faith is at least raised by the presence of the sign. One can only say that the question of faith might be put by the sign. In face of the sign it might happen that man in the Church is [261]
summoned to faith. It might happen that in the Bible whose voice still sounds in the Church man hears the Word of God, that he really hears the Word which cannot be held captive or bracketed by the Church, which cannot be integrated into the Church's own reality, which cannot by any interpretation be translated into a word of man, the Word which encounters the Church, with which the Church cannot sing a duet, but which it has simply to listen to as a full and unique solo. We cannot presuppose that this event, the event of faith, has happened. We can only relate to this event in so far as it is the content of the promise given to the Church or, as one might also say, of the command given to the Church. With reference to this event we cannot speak out of the present, the fulfilment, but only out of the recollection and the expectation. As this event takes place according to the promise, as the Church will be the Church of Jesus Christ, the Bible will be heard as God's Word. It is to this coming fulfilment of the promise received that we relate. The Word of God is the speech, the act, the mystery of God. It is not a demonstrable substance immanent in the Church and present within it apart from the event of its being spoken and heard. Thus the Church is not constantly or continuously the Church of Jesus Christ. It is this in the event of the Word of God being spoken to it and believed by it. Therefore the sign that is set up in the Church, the Bible speaking and being heard in some way, is a genuine sign, no less but also no more. If with reference to that event we could speak of a fulfilment that has already happened and is illuminating as such rather than of the promise and command of God, if we could speak of the present instead of the future, if we could argue from faith and with faith as though it were a present presupposition available to us, then the sign would cease to be a sign. Faith assumed to be present would dissolve the sign as such into a directly visible and perceptible datum. On the presupposition of that datum the Bible could then be understood directly as the Word of God. This datum with faith, or faith with this datum, would then constitute the proof of the Bible as God's Word. But by being adduced this proof would contradict what it is meant to prove.

It would lead us back exactly to where we began, namely, to the twofold construct of Roman Catholicism and Protestant Modernism. Nothing is more characteristic of either than the presupposition of the already enacted event of faith in the Word of God and therefore of an already present faith, a faith from and with which one can argue. By means of the presupposition the sign is there dissolved as a sign and therefore made possible as a proof, namely, the proof that the Word of God as an authority is not over the Church but in the

Church, that it is an authority which properly and finally is integrated into the Church and subordinated to it.

[262] The Word of God over the Church and to the Church will permit of no proof, not even and least of all this proof from the faith present in the Church. The conclusion that because I believe, and because for me as a believer the Bible is the Word of God, therefore and thus far it is God's Word, destroys the divinity of the Word of God, since it is no longer understood as the Word that stands over the Church and is directed to it. This conclusion involves *theologia gloriae*[EN11], which, in spite of its loud protestations to the contrary, does not in fact subject itself to God's Word. There is thus no question of this conclusion if the Bible is to be understood as the free and supreme criterion of Church proclamation. The reference with which this is done, the reference to the event of faith, or to God's Word being spoken and heard, does not claim to be a proof. The reference to this event does not mean that an argument is adduced, an argument operating with the ultimate force of the directly religious, an argument which puts us in a position to demonstrate the soundness of our position over against Roman Catholicism and Protestant Modernism, and to defend it by attack. We have to realise that the reference to this event might equally well be turned against ourselves, since we do not have the event in our own hands, since it is by nature a divine decision whose outcome we cannot anticipate. Whether the Bible will speak to us as God's Word, whether we will hear it, whether we will believe it as God's Word—we and those with whom we speak—is something we can neither appropriate to ourselves nor give to them. We cannot, then, presuppose it as something that has happened. We cannot argue from it and with it. What we might presuppose as our faith might even be God-forsaken unbelief and our arguing from it and with it might be powerless in the extreme. We can only point to the fact that in that event, in faith in God's Word in the Bible, a flat and irrefutable decision will be made against any view of the Bible as a court instituted and superintended by the Church, as a purely relative counter-authority to the Church proclamation of the day. Otherwise, if this decision were not made even as it takes place, it would not be this event. Now it is true, of course, that a direct pointer to this event does not achieve the reference now at issue. If we presumed to point to it directly, i.e., if we ourselves tried to come forward in the posture of Grünewald's John as witnesses to this event, we should be alleging what one ought never to think of alleging, namely, that we have its reality as it were behind us, that we are based upon it, that we can refute others by appealing to it. The word "pointer" would then be just another word for "presupposition." But we cannot speak either as prophets or as apostles. We cannot speak with the full assurance of the biblical witness: "We beheld his glory" (Jn. 1[14]). What we saw and what—we cannot say empowered us, but shall we simply say—caused us to give the pointer in question, the *ratio* of this pointer, is again very

---

[EN11] theology of glory

simply the Bible, not yet put out of the Church, not yet totally estranged from its proclamation, not yet divested of all its normativeness in relation to it, this [263] fact, this sign, as we said before. We relate to the event of faith by relating to this sign. That to which we point is thus itself a pointer. Both Roman Catholics and Modernists can and must grant that neither they nor we have fashioned and set up this sign, this pointer. But we have all found it there. Among perhaps many other signs in the Church that point in the same direction, there is in the Church which believes itself to be the Church of Jesus Christ at least this sign too, the voice of Moses and the prophets, of the Evangelists and the apostles, not completely unnoticed and not completely suppressed. What they say is the direct pointer to the event of the Word of God and faith: "We beheld his glory," and: "We have believed and known" (Jn. 6^{69}). We cannot say this in the same way of ourselves. For again we are not witnesses in the same sense as the prophets and apostles. But it is before our eyes and ears that they said it of themselves and claimed thereby to have spoken, not just a human word, but God's Word in human words, the Word which God Himself speaks to man, the Word in which God acts on man, the Word in which God's mystery is manifest. This is the sign of the Bible set up among us. And we may pay to this sign, i.e., to this utterance of the prophets and apostles, to the claim they make, the same attention, good or bad, that we do to other facts. We are in a position, and indeed we are summoned, to pay attention to it as we live in the sphere of the Church. What takes place when we perhaps do this is an act of recollection. Nothing in itself is changed if we do except that the world of our spiritual images is increased by another image. *Notitia*[EN12] has taken place; we have formed an *opinio historica*[EN13]. This does not make us prophets and apostles. It does not place us, then, in the reality of the Word and faith to which they bear witness. No development or enrichment of this image, no deepening of this recollection of ours, no systematic elucidation of its content, can bring us even a single step nearer the reality to which it points. Hence we do not refer to a method of actualisation that is placed in our hands or anyone else's hands along with the Bible when we for our part point to this sign, to this pointer that is given to us. Naturally we cannot do this pointing except as we already interpret the Bible, even if only very briefly, in a specific sense which is already our own. But this interpretation itself cannot make any other claim than that of drawing attention to the sign that has been set up as such. Interpretation itself can be only a pointer, not the discovery of the Holy Spirit or the Christian principle in the Bible, nor the mediation of the Word of God spoken in it. What may or may not take place over and above this indicating and being indicated, this recollection and *notitia*, the speech or silence of the Bible, the talking of the prophets and apostles *hic et nunc*[EN14] and the readiness of the

[EN12] understanding
[EN13] historical opinion
[EN14] here and now

[264] men of to-day to be talked to, the confirmation of the claim that this is God's Word, the decision taken, the event or non-event of faith—all this escapes our own view and grasp and that of every man. It is true by being true. It does not lie behind us but before us. Thus and only thus can we refer to it as to the decision against the relative validity and in favour of the absolute validity of the Bible as the Word of God, as the authentic and supreme criterion of Church proclamation and therefore of dogmatics as well. In making this reference we are acting as it were "irresponsibly." That is to say, we have not in any sense or in any way to answer for it that the Bible is really God's Word. Any desire to answer for it would be here a denial of what we would answer for. We can say no more than this, that the Bible can answer for itself in this matter. Just as we cannot say unequivocally, directly and generally that it does answer for itself, so we cannot say, nor can anyone say, that it cannot answer for itself. We say that it can, and in so doing we refer to the event of faith in which the decision is made that the Bible must speak and the Church must hear. If it is asked with what right we say this, we answer: By no right that we have and claim for ourselves, but by the right that proves itself to be such in the event of faith when it occurs. If we are asked why we do this, why we say No to the Roman Catholic and Modernist doctrine of the Word of God in the light of this possible self-responsibility of the Bible, our reply is that we as little know why we do this as we as we know why we got out of bed to-day with the right foot first rather than the left, and neither question finally applies to others in the same way. The fact is that we oppose the doctrine. If someone presses us and asks us whether it is an accident then that we make this objection, we would rather bite off our tongue than claim the Holy Spirit or our faith or our conscience or the like as that which grants us the required authorisation with people, and we shall answer that an accident comes from accidents. Thus it has perhaps befallen us that we should make and represent the opposition. Not because of me, but simply because there is this opposition, you have to deal with a modest fact and sign that makes no further claim. And if it is further said that this is then a secret appeal to a special grace, a Lutheran "I can do no other," a prophetic illumination, again we cheerfully reply: This opposition seeks to be nothing of all that, nothing special, no prophecy or apostolate, just a very earthly, harmless, ambivalent matter, devoid of all mystical splendour or mystery, just a little Protestantism, a sign to which we can give no signifying power, which may in fact be opposed or totally overlooked or misunderstood, and about whose unimportance among all the other signs in which the world and the Church are so rich we have no illusions. Is it a sign at all? That we can neither will nor know. With no motive or claim at all we can only act accordingly, i.e., raise our
[265] opposition. But in so doing, seeing we face the task of dogmatics, we decide, of course, to accept the Bible as the absolute authority set up over against Church proclamation. This opposition, which is simply mounted factually and with no validating proof in the light of the biblical sign, decides the point that dogmatics cannot be "dogmatics" in the sense of the Roman Catholic Church, i.e., the

development of the truths of revelation immanent in the Church, nor the "doctrine of faith" in the sense of Protestant Modernism, i.e., the exposition of the faith of the men united in the Church. This opposition implies that the possibility of seeing God's Word as an entity distinct from Church proclamation is given to us—as we have seen, actually as a possibility—in the fact that the Bible is read in the Church, and we refer to this fact when, not in Roman Catholic or Modernist but in Protestant fashion, i.e., in opposition, we take practical account of this possibility. Presupposing this opposition in the strictest sense, we imply thereby that dogmatics as the question of the Word of God in Church proclamation must be the critical question as to the agreement of Church proclamation, not with a norm of human truth or human value (the first possibility in our dilemma), nor with a standard of divine truth already known and proclaimed by the Church (the second possibility), but with the revelation attested in Holy Scripture. This is the specific point of the question of the Word of God which has to be put in dogmatics. In the light of § 4 we may also say that the task of dogmatics is to deal with the problem of the equation of the Word of God and the word of man in its form as Church proclamation with a view to the confirmation of this equation, and it does this by measuring Church proclamation as man's word by the second form of the Word of God, i.e., Holy Scripture, in so far as this itself is in turn witness to its third and original form, revelation.

Because and to the extent that dogmatics has this task, it is called dogmatics, *theologia dogmatica*[EN15]. Our translation of this is not "the science of dogmas" but "the science of dogma." Dogma is the agreement of Church proclamation with the revelation attested in Holy Scripture. Dogmatics enquires into this agreement and therefore into dogma. This brings us into conflict with the Roman Catholic definition of the terms dogma and dogmatics. According to this view a dogma is a truth of revelation defined by the Church and dogmatics is the collection of these dogmas and commentary on them.

The word "dogma" (cf. for what follows A. Deneffe, S.J., "*Wort und Begriff*," *Scholastik*, 1931, 381 f. and 505 f.) meant primarily in the usage of pagan antiquity and also of the Greek Old and New Testaments an order, statute, or decree. Thus the law of the Medes and Persians according to which Daniel was put in the lions' den is a dogma according to Dan. 6^{16}. The decree issued by Caesar Augustus in Lk. 2^{1} is also a dogma. The statutes of the OT Law are dogmas according to Eph. 2^{15} and Col. 2^{14}. But a second meaning of the term in antiquity [266]
also calls for consideration. The philosophical or the more generally academic principle of an individual teacher, school, or movement is a dogma. It is in the second rather than the first sense that the word, almost always used in the plural, seems already in the 2nd century (first in Ignatius of Ant., *Ad Magn.* 13, 1) to have passed into the usage of the Greek Church as a term for Christian truths. But Cyprian, Tertullian, Ambrose, Augustine, Leo the Great and Gregory the Great still did not know it or were not prepared to use it in this sense, and it is indeed rarely employed in this sense by Thomas Aquinas. Right up to our own time the very opposite sense has competed with it (cf. already Iren., *C. o. h.* I, 31, 3; this is perhaps the

---

[EN15] dogmatic theology

only one Augustine knew). According to this view dogmas, distinguished as such by all kinds of uncomplimentary adjectives, are the false teachings of pagans or heretics. (Leo XIII can still speak of the *prava dogmata Socialistarum*[EN16] in the Encyclical "*Quod Apostolici*" of Dec. 28, 1878.) From the 16th century, however, the term seems to have come into use with systematic emphasis in the second of the meanings given above (in the sense of *dogma fidei, dogma catholicum, dogma Ecclesiae*[EN17]). At all events, it is only along these lines that there have been serious theological attempts to define the concept in the Roman Catholic Church. Deneffe (*op. cit.*, p. 531), in agreement with Diekamp and Bartmann, sums up the results in the proposition: Dogma is *veritas a Deo formaliter revelata et ab Ecclesia sive solemniter* (by *ex cathedra* decision or conciliar degree) *sive ordinarie*[EN18] (by the fact that it has been generally taught in the Church without opposition) *definita.* (As against R. Seeberg, *Lehrbuch der Dogmengeschichte*, Vol. 1, 3rd edn., 1920, 1, we thus have to say that the Church's formal acknowledgment of the propositions in question does not exhaust the concept of Church dogma.) On the Roman Catholic view the systematic exposition of these revealed truths is then dogmatics. (Cf. Bartmann, *Lehrbuch d. Dogm.*, 7th edn., Vol. I, 1928, 2; Diekamp, *Kath. Dogm.*, 6th edn., Vol. I, 1930, 1). On the Evangelical side R. Rothe (*Zur Dogm.*, 1863, 14) understood the task of dogmatics in the same sense.

We may begin by stating that we recognise that there are dogmas in the sense of this definition, though naturally we shall have to explain more fully why we do this. In a later section of the Prolegomena we shall have to deal with dogmas, i.e., with the doctrinal propositions acknowledged and confessed by the Church and deposited in its symbols, with their relative authority and with their importance for dogmatics. At the same time—and this is our first objection to the Roman Catholic view of dogmas and dogmatics—we must deny that dogmas constitute the goal of dogmatic work or that dogmatics is called dogmatics on their account. For dogmas are not *veritates a Deo formaliter revelatae*[EN19]. In dogmas it is the Church of the past that speaks. This is venerable. It deserves respect. It is normative. It speaks *non sine Deo*[EN20], as is fitting. Yet it is still the Church. In dogmas the Church defines, i.e., limits revealed truth, the Word of God. The Word of God thus becomes the word of man. It is not an insignificant word. Indeed, it is a supremely significant word. Yet it is still the word of man. The Word of God is above dogma as the heavens are above the earth.

The proximity of *dogmata ecclesiastica*[EN21] to *dogmata haereticorum*[EN22] should be enough to remind us of the basic vulnerability of the dogma defined by the Church and also to ward off
[267] the idea of an infallible dogma of this kind. It may also be pointed out that according to Roman Catholic teaching itself not all dogmas have yet been confessed or defined by the Church, that even if revealed truth is substantially closed there is still dogmatic progress (cf.

EN16 misguided teachings of the Socialists
EN17 the teaching of the faith, catholic teaching, the teaching of the Church
EN18 a truth that has been formally revealed by God and offically defined by the Church, either by solemn declaration (papal decision *ex cathedra* or conciliar decree) or in an ordinary way
EN19 truths formally revealed by God
EN20 not without God
EN21 church dogmas
EN22 the dogmas of the heretics

Diekamp, *op. cit.*, p. 15), and that ultimately it is the material content (*sensus*[EN23]) rather than the formula that is said to be the unchangeable and infallible truth in dogmatic formulations (Bartmann, *op. cit.*, p. 38). There is perhaps an admission of the human character of dogmas in this explanation. Nevertheless, it is always the Church itself that is the subject of the expected dogmatic progress, and the *sensus* which is to be distinguished from the formulae can only be the *sensus, quem tenuit ac tenet sancta mater Ecclesia*[EN24] (*Conc. Vatic. I, Constit. dogm., De fide cath., cap.* 2). There can never be here any real disputing of dogmas, or of the Church which proclaims and elucidates them. There can never be any clear and serious distinction between dogmas and the Word of God.

In the identification of the Word of God and Church dogma as we find it in this definition of the term we can only see an example of the splendid isolation in which a church must find itself when it has seized the Word of God for itself, taken it under its own management, and lost the capability of listening to the voice of another. If in dogmatics this voice from without is to be heard as the criterion of what the Church says and does, then dogmatics cannot stop at the question of Church dogmas, nor can Church dogmas be the form in which it hears the voice from without. Otherwise dogmatics on this side too would just be a dialogue of the Church with itself, of the Church of to-day with the Church of yesterday and the day before. In the context of God's dialogue with the Church this dialogue of the Church with itself can also take on significance. As we shall still have to show in principle, there will also have to be in dogmatics this dialogue of the Church of to-day with the Church of yesterday and the day before. But if dogmatics tries to stop at this, it certainly cannot do justice to its task as the discharge of the Church's responsibility to the Word of God. Indeed, it has not even taken up this task at all. The dogma which dogmatics investigates cannot, then, be the *veritas ab Ecclesia definita*[EN25]. The *veritas ab Ecclesia definita* is itself the question of dogma. It can and should guide dogmatics. But it cannot seek to be the dogma which is the goal of dogmatics.

Our second point must be that while the dogma which dogmatics investigates is not the truth of revelation, it aims at the truth of revelation. The same may be said of the dogmas of the Church, which we shall not be dealing with more specifically at this juncture. These are propositions which grasp and reproduce the truth of revelation only to the extent that they strive after it.

Even Thomas Aquinas follows a definition of the concept of the *articulus fidei*[EN26], and therefore of the individual, concrete Church dogma, which was given by Isidore of Seville: *Articulus est perceptio divinae veritatis tendens in ipsam*[EN27] (*S. th.* II,[2] *qu.* 1, *art.* 6).

The epitome of all possible propositions of this kind, that which all dogmas [268]
are saying in their striving after the truth of revelation, is the dogma which

[EN23] meaning
[EN24] the meaning which Holy Mother Church has held and holds
[EN25] truth defined by the Church
[EN26] article of faith
[EN27] An article is a perception of divine truth that inclines toward it

dogmatics investigates. When we call it the epitome of all propositions of this kind, we are saying already that it is not itself a proposition, that it is not proclaimed by any church. Dogma is what is intended in all possible propositions of this kind. It is the dogma for the sake of which the Church proclaims dogmas. Dogma is the essence of which dogmas and also dogmatic propositions, i.e., the propositions of dogmatic science, claim to be phenomena, the essence from which real dogmas and real dogmatic propositions may arise, i.e., when they are modelled on it. For the sake of dogma dogmatics must deal with dogmas. Dogmas call upon it to pay attention to dogma. They direct it, in the way that the Church can direct it, to the question of dogma. At a third and lowest stage dogmatics then builds its own scientifically dogmatic propositions. Dogmatic propositions, dogmas and dogma have this in common: They are not the truth of revelation. Dogma aims at the truth of revelation and dogmas and dogmatic propositions seek to do so (and do, with the proviso that by the grace of God they come to do so through watching and prayer). Dogma in the true and original sense as the epitome of all dogmas and dogmatic propositions is a concept of relation, and on the basis of it so, too, are dogmas and dogmatic propositions. The only difference in their case is that there is the proviso whether they are realised concepts of relation, i.e., concepts of a relation that is really present. What this relation is we know already; we refer to the relation of the agreement of Church proclamation with the Bible as the Word of God. One may thus define dogma as Church proclamation to the degree that it really agrees with the Bible as the Word of God. To know dogma and to have dogma is to know and have the Word of God itself in a specific and specifically demonstrable form and manifestation of Church proclamation, for dogma is Church proclamation that is really in agreement with the Word of God. But a theology claiming to know and have dogma would be a *theologia gloriae*[EN28], which the dogmatics of the Church ought not to seek to be. What it is faced with is always actual Church proclamation in the whole humanity of its form and manifestation on the one hand and on the other hand the sign set up in the Church, the promise and command of the Bible. And the task it is set is to ask about the Word of God in the proclamation of the Church and therefore to ask about dogma, the necessary orientation of Church proclamation to the Bible as the Word of God. Every answer, every actualisation of this orientation and agreement, can only be one of two things, either the event of the Word of God itself which dogmatics can neither presuppose, postulate, nor effect, or one of the great illusions and prolepses of a dogmatics unaware of the fact there can be no presupposing, postulating or effecting of this event.
[269] Thus the real results of dogmatics, even though they have the form of the most positive statements, can themselves only be new questions, questions to and fro between what the Church seems to proclaim and the Bible seems to want proclaimed, questions which can be put only with the greatest modesty and a

[EN28] theology of glory

sense of supreme vulnerability if they are perhaps serious and significant questions. If questioning ceased, if dogma itself came on the scene instead of dogmas and dogmatic propositions, if the agreement of specific Church proclamation with the Word of God and therefore the Word of God itself in this specific Church proclamation could be demonstrated, then dogmatics would be at an end along with the *ecclesia militans*[EN29], and the kingdom of God would have dawned. The second possibility of the appearing of dogma or the Word of God itself can only be that of great illusions and prolepses.

To this extent one may call dogma an "eschatological concept," as I myself did in the first edition of this book (p. 112, 123).

The older Lutheran theology (e.g., Quenstedt, *Theol. did.-pol.*, 1685, I, *cap.* 1, *sect.* 1, *thes.* 3–14) made a pertinent distinction between the *theologia archetypos*[EN30] which God has and indeed Himself is, and the *theologia ektypos*[EN31] which apart from Christ according to his human nature and the angels men may also have. The *theologia hominum*[EN32] which is possible for us is then divided again into the *theologia patriae*[EN33] in eternal redemption and the *theologia viatorum*[EN34] in present temporality. In this temporality there is also another distinction *ante* and *post lapsum*[EN35], and then *post lapsum* we have *theologia naturalis*[EN36] and *theologia supranaturalis*[EN37], and in the latter there is *theologia immediatae* and *mediatae revelationis*[EN38], the former that of the prophets, apostles and Evangelists alone, the latter ours as we are directed to their writings. This theology of ours, the *theologia ektypos mediatae revelationis hominum viatorum post lapsum*[EN39], can then obviously be seen once again from two angles. On the one side it may be seen in the appropriate relation to its prototype, *theologia immediatae revelationis*[EN40], a revelation which is hidden and future for us, which we cannot achieve, and which is thus the object of our enquiry. In this case and to this degree it is dogma. On the other side it may be seen in its performance as the concrete dogmatic work which is done by the Church and in the Church in time and at specific times, the enquiry into the relation which is laid upon us for the sake of Church proclamation. In this case and to this degree we are to understand by *theologia ektypos mediatae revelationis hominum viatorum post lapsum* Church dogma on the one hand and that which occupies us here, the scientific work of dogmatics, on the other.

We shall now have to put a third question to the Roman Catholic concept of dogma and dogmatics, namely, whether the fact that the term "dogma" was adopted into the Church's vocabulary in the sense of doctrinal proposition rather than that of "command" or "decree," which is more readily suggested by biblical usage, is not the symptom of a false development of very early origin.

EN29 church militant
EN30 prototypal theology
EN31 ectypal theology
EN32 human theology
EN33 theology of the fatherland
EN34 theology on the way
EN35 before and after the fall
EN36 natural theology
EN37 supernatural theology
EN38 theology of direct and of indirect revelation
EN39 ectypal theology of indirect revelation done by humans on the way after the fall
EN40 the theology of direct revelation

Assuming that Church dogma is to be equated with *veritas revelata*[EN41]—that it aims at the truth of revelation we too admit—does it follow that *veritas revelata* is the truth of a doctrinal proposition? Is the truth of revelation—we must
[270] press the question—like other truths in the sense that it may be established as ἀλήθεια[EN42], i.e., as the manifestation of something hidden, in human ideas, concepts and judgments, that it may be, as it were, conserved in this restricted and specialised form, that it can be had as truth apart from the event of its being manifested? Such is obviously the case with the truth of a doctrinal proposition. But will the truth of revelation submit to such materialisation and depersonalisation? Can one have it in abstraction from the person of Him who reveals it and from the revelatory act of this person in which it is given to other persons to perceive? Can the possession of this truth take place otherwise than again in an act on the part of the person who perceives it, in a decision, i.e., in the adoption of a position? If the truth of revelation is the truth of a doctrinal proposition, then obviously the answer is Yes.

The truth of a doctrinal proposition can be viewed neutrally as neutral truth. It may also happen, of course, that one agrees or disagrees. But it is no part of its nature to require decision. Nor is adoption of a position an essential part of encounter with it. The Roman Catholic definition of dogma as doctrinal proposition actually excludes this. That dogma as such is only doctrine and not also command is not clear in the usage of the fathers of the 2nd and 3rd centuries nor in Eusebius and Athanasius in the 4th century. But it is clear in Cyril of Jerusalem, Gregory of Nyssa and Cyril of Alexandria, in whom dogma as the doctrine of the faith and dogma as command are kept apart as two distinct entities (cf. Deneffe, *op. cit.*, pp. 508–13). One of the most prominent characteristics of Roman Catholic dogmatics results from the fact that it not only equates dogma with *veritas revelata* but also equates *veritas revelata* with the truth of a doctrinal proposition. We have already touched on this at an earlier point. Roman Catholic dogmatics is theory *qua* theory and for the sake of theory. To be sure, it is accepted theory. By nature, however, it is pure theory according to the prevailing Thomist conception. Theory *qua* theory means that the affirmation of the *veritas revelata* is the judgment of a thinker who as such is not forced into this judgment or its opposite. In itself, it is not primarily a demand for this judgment or the constraint to adopt a position. It is pure, neutral truth. It is true in itself in the established and developed form of the proposition and then it is true for us, whatever our attitude may be, in the form of perception and understanding of the proposition in question. Theory for the sake of theory means that the theory, contemplation of the *veritas revelata*, has its goal and end in itself. There does not have to be a corresponding act, and it certainly cannot be regarded as an act itself. The whole linking of dogmatics to Church proclamation as we presuppose it here is already contrary to Roman Catholicism for the simple reason that in Roman Catholic dogmatics the search for a dogmatic task outside dogmatics itself is just as impossible as is the search for the special task of mystics, angels, or the blessed in heaven in their vision of God. The task which awaits the Roman Catholic dogmatician can only be that of grasping and expounding in its integrated wealth the divinely ordered world of specific spiritual matters that God has revealed once and for all in the *veritates revelatae*[EN43] (cf. on this E. Peterson, "*Über die Forderung einer Theologie des Glaubens,*" *Z.d.Z.*, 1925, 282).

[EN41] revealed truth
[EN42] truth (literally: un-concealedness)
[EN43] revealed truths

The very reserve with which one can confront the truth of a doctrinal proposition, the possibility of a purely theoretical attitude to it, and, in objective correspondence to this possibility, the idea of a purely material and impersonal presence of truth in the proposition—this is what makes the equation of *veritas revelata* and the doctrinal proposition suspect, and more than suspect, in our view. [271]

We might ask for a moment—and it is instructive to do so—whether our suspicions would not also be roused if we pursued the second Roman Catholic equation in virtue of which Church dogma is identified as *veritas revelata*. Even on Roman Catholic soil would not the question arise whether *veritas revelata* and therefore Church dogma can be a truth detachable from the person of the God who speaks and who acts by speaking, a truth which does not as such force to decision, to action, a truth whose acceptance as such does not mean decision or service in a task lying outside itself? In dealing with a neutral truth of this kind which allows him to be neutral too, is man really dealing with God? Can a doctrinal proposition as such really be regarded as God's Word? Even and especially on Roman Catholic soil, if dogma is equated with God's Word, will it not have to be understood primarily as command in accordance with the usage of the Bible which was at least possible in the fathers of the first centuries too? Will it not have to be understood as a truth that we can have as truth only as it is spoken to us by God and only as encounter with it is impossible without decision for a specific attitude to what is spoken to us? Will it not have to be understood as a dogma which is also a doctrinal proposition (there is no cause to rule out this meaning; why should we? Why should not a command too, and especially a command, be able to teach us?), but a doctrinal proposition which can teach us and be a dogma only to the extent that it goes out from God as the "dogma" went out from Caesar Augustus, as a decree goes out, and comes to us in the act of obedience (or does not come to us, does not teach us, does not exist for us as a dogma, in the act of disobedience), i.e., comes to us or does not come to us as a command, goes out in a divine decision and comes to us in a human decision? But we have to realise, of course, that we can enter the Roman Catholic sphere with this question or this proposal only to leave it again at once, or if we find a hearing in Roman Catholic territory with this question it will cease to be Roman Catholic territory. For is it not inevitable that this question or proposal will call in question at once the presupposed Roman Catholic equation between Church dogma and *veritas revelata*?

According to the Roman Catholic view Church dogma must have primarily the character of a doctrinal proposition in order that it may be an object of contemplation and in order that its truth may escape being made problematical either by the position adopted towards it by men or by God Himself. In a way that its character as command could not do but would rather endanger, its character as doctrinal proposition is supposed to guarantee its objectivity, its intrinsic truth, and therefore its credibility as *veritas revelata*. Roman Catholic theology would rather accept the materialising and depersonalising of revealed truth that is entailed [272] when dogma is understood as doctrinal proposition; it would rather make a virtue of necessity and declare that its very materiality and impersonality, its very abstraction from all human and divine decision, the non-paradoxical disclosure which it expresses as a proposition, are the things that characterise and accredit dogma as the truth of revelation; it would rather say this than abandon the equation. Roman Catholic theology stands or falls with the equation, with the presupposition that revealed truth is given to the Church in the form of dogmas (not in this form alone, but in this form too), that it has it and has to guard it as such, that it must be concerned theologically for its validation as such, for the credibility of its intrinsic truth. It has to make a virtue of the necessity. Or rather, the necessity is no real necessity for it. It not only accepts this; as Roman Catholic theology it wills from the very first everything that the character of dogma as doctrinal proposition entails. Only in our view and not in that of Roman Catholic theology is what happened to the word "dogma" a false development. On its view it all had to turn out as it did. It would have to betray itself if it were to come back again to the question whether the sense of command or decree should not be proposed for "dogma" and whether this would not be of decisive significance for its understanding as doctrinal proposition. If our question or proposal in this regard is taken seriously, as seriously as we naturally intend it; if the teaching of dogma is really to be understood as a command (and not the command, which is naturally not denied by Roman Catholic theology, as a doctrine for contemplation), then it will be immediately apparent that the dogma established by the Church itself cannot be this command but can only be a serious recollection of this command.

A command is what it is only in the act of the one who gives it and the one who obeys or disobeys it. One cannot give oneself a command in the way the Church gives itself Church dogmas. Nor can one have the truth of doctrine that can be received by a command in the way the Church has the truth of its dogmas. If *veritas revelata* is a command, it cannot be identical with Church dogma. Church dogma and *veritas revelata* necessarily part company. We must therefore withdraw, realising that there is no place for our concern on Roman Catholic soil.

Or rather we must say polemically that the impossibility of the Roman Catholic equation of the truth of revelation and Church dogma is betrayed for us by the fact that hereby the truth of revelation has to become what it has become in Roman Catholicism. The material and impersonal intrinsic truth ascribed to dogma, the contemplative objectivity which is the issue in Roman Catholic theology when it emphasises the sense of doctrinal proposition in the concept of dogma, this is for us the mark of a truth which is conditioned and limited not merely by the creatureliness of man but also by his sinfulness, a truth in comparison with which the truth of God in His revelation is quite different. By the very fact that as a proposition it can only be contemplated, that it is neutral and permits neutrality, that as a theory—and who can deny that Church dogma is this too?—it bears witness itself to where it belongs, namely, to the Church, its talk, its testimonies, its proclamation, its dialogue with itself—all this with great distinction, for it is not our intention to disparage Church dogma on this its proper level—and yet still to the Church and not the Word in which God addresses the Church. We do not understand and we can never understand how the truth that is put in the hands of the Church as Church dogma can be the truth of God. What we think we know as the truth of God's Word from the witness of Holy Scripture is a very different truth, a sovereign truth.

[273] Our recalling of the older use of dogma does not mean, then, that we want to equate Church dogma as command with the Word of God. To the extent that Church dogma is command—and in our view it should be pointed out that on the basis of the Old and New

Testaments it would have been more natural to introduce the word into the Church's vocabulary chiefly in this sense—it is a human command, a command of sinners even if of sinners assembled in the Church, and as such a command which is surrounded and permeated by all the ambiguity and frailty and corruption of human commanding. Heaven is as high above Church dogma regarded as command as it is above Church dogma regarded as proposition, and we are not thinking of putting the Church in possession of God's Word by the detour of this second, or rather this first, meaning of the word. On the other hand, recollection of this first meaning of the word can shed significant light on our understanding of the concept of dogma about which dogmatics asks, on our understanding of the agreement of Church proclamation with the Word of God in Holy Scripture. Remembering this first meaning of the word, we shall have to understand the relation implicit in this concept of dogma as the relation between command and obedience and only then and in this way as also the relation between doctrine and instruction. The agreement of Church proclamation with the Word of God naturally means the truth of Church proclamation as well. But truth cannot be the last word about this agreement. For what truth is must be measured by what is higher here, what God's will is. His Word goes out to the Church of assembled sinners as the Word of the Lord whose knowledge must be worked out in the form of acknowledgment. In logical if not temporal priority it must first be believed and only then and in that way can it be known as truth. *Credo ut intelligam*[EN44].

The Roman Catholic Church itself has finely expressed this in the formula: *Credimus non propter intrinsecam rerum veritatem naturali rationis lumine perspectam, sed propter auctoritatem ipsius Dei revelantis, qui nec falli nec fallere potest*[EN45] (*Conc. Vatic. I, Constit. dogm. de fide cath., cap.* 3). To be sure the *auctoritas*[EN46] is also *veritas*[EN47], but what makes it credible is not that it is *veritas*, but that it is *auctoritas.*

It would be knowledge of real dogma if we knew a form of Church proclamation which was appropriate to the will of God, in which the command of God to the Church was fulfilled, in which the faith of the Church was co-extensive with the order of its Lord. Then and to that extent it would also be perfect truth in comparison with which all other truth that it might have otherwise than in fulfilling the divine command could not make it real dogma but would rather be shown to need the enquiry into dogma, since it would always be untruth when measured by it. Now seeing that knowledge of real dogma will [274] never take place before the end of all things, this must be the point of our enquiry into dogma. It is not in the first instance the enquiry of a pupil who is anxious that his thoughts should agree with the superior thoughts of his teacher. It is primarily the question of a servant who has to ask whether his actions agree with his master's intentions and who undoubtedly in so doing will also learn something that he did not know before. When we call the dogma into which dogmatics enquires a concept of relation, we mean that it is

---

EN44 I believe in order to understand

EN45 We do not believe because the intrinsic truth of things is perceived by the natural light of reason, but because of the authority of God Himself who reveals them, who can neither deceive nor be deceived

EN46 authority

EN47 truth

the concept of a relation which exists between a demand and the decision corresponding to the demand. Dogma is the relation between the God who commands and the man who obeys His command, the relation which takes place in the event of this commanding and obeying. Hence it is not an *opus supererogationis*[EN48], a luxury, an academic game, when dogmatics is pursued in the Church. It is not at all the case that the Church carries on its proclamation properly, in good faith, and according to God's will, and then occasionally the question arises—and perhaps it is only the question of certain people with a particular intellectual interest—whether and how far this proclamation is true, and dogmatics comes into being to meet this need. It is not the case that in regard to the obedience of the Church in its proclamation everything is for the best and only a "thinking through" or explication of the faith is lacking, only the cry for a world-view, for the relating of this intrinsically excellent faith to knowledge, is unsatisfied, and along with all the other things the Church offers dogmatics must also be offered by someone somewhere to meet the demand of curiosity or the supposed need for credibility. No, the fact is that what is under debate in dogmatics is the Church's fundamental relation of obedience to its Lord in respect of its proclamation. It is not a matter of offering a little truth to those who feel especially uneasy on this score while in all else they are as satisfied as all the rest. It is a matter of the will of God whose acknowledgment or non-acknowledgment in the Church's proclamation is something that should truly unsettle the whole Church, the Church as such and in all its members. The Church stands or falls with the object of dogmatic enquiry. Hence it has to undertake this enquiry. It cannot pursue dogmatics or not pursue it. A dogmatics which it might not pursue, in whose enquiry it did not wholly participate as in the enquiry about its whole existence, a dogmatics which might let itself be crowded into the corner of religious intellectuals or the intellectually religious, could only be a poor, useless and tedious dogmatics which it would be better not to pursue at all. We pursue dogmatics because, constrained by the fact of the Bible, we cannot shake off the question of the obedience of Church proclamation. The question of its obedience includes that of
[275] its truth. But the question of its truth can be put only as the question of its obedience. As the question of its obedience it is the question of dogma.

2. DOGMATICS AS A SCIENCE

At an earlier point (§ 1, 1) we argued that when theology generally, and with it dogmatics, understands and describes itself as a science, it does not do so in principle, i.e., it does not raise the claim as one by whose recognition it will stand or fall, but it raises it without being able or even desiring to argue and

---

[EN48] work of supererogation

justify it before an external tribunal. It does not recognise the need to understand and legitimate itself as a science at all. Nor does it recognise as normative for itself the general concept of science that is authoritative to-day. Nor does it recognise any obligation to oppose to this another concept which will include and therefore justify itself. It understands and describes itself as a science because it has no interest in *de facto* self-segregation from the other human efforts at knowledge that bear this name, because it must protest against a concept of science that would exclude its own effort at knowledge, because it accepts a hidden but coming and therefore real unity of all such human efforts, because, one might also say, it affirms the Church as the hidden yet very real sphere of all such efforts. What it means by science when it calls itself a science, it defines in responsibility to the Church which it serves—and which the other sciences can and should and ultimately and conclusively will serve—in responsibility to its object and to the task imposed by this object. For it realises for one thing that in its question about dogma, i.e., about the agreement of Church proclamation with the Word of God, it has to tread a defined path of knowledge, a path defined by this particular problem. And then it realises, too, that it has to submit to itself, i.e., everyone who has a share in it, an account regarding this path of knowledge. In this twofold inner obligation to itself consists the concrete significance of its claim to be a science, which it cannot prove externally before the forum of a general concept of science. Its scientific character consists in its orientation, in its conscious orientation, in what must always be its conscious orientation, to the question of dogma which is raised by the existence of the Church. When the enquiry is pressed with this orientation, or, as we might also say, with this objectivity, then dogmatics takes place as a science.

At this point we must make a relative distinction; there is a regular dogmatics and an irregular dogmatics.

By regular dogmatics we mean an enquiry into dogma which aims at the completeness appropriate to the special task of the school, of theological instruction. If it is to be a good school, the theological school must offer training in independent enquiry into dogma. For this reason it must be as complete [276]
as possible. It must impress on the student how one question breaks up into many questions and how in every respect and from every possible standpoint all these many questions are in fact open and interrelated. Thus a regular or academic dogmatics must cover the whole field in respect of the range of concepts and themes that are significant for Church proclamation, in respect of the biblical witness in which this proclamation has its concrete criterion, in respect of orientation to the history of dogmas and dogmatics, i.e., to the concrete forms of Church proclamation existing thus far, in respect of real and possible difficulties and contradictions that one will find in every individual question, and finally in respect of the implicit and explicit distinctness of the path of knowledge. These are the demands which naturally arise if dogmatics is to be taught and if this instruction is to be planned guidance, i.e., guidance

to independent dogmatic work, and not just the imparting of the specific results of the work of a specific teacher.

Origen's *Περὶ ἀρχῶν*, the great "*Discourse*" of Gregory of Nyssa, the *Catecheses* of Cyril of Jerusalem, Augustine's *Enchiridion* and the *Ἔκδοσις ἀκριβὴς τῆς ὀρθ. πίστ.* of John of Damascus are dogmatic works in this sense in the early Church, while in the Middle Ages we have the writings of Anselm of Canterbury (as a whole and according to their intent), the *Sentences* of Peter Lombard, and naturally the *Summas* of the great Dominicans and Franciscans. The increasingly academic character which one unmistakably finds in the Scholastics as compared with the fathers is repeated in the Evangelical world when one compares the regular dogmatic works of the Reformation period itself (Melanchthon's *Loci*, at least in the later editions, Zwingli's *Commentarius de vera et falsa religione* and especially Calvin's *Institutio*) with the orthodoxy of especially the 17th century, which was so very industrious and fruitful in producing both comprehensive text-books and compendious outlines, and which was opposed by a Roman Catholic theology by no means inferior in learning. A slow but clear decline began with the 18th century. Roman Catholic dogmatics recovered from this after the middle of the 19th century, chiefly by a common and deliberate return to Thomas Aquinas. Thanks to the achievement of Schleiermacher, and under his influence, e.g., in the works of A. Schweizer, A. E. Biedermann and J. A. Dorner, Evangelical dogmatics enjoyed a new golden age even before the Roman Catholic revival. But this incontestable formal rise of Evangelical dogmatics in the first half of the 19th century had too little inner necessity, was too little due to a fresh understanding of the matter of Evangelical theology, was too much impelled by a mere acceptance of the achievements of contemporary philosophy, and in this connexion was too much influenced by a wholesale surrender of the theme of Evangelical theology, to be able to stand the test. It was a tired age that thought it could see a gleam of hope in the theology of A. Ritschl, which in the event merely reached back over Idealism and Romanticism to the quintessence of the Enlightenment. The end of the spasmodic concentration that made the dogmatics of this school impressive for a time was simply an individualistic simplification and abridgement of all questions which has given a journalistic impress to modern Evangelical dogmatics even as compared with its own past in the age before Ritschl.
[277] To see what is meant one should compare, say; the *Glaubenslehre* of Troeltsch, the leading figure of the post-Ritschlian period, with the dogmatics of A. E. Biedermann or the achievement of a follower of that age like H. Lüdemann, who is so worthy of respect in his own way. Let us be under no illusions; this decline has not been arrested even to-day. In terms of academic exactitude, nothing we are producing now can stand comparison with the achievements of mediaeval and post-Reformation dogmatics, nor with Idealistic dogmatics, nor with Thomistic, let alone with the dogmatics of the Reformation. Would that we had even reached the point where we again regarded regular dogmatics as at least an admonitory ideal worth striving after!

It is part of the human reality of the Church that there has to be in it not just theology but also the theological school or the theology of the school (*theologia scholastica*), i.e., the theology which is practised not just for free intellectual exchange but also for instruction. It was a fateful theological error, for which Anabaptist spiritualism must share some blame, to think that this could be dispensed with. If we face the fact of the Church's humanity, we cannot release it from the task of pursuing academic theology and we must thus accept in principle the task of a regular dogmatics.

By irregular dogmatics, on the other hand, we mean the enquiry into dogma in which there is no primary thought of the task of the school and there is thus no primary concern for the completeness mentioned above. Dogmatics as free discussion of the problems that arise for Church proclamation from the standpoint of the question of dogma can and must be pursued in the Church outside the theological school and apart from its special task. Such free dogmatics existed before there was the regular dogmatics of the school, and it will always have its own necessity and possibility alongside this. It will differ from it by the fact that it does not cover the whole ground with the same consistency, whether in respect of Church proclamation itself, the decisive biblical witness, the history of dogma, detailed systematics, or strictness and clarity of method. Perhaps for specific historical reasons it will take up a specific theme and focus on it. Perhaps it will be relatively free in relation to the biblical basis or its choice of partners in discussion. Perhaps it will be more of an exposition of results, and will take the form of theses or aphorisms, and will observe only partially or not at all the distinction between dogmatics and proclamation. Perhaps it will leave much to be desired as regards the explicit or implicit distinctness of its path of knowledge. In one respect or another, or even in many or all respects, it will be, and will mean to be, a fragment, and it will have to be evaluated as such.

The dogmatic work that has come down to us from the early Church, even from the pens of its most significant and learned representatives, is not for the most part regular dogmatics but irregular dogmatics in the sense described. In distinction from Origen and John of Damascus, Athanasius wrote no true dogmatics. Luther in contrast to Melanchthon and Calvin was a typical irregular dogmatician. From the more recent and less classical past one [278]
might also recall men like J. G. Hamann, G. Mencken, H. F. Kohlbrügge, J. C. Blumhardt, and H. Kutter, whose work undoubtedly belongs formally to this category. From early times and on into our own day irregular dogmatics has been produced in dogmatic treatises, Bible commentaries, historical accounts, sermons, pamphlets and other forms of what is called devotional literature. Tacitly or even openly everyone does a little irregular dogmatics if he is interested in the problem of dogmatics but does not have the call or the desire or the time or the equipment to take part in regular dogmatics. On the whole it must be admitted that in spite of its name irregular dogmatics has been the rule, and regular dogmatics the exception, in every age of the Church. It should also be noted that regular dogmatics has always had its origin in irregular dogmatics, and could never have existed without its stimulus and co-operation.

If we keep clearly in view the complete difference between the two both materially and historically, we shall be on guard against overhasty estimation or disparagement of either the one or the other. In particular we shall refrain from immediately ascribing a scientific character to regular dogmatics and a non-scientific character to irregular dogmatics. If the scientific nature of dogmatics lies in its special objectivity, namely, in its orientation to the question of dogma, then there is no obvious reason why both regular and irregular dogmatics should not be either scientific or non-scientific.

It has happened, of course, and this was especially true in the age of orthodoxy, that the scientific character of academic dogmatics has had to be vindicated against free-lances. But it has also happened that the scientific character of dogmatics has had to be vindicated by free-lances against the dogmatics of the schools. Naturally it cannot be denied that the aversion to the dogmatics of the schools which may be found a little in every age has often rested on enthusiasm of some sort and not on solid Christian insight, that it has had little or nothing to do with the seriousness of the question of dogma, and that it is not, therefore, a sign of scientific concern. But it is also impossible to deny that the transition from irregular to regular dogmatics—when perhaps the school has ceased to be aware that it had to serve life, i.e., the Church—has often been accompanied by a decline in the seriousness, vitality and joyfulness of Christian insight, by a lameness in the enquiry into dogma, and therefore by a loss of the true scientific character of dogmatics.

At this point there must be openness and readiness on both sides. No general statement can be made, but it should be asked from time to time whether the aphoristic style of irregular dogmatics or the systematic style of regular dogmatics does more or less justice to the task of dogmatics. The call for the one or the other may become a necessity, just as it may also be necessary to confine either the one or the other to its proper limits.

What is to be attempted here is regular dogmatics. At no time, even and especially in times of greatest flux, can the Church do without this, and on every hand there are indications that especially for Protestantism to-day an
[279] orderly school dogmatics might be healthier than a further plethora of irregularities in which it has always been so dangerously rich, particularly in the modern period. The results of irregular dogmatics are more exposed than those of regular dogmatics to the danger of being purely accidental, for in form at least they nearly always tend to be strongly influenced by the person and biography of their authors. The seriousness of their significance for the Church must at all events be proved by the fact that they can be presented not merely as the results of irregular dogmatics, e.g., in the form of sermons or the tone of pamphlets, not merely as the expression of religious and perhaps even prophetic experiences and impressions, but also in the stricter form of deliberations that can be tested academically. Almost all the insights in our field have first seen the light in the form of aphorisms and in the tone of proclamation. Dogmatics, i.e., the criticism and correction of previous proclamation, usually has its origin in proclamation itself. But an insight that is tied to the form of aphorisms or the tone of proclamation, an insight that cannot be taught as well, is no true insight, and hence dogmatics must develop as regular dogmatics even if it cannot begin as such. Nothing that can claim to be truly of the Church need shrink from the sober light of "scholasticism." No matter how free and individual it may be in its first expression, if it seeks universal acceptance, it will be under constraint to set up a school and therefore to become the teaching of a school. Fear of Scholasticism is the mark of a false prophet. The true prophet will be ready to submit his message to this test too.

The phenomenon of Luther's theology, which might be given a very different name, is instructive enough as regards the dangers to which irregular dogmatics is exposed. But it is a sign of its significance for the Church that it could survive being put in the school theology of Melanchthon and Calvin and their successors, and all that it possibly lost in the process should not prevent us from recognising that the process was a necessary one for the sake of the Church character of the Reformation.

Anyone who wants to pursue regular dogmatics will have, of course, special cause to remember that this way of doing the task cannot claim a monopoly, even or especially as regards scientific character. It is certainly as well to reflect that at any moment it is possible that the question of dogma may be put and answered much more seriously and fruitfully in the unassuming Bible class of an unknown country parson than in the most exact academic discussion imaginable. School dogmatics should not try to regard itself as better dogmatics, only as a necessary second form of dogmatics. And it should not disdain to listen time and again to the voice of free dogmatics.

It has had disastrous results that the dogmatics of the 19th century Protestant schools, which was much prouder at this point than that of the age of orthodoxy, did very largely disdain to listen in this way, and it was thus able simply to sleep through the existence of phenomena like Kohlbrügge and Blumhardt.

Whether or not regular or irregular dogmatics is scientific depends on the answer to the question how far they stick to their task and are not distracted by very different things. But their task consists in criticism and correction of Church proclamation regarding its agreement with the revelation attested in Holy Scripture. Three things may thus be demanded of a scientific dogmatics, whether regular or irregular. [280]

1. It must devote itself to the problem of Church proclamation as such and not to problems of thought which might arise in proximity to certain concepts in Church proclamation but which have nothing to do with proclamation itself. A system of Christian truth can be the task of dogmatics only to the extent that we are dealing with Christian truth that is proclaimed and is to be proclaimed, so that the exposition of it is less a system than the report of an event. Dogmatics as gnosis without regard for the task of Church proclamation, dogmatics as self-motivated and self-grounded metaphysics is unscientific as dogmatics no matter how profound, erudite and logical it may seem to be. When and where the transition to this type of metaphysics takes place, it is, of course, impossible to say generally. It should be realised that the concepts of pure metaphysics can become the concepts of proclamation and *vice versa*, so that the range of legitimate subjects in dogmatics is variable *in concreto*[EN49].

It is a mistake one cannot respect when uneasy and limited scholars or those whose reading is fundamentally cursory think they should reject a theological exposition out of hand because it uses concepts that they find elsewhere in metaphysical usage. The legitimacy of such use must be decided by the context in which the concepts occur. But the context must also decide the legitimacy of all concepts, even those that seem to belong to proclamation. They, too, might become the concepts of a metaphysics that has nothing whatever to do with proclamation. And one may well ask whether this is not pre-eminently the case with Ritschl, from whom the anxious and others received their cue.

[EN49] concretely

Nevertheless, this does not alter the fact that at this point a question is always put to dogmatics and a boundary drawn for it. Not all the statements of dogmatics are adapted to become directly statements of Church proclamation. To be precise, we must even say that no single statement in dogmatics is adapted to be a statement in proclamation. Dogmatics is preparation for Church proclamation. It formulates statements that have to be pondered before Church proclamation formulates its statements. But it is by this relation that the statements of dogmatics must be tested. They should never stand in the air (perhaps as statements constructed merely for the sake of logical or philosophical or moral completeness) in such a way as to be unintelligible as preparation for Church proclamation and intelligible only as pure gnosis. There are border-line cases (we shall meet them in the doctrine of God, the doctrine of creation
[281] and eschatology, least of all in the doctrine of reconciliation, but there too in Christology) which cannot be avoided, but which are to be handled with extra caution. Yet when we say that there are border-line cases we are admitting that there is a border. It is sometimes easier to find and sometimes harder, but it must always be borne in mind and it will never be crossed with impunity.

The question of being unscientific in this respect arises with regard to the parties in mediaeval and the older Protestant dogmatics in which it seems to have been more a matter of satisfying the formal need of the general scholar or teacher for completeness than of the consistency and exactitude of the scholar or teacher in the Church. But it arises even more in respect of certain enterprises in modern dogmatics which do not seem to be concerned with the Church's task as such but with all kinds of accommodations respecting its possibility in relation to this or that general view. What seem to have been the loftiest peaks of learning in our field, both ancient and modern, always seem to have been most exposed to the danger of being unscientific in the form of the ever-threatening transition to pure gnosis.

2. Scientific dogmatics must devote itself to the criticism and correction of Church proclamation and not just to a repetitive exposition of it. Dogmatics cannot just be a historical account of the classical expression of the faith proclaimed by this or that period in the Church's past. Nor can it just be the clarification and presentation of the faith as the dogmatician concerned personally thinks it should be proclaimed. Nor again can it be just the phenomenology of a cross-section of the common faith proclaimed in a given present.

The first of these was the task of dogmatics according to R. Rothe, the second was its task according to Schleiermacher and Hofmann, and the third was its task according to A. Schweizer. Against all these approaches one may make the objection that in them the Church is, as it were, seen from without, or it is its own spectator. But the true Church exists in the act of the hearing and proclaiming of God's Word by men. The only dogmatics to answer the question of this true Church is the one which examines the problematic nature of its own existence, which does not merely aim to say something, but by saying something aims to serve, to help.

Repetitive exposition according to the intentions of the theologians named will, of course, be indispensable for dogmatics at every step. But dogmatics cannot be only exposition. Its scientific character consists in unsettling rather than confirming Church proclamation as it meets it in its previous concretions and especially in its present-day concretion. It consists in putting it at variance with itself as is proper, in driving it outside and beyond itself. The historical account and the personal confession of faith in the name of contemporaries can only be means to this end. Dogmatics becomes unscientific when it becomes complacent. But it becomes complacent—even when pursued with lively feeling and great perspicacity—when it limits itself to the unfolding and [282] display of a possession already to hand. It is not only what is called the "rigid" dogmatics of the old style (often the Roman Catholic style) that is to be called unscientific in this sense. The same can and must be said of the most fluid, mobile and pious modern dogmatics to the degree that its critical nerve is perhaps dead, to the degree that for the Church around it its significance is merely that of a pleasant certification that all is well and can go on as it has been. So long as the Church on earth is a Church of sinners and its proclamation is thus beset by the most serious problems, one can say very definitely that a dogmatics which takes this attitude and produces this result is wrong. The true Church is waiting for something far different from certification. Again we must say that the line between a purely historical dogmatics and one that is, as it ought to be, critical, is a line that cannot be fixed in general. In all seriousness a critical dogmatics too, and especially, will simply have to give historical accounts over wide stretches, and it is precisely in so doing that it will criticise and correct.

It is obvious that in some circumstances more can be done for dogmatics by adducing a single passage from the Bible or the fathers than by the most penetrating dialectical discussion.

On the other hand a dogmatics that criticises and corrects at every step might end up as a mere historical record.

The *Glaubenslehren* of Schleiermacher and A. Schweirer contain a veritable wealth of criticism and correction and yet one might well ask whether all the criticism and correction do not finally end up, and are not meant to end up, as a grandiose certification, in remarkable harmony with the Roman Catholic conception of dogmatics.

Appearances may deceive on both sides and there is no firm guarantee against slipping into the forbidden opposite. Nevertheless, the question is put here too, and it must be answered by every dogmatics, whether dogmatics is a part of Church history or of information about the present-day Church, or whether it is itself a part of the Church's action. Only in the latter case is it a science in the sense of its commissioned task.

At the beginning of his work *Die Theologie der Tatsachen wider die Theologie der Rhetorik* (4th edn. 1876, 1) A. F. C. Vilmar tells of a certain teacher of dogmatics he heard in his youth who used to accompany and conclude certain sections of his discipline with the words: "*In futuram oblivionem*[EN50], gentlemen." Remarkably enough these sections included those on

---

[EN50] with an eye to future oblivion

faith, justification, the person of Christ, the sacraments and the gifts of the Holy Spirit. But be that as it may, whatever can be taught and learned in dogmatics *in futuram oblivionem*, as the mere material of knowledge, whatever can be had in black and white and confidently carried home, has certainly nothing to do with science. Dogmatics is a science, not as the
[283] offering of all sorts of material, though it must be this too, but as the movement of this material or as this material in motion. So long and so far as this movement or state of movement has not started, dogmatic work itself has not begun.

3. Scientific dogmatics—and now we come to the decisive point—enquires into the agreement of Church proclamation with the revelation which is attested in Holy Scripture. This is what we called the meaning and point of dogma in the first sub-section. If the scientific nature of dogmatics consists in its specific objectivity, i.e., in its orientation to the question of dogma, then we have here the decisive test by which its scientific character has always to be proved. We have already seen that Church proclamation could and can be criticised and corrected from very different standpoints too. What might happen when this is done could even be science from these different standpoints. But it would certainly not be dogmatic science. The two aberrations mentioned above do not have to be fatal to dogmatics. Both a gnostic and also an uncritical dogmatics might incidentally at least do justice to the task of dogmatics. But this is ruled out in the case of the third error, namely, the confusion of the criterion of dogmatics with other criteria. Humanly speaking, and this is the only way we can speak, the result in this case can only be perversion. Dogmatic work stands or falls by whether the standard by which Church proclamation is measured is the revelation attested in Holy Scripture and not a philosophical, ethical, psychological or political theory. Now it is obvious that everyone who works at dogmatics works more or less with specific intellectual presuppositions. The only question is whether in addition to these he also knows the sign of the divine promise which is set up in the Church and whether he is able and willing, in a way that admits of no proof, to take this sign so seriously that in this context its direction takes absolute precedence over all the directions he might owe to the humanities. If and so far as this is so, his work is scientific, and if and so far as it is not so, his work is not scientific, no matter how scientific it may be considered from other angles. It is quite right—and we are not questioning this here but emphatically underlining it—that an education in the arts and a familiarity with the thinking of the philosopher, psychologist, historian, aesthetician, etc., should be demanded of the dogmatician or the theologian. The dogmatician, too, must think and speak in a particular age and should thus be a man of his age, which also means a man of the past that constitutes his age, i.e., an educated man. Nevertheless, the only element in education that makes him a dogmatician is the one which is not provided in all these other disciplines and which consists in indemonstrable and unassuming attention to the sign of Holy Scripture around which the Church gathers and continually becomes the Church. By this attention,

and by nothing else, the theologian becomes a theologian. It is not a question, [284] then, of depreciating other disciplines. It is sheer nonsense to talk of criticising culture in this regard, for in the last resort attention to Holy Scripture might be called an element of culture or education. Nor is it a question of the barbarous demand that the problem of culture as such must be indifferent to the theologian. The problem of culture is the problem of being human, which undoubtedly exists for the theologian too, since theology is a specific activity of humanity. The problem of theology and dogmatics can also be seen as wholly set within the framework of the problem of culture. What is at issue is just the simple insight that this special problem, like all the other problems of culture, has its own set of laws which is not to be confused nor intermingled with any other.

Once when Luther wanted to show why theology like jurisprudence and medicine has and must have its own vocabulary, the *phrasis Spiritus sancti*[EN51], he formulated the issue in the statement: *Non debet ars artem impedire, sed unaquaeque debet retinere suum quasi cursum et uti suis terminis*[EN52] (*Comm. on Gen.* 1[14], *W.A.* 42, 35, 35). Why should we want it to be otherwise? Dogmatics is in fact an *ars* among other *artes*[EN53] and can be taught and learned like them, but it is the art whose law points us to Holy Scripture as the decisive norm without whose validity and observance it becomes sheer bungling.

Certainly this problem is a very special and extremely distinctive problem. We must beware of trying to level it down or to deduce or prove the fact or extent that it can be viewed as set within the framework of the problem of culture generally. The man who argues that this is so and who knows what he is saying in so doing can only believe that we are dealing here with *the* problem of culture, with the framework of all cultural problems. He has to realise, then, that he must not only grant this problem its own laws but must also refrain from deriving these from a superior general law, though he must also refrain, of course, from trying to prove as a general necessity the superiority of this problem over all other problems, e.g., in the form of a theological philosophy of culture. He will know the nature of this problem well enough to realise that this is all forbidden. We cannot postulate of any man that for him, too, this problem is posed in the context of the problem of his humanity and indeed as the problem that dominates the context, just as we cannot postulate of any man that he knows he is in the Church when he does not know that he is. But when a man says he is stirred by this problem, and when he wants to take part in the work of dogmatics, we may postulate that he will observe the proper laws of this problem no matter how remarkable they may be, just as in any other field he would observe the relevant if possibly less remarkable laws of the field. We may postulate that he will conduct himself as an expert in the field and not as a bungler. Without any arrogant criticism of culture we may postulate that

---

[EN51] terminology of the Holy Spirit

[EN52] One art should not obstruct another, but each art ought to hold to its own course, so to speak, and use its own terms.

[EN53] art among other arts

[285] he will realise that in this sphere the criteria of other philosophies cannot play the role which they might perhaps be assigned in every other sphere.

If anyone resolutely refuses to accept this but insists on deriving the final standard in this field, too, from this or that logic, ontology, psychology, or sociology, his attention must be kindly called to the fact that all the rest of the land is open to him but he should desist from working here, where he can only cause confusion with these other final standards.

The time has come to lodge a protest in the name of purity and propriety against the corruption of theology which has now been in full swing so long and which has been brought about by trying to understand and treat it simply as a branch of the humanities in general. To give this protest inner justification more will be needed, of course, than phenomenological interest in the respecting of existing orders and categories or the jealousy of an intellectual trade unionism insisting on its special rights. The formal need for the autonomy of theology can and should be pointed out, but one should not forget that the seriousness of the reference stands or falls with the attention that is actually paid to the witness of Holy Scripture and not just with speaking about it. The truly effective summons to theological relevance can in fact be issued only by a wholly relevant theology and in the last resort it can indeed consist only in the work of this wholly relevant theology. Not the description but the existence of such a theology says what has really to be said here and can be heard as what has really to be heard here, namely, that at no time and in no situation and under no pretext can theology know any more urgent concern than always remaining true to itself and always becoming truer to itself as scriptural theology. Without the existence of such a theology it is futile and unprofitable to debate the question of correct theology even though the answer we propound be ever so powerful and impressive in theory. Only he who actually pursues this theology knows and can effectively advocate what is meant by purity and propriety here, not he who on some ground thinks he knows in general that in theology, as in all else, everything should be done with purity and propriety and that Scripture should thus be and become and remain the master in theology's house. A single attempt to think and speak on this presupposition in a concrete question is far more cogent that the most exact discussion of the fact that one should think and speak in this way, of why one should do so, and to what extent. At this point the question becomes an urgent one whether it has not more often been irregular dogmatics rather than regular dogmatics that has simply existed in this sense as true theology and thus done the decisive thing to establish the scientific character of dogmatics. But be that as it may, i.e., no matter how this third mark of the scientific character of dogmatics be established, it is beyond question that we have here the mark where the roads
[286] diverge most pitilessly and momentously to the right hand and the left. So fully is everything involved here that if the boundary between a dogmatics that is finally determined by Scripture and a dogmatics that is finally determined by other authorities could be generally traced all further discussion between the

one side and the other would be cut off. One could only admit on both sides that under the same name we were engaged in matters that differed *toto coelo*[EN54] and that we had nothing to learn from one another apart from a warning against what is absolutely forbidden, which would mean giving a share to the other side. Let us be under no illusions! The sword of this total separation does hang over both our opposition to Roman Catholicism and also our opposition to Protestant Modernism, and something of its threat will always be discernible in the necessary discussions with both. The only point is that in reality the course of this boundary cannot be traced in a general way but has always to be found in each individual case and in the last analysis it is indeed completely hidden from us.

Dogmatic work which truly sets itself under the criterion of Holy Scripture is finally and properly a matter of calling whose presence and continuation are outside human influence in just the same way as is the call to real proclamation of the Word of God. In relation to the possibility of this calling as it is suggested by the biblical promise itself this work may be the matter of a constantly renewed intention. Only to this extent can it be a programme as well. But no programmatic orientation to this decisive mark of scientific dogmatics can be a mechanical safeguard against slipping into a non-scientific or non-scriptural procedure. In fact there has never been, not even in the Reformation, an unequivocally scriptural dogmatics that has not been determined at all by other authorities. On the other hand one must admit that determination by Scripture, and therefore a truly scientific character, can be achieved in part in dogmatics, and by good fortune has been achieved, even when this basic insight, and therefore programmatic regard for this sign, have been more or less seriously lacking. This twofold truth explains why discussion with Roman Catholicism and Modernism has not been broken off but is always possible and necessary in practice, why, even when both sides can only view each other as heretics, they must still reckon with the presence of the sphere of the Church that embraces the heretic, so that for all the menace of the situation they cannot utterly separate from one another.

But once again and even here the fact that the boundary cannot be traced in a general way, that all concrete judgments will be provisional, that the actual course of the boundary will always be a matter for decision in which the first might become last and the last first—this fact cannot mean that the boundary is not drawn in specific instances. For here again the question is put to dogmatic work, and, as we must emphasise once again, it is put in such a way that the real answer, the actual meaning that a particular dogmatics has or has not when considered from this standpoint (however much or little we may know about it *in concreto*), means a verdict of life or death on its scientific character. We have every cause to be cautious in judging whether a given dogmatics has [287]
or has not as its standard the revelation of God attested in Holy Scripture. There can be no doubt that in every age men have been much too ready with both positive and negative judgments in the heat of the controversy. It is as well to realise that even when it seems that a verdict can and should be given in a specific case, we can only make, as it were, a judgment for the moment, for

---

EN54 totally (literally: by the total extent of heaven)

to-day, and tomorrow we must give another hearing to find out whether we have perhaps been deceived in some respect and ought thus to alter the judgment. Such judgments, even those that are well-founded, even those that the divided Church has solemnly laid down in its mutually opposed and mutually accusatory confessions, must always be regarded in principle merely as very sharply put questions and not as God's own judgments. But when all this is seen and said, it must also be seen and said that the sword of God's real judgment does hang over our heads—over our own heads as well as those of our heretical partners in the controversy—when we take up and pursue this work. The ultimate question cannot be whether we are doing regular or irregular dogmatics. Nor can it be whether we avoid the mistakes of a gnostic or uncritical dogmatics to which we referred earlier, though these mistakes must certainly be kept in view and avoided so far as possible. What finally counts is whether a dogmatics is scriptural. If it is not, then it will definitely be futile, for we shall definitely have to say regarding it that in it the Church is distracted, i.e., it is busy about other matters and is not doing justice to the scientific task set for it by the problematic nature of its proclamation.

3. THE PROBLEM OF DOGMATIC PROLEGOMENA

We have now reached the real goal of this section. Dogmatics, we have said, understands and describes itself as a science. This means that it consciously and explicitly treads its own very specific path of knowledge as specifically defined by its object. But what this specific path is, is something on which agreement cannot be presupposed in the situation in which the Church has found itself for the last four hundred years. The path of Roman Catholicism and the path of Protestant Modernism differ from the path of the Evangelical Church. Evangelical dogmatics has to explain to itself why it thinks it should go its own distinctive way and what this way is. According to our deliberations in § 2 this is the task of the prolegomena to dogmatics. What we have done thus far in relation to this task is to define the criterion of dogmatics. But we have not yet spoken of the application of this criterion. This means—and to this extent we cannot break off at this point, but the greater part of the task is still
[288] ahead—that we have not yet spoken of the path of knowledge as such which must be taken in dogmatics. Definition of the criterion of dogmatics—and this was the purpose of the first chapter that is now drawing to a close—resulted from a consideration of the promise and task of proclamation given to the Church. We have seen that it is the promise and task of this proclamation to be God's Word to men. We first put and answered the formal questions where and how the Word of God is to be found, what it is, and how it may be known. We did all this on the presupposition that its promised and commissioned identity with Church proclamation is called in question by the fact that the latter is always the work of man. Church proclamation has to become what it is when

seen from the standpoint of the promise and the task. From this "becoming what it is" there develops for the Church another task alongside that of proclamation, namely, that of dogmatics, i.e., the task of testing, criticising and correcting the actual proclamation of the Church at a given time. We then saw that God's Word concretely confronts Church proclamation in the form of Holy Scripture as the witness to God's revelation given to the Church. Church proclamation in agreement with Scripture is the fulfilment of the concept of dogma which dogmatics is concerned to know. Thus far we have not gone beyond this definition of the criterion of dogmatics. How are we now to go on to define its path of knowledge as such, to define the employment of this criterion? The choice which must be made here cannot be an arbitrary one. It arises out of the matter itself, as we have already learned. If we were on the right track in bringing the problem of proclamation and the Word of God under the denominator of proclamation and Holy Scripture, we must now go back to that point in our enquiry where we have already encountered proclamation and Holy Scripture in their interrelationship. This encounter took place in § 4, which dealt with the three forms of the Word of God. In the relationship shown there between proclamation and the Word of God there is obviously implied the theme of our present enquiry, namely, the path of knowledge to a critical investigation of the agreement of proclamation with Holy Scripture. We were then dealing with proclamation and Holy Scripture as such, or rather as two forms of the Word of God. We had not yet taken up the question how the former is to be measured by the latter, how it is to be criticised and corrected by it. To answer this question, then, we must go back to that relationship. If the path of knowledge which we are now beginning to seek is to be plain, the following points that have not yet been clarified obviously demand clarification.

1. We must show how we are to understand it when we understand the Bible as the sign of the promise set up in the Church, namely, as the witness to God's revelation and to that extent as the Word of God by which proclamation is to be measured. We must show what it means to have this sign as the Church and [289]
in the Church, and to hear and accept it as such. And we must show how men can come to the point of accepting this sign. In other words, we must offer an explicit doctrine of Holy Scripture.

2. We must also show how we are to understand the fact that man's word in Church proclamation can and should become God's Word in virtue of the promise. We must exhibit the norm to which man's word is to be subject in view of this promise. And we must describe the nature of a thinking that is ready to subject itself to this norm. In other words, in strict correspondence to the doctrine of Holy Scripture that needs to be set forth, we must attempt an equally explicit doctrine of Church proclamation. If we succeed in exhibiting the correspondence then we are obviously saying what needs to be said generally about the use of the criterion of dogmatics or the path of knowledge in dogmatics.

3. But investigation of this correspondence and the actual doctrines of Holy Scripture and Church proclamation would be left strangely in the air if finally and supremely the question of the Word of God itself and as such were not also raised again in a completely new way. The whole point of the correspondence between Holy Scripture and proclamation, and therefore the whole point of the path of knowledge in dogmatics, consists in the fact that in both Holy Scripture and Church dogmatics we are dealing with the Word of God. There is the distinction that in the one (in Holy Scripture) we have simply to find it so far as concerns the task of dogmatics while in the other (in proclamation), at least in connexion with the task of dogmatics, we have not so much to find it as to ask after it, to investigate proclamation with reference to it. Nevertheless in either case we are still dealing with the Word of God. If the correspondence is not just asserted but is to be understood as intrinsically meaningful, we cannot evade the question how this correspondence can arise, and what we mean when we speak of finding the Word of God in the Bible and of the question of the Word of God in proclamation. One can hardly leave it as a presupposed thesis that both of these come into consideration, and that dogmatics has to reckon with the problem of this identity. Certainly no external basis is needed for it, nor can any such be given. But an inner basis is both necessary and possible. And if there is really this correspondence between the Bible and proclamation, if a dogmatic path of knowledge is thus brought to light, this can hardly be seen as an accident or as the result of general didactic considerations. It must arise out of the matter itself, i.e., out of the fact that the Bible and proclamation are or can become God's Word. It must be shown how and how far the questions already put with reference to the Bible and proclam-
[290] ation are not spun out of the void, are not those of random curiosity, do not spring from a logical schematism which can be applied here as elsewhere, but necessarily result from the fact that both the Bible and proclamation are or can become God's Word. It is for this reason that the question of God's Word in itself and as such must be raised again in a completely new way. In a completely new way! The fact that God's Word exists in three forms, that it is God's speech, God's act and God's mystery, that it may be known by men, and how far, does not need to be repeated explicitly. We shall refer in the future to this definition of the criterion of dogmatics—and it will be of real importance at every point—as to an insight that is for the moment presupposed. There is, however, one point in our deliberations thus far which in the interests of an answer to the question of the path of knowledge needs new and very thorough clarification. We have spoken in § 4 of three forms of the Word of God, proclamation, the Bible, and then thirdly (although secretly first and decisively) revelation, the whence of God's Word in the Bible and proclamation, the primary form of the Word of God, in relation to which and by participation in which the Bible and proclamation can also be God's Word. We have called this God's Word in an absolute sense apart from any becoming, the event of God's Word in whose power the Bible and proclamation become God's Word. As the

Word of God reveals itself, the Bible and proclamation are the Word of God. Hence it is the concept of revelation which must give us the key to an understanding of the relations between the two and from which we must also take the very questions with which we approach the two. It alone can show us what it means that preaching to-day and yesterday is measured by the Bible. But we cannot enquire into revelation generally. We cannot enquire into that which is common in all religions so that what the religion of the Bible and Christian proclamation calls revelation must even in its distinctiveness be integrated with it. By putting such general questions we should show already that we were not asking about the revelation of the Word of God and we could certainly not give any answer to this question. And in any case what reason have we in this context to ask generally about revelation or to ask about a revelation in general? We are asking about the revelation in terms of which proclamation can and must be measured by the Bible and to which the Bible and proclamation both relate in what is also, then, a mutual relation. We have to do with the concrete concept of revelation which the Bible attests to have taken place and proclamation promises will come, with the concrete bracket which embraces a specific past, the epiphany of Jesus Christ, and what is always a specific future, the moment when men will hear God's Word, in the Scripture that is adopted by the proclamation of the Church or in the proclamation of the Church which is set in motion by Scripture. We are asking about the con- [291] crete present of God's Word between the times, a present that is as certain as it is inconceivable, as unique as it is ever new. Naturally the reality of revelation stands beyond the concept, even and precisely the concept derived from the Bible and proclamation. We cannot try to deal with the reality. Neither in proclamation nor in dogmatics can we produce the attested past and promised future as a present. Nor can we think that in any present that we can produce we are producing this past or this future. We are dealing with the concept of revelation, i.e., with the present of God's Word between the times. But we are still dealing with a concrete concept of revelation, with a concrete present of God's Word. We are dealing with the concept of the revelation of the God who according to Scripture and proclamation is the Father of Jesus Christ, is Jesus Christ Himself, and is the Spirit of this Father and this Son. Naturally one might also investigate the concept of completely different revelations and perhaps even a general concept of revelation. But in so doing one would abandon the task of dogmatics. For it is the concept of this God, and this concept alone, that interests dogmatics. From this concept and this concept alone can it expect light on the relation between the Bible and Church proclamation and guidance in criticism and correction of the latter. If we are not to make a transition to some other discipline which may well be good and necessary but is not dogmatics, then at this point where the relation between the Bible and Church proclamation is in question we can only investigate this concrete revelation.

But how can we perform this investigation? Clearly only by first considering and analysing the fact of this revelation—obviously the revelation which is attested to have taken place in Scripture and is promised as coming in proclamation; clearly only by analysing how the fact "God reveals Himself" is itself brought before us in the Bible and revelation; clearly only by analysing it as required by the fact itself and by the way it makes itself known to us. Again it is from the fact itself that we are to learn how far it may be understood as intrinsically possible and as self-actualising. But analysis of this fact itself can only be a development of what has always played a distinctive role in dogmatics under the name of the doctrine of the Holy Trinity. The answer to the question of the inner possibility of this fact will be provided on the one hand by the basic propositions of Christology and on the other hand by the basic propositions regarding the work of the Holy Spirit. But we shall first investigate the concept of revelation in order to clarify the presuppositions of the doctrine of Holy Scripture and the doctrine of Church proclamation which are our practical concern. The concept of revelation will have to show us how far the Bible and
[292] proclamation are to be understood as God's Word, what correspondence there is between them, and how the latter is to be measured by the former. Investigation of the concept of revelation belongs, therefore, to the beginning of the whole. In the further course of our prolegomena we shall have to have three chapters on revelation, Holy Scripture and the Church's proclamation in which we shall speak of them in such a way that the whole can be regarded as an exposition of the doctrine of the three forms of the Word of God intimated in § 4. The only point is that we shall no longer be concentrating on a demonstration of the forms but rather on their inner structure and mutual relations. We shall thus have to reverse the order. Previously we began with proclamation as the problematic factor in the whole nexus. Revelation must now form the starting point and proclamation the goal.

INDEX OF SCRIPTURE REFERENCES

INDEX OF SUBJECTS

INDEX OF NAMES